THE LEVITTOWNERS

*Ways of Life and Politics in
a New Suburban Community*

THE LEVITTOWNERS

Ways of Life and Politics in a New Suburban Community ⊠ by HERBERT J. GANS

ALLEN LANE THE PENGUIN PRESS · LONDON · 1967

First published in Great Britain 1967
Allen Lane The Penguin Press, Vigo Street, London W.1.

Manufactured in the United States of America
by Vail-Ballou Press, Inc., Binghamton, New York

Design by Kenneth Miyamoto

Preface

THIS BOOK IS ABOUT A MUCH MALIGNED PART OF AMERICA, SUB-
urbia, and reports on a study conducted by an equally maligned
method, sociology. The postwar suburban developments, of which
the Levittowns are undoubtedly the prototype, have been blamed
for many of the country's alleged and real ills, from destroying
its farmland to emasculating its husbands. Sociology is accused of
jargony or statistical elaboration of the obvious *and* of reporting
unpopular truths; of usurping the novelist's function *and* being
too impersonal; and most often, of making studies which uphold
the conventional wisdom. (As I write this, a *New York Post*
columnist commenting on Frank Sinatra's marriage to a woman
thirty years his junior, notes: "Sinatra and his new wife would
confound the . . . sociologists who smugly branded so large an
age gap unbridgeable." It was probably an unconscious aside,
but to the best of my knowledge, no sociological studies have
ever been made of "December-May" marriages, and whatever
may be wrong with sociological writing, it is rarely smug.)

My book is not a defense of suburbia, but a study of a single
new suburb, Levittown, New Jersey, in which I lived as a "participant-observer" for the first two years of its existence to find
out how a new community comes into being, how people change
when they leave the city, and how they live and politic in suburbia. Nor is it a defense of sociology, but an application of my
own conception of it and its methods. The essence of sociology, it

seems to me, is that it observes what people really do and say. It looks at the world from their perspective, unlike much literary writing, which often boils down to cataloguing their shortcomings from the author's perspective. Sociology is a democratic method of inquiry; it assumes that people have some right to be what they are.

Much of the maligning of both suburbia and sociology has come from the people whom I had in mind while writing this book. Of course, it is a sociological research report, addressed to colleagues, students, and other social scientists interested in community, class, politics, and social structure. It is also a report to another set of colleagues: city planners and social planners, educators, and other service-giving professionals who plan and provide a variety of services to communities like Levittown. But I hope the book will also be of interest to people publishers describe as "informed laymen" and sociologists call "the upper middle class." Although this group is probably the single most influential set of opinion leaders in American society, its knowledge of that society is often sadly deficient. It sees the lower middle and working class people with whom I lived in Levittown as an uneducated, gullible, petty "mass" which rejects the culture that would make it fully human, the "good government" that would create the better community, and the proper planning that would do away with the landscape-despoiling little "boxes" in which they live. This is upper middle class ethnocentrism, and since upper middle class people—as marketers, teachers, bureaucrats, professionals, and consultants—make decisions which affect the lives of people like the Levittowners, they need to understand them better. I am not looking for illusory harmony between the classes, but am only saying that the class conflict could be fought more productively if all sides were better informed about each other.

We know so little of our society and do so little research about it that every study of one of its parts is almost always used to interpret the whole. This book is not about America, however. For one thing, it only describes how people *live* in one suburb, and ignores how and where they *work*. Although I have sought to report findings which apply to many other communities and to people like the Levittowners wherever they live, it is also not about a cross section of Americans, but only about one significant group of them. The Levittowners are young people (in a society which values youth) who hold the new technical and service jobs that are transforming our economy; who are principally working class and lower middle class (and so neither rich nor poor); who are giving up ethnic and regional allegiances and are gradually moving toward the triple melting pot in religion. They are Protestants, Catholics, and Jews who believe in an increasingly similar God, share an increasingly similar Judeo-Christian ethic, and worship in an increasingly similar way with similarly decreasing frequency.

But if Levittowners are at all typical of America, it is because people like them are the principal market for the consumer goods offered by big national corporations, the entertainment and information provided by the mass media, and the political appeals that come out of Washington. They are the customers for whom these agencies create their product—and they are the people who converse about soap and aspirin in the television commercials. People like the Levittowners are wooed by the national churches and voluntary associations and are the independent voters whom both national parties are courting assiduously. In short, they are the people whom the major creators of America's products, services, and ideas believe to be most important or most typical—another reason why I hope the book interests the informed laymen, who often work for them.

Needless to say, Levittown is not a typical American community either. It is a suburb, located beyond the Philadelphia and Camden city limits, and it is a bedroom community, for almost all its residents work outside Levittown. But unlike most suburbs, Levittown was developed by a single builder. Also, the Levittowners account for about 98 per cent of the population of the township within which Levittown is located, so that the usual conflict between old residents and newcomers is quite onesided. And most important, Levittown is a new and still growing community. Even now, new Levittowners are arriving daily, and the community may not be completed entirely until the end of the decade. Consequently, I do not expect my findings to fit all suburbs, and certainly not all established communities. Indeed, how many of my observations apply to other communities remains to be seen.

Although it is standard practice for the sociologist to hide the community he has studied behind a pseudonym, Levittown is distinctive enough to make that impossible, and my approach such that it is unnecessary. Being interested in group behavior and group influences on individual behavior, I am rarely writing about people as individual personalities and I mention no names. Besides, most of the events described here took place between 1958 and 1962 and are now ancient history. Moreover, Levittown, New Jersey, no longer exists; after my research was completed, the voters decided to call it by the original name of the township, Willingboro. I call it Levittown because my study is not of the township but of the Levitt-built community that accounts for almost all of its population.

Acknowledgments

MY PRIMARY DEBT IS TO THE INSTITUTE FOR URBAN STUDIES OF THE University of Pennsylvania, under whose aegis the research and much of the writing was done, and which paid my salary when no grant monies were forthcoming. I am especially grateful to William L. C. Wheaton, now at the University of California at Berkeley, who, as the Director of the Institute, kept financial aid and moral support coming for long years, and to Robert B. Mitchell, who relieved me from teaching duties. A first draft of the book was completed while I was on the staff of the Institute of Urban Studies of Teachers College, Columbia University; and the final one, at the Center for Urban Education. I am grateful to Robert A. Dentler, Director of both, for giving me time to write.

Portions of the study were supported by grants. A mail questionnaire survey was aided by small grants from the National Institute of Mental Health and the Social Science Research Council. Part of an interview survey was financed by a grant-in-aid from the American Philosophical Society, and one year's data analysis and writing was supported by Penjerdel (the Pennsylvania-New Jersey-Delaware Metropolitan Project, Inc.). The Statistical Laboratory of the Wharton School of the University of Pennsylvania punched and tabulated the questionnaire data without charge, and I am grateful to Nancy Schnerr and Ronald Cohen for doing so.

■ *ix* ■

Most of the research I did myself, and am therefore responsible for all its shortcomings. My then wife, Iris Lezak MacLow, helped with the fieldwork; Ruth Blumenfeld did many of the interviews; and Phoebe Cottingham, the coding and statistical computation of the mail questionnaire data. William Michelson conducted a special study of voluntary associations under my supervision, and Alice Pierson asked some of my questions in another Levittown. Several past and present executives of Levitt and Sons, Inc., gave information on the firm's plans and activities, and made it possible to send the mail questionnaire to homebuyers. A number of colleagues made helpful comments on earlier drafts of the book, among them Martin Meyerson, Peter Marris, H. Laurence Ross, William Michelson, Peter Willmott, and particularly Margaret Latimer. I am especially grateful to Judy Engelhardt of Pantheon Books, whose careful and close editing of a very long previous draft helped me cut the book without loss of substance; and to Martha Crossen Gillmor, for her thorough last-minute review of the final version. The major share of manuscript typing was done by Leona Cohen, Mary Ellison, Jacqueline Ferguson, Marcia Hyman, Thelma Johnson, Mae Kanazawa, and the late Theresa Barmack. But the principal co-workers of the study were the Levittowners, with whom I lived for two enjoyable years, who provided information in my endless rounds as a participant-observer, and let themselves be questioned by interviewers and by mail. I hope they will find my report on their community useful.

H. J. G.

New York City
August 1966

CONTENTS

TABLES

Introduction

THE SETTING, THEORY, AND METHOD OF THE STUDY

THIS STUDY HAD ITS BEGINNINGS SIXTEEN YEARS AGO WHEN I CONcluded some research in the new town of Park Forest, Illinois, near Chicago. Having come to Park Forest when it was fourteen months old and already a community, I decided that someday I would study a new town from its very beginnings. Soon after I left Park Forest, it and other postwar suburban developments suddenly became a topic of widespread popular interest. Journalists and critics began to write articles suggesting that life in these new suburbs was radically different from that in the older cities and towns and that these differences could be ascribed both to basic changes in American values and to the effects of suburban life. In the first and most perceptive of these reports, Whyte's articles on Park Forest, the author described drastic increases in visiting and club activity, shifts in political party affiliation and church-going habits, and a more equalitarian mode of consumer behavior and status competition (keeping down with the Joneses) which he explained as a decline in individualism and the rise of a new Social Ethic—most evident in and partly created by the new suburbs.[1]

Later reports by less searching and responsible writers followed,[2] and so did a flood of popular fiction,[3] eventually creating what Bennett Berger has called the myth of suburbia.[4] Its main theme took off where Whyte stopped: the suburbs were breeding a new set of Americans, as mass produced as the houses they lived in, driven into a never ending round of group activity ruled by the strictest conformity. Suburbanites were incapable of real friendships; they were bored and lonely, alienated, atomized, and depersonalized. As the myth grew, it added yet more disturbing elements: the emergence of a matriarchal family of domineering wives, absent husbands, and spoiled children, and with it, rising marital friction, adultery, divorce, drunkenness, and mental illness.[5] In unison, the authors chanted that individualism was dying, suburbanites were miserable, and the fault lay with the homogeneous suburban landscape and its population. John Keats, perhaps the most hysterical of the mythmakers, began his book as follows: *"For literally nothing down* . . . you too can find a box of your own in one of the fresh-air slums we're building around the edges of American cities . . . inhabited by people whose age income, number of children, problems, habits, conversation, dress, possessions and perhaps even blood type are also precisely like yours. . . .]They are[developments conceived in error, nurtured by greed, corroding everything they touch. They . . . actually drive mad myriads of housewives shut up in them."* [6]

Subsequently, literary and social critics chimed in. Although they wrote little about suburbia per se, articles and reviews on other subjects repeated what they had learned from the mass media, dropping asides that suburbia was intellectually debilitating, culturally oppressive, and politically dangerous, breeding bland mass men without respect for the arts or democracy.[7] They were joined by architects and city planners who accused the suburbs and their builders of ruining the countryside, strangling the cities, causing urban sprawl, and threatening to make America into one vast Los Angeles by the end of the century.[8]

I watched the growth of this mythology with misgivings, for my observations in various new suburbs persuaded me neither that there was much change in people when they moved to the suburbs nor that the change which took place could be traced to the new environment. And if suburban life was as undesirable and unhealthy as the critics charged, the suburbanites themselves were blissfully unaware of it; they were happy in their new homes and communities, much happier than they had been in the city. Some of the observations about suburbia were quite accurate, and the critics represented a wide range of political and cultural viewpoints, so that it is perhaps unfair to lump them all together—although I do so as a shorthand in the chapters that follow. Nevertheless, it seemed to me that a basic inaccuracy was being perpetrated by those who give American society its picture of itself, and when I learned that city planners also swallowed the suburban myth and were altering their professional recommendations accordingly, I felt it was time to do a study of the new suburbs. Lacking the grants to do a large comparative study of several communities that was—and still is—needed, and leaning toward participant-observation by my training, I decided the best way to do the research was to live in one such community. That community turned out to be Levittown, New Jersey.

THE SETTING

When I first began to think about the study, I learned that Levitt and Sons, Inc., then building Levittown, Pennsylvania, were planning to build yet another new community in the Philadelphia area. The firm was then, as now, the largest builder in the eastern United States, and Levittown was even then a prototype of postwar suburbia.[9] Hair raising stories about the homogeneity of people and conformity of life in the first two Levittowns made it clear that if any of the evils described by the critics of suburbia actually existed, they would be found in a Levittown. Moreover, Levitt was building communities and not just subdivisions, which meant that the entire range of local institutions and facilities typically associated with a community would be established *de novo;* the firm was offering relatively inexpensive houses, which meant that the community would attract both middle and working class people.[10]

In 1955, Levitt announced that he had purchased almost all of Willingboro Township, New Jersey, a sparsely settled agricultural area seventeen miles from Philadelphia, and that building would begin as soon as Levittown, Pennsylvania, was completed. The newest Levittown was to be a full-fledged community, with at least 12,000 houses, and because Levitt had bought almost the entire township, with its own government as well. Three basic house types, costing from $11,500 to $14,500 would be built on the same street and organized into separate neighborhoods of about 1200 homes, each served by an elementary school, playground, and swimming pool. The complex of ten or twelve neighborhoods would be complemented by a set of community-wide facilities, including a large shopping center, some smaller ones, and of course high schools, a library, and parks; and some of these would be provided by the builder.

On a sunny Saturday in June 1958, Levittown was officially opened to potential purchasers, and that day my wife and I were among hundreds of others who looked over the houses. Since I wanted to be among the very first residents, we selected the model we liked best, a four-bedroom "Cape Cod," and made the required down payment of $100. A few weeks later, the first group of about 100 purchasers was asked to come to Levittown to pick a lot, and we chose one in the middle of a short block—to make sure that we would literally be in the middle of things. During the second week of October, we were among the first 25 families who moved into the new community—none of them, I was pleased to discover, coming to study it.[11]

THE THEORY OF THE STUDY

The study I wanted to do focused around three major but interrelated questions: the origin of a new community, the quality of suburban life, and the effect of suburbia on the behavior of its residents. Later, I added a fourth question on the quality of politics and decision-making.

My first task was to determine the processes which transform a group of strangers into a community, to see if I could identify the essential prerequisites for "community." But I also wanted to test the critics' charge that the Levittowns were inflicted on purchasers with little choice of other housing by a profit-minded builder unwilling to provide them with a superior home and community. Consequently, I intended to study how the community was planned: to what extent the plans were shaped by Levitt's goals and to what extent by the goals of the expected purchasers. For this purpose, I needed also to study the purchasers—why they were moving to Levittown and what aspirations they had for life in the new community. Once they had moved in, I wanted to observe the community formation process from the same perspective: how much specific groups were shaped by their founders, how much by their members, and how much by the group's function for the larger community. I hoped to know after several years to what extent the emerging community reflected the priorities of builder, founders, and other community leaders and to what extent the goals for which people said they had moved to Levittown.

These questions were grounded in a set of theoretical issues of relevance to both social science and public policy. Sociologists have long been asking what and who bring about innovation and social change, and what role elite leaders and experts, on the one hand, and the rank-and-file citizenry, on the other, play in this process. As a policy matter, the same question has been raised by the concept of mass society, which implies that many features of American society—whether television programs, Levittowns, or Pentagon policies—are imposed by an intentional or unintentional conspiracy of business and governmental leaders acting on passive or resigned Americans who actually want something entirely different.

This issue is of more than academic interest to makers of community policy, be they politicians or city planners. The city planner is an expert with a conception of the ideal community and good life, which he seeks to translate into reality through his professional activities. If a small number of leaders shape the community, he need only proselytize them effectively to establish his conception. If the residents themselves determine the community, however, he is faced with a more difficult task: persuading them of the desirability of his plans or somehow changing their behavior to accord with them. The further and normative issue is even more perplexing: whose values *should* shape the new community, the residents' or the planner's? [12]

The second question of the study sought to test the validity of the suburban critique, whether suburban ways of life were as undesirable as had been claimed. Are people status-seekers, do they engage in a hyperactive social life which they do not really enjoy, do they conform unwillingly to the demands of their neighbors, is the community a dull microcosm of mass society? Are the women bored and lonely matriarchs, and does suburban life produce the malaise and mental illness which the critics predicted? And if not, what dissatisfactions and problems *do* develop?

The third question followed logically from the second: were undesirable changes (and desirable ones too) an effect of the move from city to suburb or of causes unrelated to either the move or suburbia? My previous observations led me to suspect that the changes were less a result of suburban residence than of aspirations for individual and family life which encouraged people to move to the suburbs in the first place. Consequently, I wanted to discover whether the changes people reported after coming to Levittown were *intended,* planned by them before the move, or *unintended,* encouraged or forced on them afterwards by the community. If unintended changes outweighed intended ones, the community probably had significant effects on its residents. And if so, what *sources* and *agents* within the community created them—the physical environment of suburbia, the distance from urban facilities, the social structure and the people who made it, and/or the builder or organizational founder?

The theoretical issue about the impact of the community has long been debated within sociology, the ecologists arguing that the local economy and geography shape the behavior of the community's residents; the cultural sociologists suggesting that the community and its residents' behavior are largely a reflection of regional and national social structures.[13] The policy issue is related to the previous one. If there is no change in people's behavior when they move to the suburbs, then public policy which alters only the community, such as city planning, may be ineffective. The same is true if changes are mainly intended. If they are mainly unintended, however, and the community has impact on people's lives, then policy to change the community will also change their lives. And if the sources of change can be traced to the physical environment, the city planner's concern with altering that environment is justified; if they lie in the social environment, then social planning would be more effective. But if intended changes predominate, public policy would have to affect the aspirations with which people come to the community and the more fundamental sources of these aspirations. Of course, all this assumes that policy change is needed, which requires a prior determination of what is harmful or in need of improvement in suburban life.

As part of my study of the quality of life, I had intended to research political life as well, and as part of the inquiry into origins, to find out how much attention elected officials paid to feedback from the voters—whether the body politic was being created by political leaders on their own or in response to resident demands. In the course of my research I became aware of what should have been obvious all along: that the community was also being shaped by the decisions of its governing body, and that I

needed to study who was making them and how, and to determine what role the planner and other kinds of experts played in
the decision-making process. I wanted particularly to find out
how much leeway the decision-makers had for unpopular decisions, especially those termed "in the public interest" by experts
and planners. Underlying the empirical question was another
normative one: whether government *should* be responsive and
democratic, and when it should make unpopular decisions to
preserve the public interest as well as the rights of powerless
minorities.

All four questions ultimately boil down to a single one about
the process of change and the possibility of innovation in a social
system. They all ask how change can be brought about, whether
the major initiators are the leaders or the led, and what role the
planner or any other expert policy-maker can play. And they also
ask, normatively speaking, what changes are desirable, particularly when they conflict with the actions or wishes of the majority of residents. These questions are, of course, relevant to any
community, but they are raised more easily in a new community,
where all social and political processes can be traced from their
very beginning.

I should note that when I began my research, I had not formulated the questions as clearly or compactly as they are here written, and I had no intention of limiting myself only to them. One
of the major pleasures of participant-observation is to come upon
unexpected new topics of study, and these are reflected in the occasional tangential analyses that occur throughout the book.

THE METHODS OF THE STUDY

The main source of data was to be participant-observation. By
living in the community for the first two years, I planned to observe the development of neighbor relations and social life and to
be on hand when organizations and institutions were being set
up. In addition to observing at public meetings, I would also be
able to interview founders and members, and once having gotten
to know them, follow their groups as they went through their
birth pains. Meanwhile I would do much the same with
churches, governmental public bodies, and political parties; I
would talk to doctors, lawyers, local reporters, and the Levitt executives, as well. Eventually I would get to know all the impor-

tant people and a sizeable sample of other residents, and interview them from time to time as the community building process unfolded. The nature of everyday life I would discover principally on my own street, where I could observe my neighbors and myself in our roles as homeowners and block residents. These plans came to fruition, and I spent most of my days making the rounds of the community to find out what was happening, much like a reporter. For a year after organizations first sprang up, I went to at least one meeting every week night.

Although observation would also provide some data on the community's effects on people, and on their feelings about Levittown and their problems, it would not allow me to contact a large and random enough sample. Consequently, I planned to interview such a sample shortly before moving in, to find out what aspirations they were bringing to the community, and again two years later, to determine what intended and unintended changes had occurred in their lives. The shortage of funds made the sample smaller than I had wished, but forty-five respondents were interviewed twice, mainly by graduate students from the University of Pennsylvania. As the sample included too few former city dwellers for even a rudimentary statistical analysis, fifty-five ex-Philadelphians were interviewed as well, but only once. And being unable to persuade the builder to give me the names of purchasers before they moved in, I had to schedule the initial interview with the first sample shortly after they arrived.[14] The builder did, however, send out a prearrival mail questionnaire for me, which ultimately went to 3100 purchasers (a record-breaking two thirds of whom filled it out), and provided much of the data on the Levittowners, their moving reasons, and aspirations reported in Chapter Two.[15] Whenever I report statistical findings about people's behavior, the data come from the mail questionnaire (particularly in Chapter Two), and from the interviews (particularly in Part Two). Further details about the questions themselves and about the limitations of the mail questionnaire, interview, and participant-observation findings will be found in appropriate places in the text and in the Appendix.

My previous participant-observation research had convinced me that my role in Levittown would be more an observer's than a participant's. Participating is undoubtedly the best way to discover what is really going on, but becoming a participant in one group automatically excludes the researcher from learning anything about what is going on in competing or opposing ones. Consequently, I decided I would participate only in the life of my own block and as a member of the public at meetings, but that otherwise my role would be that of an observer and informal interviewer.

As soon as I moved in, I told people I was on the faculty of the University of Pennsylvania and that I would do a study of the community formation process in Levittown. Having learned from previous experience that it is difficult to explain sociology meaningfully to people, I usually described my research as a historical study. I did not go into detail about it—I was rarely asked to—and I did not tell people on my block that I was keeping notes on their (and my) activities as homeowners and neighbors. To have done so would have made life unpleasant for them and for me. I disclaimed association with the mail questionnaire or the interviews on behavior change, fearing (probably unnecessarily) that I might be rejected as a participant-observer. Finally I did not tell people I had moved to Levittown in order to do the study. Actually, it would not have occurred to them that I was not simply interested in a good low-priced house and the chance to enjoy suburban living.

Aside from these deceptions, being a participant-observer was almost always enjoyable and often exciting. I liked most of the people I met and had no trouble in getting information from them. Identifying myself as a researcher did not inhibit them from talking, but then I asked few personal questions; being as curious as I about the evolution of a new community, they were willing and often eager to have me sit in at meetings or interview them. After a while, I became a fixture in the community; people forgot I was there and went on with their business, even at private political gatherings. I was always welcomed at public meetings, especially when citizen attendance was low. Needing an audience, public officials were glad to forget I was there as a researcher. Indeed, I was once publicly praised for my steady attendance.

Most people enjoy being studied; it means they are important and it flatters them. Since I was always collecting information but never published anything, however, people could not check on me as they can on a reporter, and some of the politicians became suspicious of what I would eventually write. "Will it be like

Peyton Place?" a couple of them once asked jokingly. I wise-cracked back that I would be glad to include similar material on local incest if they could provide the data, but realizing that their jokes hid some concern about my publishing political and other community intrigues, I made it clear that I would not use names in the book.

I tried not to act like a formal researcher and rarely took notes during the thousands of informal conversational interviews. Instead I memorized the answers, made quick notes as soon as I could, and later wrote the whole interview in my field diary. (Although a famous novelist has recently garnered considerable publicity for memorizing his interviews, this has long been standard practice for many sociologists.) Social occasions were a fruitful source of data about community attitudes, but I was always careful not to ask too many questions or questions inappropriate to the neighborly role. I recall feeling frustrated about this at one social gathering, only to hear a neighbor ask exactly the questions I felt I could not ask. This made me wonder about the similarity between sociology and gossip, but then she was the block's nosy neighbor. Actually, in life on the block I often acted spontaneously as a neighbor, and only after I got home would I become the researcher again, writing down my and my neighbors' conversations and activities.

The main problem in being a participant-observer is not to get people to give information, but to live with the role day after day. As a researcher, I could not afford to alienate any present or potential sources, or become identified with any single group or clique in the community. Consequently, I had to be neutral, not offering opinions on controversial local issues or on national politics if they were too different from prevailing opinions—as they often were. Even in social situations, I could never be quite myself, and I had to be careful not to take a dominant role. The life of the party makes a poor participant-observer, but being shy anyway, I did not have to pretend. I also had to restrain the normal temptation to avoid people I did not like, for had I given in, my sample would have been biased and my conclusions inaccurate. The participant-observer must talk to a fairly representative cross section of the population. I had to be sure not to act like a professor, for fear of losing access to people who feel threatened by academic degrees or by their own lack of education. This was not too difficult, for I am not entirely comfortable in a professorial role anyway. And having enough interest in small talk about sports, sex, automobiles, weather, and other staples of male conversation, I had no difficulty in participating in the regular evening and Saturday morning bull sessions on the front lawn. Relaxed conversation with women was more difficult, except in a group of couples, and observing women's meetings was out of the question. Perhaps they would have let me in, but we would all have been uncomfortable. However, women enjoyed being interviewed—they liked having their housework interrupted—and I could always go to see anyone I wished to find out what happened at their meetings.

A participant-observer is much like a politician, for he must always watch his words and his behavior, think about the next question to ask, and plan strategy for studying a prospective event. There was anxiety too, about figuring out what to study and what not to study, and particularly about the possibility of missing something important that could not be retrieved in the rapid flow of events. I also felt guilty sometimes about not telling people why I was asking questions and about the deceptions that inevitably accompany the research role, but I felt secure in the knowledge that none of the information so gathered would ever be used against anyone.

Yet even the strain of playing a role that inhibits one's personality is more than matched by the excitement of doing research, watching society from close up, seeing the textbook social processes in operation, and constantly getting ideas about social theory from what people say and do. There was enjoyment in meeting many hundreds of people, and above all, in being in the middle of and in on things. Often, I felt I was watching dozens of continuing serials, some pitting heroes against villains, others with temporary cliff-hanger endings, but all of them stimulating my curiosity as to how they would come out. And before one serial was over, several others were sure to have begun. This is why I could never answer properly when city people asked me whether I *really* enjoyed living in Levittown. I did enjoy it, but as a researcher, I was not a normal resident. Had I been one, I would have enjoyed the many opportunities for community activity which came my way (partly because of my training in city planning)—all of which I had to turn down as a researcher—but sometimes I found the community personally unsatisfying because of the shortage of people and facilities to meet my own intellectual and cultural needs. Even so, I would not judge Levit-town, or any community, negatively simply because it could not fully satisfy my personal needs.

Studying the quality of life implies evaluation, and this means personal value judgments. I was guided by at least three. First and foremost, my evaluation reflects the standards of the residents themselves, for I begin with the judgment that, more often than not, they are the best authority of the quality of their own life. In a pluralistic society, there is no single standard for the good life, and in a democratic one, people have the right to set their own. For example, if Levittowners report that they find their community satisfying, as they do, their opinion ought to be respected. Although the suburban critics insist that these satisfactions are spurious and self-deceptive, they offer no valid evidence, so that their charge only indicates their differing standards for the good life. Of course, if the Levittowners' statements include latent suggestions of dissatisfaction, something is clearly wrong.

Implicit in this value judgment is a second which goes beyond the dictates of pluralism and democracy. Specifically, I believe that there are an infinite number of ways of living well and of coping with problems, all of them valid unless they hurt the people practicing them or others. Our society generates too much social criticism consisting essentially of complaints that people are not behaving as the critics would like or themselves behave. Without proof that certain behavior is pathological for individual or society, such criticism can be rejected for what it is, an objection to diversity and pluralism.

But it would be foolhardy to base an evaluation solely on what people say, for if sociology has discovered anything, it is that often people do not know all they are doing or what is happening to them. The observer always sees more than anyone else, if only because that is his job, but if he evaluates what he alone sees, he must still do so by the standards of the people whom he is observing. Of course, here and there I make personal judgments which do not practice what I have just preached and which reject one or another of the Levittowners' standards. At the conscious level, I have limited myself to those judgments which I consider of higher importance than the Levittowners' standards—including the practice of democracy—but unconscious judgments surely creep in too. One cannot live intimately with a community for several years without making them, and I only regret not being aware of those that might bias the study unduly.

In later chapters, I also make a number of recommendations. Most are not spectacular, for although I can be as radical as anyone else, I feel that proposals which run totally counter to the standards of the people who are asked to implement them and which have little chance of implementation in the foreseeable future are utopian in the negative sense. Being radical can sometimes be a conformist ploy to maintain one's social standing and self-image in radical circles. Most of the proposals relate to Levittown as it existed during the time of my fieldwork, and should not be taken as recommendations for today, unless a restudy indicates (as it probably would) that the community has not changed significantly since the beginning of the decade. Finally, I have tried to keep analysis and evaluation separate, because I believe that the former is more than a rationalization or elaboration of my value judgments; most of my findings would have been reached by another social scientist starting from different value judgments. Obviously, the analysis is objective only in relation to the methods and concepts I have used and to the judgments which determined them, but in that sense, I believe it is objective.

The book tells, then, what I learned during the two years I lived in Levittown (October 1958–September 1960), in the year I did additional fieldwork without living there (September 1960–June 1961), and in the years covered by the effects interviews (1960–1962). Wherever possible, I have used newspaper articles and data from Levittown informants to report important events that have occurred since then.

NOTES

1. The articles appeared originally in *Fortune* in 1953, and in Whyte (1956), Part III. For full citation of works referred to in the notes by author's name only, see References, pages 452–462. Where several works by the same author are cited, the note reference is followed by the appropriate publication date.
2. Among the principal contributors to the popular image of suburbia were a 1950 novel by Charles Mergendahl, *It's Only Temporary* (perhaps the first of the flood of fiction and nonfiction about the suburbs) and Henderson, Allen, Burton, Spectorsky, Keats, and more recently, Wyden. A Sunday supplement, *Suburbia Today,* was filled with articles about suburbia, pro and con.
3. There were dramatic novels, mostly about upper middle class

suburbs, like Otis Carney's *How the Bough Breaks;* melodramatic
ones like John McPartland's *No Down Payment,* later made into
a movie; and humorous ones like Mergendahl's; plays, for example, *Man in the Dog Suit;* and even an opera, Leonard Bernstein's
Trouble in Tahiti. Levittown was often the site, by implication
in Mergendahl's book, and explicitly in a half-hour television
comedy series, (never produced) called *The Man Who Came to
Levittown.* While most of today's television situation comedies
are set in the suburbs, they are not so identified and do not deal
with problems they describe as suburban.

4. Berger (1960), Chap. 1. For other analyses of the popular image
   of suburbia, see Strauss, Chaps. 10 and 11; Dobriner (1963), Chap.
   1; Riesman (1964); and Berger (1966).

5. On mental illness see James, and a full-length study which became
   a best-seller, by Gordon, Gordon, and Gunther. The myth of suburban adultery, which can probably be traced to century-old
   novels about upper and upper middle class unfaithfulness, has
   spawned a flood of strenuously erotic paperbacks which still keep
   coming, although the output of other suburban literature has now
   abated. See e.g., John Conway's *Love in Suburbia,* subtitled
   "They Spiced Their Lives with Other Men's Wives," or Dean
   McCoy's *The Development,* advertised as "a biting novel which
   strips bare the flimsy façade of decency concealing unbridled
   sensual desires of America's sprawling Suburbia."

6. Keats (1957), p. 7.

7. Although most sociologists doubted the myth, some accepted
   parts of it, e.g., Gruenberg, Duhl, Riesman (1957), and Stein,
   Chaps. 9 and 12. Interestingly enough, "serious" novelists have not
   written about suburbia. George Elliott's *Parktilden Village* and
   Bruce Jay Friedman's *Stern* are set in suburban housing projects
   and reflect the suburban myth, but deal even less with representative and recognizable suburbanites than the popular novelists.

8. For example, Mumford, Chap. 16; Blake; and Gruen, Chap. 5.

9. Actually, most of the suburban building had taken the form of
   subdivisions on the fringe of established communities rather than
   new communities, so that Levittown was in many ways atypical.
   It was a prototype largely because it had become the symbol of
   modern suburbia among the critics, journalists, novelists, and
   moviemakers concerned with the subject.

10. My study was formulated in the affluent society of the mid-1950s
    and I was then especially interested in whether (and how) working
    class people were acculturating to middle class life styles. If the
    move from city to suburb created major changes in people's lives,
    I thought they would be most apparent among working class
    people moving to a middle class suburb and could best be studied
    there, provided one could distinguish between changes resulting
    from social mobility and changes resulting from the move. There
    were too few working class Levittowners to limit my research to

    them, but some years later, Berger (1960) studied a working class suburb, covering many of the topics in which I was interested.

11. Later, I would have welcomed sharing my task with other participant-observers, but at that time, I was unsure about people's feelings toward a resident researcher and thought that more than one sociologist in the community would make the research too visible. I was wrong, because the community was large enough and the neighborhoods separate enough, and because after a while the researcher became part of the daily scene and faded into invisibility.

12. This question was also evoked by a study I had just participated in: on the issue of whether municipal services ought to be planned according to the priorities of those who supplied them (the professional educators, recreationists, public health officials, and social workers), or of those who used them (their "clients"). My own research, which dealt with public recreation, concluded that parks and playgrounds ought to be planned for their users, and undoubtedly left an a priori bias in studying the larger issue in Levittown.

13. See, e.g., Duncan and Schnore.

14. The builder was my only source of purchasers' names, but he had a policy of not giving them out to discourage milk salesmen and other merchants from bothering people before they moved in. The firm also had little interest in research, and some officials feared that several purchasers might change their minds about buying if I interviewed them about it. Consequently, I had to ask people to recall the aspirations with which they came, but they mentioned the same ones which appeared in the mail questionnaire that was filled out before arrival in Levittown.

15. The questionnaire was on University of Pennsylvania stationery, and answered ones were to be returned to the campus, thus alleviating any suspicion that it was a Levitt research project.

Part 1 ▪ THE ORIGIN OF
A COMMUNITY

Chapter One

THE PLANNERS OF
LEVITTOWN

IN ORDER TO DESCRIBE LEVITTOWN'S ORIGIN, ONE MUST BEGIN WITH its planners: who made the critical decisions for the conception of the community, with what goals in mind, and for what kinds of residents and aspirations? The most important role was, of course, played by the builder, Levitt and Sons. The firm was founded during the Depression by the late Abraham Levitt, a "self-made" son of Russian-Jewish immigrants who had practiced real estate law for a quarter of a century before going into the building business, and by his two sons, William and the late Alfred. Until the beginning of World War II, the firm built a number of small suburban subdivisions on Long Island, priced to appeal to the upper middle class then streaming to the Island. After World War II, as a result of experience gained in building Navy housing, the Levitts developed a mass production scheme that allowed them to build inexpensive housing for the postwar flood of veterans and their families.[1]

Most of the concepts that went into planning Levittown, New Jersey, were evolved in the two earlier Levittowns, in New York and Pennsylvania. Levittown, Long Island, begun in 1947, was built in traditional subdivision style, with the builder buying a piece of land—much larger than most others, to be sure—and then acquiring further acreage as sales continued to go well. The houses in Levittown were smaller versions of the expensive suburban ones the Levitt firm had built previously, but included an array of home appliances and were located around Village Greens that consisted of neighborhood shops, a playground, and a swimming pool.² Perhaps these additional items were provided because of the builder's uncertainty that the house alone was salable. Levittown was, after all, an experiment, begun when the housing industry as a whole had known only lack of demand and when fears of a postwar depression were still prevalent. But the firm also had an additional goal: to create a community. This emerged more clearly when Alfred Levitt, who was trained in architecture, proposed his scheme for Landia, a 675-acre community elsewhere on Long Island.³ It was planned to provide separate residential neighborhoods without through streets, a town center, and a complete set of community facilities, including parks.

Landia was never built, partly because of the moratorium on housing at the start of the Korean War, but some of its ideas were incorporated in the building of the second Levittown, in Bucks County, Pennsylvania, in 1951. Although the Levitt firm was secure enough by this time to buy a much larger amount of land at the start, the community was still not totally planned in advance, the individual neighborhoods being laid out just before their construction. The plan for this second Levittown called for about 17,000 homes, and neighborhoods free from through traffic, with elementary schools, playgrounds, and pools at their center. The local shopping centers were almost entirely eliminated after the firm learned to its dismay that a large shopping center in the Long Island Levittown—not built by the firm—was drawing most of the sales away from shops on the Village Greens. Instead, the Levitts built a huge "regional" shopping center on the edge of their new Levittown, hoping to attract not only their house buyers but people from other communities as well. The firm also gave land to a number of churches, institutionalizing a practice that had begun on an ad hoc basis in the initial Levittown when a church came to the builder with a request for free land.

But Levittown, Pennsylvania, like Levittown, Long Island, had one major drawback. Because of the way land had been purchased, the final community was spread out over four townships and many other governmental units, and in developing the land the builder had to negotiate separately with each unit. This not only took considerable time and energy, but required changes in the initial plan, particularly in the design of neigh-

borhoods and location of schools, and also forced the firm to administer recreation areas so as to limit their use to purchasers of
Levitt houses. As a result, the firm's executives were frequently
diverted from the business of building and even became embroiled in community conflicts.

Not long after the Bucks County development had gotten off
to a successful start, the firm began to consider yet a third Levittown, and this time it sought to eliminate the difficulties it had
encountered previously by purchasing land within a single township. Ultimately, the choice fell on Willingboro township in
New Jersey. Willingboro township was an area of small farms,
producing peaches, plums, and tomatoes on the region's sandy
soil. Just outside the ring of postwar surburbs that had sprung up
around Philadelphia, and only about ten miles from Levittown,
Pennsylvania, it was eminently "ripe" for residential development. It was particularly suitable for Levitt and Sons because it
was inhabited only by individual farmers, a few owners of what
had once been a summer home colony, and the village of Rancocas, a nineteenth century Quaker settlement of less than 500
people. Soon after the firm bought the land, it had the township
boundaries changed so that Rancocas was incorporated into the
neighboring township of Westampton. Thus it had obtained a
large acreage, located entirely within one township and occupying most of it. Once Rancocas had been moved out, only about
600 people were left in the township, and they, the builder felt,
could be persuaded to give him a free hand to build as he
wished. Willingboro would provide a virtual *tabula rasa* for
realizing William Levitt's goals and plans.

THE PLANNING PROCESS

By the time the planning for Levittown, New Jersey, began, control of the firm was entirely in the hands of William Levitt.
Abraham Levitt had retired because of increasing age, and Alfred
Levitt had left the firm, selling his share of the stock to his
brother, reputedly because they could not develop a method for
making decisions jointly. Working with William Levitt were half
a dozen executives, many of whom had been with the firm since
the late 1940s, but the final decisions were his.[4] Like his brother,
he was open to advice, but he was known as a man who rarely
changed his mind once he had made it up.[5] William Levitt's

goals were to build another profitable development and a better community, more comprehensively planned in advance and more completely stocked with public facilities. He also sought to end the attacks by planners, architects, and social critics against the firm and the past Levittowns. Known for his low opinion of the city planning profession, however, and lacking Alfred's interest in its concepts and schemes, he had no intention of building the community to please the planners. Nor was he especially concerned about how to satisfy the buyers and meet their aspirations. As the most successful home builder in the East, with a decade's reputation for providing "the best house for the money," he felt he knew what they wanted. Unlike his father, he had no desire to involve the firm in the life of the community or to uplift the cultural level and civic performance of the residents. He wanted only to build what he deemed to be a better Levittown, what he often called a "showplace."

Because of the success of the Bucks County community, Levitt felt secure enough to buy 80 per cent of the land he would need for the entire community, with options on the remaining portion. A fairly complete plan of the eventual community was developed, including an overall road system, a community-wide sewage and water supply system to be built before the community was occupied, and a generalized scheme for shopping, including both a regional retail center and a series of local ones, and for locating schools and churches. The plan was generalized in that preliminary locations for these facilities were included in the site maps with which the firm worked, but final locations and facility designs were not made until just before actual construction. No longer needing to accommodate his ideas to several township boundaries, the builder could plan the community as a set of residential "parks," with school, playground, and pool located at the center in true neighborhood planning tradition.

There were other innovations in the plan for the third Levittown. The elementary schools would be provided by the firm and their cost incorporated into the house price. They could be "donated" to the community, thus keeping taxes down, and would be open when people moved in. The previous pattern of neighborhoods with only one house type was dropped. From now on, the three types of houses were to be mixed on each street: a four-bedroom "Cape Cod" initially selling for $11,500; a three-bedroom, one-story "Rancher" for $13,000; and a two-story "Colonial," one with three, another with four bedrooms and costing $14,000 and $14,500 respectively. Each house type was built in two elevations, but with the same floor plan, and was varied in external color to effect yet more visual heterogeneity. Whereas the houses in Levittown, Pennsylvania, were of a fairly severe modern style, those in New Jersey would be in the pseudo-Colonial style popular all over the Eastern seaboard. The shopping center, again located at the edge of the community, was designed by a nationally known architect who had built a prize-winning center in the Middle West, providing a considerably more attractive shopping area than in the Pennsylvania Levittown.

During the initial planning phase, Levitt employed an engineer with city planning experience to develop the overall plan, and also brought in a number of nationally known consultants to design detailed plans for educational and recreational facilities; but no city planners were included among the consultants. Subsequently, he did work with the planner hired by Willingboro township, and in 1964, when the firm was building developments of varying size in a number of locations all over the world, it finally hired a city planner to help select sites and make preliminary master plans.

The executives themselves were divided into two relatively stable factions, the self-styled "idealists" who wanted to build what they considered the best possible community, and the "realists," concentrated mainly in the comptroller's office, who were concerned with economy and sometimes questioned innovations that might increase costs or affect sales. Levitt himself seems to have mediated between the two groups. In the initial phases of planning he sided with the idealists, but later, when plans were about to be implemented, he became more conscious of cost and market considerations and often supported the realists. Generally speaking, the plans put forth by the idealists and their consultants were accepted when they contributed to the development of the best community at the lowest cost, and rejected when they were too expensive or added "frills" that would not help sales. Although Levitt had been traditionally hostile to outsiders, he accepted many of the consultants' proposals—often because they agreed with his own ideas. The consultants had been chosen initially because of their national reputations, and the agreement between them and Levitt was often fortuitous. For example, the concept of the school at the center of the neighborhood, originally brought into the firm by Alfred Levitt, was also part of traditional planning ideology and was favored by the school consultants as well. Similarly, because the firm wanted to divest itself of control of the recreation facilities and believed that the school and playground would be used by the same people and should therefore be administered jointly, it proposed a combined school-playground-pool area. When the firm asked the National Recreation Association for technical help, it did not know that that organization had advocated such a combination for almost forty years.

But some plans were rejected. One Levitt official wanted a new and comprehensively planned educational system to be designed under the aegis of the Ford Foundation, but when Foundation funds for this scheme were not available, a more conventional school system, more akin to existing county and township values and practices, was developed instead. The ambitious recreation plan of another firm member, providing for a large park and playground system around the school and more than one swimming pool for each neighborhood, was similarly cut down to make more land available for houses. As the time for building drew closer, both of these officials who stood for a maximum investment in community facilities could not agree with the emphasis on housing, and eventually they were fired, although not for this reason alone.

Perhaps the principal innovation in the new Levittown was the mixing of house types. This idea, originally suggested by Mrs. Levitt, debated within the firm for several months, and finally carried out by Levitt over the strong objections of all his executives, stemmed indirectly from the criticisms of the city planners, particularly Lewis Mumford. During the 1950s, when attacks on the physical and demographic homogeneity of the postwar suburban subdivisions began, Levittown was frequently mentioned as the prototype. At first, the firm shrugged off this criticism. As it continued to mount, however, and spread into the mass media, Levitt became concerned that Levittown's image would be impaired and even that sales might be affected, particularly when, later in the decade, the sellers' market was starting to become a buyers' market. By the time he was ready to start the third Levittown, Levitt also wanted a reputation for building the best possible communities.

In addition, the firm was beginning to upgrade the image of the purchaser it was seeking. In Long Island it had built for veterans and had attracted predominantly lower middle class buyers. In Pennsylvania, however, Levittown also drew a number of blue collar workers and what Levitt officials worriedly called "marginal" buyers, people who could not really afford the house but were able to take it because no down payment had been required under Veterans Administration mortgage insurance regulations. The firm did not want marginal buyers in the new Levittown, and, in fact, hoped to build somewhat more expensive houses which would increase its profit margin. If it was to do so, and bring in middle and upper middle class home buyers, Levitt wanted to prove incorrect the critical magazine articles on suburbia read by this population. When the idea of mixed house types was approved, one of the Levitt executives pointed out, "Now Lewis Mumford can't criticize us any more"; later, the firm promoted the innovation as a sales device. In the press release announcing the opening of the new Levittown, Levitt said, "We are ending once and for all the old bugaboo of uniformity. . . . In the new Levittown, we build all the different houses . . . right next to each other within the same section."

The struggle against criticism affected other features of the plan. Although the Levitts personally identified so much with their developments as to give them the family name, William Levitt was quite aware that some people considered "Levittown" a symbol of the worst in suburban development, even if others saw it as a brand name for good and inexpensive houses.[6] Several executives urged strongly that the name be dropped, but Levitt rejected the idea. As a compromise, the merchandising was to stress the individual parks into which people would buy. A Levitt official pointed out, "One of the major reasons for the neighborhood plan was to answer the critics of Levittown who say that it is one huge mass of homogeneous mass-produced housing, all preplanned to standardization and mass production."

Shortly before Levittown, New Jersey, opened for occupancy, an article by William Levitt entitled "What! *Live* in a Levittown?" appeared in *Good Housekeeping*.[7] In it, the builder argued—and quite rightly so—that mass-produced housing did not lead to conformity or homogeneity among the population. After Levittown opened, many tongue-in-cheek advertisements appeared in the Philadelphia papers which sought to give the impression that Levittowners were diverse, respectably middle class, but not overly sophisticated. One ad, headed "Wanted: Zoologist for a Neighbor," indicated that all occupations were represented in Levittown but listed mostly professional ones. Another, entitled "Hi and Middle Fi," suggested that the Levitt house could be rigged up for hi-fi enthusiasts, but poked fun at such sophisticated taste and concluded, "You'll find all kinds of music lovers in Levittown, but we've discovered that most of them are middle-fi, like ourselves." [8]

When it came to planning the houses, however, there was less concern with status than with livability and effective use of space. The houses built in the third Levittown were radically improved versions of the models built in the earlier ones, altered frequently and sometimes annually in a process of trial and error that responded partly to market reactions, partly to technological innovation and cost-cutting opportunities, and partly to a desire for change within the Levitt firm. The basic construction concepts and layouts have remained remarkably stable, however. The Levitt house is built on a concrete slab with precut materials and is put together on an assembly line basis. [9] The layout provides a relatively open house plan, with maximum space for rooms and for storage, and a minimum for circulation or symbolic, nonutilitarian space such as a foyer.

In the initial planning phase, Levitt considered a total revision of the basic house types, and asked two world-famous architects to submit sketch plans. When their houses turned out to cost about $50,000, they had to be dropped, and the firm's own small architectural department, with assistance from Levitt executives, was given the job of revamping the designs used in Levittown, Pennsylvania. When models of the houses were erected, Levitt himself looked them over and suggested changes. After the model was opened to the public, criticisms and suggestions for it were recorded at the sales desk. If a model did not sell, it was redesigned at once. Usually the models were not altered until the annual model change or until sales dropped to a point where alteration was considered necessary. [10]

The improvements made in the houses over time have increased their spaciousness and efficiency, with little concern for fashion except in inexpensive externals. Despite the popularity of basement or split-level designs, the firm refused to consider them until 1965, when it built some basement houses in a new Long Island project. Likewise, Levitt officials chose the pseudo-Colonial design for New Jersey, not because of its popularity, but because they felt it would help them attract higher-income purchasers, and because they themselves disliked the starkly modern designs they had initially built in Levittown, Pennsylvania. The design of the Levittown houses proceeded, then, on an ad hoc basis, with periodic improvements based on what the firm thought best and with recognition of the vetoes expressed in the market. Beyond this point, there was no catering to the customers.

For this reason, no market research of any kind went into the planning of Levittown, New Jersey, although just before the community opened some of the less optimistic Levitt officials commissioned a prominent land economist to estimate the market for the community. His report was extremely pessimistic, noting that the metropolitan area market for low-priced, single-family housing was almost saturated, and that the new Levittown was located outside of what were then considered the boundaries of Philadelphia's suburban commuting zone. As it turned out, the consultant's prediction was accurate, for by 1960 the soft market conditions he had forecast began to appear, forcing a slowdown in the construction schedule that has continued until the present. Although the firm expected to build 12,000 houses by 1965, it had only put up about 6000 by that date—and it had also established a market research department.

In planning for the new Levittown, however, Levitt had no inkling of what was to come. His mass production techniques had previously enabled the firm to undersell its competitors in the area, and in a seller's market it did not need to think about the buyers. The Levitt officials' ability to make decisions without consulting them was aided considerably by their consensus with and similarity to their customers. Most of the Levitt executives were born and raised in the suburbs, and had little or no use for the city, other than as a place for occasional recreational and shopping trips. They favored single-family housing and could not understand why anyone would want to live either in apartments or in the row houses that had been Philadelphia's dominant building type. They believed that the utility of the house for family living came first and that style was secondary. Their taste was not much different from that of their customers; both rejected the abstract and severe contemporary design that dominated the architectural magazines of the late 1950s.

If anything, the firm's official style was a more exuberant version of its customers', in much the same way as movie stars are often exaggerated versions of what their fans would like to be. Indeed, a decade earlier, Eric Larrabee had described the first Levitt office building as "Selznick Colonial." [11] The new headquarters building the firm put up in Levittown, New Jersey, was furnished in what one might call Dionysian-Modern, a vivid and often garish mixture of bright colors, strong textures, and antique as well as modern knickknacks. Levitt's office had white rugs and gold-plated bathroom fixtures, and the model homes, furnished to entice purchasers, displayed a similar, if less expensive, Dionysian motif.

About their purchasers' aspirations for life in Levittown, the Levitt officials thought only rarely. Some looked down on them as being of a lesser status, but others saw them as smart, young, socially mobile couples who really wanted to live in high-status suburbs but could not afford to do so. Mostly, the firm viewed them as people who needed a new house and were obviously sensible in their choice of Levittown, because they realized that Levitt's houses were the best value for the money. It also felt that most of their buyers were moving to Levittown only because of the house and had little interest in the wider community. As a result, whenever Levittowners objected to conditions in the community, firm officials were quick to argue—whether the firm was responsible or not—that the objections were those of a minority, "self-seeking politicians," or "sick" people who just wanted to show off for psychological reasons. Suspicion of community participation was a tradition of the Levitt organization, even though there had been much less builder-buyer conflict in the Levittowns than in most other new housing developments.[12]

Marketing the House

The only deliberate planning vis-à-vis the eventual purchasers took place in marketing the house. That process was aimed at attracting the young family buying its first home, a group to which the builder had appealed ever since he began to build the first Levittown. The houses were designed with young children in mind, with bedrooms just large enough to serve as playrooms as well, an extra bathroom for them, and the kitchen located so mothers could watch their children play outside.[13] In addition, Levitt provided all the necessary kitchen appliances, eliminating extra initial expenditures. He absorbed settlement costs, which often come to 5 per cent or more of the house price, and he simplified the sales procedure so that buying a house was almost as easy as buying a washing machine. His advertising stressed that there were "no hidden extras, and the price you pay is the price we say." Unlike builders of higher-priced houses, he emphasized the size of the down payment—which thanks to FHA insurance was low—and the monthly payments, so that prospective purchasers could readily figure exactly how much the house would take out of the paycheck.

The firm went to a considerable effort to keep the monthly payment figure as low as possible. As already noted, the builder "donated" the schools to the community. During the first years, he subsidized the schools' operating costs as well, holding taxes, which were added to the monthly payment, at a level that would not frighten away the family earning $6000 or $7000 a year. Thanks to the scale on which the firm was operating, the cost of schools, utilities, and road system could be added to the house price without raising it beyond what other builders in the area were charging.

While all the ads mentioned the schools, churches, and pools, the major emphasis was on the size and value of the house, presented in a confident yet catchy style as if to dare skeptics to come to see whether Levittown's values were real. Many ads were written by William Levitt himself. When the prospective purchaser came out to the model homes area, his attention was focused on the house, and the sales process itself was muted as much as possible. The salesmen were carefully selected and trained to contradict the image of the fast-buck, easy-talking salesmen traditionally associated with real estate. "Courteous representatives are on hand to answer your questions," the ads read. They were dressed in conservative dark clothes—to look like bankers, as one Levitt official put it—and they were instructed by a professional speech teacher to talk in a sedate but friendly manner.

While everyone was welcome to buy in Levittown, the firm did try to screen out two types of people: the marginal buyers and the socially undesirable or emotionally disturbed. Partly because of FHA regulations, the firm had set an income floor for purchasers: people who wanted to buy had to have a weekly income 10 per cent above the monthly carrying charge—more if they had many children or large outstanding debts. Those who could not meet this figure were asked for a larger down payment or were advised against putting down the deposit, and some were excluded by the subsequent credit check. The salesmen were not to sell to disreputable or especially unkempt people, and the credit check excluded people with a record of job instability or legal difficulties.[14] The "social filtering" process was, however, less effective than the income check, for some people with serious—but not visible—problems were able to buy into the community.

Until the state enforced a nondiscrimination law, salesmen refused to sell to Negroes and assured whites who asked about Negroes that the community would be as lily-white as the other Levittowns. After the law was enforced, the salesmen protected themselves by citing the law, and promised to locate people who did not like to be near Negroes away from them, but also discouraged those who were strongly biased against Negroes from buying in Levittown. (The story of Levittown's integration is told in Chapter Fourteen.)

LEVITT AND WILLINGBORO TOWNSHIP

The Levitt planning did not take place within a vacuum, of course. Perhaps the most important outside influences were the federal government, which through FHA insured the mortgages of the purchasers, and the banks who purchased them. Without the FHA, Levittown could not have been built, for the banks would not take the uninsured mortgages of middle-income, young home buyers whose long-term financial status was, at best, unpredictable. Levitt had to meet the FHA regulations, both for the design of the house and the community, and the expectations of the bankers and savings and loan association officials, but since the previous Levittowns had met FHA standards, this created no problem. Indeed, thanks to his previous success, Levitt was able to quiet the fears of his bankers that the mixing of house types on the street would inhibit sales.

The other group which played a role—even if not a major one—in the early planning of Levittown was the government and the old residents of Willingboro township. Willingboro township was a sleepy farming area with a history—albeit uneventful—dating back to William Penn's arrival in the Philadelphia area in 1681. Its political and civic life was in the hands of a few families some of whom had been in power for at least 125 years. Although one or two were wealthy, most of them were friendly and easygoing lower middle class people, who explained guilelessly that they were running township affairs because no one else was interested and someone had to do it. Yet newcomers to the township, and especially those with dissident views, were often denied access to the political and social elite.

In 1952, the township had set up a Planning Board, mainly because, in the words of its founder, "We just went along with the crowd; everybody was doing it." Also, it was feared that eventually subdividers would come to the area, and the township ought to protect itself. A zoning ordinance was passed, designating the land as agricultural, but nothing else was done until 1955, when it became known that land was being purchased by unknown buyers. At that time, the chairman of the Planning Board decided to hire a planning consultant.

The planning consultant was a professional who had been active in other parts of Burlington County for several years and saw his role as one of educating this predominantly rural area to the virtues of master planning. His ideas reflected those traditional among planners: orderly and effective use of the land to prevent patches of vacant land amidst other development that would lead to urban sprawl, and an esthetically pleasing landscape. He was particularly concerned with the elimination of "strip shopping," believing stores strung out on major streets and highways to be a "commercial cancer growth," which might blight residential neighborhoods near them. A crusader on this topic, he was especially intent on keeping out essential but unsightly enterprises such as ice cream parlors, hot dog stands, and commercial garages.

Once hired by the township, the planner persuaded it to have him draw up a master plan which he hoped the Levitt organization would also follow. Initially, Levitt was hostile; he wanted total control and was fearful of any outside interference, especially by a city planner. Consequently, he urged the Planning Board to fire the planner, but was persuaded that this was an inauspicious beginning for Levitt's relationship with Willingboro township. Since the firm was sensitive to criticism about the lack of planning in earlier Levittowns, the planner was eventually able to persuade the Levitt organization that a master plan would be to its benefit. On the other hand, the planner realized that his master plan would be largely dependent on Levitt's building program. He soon concluded that the cause of planning and his own efforts could best be advanced by siding with the builder, whom he considered an agent of progress, rather than with the existing residents, some of whom would probably be opposed to the new community.

The township Planning Board knew little about city planning, but its members were sincere and earnest enough to feel that planning, whatever it might be, was a good thing. The consultant's first recommendation was a revision of the zoning ordinance which would enable it—or the consultant—to prevent strip shopping on the major highway on which Levittown fronts. Naturally, the people who owned this land objected strenuously. This zoning ordinance crystallized the township into pro- and anti-Levitt factions. Generally speaking, the people whose land Levitt had bought—mostly the bigger landowners, since he was interested only in large acreage—were, if not in favor of Levitt, at least amenable. Conversely, those who had not been approached by Levitt—people who owned only two or three acres—or did not want to sell to Levitt made up the anti-Levitt faction. From this time on until the arrival of the new Levittowners, the once peaceful politics of the township were no more; old friendships and alliances disintegrated as some sided with, others against Levitt.

The hateful zoning ordinance was rescinded after the people on the highway started court proceedings. This, as well as the general antagonism to Levitt by some of the community leaders, helped to bring the planning consultant firmly on Levitt's side. He decided that the old residents were interested only in making as much money as they could from Levitt's presence and that they had no interest in good planning. From then on, the consultant worked so closely with the builder that it caused him some difficulty in obtaining the community's trust. Because of this relationship, the planner knew the firm's still confidential building plans and was therefore reluctant to talk to citizens, which also affected his relationship to the community. Indeed, when I asked him for an interview to learn about the master plan, I was refused, only to receive a call from a Levitt vice-president who asked why I wanted the interview. Once I had explained my study to him, I had no trouble in obtaining an interview with the planning consultant.

Levitt had never favored the ordinance against strip shopping as much as the planner, and once it had been rescinded, the firm had little difficulty in persuading the township fathers to approve his building plans. There were several reasons for this. First, some of the people in the pro-Levitt faction planned to remain in Willingboro township even after Levittown had been built and believed that the interests of their community could best be served by letting Levitt go ahead with his development without undue harassment. They wanted to live in a good-looking and well-planned township, and had been persuaded that the anti-Levitt faction would sell its land to speculators who would put up hot dog stands, small factories, and the other low-status outlets against which the planning consultant had been campaigning. Some had more immediate motives; they hoped to work in the township, either in the government or in stores which they would open to serve the new residents.

Also, the firm's intention to build—and pay for—most of the municipal facilities relieved public officials of the need to worry about them. Unlike small subdividers elsewhere in the county, Levitt was providing the schools, roads, water and sewage plants, and other facilities, and because he was doing so—and because the new Levittowners would be paying for them—the older residents of the township felt he ought to have the right to determine the character of those facilities. They all realized that whatever he provided would be far superior to what had existed before, and possibly even better than what would be built with public funds. As a rural area, Willingboro township—and Burlington County—had not been noted for lavishness in the provision of public facilities in the past.

The public officials who had to approve the Levitt building plans could, of course, have asked for better or more expensive facilities. In some instances, however, they had no legal basis for such requests, since the township and county both lacked modern building and other codes. Yet even when they had effective veto power over Levitt's operations, they did not often think to exercise it, because they felt Levitt was trying to do a good job and would make the township the best in the county. Cooperation with the builder would be far more pleasant than conflict, they concluded, particularly since they had little chance of winning such conflict.

Most of the old residents were farmers, without the knowledge and skills to stand up against the builder. For example, the ablest member of the Planning Board thought that the township would look better if Levitt were required to build on 75-foot lots rather than on the 60-foot lots he wanted to allow for in the subdivision ordinance. He could not, however, make his argument stick, and after Levitt had promised that he would never build on less than 65-foot lots, he gave in.

The Levitt firm itself was not passive in the face of opposition. Its officials had had two decades of experience in dealing with local opposition, and they had a reputation for brilliant tactics as well as the application of campaign funds in the right place at the right time. When Levitt first arrived on the scene, the firm engaged some prominent county figures to buy land, and before the planning was over, it had hired, for one reason or another, most of the politically influential lawyers in the county and many who had influence in the state capitol as well, principally for the alteration of township boundaries. Although the firm never interfered officially in county or township politics, and usually sent campaign contributions to both parties, it gave more to defeat candidates it thought could cause trouble for the firm. Every new community is flooded with rumors that some local officials are on the builder's payroll, and Levittown was no exception, but one Levitt executive indicated that the township leaders were so willing to go along with the firm's wishes that such distasteful tactics were not necessary.

Even if local politicians had wanted to fight Levitt, they had little political incentive. Their remaining old constituents did not really care about matters that concerned only the new community, and the new constituents were not yet on the scene. Even if the politicians could agree among themselves to put up a united front against Levitt (which was not often the case), there was always the possibility that he would intervene against them at higher political levels in the county and state. But when the township officials did question the Levitt proposals, it was almost always on matters of detail. On the larger issues they agreed, for they shared some basic values with the firm, and they united against a common enemy. Both were antiurban, and both resented the *cosmopolitan,* upper middle class, intellectual values they associated with the big city, believing that planning should uphold the *local* values of the small middle or lower middle class community.[15] This consensus was demonstrated in the planning of the new school system.

The Ford Foundation, which had suggested a comprehensive planning program for the Levittown schools, had urged that the superintendent of an upper middle class New England suburban school system of national repute be hired to head it, to plan an educational program whose graduates would presumably head toward the most cosmopolitan of the country's colleges. When funds for this plan were not forthcoming, Levitt turned the job of designing the schools over to a national firm of school consultants, and asked the county Superintendent of Schools to develop the curriculum and hire the staff. Both the consultants and the superintendent defended more traditional local approaches. The consultants disliked big-city schools and were conservative about educational innovation. "If you are going to try something new," the principal consultant pointed out, "you need someone to bounce your ideas against," but the new Levittowners had not yet arrived and the township Board of Education was hesitant to speak for them. As a result, the final architectural program was the consultants' standard package. The county superintendent had spent most of his professional life in Burlington County, was personally interested in rural education, and did not favor teachers from the big cities or from high-status suburbs who might question the township's rural, lower middle class values.

I do not know how the Levitt organization felt about the Foundation's cosmopolitan educational concepts, but it had no educational aims of its own, and judging by its feelings toward the intellectuals then criticizing suburbia, it was not distressed over the change in plans. In any case, the firm supported the consultants and the superintendent fully, allowing the township Board of Education to feel that its essentially rural educational values would be perpetuated in the new Levittown. Subsequently, the county superintendent was hired to run the Levittown schools, and in the years to come, when the conflict about upper middle class cosmopolitan and lower middle class local education raged among the Levittowners themselves, the builder was usually found on the side of the latter.

As it turned out, then, the goals of the Levitt organization and the township were never far apart, and even if Levitt sought to accommodate some of the criticism of suburbia in his planning, he was not ready to build the kind of urbane new town that intellectuals would approve. Both in their business judgments and in their personal inclinations, the Levitt officials sided with the young, middle class purchasers with whom they had been dealing successfully in the past and who, they were sure, would approve the innovations they had made in their aim to create a showplace—but a profitable one—in the newest Levittown.

NOTES

1. For an early history of the Levitt organization, see Larrabee.
2. Larrabee. For a more detailed description of Levittown, New York, see Liell (1952), Wattel, and Dobriner (1963), Chap. 4.
3. See Alfred S. Levitt.
4. In the pages that follow, I will for this reason use Levitt, meaning William Levitt, as a synonym for the firm, although he did not always make personally all the decisions thus ascribed to him.
5. The material in the following section is based on interviews with a number of Levitt executives. Unfortunately, I was never able to obtain interviews with either William or Alfred Levitt.
6. Early in the building of Levittown, Long Island, a group of Levittowners tried to get their post office address changed to Hicksville. Later, in Levittown, Pennsylvania, the people who had bought the high-priced houses also wanted to detach themselves from Levittown, and at one point tried to buy the neighborhood pool for their own use.
7. William J. Levitt.
8. *Philadelphia Evening Bulletin*, March 1, 1959, and February 26, 1959, respectively.
9. The firm's building methods are described in Levitt and Sons, and in *Practical Builder*.
10. Often, the saving is passed on to the purchaser, for the cost of the house on a square-foot basis has not increased significantly since the first Levittown. The houses themselves have grown in size; the Levittown, Long Island homes had only two bedrooms and an unfinished attic; in Levittown, New Jersey, they initially had three or four bedrooms, and a minimum square footage of over 1200 square feet even in the smallest one. In 1963, the firm began to experiment with five-bedroom houses, and in 1964, to build them.
11. Larrabee, p. 81.
12. On earlier manifestations of this suspicion, see Larrabee, p. 84, and Liell (1952).

13. Conversely, the house was less suited to families with teenage children, for the bedrooms were not large enough to serve their needs, and the compact design of the house and its lack of soundproofing made it difficult for teenagers and adults to have privacy from each other.

14. One Levittowner tested this by coming in shabby clothes and several days' beard to buy a house, only to be refused. The next week, he came back clean and clean-shaven and was sold a house.

15. On the conception of cosmopolitans and locals, see Merton (1957).

Chapter Two

THE LEVITTOWNERS—AND WHY THEY CAME

IN 1958, BEFORE LEVITTOWN, NEW JERSEY, WAS OCCUPIED, THE township contained about 300 households. By 1960, the number had risen to 2978 (totaling 11,861 individuals), and by 1964, to about 6200 households (with about 25,000 individuals). The people to be described in this chapter are the first 3000 families who came to Levittown between October 1958 and June 1960.[1]

These Levittowners were, like many other suburbanites, primarily young families who came to the new community to raise their children.[2] At the time of their arrival in 1958–1960, almost four fifths of the men were under forty; 44 per cent were between the ages of thirty and forty.[3] Ten per cent were as yet childless couples; another 6 per cent, in which the wives were over thirty-five, were probably permanently childless. Median family size, according to the 1960 Census, was 3.90, but at the time of arrival, in 1958–1960, almost a fifth of the families had three children, and another 11 per cent had four or more. A third of the families had only children of preschool age; 5 per cent had a majority of the children in high school.

At time of arrival, the median family income of the population was $7125; 11 per cent earned more than $10,500 and about 20 per cent earned less than the $5500 required for buyers making the minimal down payment.[4] Eighteen per cent of the men were professionals, 56 per cent were white collar workers, and 26 per cent were blue collar workers. Among the white collar workers,

13 per cent were managers and minor officials; 18 per cent were technicians and semiprofessionals; and the remaining 25 per cent were in clerical and sales work. The blue collar workers were divided into 7 per cent foremen, 10 per cent skilled workers, and 9 per cent semiskilled and unskilled workers. Most of the Levittowners worked in the offices, stores, and electronics and other manufacturing and research plants in Philadelphia and Camden, but 12 per cent were in the armed forces, principally as Air Force pilots. Being mainly young people, their educational levels were fairly high. According to the 1960 Census, 43 per cent had attended college, 27 per cent graduating; only 28 per cent had not received a high school diploma.

Although these statistics suggest that most Levittowners were lower middle class, they still overestimate the upper middle and working class populations. Most of the professionals were teachers and social workers; only 10 per cent of them were doctors or lawyers. Also, the majority of those who attended college had gone to junior and community colleges, small private schools, and state universities; probably less than 10 per cent had attended the "name" universities of high educational and social status. I would guess that no more than 5 to 10 per cent of the Levittowners could be considered upper middle class.

Conversely, most of the blue collar Levittowners were in the highest-skill, highest-status manual occupations, such as foremen, printers, electricians, and plumbers, and 10 per cent had attended college. Many were trying to raise their children for middle class careers, and I suspect that the proportion of families who were working class in terms of family culture was smaller than the proportion working at blue collar trades—perhaps only 20 per cent of the total population. Thus, about 75 per cent of the community might be considered lower middle class, culturally speaking.

Thirty-seven per cent of the families were Roman Catholic; 47 per cent were Protestant—with Methodists, Lutherans, Presbyterians, and Baptists in the majority; and 14 per cent were Jewish, the majority Conservative. This distribution is similar to that of Levittown, Pennsylvania, and of the Philadelphia metropolitan area generally. The vast majority, 66 per cent, were third and fourth generation Americans; 28 per cent were second generation (native born of foreign parents) and 6 per cent were foreign born. Thirty-seven per cent reported being of Northern

European origin (English, German, or Scandinavian); 17 per cent were Eastern European (mostly Russian Jewish with a scattering of Poles); 10 per cent, Irish; 9 per cent, Southern European (mainly Italian), and the remainder a heady mixture of all of these backgrounds. Most came from acculturated homes, however, with little evidence of ethnic culture remaining except among Jews and a handful of Greeks, Chinese, and Japanese. In 1964, less than 1 per cent of the population was Negro, most of these families having moved in after my study was completed.

MAJOR SUBCULTURES AMONG THE LEVITTOWNERS

Statistics do not provide a complete picture of the Levittowners and how they vary, and figures must be fleshed out by ethnographic description. Age and life-cycle position are important sources of diversity in American society, but most Levittowners are young couples. Given the declining influence on behavior of regional origin, religious preference, and ethnic background, the crucial source of variety in Levittown is *class* and *class subculture.*

Classes are strata-with-subcultures that grow out of the structure of the national economy and society.[5] By class subcultures I mean *sets of responses* that have developed out of people's efforts to cope with the opportunities, incentives, and rewards, as well as the deprivations, prohibitions, and pressures, which the natural environment and society offer to them.

From another perspective, subcultures are *predispositions* to behavior, ways of acting to be followed when the social situation permits it. For example, the desire for community activity is a major source of differentiation between lower middle and upper middle class subcultures. People of the latter class are more predisposed to routine involvement in civic ventures; those of the former participate only when there is a political threat to their homes and families or when occupational roles require it, as in the case of a lawyer or insurance salesman who must advertise his services through community activities in order to earn a living. The social situations with which people must cope and the roles they normally play are, of course, the most important determinants of behavior, but cultural predispositions help to explain why people act differently in the same social situation or role. Finally, subcultures are *aggregates* of predispositions, so that where one is found (for example, civic activity), another (buying gourmet foods or reading a magazine like *Harper's*) is also likely to be present. Predispositions are related or aggregated, sometimes into a fairly stable system, because the situations which people face and the responses they make are often similar, and it is these similarities which are estimated when class is measured by income, occupation, or education. At one time, occupation was an easy clue to the rest of a person's culture, but among the Levittowners education is probably the best index, for years of schooling and the quality of the school attended influence strongly the job for which a person is eligible, the amount of money he has to spend, the kind of woman he marries, and the way he and his family will spend their leisure hours.

The people who came to Levittown may be distinguished as "belonging" to three major class subcultures, which can be labeled as working class, lower middle class, and upper middle class. They must be described in very general terms, ignoring for the sake of clarity the many nuances and diversities which each individual, by virtue of his upbringing and experience, expresses in acting upon his own predispositions. At best, then, the descriptions that follow are brief profiles; at worst, they are only stereotypes.[6]

The Working Class

The way of life I call "working class subculture" is to be found not only among blue collar workers, but also among lower-echelon white collar workers and among people who did not graduate from high school. In the white population, many are Catholics, and of Irish, Italian, and Southern or Eastern European peasant backgrounds. The vestiges of this origin are especially strong in family life. The typical working class family is sexually segregated. Husbands and wives exchange love and affection, but they have separate family roles and engage in little of the companionship found in the middle classes. The husband is the breadwinner and the enforcer of child discipline; the wife is the housekeeper and rears the children. Whenever possible, husbands spend their free time with other male companions, women with other women. Entertaining is rarer than in the middle class, and most social life takes place among relatives and childhood friends. When they are not available, there is occasional visiting with neighbors and also a tendency for husband and wife to draw closer to each other.[7] Even so, it is significant that the first organization to be founded in Levittown was the Veterans of Foreign Wars, its predominantly working class membership quickly making it a suburban substitute for the city's neighborhood tavern.

Parent-child relationships are *adult-centered*. Children are expected to behave according to adult rules and are often disciplined when they act as children. Therefore, the young child is supervised strictly and his life is bounded by a large number of rules, deviation from which is punished affectionately but, by middle class standards, harshly. The main purpose of child-rearing is to make sure that the child stays out of trouble—that is, does not get into difficulties with the school or the police. For this reason, working class parents expect the school to enforce discipline. Children react to these parental demands by seeking to get out of the house at an early age and to give up the family for the peer group as soon as possible. For some years there is familial conflict over this move, but, generally speaking, working class parents give their children freedom sooner than middle class parents do. They often expect the child to get into trouble by the time he reaches adolescence, and accept its occurrence fatalistically. By then the child, especially the boy, is expected to be a near-adult and responsible for himself.

Socially mobile working class families attempt to prolong adult control, especially over school behavior. Since parents know that mobility can only be achieved by educational success, they put pressure on their children to do well in school. Not being well equipped to help the child, however, they can only continually urge him to work harder at his studies. Often, this kind of pressure is ineffective, and mobile families find to their disappointment that the child does poorly in school. In nonmobile families, children are expected to finish whatever schooling is necessary to obtain good—that is, secure and stable—jobs. By now high school graduation is considered desirable, and if a boy is academically successful, the parents will make an effort to send him to college. However, there are usually so many opposing peer group influences and other pressures that by the time the child reaches college age he is neither able nor willing to go on.

Working class culture provides few of the skills and attitudes needed for organizational activities. People find it extremely difficult to accept the validity of values and interests which conflict with theirs; they have trouble relating to strangers and making decisions in a group—or for the group. Also, they tend to view political and other organizations with the same moral measuring stick as the family, and expect similarly altruistic behavior from such organizations. This produces a highly personalistic view of government and associations, and when their actions are undesirable, they are seen as tools of unscrupulous individuals out for personal gain. More generally, working class people believe—with some justification—that these agencies are established to benefit the business community and the middle class, and to deprive "working people" of their rightful share of goods and privileges. As a result, they are highly suspicious of private and governmental organizations and reject them when their aims do not accord with working class priorities. In a middle class community then, people of working class culture stay close to home and make the house a haven against a hostile outside world.[8]

The Lower Middle Class

Probably three quarters of the Levittowners follow the predisposition of lower middle class culture. They are some of the blue collar workers, the white collar ones, and even many of the professionals; they are people who have completed high school and perhaps a vocationally or a nonintellectually-oriented liberal arts college.

The lower middle class family is sexually less segregated than the working class one. Husbands and wives are closer to being companions, for both sexes have learned to share a few common interests and to participate to some extent in each other's world. Since neither man nor woman is likely to have an intense outside avocation, the home and the family are the focal point for mutuality. Partly because the common interest is in the home, the lower middle class family is *child-centered*. This characteristic must not be exaggerated, however, for the image so popular in the mass media—of impotent parents dominated by their demanding children—is inaccurate, except perhaps among families from extremely poor beginnings, who want their children to have everything they missed and then cannot cope with their ceaseless requests. Most lower middle class families are child-centered only to the extent that the home is run for both adults and children, and the children are allowed to be themselves and to act as children. At the same time, they are raised strictly, for parents are fearful of spoiling them. Lower middle class parents play with their children much more than working class parents do. Partly for this reason, they do not relinquish control over their children so quickly. They believe in the value of school and church, but do not want these institutions to transform the child or to make demands that would alienate it from the home. The working class sees these institutions as keeping the child in line; the lower middle class wants them to support the home and its values.

In education the lower middle class prefers a modern approach without undue pressure on the child, with every child treated as an individual—but not as a unique or different one, as upper middle class parents favor. Social adjustment is as important as academic success: it is hoped that the children will be accepted by peers of equal status. Educational achievement is important; lower middle class parents want their children to go to college, because higher education is a prerequisite to a respectable and well-paid job and a good marriage.

One reason for the child-centeredness of the lower middle class family is that such a family type is nuclear—that is, consisting only of parents and children. In America, the clanlike extended family is highly valued only in the working class, in some ethnic groups of all classes, and for other reasons, in the upper class. Lower middle class people still love and visit their relatives, but if they are too far away to visit, they are not especially missed, for lower middle class people are able to make friends. Their social life is informal and involves primarily neighbors and friends met through organizational activities.

Many lower middle class people are also active in church and in voluntary associations. The church reinforces their view of the world as run by morality, in which goodness, kindness, honesty, and altruism are important motive forces to action, and evil is the result of evil impulses. Of course, the church is important also as a source of fellowship; here people can find friends with similar viewpoints, and of similar class level as well, and without having to admit this aim as a motivation. Parents support such organizations as the PTA and the Scouts, which uphold the cultural values of orderliness, self-reliance, constructive leisure, and above all, the primacy of the home and its moral strictures. People also belong to purely adult associations, many still sex-segregated, which combine sociability with community service. As in the case of the working class, the lower middle class normally has little interest in government. The working class distrusts politicians because they are seen as enriching themselves; the lower middle class is wary of politicians as dishonest and opportunistic. If government is immoral, the best solution is to keep its functions and power minimal; the ideal is a businessman or a city manager who will do away with politics and will also keep taxes low.

Today, the lower middle class must be divided into *restrictive* and *expansive* subgroups. The former includes most Protestants and those Catholics (especially of Irish origin) who have adopted the Calvinist-Puritan tradition of pre-twentieth century America. This tradition arose in the small towns of America, and its adherents still harbor considerable suspicion of the city and its people, but especially of the "action-seeking," adventurous working class and the urbane and cosmopolitan upper middle class. They try to lead sober and controlled lives, with little drinking or partying other than the ubiquitous card parties. Ostentation and gaudiness are shunned, as are excitement and sensuality, which may be enjoyed only vicariously in the mass media. The expansive group includes other Catholics, Jews, and those Protestants who share their European, non-Puritan origins, particularly those who have moved into the middle class from urban working class and ethnic origins. Members of the expansive subgroup buy more impulsively, enjoy an aggressively active social life, and are willing to drink, gamble, and enjoy openly the offerings of modern show business.

Lower middle class culture is often accused of being overly concerned with respectability and keeping up appearances. This is probably truer of the restrictive than of the expansive group, for the former is essentially attempting to maintain a past tradition. Even so, there is more of a conflict between the ideal and the real in the lower middle class than in the working class. The latter has few pretensions about the world and expresses its idealism as cynicism; working class people have suffered too much from reality to believe that things could be much different. Lower middle class people, however, still defend a preindustrial moral code which sometimes requires the hypocrisy that has been noted in contemporary lower middle class life.

The Upper Middle Class

A small proportion of managers and professionals have found their way to Levittown, at least temporarily, and although many are not yet upper middle class in income or status, they will be in years to come. Theirs is already the culture of the college-educated, cosmopolitan population, trained to be interested in and to participate in the larger world. Home and family are somewhat less important to this than to the other classes. The upper middle class family has shed almost all sexual segregation, for college attendance has trained women for organizational and occupational skills which they can and want to pursue even while being mothers and housewives. The wife still does the house-work—though she is likely to have domestic help to release her for other activities—but many of the child-rearing functions may be shared with the husband. Interests other than those of the home can also be shared by the spouses and, conversely, each can have interests that take them away from the home. One—but not the only one—of the shared interests is the children. The upper middle class is concerned with the development of the child as a unique individual, one who can perform autonomously in all spheres of life valued by the upper middle class, especially a re-warding professional career. In order to achieve these aims, parents provide direction for the lives of their children, so that while family life is child-centered, it is also *adult-directed*. The children are encouraged and even pressured to do well in school and parents are concerned that the school their children attend not only provide a good education but also demand a high level of performance.[9]

Since most upper middle class people (at least in Levittown) have achieved their present position by their own individual achievement, the relationship with the extended family is even more tenuous than in the lower middle class. Upper middle class people are good at making friends, and choose them on the basis of shared interests. There is a considerable amount of social life, although the parties and entertaining may be devoted as much to shop talk and civic affairs as to the gossip and small talk that con-stitute the staple of social conversation among other groups.

Upper middle class people participate not only in voluntary associations but in the entire community. As cosmopolitans, they want to shape the community by national values which may not respect local traditions.[10] For example, they are less interested in having the school system be superior to that of nearby commu-nities than in making sure that foreign languages are taught in the elementary grades. For this population, community participation is almost a cultural duty. Although upper middle class people are as distrustful of politicians as others, they have both the skills and the status to become involved in government and to fight for what they think is desirable. Needing the community's public institutions to provide cosmopolitan educational and cultural services that cannot be made available at home, they favor a high level of public expenditure, to be parceled out by well-educated, nonpartisan political leaders of their own class.

Upper middle class culture can also be divided into two subgroups which might be called *conservative-managerial* and *liberal-professional*. The former is often thought of as "the business community," and its people are likely to be politically and culturally conservative. The latter are frequently Jewish, and politically and culturally liberal, and are employed in the community-centered professions such as education and social work. In some ways, the distinction between the two groups is similar to the restrictive and expansive distinction in the lower middle class. The conservative-managerial upper middle class has also come from Protestant origins, although its behavior is less restrictive. The liberal-professional upper middle class is unusually active in the community. Aside from its personal interest in good schools—a characteristic it shares with the managerial group—it also fights for well-known liberal causes such as better race relations, community planning, mental health, and the United Nations. Indeed, it is much more cosmopolitan than the managerial group, more sensitive to "ideas" in the abstract and to national issues than the latter. The managerial group may often oppose the professional group here, for the former, being allied with business, favors low taxes and opposes the liberalism that is inherent in the cosmopolitan stance. Liberal-professionals are the main audience for high culture. They go to concerts, plays, and museums in the big cities; they organize lectures, art exhibitions, and visits from famous performers in the suburbs. The managerial group is more likely to put its energies into golf and the country club which the liberal-professionals shun.

MOVING TO LEVITTOWN

Most New Jersey Levittowners who bought in the first two years—77 per cent altogether—came from the Philadelphia metropolitan area, nearby New Jersey counties, and the states surrounding New Jersey. Almost half (46 per cent) had previously lived in what they described as suburban neighborhoods (including 8 per cent from Levittown, Pennsylvania); a third came from urban areas (19 per cent from Philadelphia); and 19 per cent came from small towns. (The rest came from farms or from army camps, here and abroad.) Although 60 per cent had been renters before, only 39 per cent moved to Levittown from apartments; for 53 per cent Levittown was their first house purchase, and for another 32 per cent, their second.[11] Many purchasers were mobile, the median Levittowner having moved once for every two and a half years of married life, and 17 per cent, once for every year of marriage. Some were quite stable, however, 13 per cent having moved less than once for every five years of marriage.[12]

People's reasons for moving *to* Levittown were primarily the need for more spacious housing and the desire to own a freestanding house—"to own our own home," as many put it.[13] Table 1 shows that these reasons, together with transfers to the Philadelphia area by the purchasers' employers were volunteered most frequently as the principal reason for moving *out of* the previous residence.[14] More important, the vast majority were moving because of the inadequacy of the housing. Only 9 per cent volunteered the inadequacy of the neighborhood or community as the most important reason, mostly city dwellers.

The purchasers could have moved to Levittown either because they needed to leave their prior residence or because they were attracted by suburbia and by Levittown—because they were *pushed* or *pulled*.[15] An analysis of how they worded their volunteered reasons for leaving their previous residence indicated that more were pushed than pulled, 55 per cent indicating the former, 34 per cent the latter. The people with the most urgent space needs, large families and blue collar workers, were pushed most often, but only among childless couples did those pulled outnumber those pushed. Even apartment dwellers and tenants, who might have been expected to want home ownership, were pushed more often than they were pulled, indicating again that the need for space was more urgent than all the possible attractions of suburbia in explaining why people moved to Levittown.

The major reason for choosing Levittown specifically, people explained, was that it offered "the best house for the money";

PRINCIPAL REASON FOR MOVING FROM PREVIOUS RESIDENCE, BY TYPE OF COMMUNITY

PRINCIPAL REASON	PERCENT OF PURCHASERS		
	Previous Community		
	Urban	Suburban	All [1]
HOUSE-RELATED REASONS	60	58	58
Need for more space	24	27	26
Want homeownership and free-standing house	17	21	18
Dwelling too hard to maintain, or want new and modern house	9	4	7
Moving out of parents' house	4	2	4
Evicted, need less space, etc.	6	4	3
COMMUNITY-RELATED REASONS	19	6	9
Inadequacy of schools, other facilities for children	2	1	1
Dirt, noise, other physical inadequacies	2	1	1
Racial change in neighborhood	4	0	1
Other dissatisfactions with social aspects of neighborhood or community	1	1	1
General dissatisfaction with neighborhood or community	10	3	5
JOB-RELATED REASONS	19	34	29
Transfer by employer	11	17	15
Change of job	7	11	9
Want shorter journey to work	1	6	5
OTHER	2	2	4
N	(170)	(238)	(520)

that is, a new single-family house which was the best value within their price range.[16] Many had shopped around, 52 per cent having inspected ten or more other developments, and 38 per cent having looked at houses for from one to five years before buying in Levittown. Table 2 describes in more detail their reasons for choosing Levittown. Eighty-four per cent came primarily because of factors relating to the house; only a few considered the facilities and social quality of the community their major reason for coming. No one volunteered as a reason for purchase the mixing of house types, and even the availability of schools at time of arrival was mentioned by less than 0.5 per cent. When people were asked to check a list of "other reasons" for moving, however, 84 per cent checked off the availability of schools; 81 per cent, of pools; and 87 per cent, of shopping. Seventy-two per cent approved the mixing of house types, but only 44 per cent, the 6500 square foot lots, and no more than 40 per cent considered the kinds of neighbors they could expect in Levittown as a reason for buying there. Clearly, some features of the community were not unimportant, but they were hardly the most important reason for buying in Levittown.

Although husbands and wives generally agreed on the need for the move, the men more often decided on Levittown, largely for reasons of economy, whereas the women seem to have wanted a more expensive community.[17] Even so, for an estimated 80 per cent of the buyers, the move meant an increase in housing expenditures. Roughly speaking, it cost $125 to $150 a month to buy in Levittown during the early years, and $140 to $165 when taxes rose later.[18] On the average, Levittowners were paying about 33 to 50 per cent more for housing than before. Still, they were not paying very much; the median Levittowner devoted only about 15 per cent of his income to housing before the move and about 21 per cent afterwards, well within the 20 to 25 per cent generally considered reasonable by the experts. However, among the 21 per cent earning less than $5500, those without other sources of funds must have been paying at least 28 per cent of their income for the new house, and they were confronted with financial problems when living costs and taxes went up.

Many of the buyers had come to Levittown to settle down. At the time of arrival, 44 per cent said they intended to settle permanently; 20 per cent knew already they would be transferred again by their employers; 12 per cent thought they wanted to

TABLE 2

PRINCIPAL REASON FOR BUYING IN LEVITTOWN, BY TYPE OF PREVIOUS COMMUNITY

PRINCIPAL REASON	PERCENT OF PURCHASERS		
	Previous Community		
	Urban	Suburban	All [1]
HOUSE-RELATED REASONS	85	84	84
Value: "Best house for the money"	48	48	48
Low price	16	21	16
Low down payment	6	7	7
Amount of space	2	1	2
Modernity, other qualities of house	13	7	11
COMMUNITY-RELATED REASONS	5	2	3
Provision of schools	*	*	*
Playgrounds, pools, other facilities for children	2	0	1
Shopping, other facilities for adults	2	1	1
Neighbors, other social aspects of community	1	1	1
JOB-RELATED REASONS	5	8	8
Journey to work	4	6	6
Business and professional opportunity in Levittown	1	2	2
OTHER	5	6	5
N	(159)	(222)	(484)

* Less than 0.5 per cent
[1] Also includes people from small towns, farms, army camps

move again, hopefully to a more expensive house; and 24 per cent were undecided.[19] Those whose plans were firm at this stage can be divided into Settlers, 57 per cent; Transients, 27 per cent; and Mobiles, 16 per cent. The Settlers were somewhat older than the average Levittowner, with more children, lower incomes, and less education. Only 13 per cent had gone to college, compared to 80 per cent of the Mobiles and Transients; 40 per cent were blue collar workers, but only 12 per cent of the Mobiles were; and 13 per cent were professionals, as compared to 31 per cent of the Mobiles and 21 per cent of the Transients. Forty-two per cent of the Settlers were Catholics, whereas 65 per cent of the Transients were Protestants, indicating the extent to which the armed forces and the large national corporations still select or attract from the latter religious group. The Settlers come by the label rightfully; only half had recorded a move for every three years of marriage, as compared to 83 per cent of the Mobiles and fully 91 per cent of the Transients. In fact, 78 per cent of the Transients had moved at least once for every two years of marriage.

(These data would suggest that in the long run, if the Transients and Mobiles do leave and are not replaced, Levittown could become a predominantly working class community. Although this may be taking place in the first of the Levittowns, now almost twenty years old, it is too early to tell whether it will happen in Levittown, New Jersey, particularly since the rise in house prices during the 1960s attracted a somewhat higher-income population than the initial arrivals I studied.[20])

The Move from City to Suburb

The third of the Levittowners who came from cities or from areas they described as urban neighborhoods were slightly older than previous suburbanites, more often apartment dwellers and tenants, Catholics, less mobile, and more likely to want to settle. They moved out of the cities principally for more space and in order to own a single-family house, although those who came from aging apartments and row houses placed special emphasis on getting a brand new house and having a yard for the children.

As Table 1 indicates, they were slightly more impelled to move by community conditions than were suburbanites, for 19 per cent of them gave such conditions as the major reason for moving. Both in their volunteered reasons and in those they checked off, their main complaint was a general one; 49 per cent checked "we just wanted to get out of the city" and 34 per cent, "the neighborhood is poor for raising children." An equal number mentioned lack of playgrounds and "urban dirt, noise, and traffic."

The reasons most often advanced for the so-called flight to the suburbs were of less concern to the city dwellers who came to Levittown. Fewer of them than those already in the suburbs complained about a long journey to work. Only 4 per cent volunteered racial change in the neighborhood as their most important reason, although 20 per cent checked it as one reason among many, and yet others may have been reluctant to do so or considered racial change one reason why the neighborhood was poor for raising children. Less than 2 per cent volunteered the low quality of schools as their first reason for leaving the city; 20 per cent checked it as one of the reasons—but that was 14 per cent less than those concerned about lack of playgrounds.

Nor were they leaving the city only to benefit their children.[21] When I asked the purchasers whether "they would prefer to live in the city if it were not for the children," 87 per cent responded negatively (86 per cent of the urbanites and 90 per cent of the suburbanites). The college educated were only a couple of percentage points more favorable to the city than those who dropped out of high school, and sex made no difference at all, but religious preference did. Jews were the most favorable to the city, and Protestants the least: 23 per cent of Jewish women, 19 per cent of the men, 14 per cent of all Catholics, and only 8 per cent of all Protestants expressed preference for the city.

Of course, this question was asked of a population which had just bought a house in the suburbs. Still, they did not regret leaving the city, nor did they flee from it. And they certainly did not move to "suburbia" to find the social and spiritual qualities that various writers have assigned to it. They were not looking for roots or a rural idyll, not for a social ethic or a consumption-centered life, not for civic participation or for "sense of community." They wanted the good or comfortable life for themselves and their families, and the anticipated peacefulness of outdoor living, but mainly they came "for a house and not a social environment."[22]

ASPIRATIONS FOR LIFE IN LEVITTOWN

Although only about a third of the people who filled out the mail questionnaire said they had given "a lot of thought" to what they wanted their life in Levittown to be like, 90 per cent of all mail questionnaire respondents volunteered things they "especially looked forward to about (their) life in Levittown," and the list of aspirations was the same for those who had and those who had not thought seriously about the future.[23]

Essentially, they wanted more comfortable and modern surroundings, but they did not want to change their old way of life or to make a new one in the new community. About half bought in Levittown because it was a new community, but their reasons indicate they were referring to the new house; about 40 per cent wanted to make some changes in their lives, but the changes listed also had to do mainly with the house.

The aspirations people volunteered before moving to Levittown, summarized in Table 3, express the same themes in more detail. The largest number of purchasers hoped that a new house would give them a more comfortable and less crowded place, and that owning their home would provide privacy from neighbors and freedom of action and self-expression. As one respondent wrote, "I wanted a more casual way of life and a less cramped one. In your own home you can do as you please." While some hoped the new house would enable parents and children to spend more time and do more things together, an equal proportion looked forward to continuing their accustomed family duties as "homemakers" and providers. In fact, the desire for newness and change was limited to meeting new people and making new friends.

The major source of diversity in aspirations was by sex. The men especially looked forward to "the peace and quiet of the country after the day's work," what some called "outdoor living," as well as the opportunity to "putter around the house and yard." The women placed most stress on making new friends and "having nice neighbors." In response to a checklist question to test attitudes on various kinds of social relations, 80 per cent of all respondents checked looking forward to meeting new people; 71 per cent, to "having neighbors of similar age and interests"; 55 per cent, to "meeting people with different interests and backgrounds"; and 54 per cent, to "having more desirable neighbors." On all items, Jews and Mobiles scored highest. The desire for homogeneity was greatest among women, for heterogeneity among the well educated, and for "desirable neighbors" among those with least status—the blue collar workers and the least educated. Urban residents also looked forward more to home ownership and its consequences for family life and relaxation,

PRINCIPAL ASPIRATION FOR LIFE IN LEVITTOWN, BY SEX

PRINCIPAL ASPIRATION	Per Cent	
	Women	Men
Comfort and roominess for family members in new house	25	15
Privacy and freedom of action in owned home	15	18
Furnishing and decorating the new house	4	1
Working around the house and yard, in garage and workshop	1	10
Carrying out normal family roles: being a homemaker (W); providing for family (M); a better place to raise children	8	7
Better family life: more time with and joint activity among family members	5	6
Better social life: making new friends, having good and sociable neighbors	10	5
Relaxed peaceful outdoor living	4	7
Using Levittown's recreation and shopping facilities; enjoying the convenience of its facilities	4	1
A new start or a better life; being part of a new community	1	1
Settling down in a community	*	1
Being active in churches and clubs	1	1
Being active in civic affairs; having a voice in the community	*	2
A shorter journey to work	7	5
Other	7	5
None	12	15
N	(924)	(864)

* Less than 0.5 per cent

whereas those who had already lived in the suburbs and had achieved these goals anticipated the comfort and modernity of the new house.

Altogether, about 95 per cent of the respondents who volunteered aspirations hoped for improved individual, family, and social life; and less than 5 per cent for identification with and activities in the wider community. A checklist question distinguishing between different types of community activities, however, showed that 55 per cent looked forward to "having a voice in community affairs"; 45 per cent, to "being active in civic groups"; but only 28 per cent to "joining clubs." Interest in political and civic activity was greatest among the higher-status and better-educated residents, but also among the Settlers and those who expected to be a minority in the community—the childless, Jews, and other ethnic group members. Those who moved to Levittown as a new community and those who occupied its first neighborhood were more interested in joining civic groups, whereas those who moved into the second and third neighborhoods were more concerned with having a voice in community affairs, perhaps fearful that the earliest residents would take over the government. Club activity was mentioned more often by low-status respondents.[24]

That individual and family aspirations were more important than community ones is neither a novel finding nor one that should be attacked on moral grounds. The same priorities would probably be assigned by any other group studied, including even the people who bemoan the modern lack of interest in "community." In part, the findings are a result of the method. The questionnaire asked only for the "most important" aspirations. Presumably, if people had been asked to list *all* their aspirations, more would eventually have mentioned community values.[25] Also, such aspirations are difficult to think about before the move, especially to a new community as yet without organizations. If the same question had been asked after a year's residence in Levittown, people would probably have mentioned community aspirations more frequently.

Nevertheless, both the reasons for moving and the aspirations suggest clearly that when people move into a new community they do so primarily for a house. Half the volunteered aspirations, two thirds of the moving reasons, and four fifths of all reasons for buying in Levittown were house-related; to put it another way, for 80 per cent of the purchasers, the house was the major reason for coming. This would justify Levitt's emphasis on providing "the best house for money." One could even argue that from a market point of view, the firm's site planning and other community innovations were not necessary, at least to attract the original set of purchasers. That people did not move because of the availability of schools suggests not that they were uninterested in schools, however, but only that they knew schools were being provided and were not particularly concerned about the quality of the education their children would be receiving.

House-related reasons for moving and aspirations may have been higher in Levittown than elsewhere because the Levitt houses were thought to be such an unusual value. Even so, the data permit one to suggest that any plan for a new community which does not make sure that the house is as good as any other in the market area is bound to run into difficulty, particularly if novel and as yet unaccepted ideas on community planning are tried out. In the last analysis, most people spend most of their time in the house and the community is of secondary importance.

The data also suggest that the evolution of a new community may not be affected by the aspirations with which people move into it. Being most concerned with individual and family goals, they will leave the development of the community to others, reserving for themselves only the veto power over their actions. What actually happened when the purchasers moved in will be told in the next five chapters.

NOTES

1. Unless otherwise indicated, these data are from a mail questionnaire returned by two thirds of the first 3000 home buyers. Generally speaking, older, poorer, and poorly educated buyers were less likely to answer, and although this was corrected for in the analysis, the findings still underemphasize that portion of the population. The method by which the questionnaires were sampled and analyzed is described in the Appendix.
2. They were also quite like the residents of the earlier Levittowns. For the population characteristics of Levittown, New York, shortly after the purchasers' arrival, see Liell (1952); for today, see Dobriner (1963), Chap. 4. An early demographic analysis of Levittown,

Pennsylvania, is in Institute of Urban Studies, Vol. I, Table 54.

3. The 1960 Census showed 71 per cent of the men to be under forty, 43 per cent to be between thirty and thirty-nine, and only 6 per cent to be over fifty-five.

4. According to the Census, by 1960 median family income was $7654; by 1962 it was $8500, according to an unpublished study, with 13 per cent of the families still earning less than $6000. As I indicated earlier, people who earned less than $5500 had to make higher down payments.

5. For the reasoning behind this definition of class, see Gans (1962a), pp. 242–252.

6. For another description of suburban classes, see Dobriner (1963), Chap. 2.

7. Mogey (1956), Chap. 4.

8. In this connection, see Rainwater. For more general descriptions of working class culture in the suburbs, see Rainwater, Coleman, and Handel; Berger (1960); and Willmott (1963).

9. For a more detailed analysis of upper middle class culture and its family, see Seeley, Sim, and Loosley.

10. Merton (1957).

11. The high proportion of renters who had lived in houses, 40 per cent, is a peculiarity of the Philadelphia area, which is built up mainly with row houses, so that apartments are scarce.

12. These figures underestimate the mobility somewhat, for they include only couples married for three years or more.

13. Most people wanted both ownership and a free-standing house, but the desire for ownership was stated more frequently than desire for the single-family house, even among previous apartment dwellers. Of course, at the end of the 1950s, suburban builders were not yet offering "town houses," and I did not ask Levittowners how important the single-family house was to them. However, 43 per cent checked as one of their reasons for moving the desire for more privacy, by which they presumably meant a free-standing house.

14. These were also mentioned most often as second and third most important reasons.

15. The conception of push and pull factors in residential choice comes from Rossi. His study, like subsequent ones of residential mobility, also showed that space needs were most important in moving decisions.

16. A 1956 study of Levittown, Long Island, reported that 41 per cent gave as their first reason for coming, "the best house for the money." See Citizens Committee for a Better Levittown.

17. Eighteen per cent of the women said they were "more in favor" of buying in Levittown than the men, 42 per cent of men said that *they* were more in favor, and 40 per cent indicated agreement.

18. The figures vary, depending on the model purchased, and include the cost of heating (which came to about $300 a year) but not other utilities.

19. After about three years' residence in Levittown, Long Island, 50 per cent of the homeowners considered themselves permanent residents; 17 per cent, temporary; and a third were undecided. See Liell (1952), p. 267. In a new working class suburb, 84 per cent of the semiskilled and a third of the foremen saw themselves as permanent residents, Berger (1960), p. 20.

20. Dobriner (1963), pp. 98–102.

21. For similar findings in Levittown, New York, see Dobriner (1963), pp. 64–66.

22. Clark, p. 110, and Chaps. 3 and 4, which report strikingly similar findings about suburban movers and moving reasons in the Toronto area.

23. Interestingly enough, the least educated and blue collar workers had thought more about their future than the well educated and the professionals, although other studies usually describe them as less able and willing to think ahead. The probable reason is that the former, moving into what they could expect to be a middle class community, would have to make more adjustments than other purchasers, as would the Settlers and those most eager to leave the city, who were also most "future-oriented."

24. By low status, I mean people lowest both in educational and occupational level, i.e. blue collar workers and people without high school diplomas. I shall use the terms low or lowest status hereafter when statistical findings are similar for both blue collar and high school dropouts. It should be noted, however, that I did not develop a single class index, and when I use these terms, I mean not blue collar people without high school diplomas but blue collar and diplomaless ones analyzed separately.

25. Even so, as the second most important aspiration volunteered by the respondents, the house, home, family, and friendship goals turned up as often as in the first.

Chapter Three

THE BEGINNINGS OF
GROUP LIFE

THE FIRST LEVITTOWNERS OCCUPIED THEIR HOMES IN THE SECOND
week of October 1958. Awaiting them was a township government which in the past had only to maintain the roads, and a
school system which in the previous year taught 85 pupils in
grades 1 through 9. The township also boasted a Methodist
church with attached social organizations, a YMCA with its own
(but ramshackle) building, a PTA for the local school, and a
Levittown Civic Association, founded the year before to prepare
for the newcomers and to integrate them into the existing community. Township and county residents, most of whom were
Protestants, were eyeing the new community with some trepidation, because rumors had it that many of the newcomers were
Catholics leaving Philadelphia slums to escape Negroes, and some
were Italians who carried knives. Elected officials were equally
fearful, for the township and the county had always been Republican, and most Levittowners were expected to be Democrats.
Even so, everyone was waiting to welcome, and if possible to
coopt, the 25 families who moved in that October week and the
3000 others who followed them during the course of this study.

Among the Levittowners themselves, the first signs of group
life began to appear even before they moved in. As they inspected the model homes, many were also inspecting the other
people who were looking at the homes with them. Those who decided to buy were called back to Levittown a few weeks later to

select their lots, and at that time some met the people who would live near them. Most did not, but even so, they were ready to assume that they would be agreeable neighbors and perhaps even good friends. Later, only 9 per cent recalled being "very much concerned about not knowing [their] neighbors beforehand." Reassured by the people they had seen around the model homes area and by the builder's credit check, they felt, as one man put it, "the people who could afford this type of house would be good people." Besides, everyone was looking forward to occupying his new home, and this engendered a spirit of optimism and the trust that other purchasers shared this spirit. After all, Levittown would be a new community, and newness is often identified with perfection in American culture.

Before moving in, only a few people were looking forward to getting together with their neighbors, at least according to the mail questionnaire results. However, once they had occupied the house and had gotten it and themselves settled, they began to look for playmates for their young children and then to find companions for themselves among their new neighbors. For the first two weeks they worked mainly at getting the house in shape, limiting themselves to exchanging cheerful hellos across the street or backyard. Once the initial nest-making period was over, however, people were ready to meet and, in this process, they got some help from an unexpected source—salesmen.

On moving day the first people to greet the new homeowners had not been their neighbors but an unending parade of milkmen, bread salesmen, and other merchants hoping to sign them up for home delivery until the shopping center was completed. At first, the constant callers were a bother, but when the moving-in chores were over, the salesmen became social intermediaries, telling people about their neighbors, and pointing out the ones with similar backgrounds or interests. Children, too, were a catalyst. They were let out of the house at once to allow mothers to get the house settled, and immediately began to find age mates on the block. This brought parents of roughly similar age together. Where such playmates were not available, or if the children were too young, mothers would take them in hand and knock on a few doors to find out if children of similar age were nearby. The women then had an excuse to meet their neighbors.

The speed with which people met depended in part on the season. Winter arrivals could not get out of the house much and in some cases had to wait until spring, being lonely in the meantime. But the initial section was occupied when the weather was still warm, and the very first Levittowners came together quite quickly. Bad weather does not prevent socializing; it is, rather, that most people need an excuse to meet each other. The intrepid and extrovert few can go up and introduce themselves, but for most people such a frontal assault, with its tacit admission of loneliness and the possibility of being rejected, is impossible. In good weather, however, opportunities and excuses were at hand. One could take the children outside, and spend some time with them until a neighbor appeared, or one could work on the lawn for the same covert purpose. If these methods did not work, people could—and did—walk up and down the street with baby carriages or tricycling children as a way of extending the exchange of hellos to a meeting. Since everyone was dying of curiosity, such excuses were acceptable forms of breaking the isolation.

The feeling of optimism that neighbors would be friendly was not enough; there had to be some sign that there would be no rejection. Women asked, "Are you settled yet?" If the answer was positive, then invitations could be exchanged to look at each others' houses. Being settled meant that the house was in sufficient shape to express the image that the women wanted to create among their neighbors. The men, knowing that they would be less dependent on their neighbors for social activities, could be more casual, although they did help their wives, working on the front lawn to make sure that the image outside was as good as that inside.

Once the image was ready, and an initial meeting produced no rejection, people were prepared to exchange information and to look for common backgrounds or interests that would bind them together. They described where they had come from, and their— or their husbands'—occupations, and went on to cover child-rearing methods and plans for fixing the house (women), the lawn, cars, and work (men). Every topic served either to bring people closer together or to pull them apart, by indicating where differences existed and what topics were taboo. For example, one of my neighbors was an Army pilot, and on our initial meeting— produced by a washout on our front lawns—we exchanged occupations. After I mentioned being a professor, he made a crack about another neighbor, a blue collar worker, to indicate that, although he referred to himself as "a glorified truck driver" he was, nevertheless, a white collar worker like me. He went on by talking about a relative who was studying for his Ph.D., but, aware that most professors were liberal and agnostic, he also let me know that he shared Southern race attitudes and was a fundamentalist Baptist. Disagreements would surely come up about race and religion, and if we were to be good neighbors, these subjects should not be discussed.

After the first bits of personal and family information had been exchanged, adjacent neighbors traded invitations to come in for coffee. If a social entrepreneur had moved onto the block, there might even be a block party, but as a rule, large gatherings needed another rationale so as to leave enough social distance between potentially incompatible people. One such device was a card party; another was a party at which a national manufacturer of plasticware or small appliances exhibited and sold his products to a group of invited women. Although the hostess of such a party might appear to trade on her social contacts in order to obtain material benefit—she received free products for holding the gathering—it was never interpreted in this fashion. "It gives me a chance to meet people I've wanted to meet," one such hostess explained. "It's just not right to go up to someone to say I want to meet you; that you only do with next-door neighbors. I'm not out to make money; it's just an excuse for partying." On the blocks that settled later, people got together after attending community-wide meetings or were introduced to each other through the charity fund drives. These were usually run by women experienced in community activity or by those who could knock on doors without trepidation, but even for the less courageous, collecting for the heart or cancer fund was an entree and, of course, a chance to meet the neighbors. Finally, such holidays as the Fourth of July, Halloween, and Christmas allowed neighbors moving in just before then to throw a party without seeming too bold socially.

All of these occasions were structured to make overtures as successful as possible. Initial rejection was, of course, rare, for no one could be curt to a neighbor who would be living on the same block for several years. Too much social aggressiveness was out of the question, however, for most Levittowners were uncomfortable with "forward" people.

First encounters took anywhere from two weeks to a month or two; they were followed by a period of considerable informal visiting and entertaining, lasting perhaps two to six months. These visits provided companionship and mutual support in the early period of living in a new community, for a new house in a still almost rural area created not only loneliness but also a variety of problems which were solved by getting together and "sharing ideas."

Each contact between neighbors could advance people closer to friendship, or it could bring out differences that would indicate that friendship was not possible. Both alternatives developed quickly. On one block a group of women had established a bridge club a month after arrival; on another, four women had a daily coffee-klatsch after about two months. On my block all of this happened so precipitously that by mid-December, one neighbor could say, "I feel I have been in Levittown for years, the place is so settled."

The culture of the block jelled quite rapidly too. Standards of lawn care were agreed upon as soon as it was time to do something about the lawn, and by unspoken agreement, the front lawn would be cared for conscientiously, but the backyard was of less importance. Those who deviated from this norm—either neglecting their lawn or working on it too industriously—were brought into line through wisecracks. When I, in a burst of compulsive concern, worked very hard on my lawn at the start, one of my neighbors laughed and said he would have to move out if I was going to have "that fancy a lawn." Since I was not interested in a "fancy lawn," I found it easy to take the hint, but those who wanted a perfect lawn stayed away from the talkfests that usually developed evenings and on Saturday mornings when the men were ostensibly working on the lawns, so as not to be joked about and chastised as ratebusters.

Perhaps the best illustration of the rapid definition of block norms came at a party around Christmas time. A former New York suburbanite invited everyone to a stand-up cocktail party, but within an hour it had turned into an informal gathering, climaxed by a slightly drunken group sing. The almost immediate transformation from an upper middle class party to a lower middle class get-together took place for several reasons. Most of the guests were unfamiliar with cocktail parties and were not willing to stand up in the prescribed fashion. The hostess was dressed up in bright Capri pants, but one of the neighbors, of working class background, had never seen such pants, and thinking they were pajamas, concluded the party had been called off. Only when guests started arriving did she realize her error and later everyone, she included, laughed about it. The hostess' husband had objected to what he called a "Westchester County party" from the start, and the hostess went along with the dramatic metamorphosis too. She had not been putting on airs, but had thought her neighbors were like those in New York. From then on, social life on the block followed the norms of lower middle class entertaining.

Informal Clubs

As people decided how they felt about their nearby neighbors, a sorting and departure process developed. Those who had become friends set up block cliques, others moved into multiblock ones, and yet others looked for friends elsewhere, particularly for evening visiting. The earliest departures took place among social and cultural *minority groups,* especially working and upper middle class people, older ones, and Jews—and all others who felt themselves out of place among their neighbors and needed or wanted to find their social life elsewhere. With this departure, the community stratification process began in earnest.[1]

Many of the Jewish women had come from predominantly Jewish areas in the cities and for a significant number, Levittown was the first real contact with non-Jewish neighbors. Some made friends, but many were not comfortable enough and began quite early to search for other Jewish women. The salesmen helped, but the process was immeasurably hastened by an unpredictable factor. One of the ministers who was forming a church had long admired the Jews. As he made the rounds looking for people for his church, he ran into a Jewish couple who mentioned the need for a synagogue in Levittown, and thereafter he passed on the names of all Jews he encountered. As a result, only five weeks after the first Levittowners had arrived, the twenty-six Jewish families among them met to discuss the formation of a synagogue. The meeting acquainted Jews with each other, and the first Levittown organization was set up a few days later—a mahjong club for Jewish women. It was not really a formal club, but by this time the county daily newspaper had added a society column, and the society editor was so short of news that she pounced on any grouping and promptly dubbed it a club.

Another sorting process occurred among a group of women on a block adjacent to mine. Although people chose their lots individually, the high proportion of Catholics brought it about that four women of that religion, all of them from working class backgrounds, lived close to each other. Since they differed from the evolving block culture, they began to meet every day for lengthy coffee-klatsches, partly in common defense against the middle class ethos. In fact coffee-klatsch cliques sprang up all over Levittown, although not half as many as the suburban myth claimed or as I had expected. Women not of a minority culture took occasional coffee with their neighbors, but they did not need to huddle together as closely.

Some of the coffee-klatsch groups expanded into block clubs, involving a dozen neighbors on adjacent blocks, which met fortnightly or monthly for conversation and/or cards, with individual members getting together in between. Some were formed by enterprising women who had belonged to similar clubs in other suburbs, but most developed among people with minority backgrounds or interests. They usually evolved after the summer, as block sociability waned and women wanted to make sure that they would see each other in winter, when people who do not visit each other regularly have little opportunity to meet. On one block, it was a group of older women; on another, a group of women interested in civic activities or in politics; on yet another, a group of wives with traveling husbands—salesmen, pilots, or merchant seamen. Elsewhere, it was a group of Catholic women whose men had become involved in the organization of the Catholic parish and had told their wives, "You'd better get busy if you want companionship." Indeed, the clubs were often formed by women whose husbands were away from the house a lot. Most clubs were strictly female, although sometimes the men later formed card-playing clubs. One informal group, called the Happy Hours club, consisted of previously urban and primarily Italian couples who liked to stay up late and complained that their neighbors went to bed at 10 P.M. every night.

Most of the groups remained together for at least the three years that I was in touch with them. Some had become regular clubs when the group lost its initial enthusiasm and structure was needed as an adhesive. Sometimes, the organization was involuntary, as when the society reporter from the county daily wanted to write about them and asked them to take a name and become a club. Usually, the women did not want publicity, partly because neighbors who had not been invited to join would feel excluded.

Other minority group members had a more difficult time in finding friends close by and had to enter the larger community. Among these were professional and upper middle class people and, especially, college-educated women. They felt isolated on the blocks, and of course their dissatisfaction separated them further from the neighbors. Their feeling of estrangement in the pervasive lower middle class culture encouraged them to establish community-wide voluntary associations which could attract other Levittowners with similar social and cultural interests.

The Evolution of Social Life

The development of social relationships reached an equilibrium rapidly, for 75 per cent of the interview respondents reported having settled down both in the house and in the community within six months, and fully half indicated it took even less time than that. After two years in Levittown, 47 per cent reported that they were doing about as much individual visiting with neighbors as they had after six months; 30 per cent said they were doing more. Nighttime visiting with other couples increased, 43 per cent reporting more, 34 per cent about the same, and the rest, less. About a third indicated the couples they spent most of their time with were neighbors, while 24 per cent mentioned people they met in community organizations, and 13 per cent, those met at church. Only 20 per cent indicated that none of their friends were neighbors. The people who did more visiting with other couples than after arrival also said they visited with neighbors more, and vice versa. About a quarter of the respondents reported less visiting with couples and neighbors than before, however, and these respondents were primarily low-status people with less than a high school education, and with blue collar jobs.

Over time, the block social system had stabilized as well, ranging from close friendship among some to open hostility among a few, but mostly calling for friendly coexistence and occasional visiting among those who were not friends. Holiday parties increased cohesion temporarily, and if an accident or illness befell a neighbor everyone pitched in to help as much as he could, regardless of how people felt about the family.

The prevailing equilibrium was most often interrupted by two phenomena: the turnover of residents and fights among neighbors. The latter were not frequent, but when they happened, they could produce lasting feuds. Most squabbles generated over the children. If children quarrel—and they often do—parents naturally take sides. If one set of parents feels that the other child is in the wrong and has not been sufficiently punished or that his wrongdoing is a result of what it considers poor parental supervision, the children's conflict is likely to become one between parents. This may continue long after the children have forgotten the fight. Parental conflicts, of course, expressed deeper disagreements between neighbors; friends do not fight over their children's battles. Sometimes there was an eventual reconciliation, but often people just stopped talking to each other.

Turnover was then slight and stemmed largely from transfers by employers, but if the relationship with neighbors had been intense, the family who took over the house was not invited to join the group. If ties were less close and the newcomer amicable and of similar age and background, she was usually welcomed. As one pointed out, "I had to push a little at first to get people to talk to me, but now there's no problem. There isn't much coffee-klatsching here, we are all too busy cleaning. But I'm pregnant, and the gal next door just had a baby too, so that made for a common interest."

The arrival of a baby was always an event in Levittown—where it was an everyday occurrence—and there was likely to be a baby shower and renewed interest in the mother among the neighbors. A first pregnancy also incorporated old-time residents into the block society. One of my neighbors had worked prior to her pregnancy, and had not been around for the weekday exchange of coffee visits. When the baby came, she was at once visited by another neighbor, also pregnant, and then became part of the block, even though it had been two years since they had all arrived.

THE FOUNDING OF VOLUNTARY ASSOCIATIONS

In a new community, organizations can be started by outsiders or by residents, that is, by *external* or *internal* initiative. The residents can act *intentionally* to achieve community aspirations held before arrival, or *unintentionally*, responding to community conditions of the moment. This suggests three types of origin: *External, Internal-Intended,* and *Internal-Unintended.*[2] For simplicity's sake, I will call the first *External,* the second *Internal,* and the third *Unintended.*

In Levittown, almost a third of all organizations set up in the first two years were External. These were usually branches of nationwide associations, especially service clubs, veterans' groups, and women's social clubs. Since Levittown's opening had been widely heralded for some time, and a community of 12,000 or more families were expected, the associations saw a golden opportunity to expand their roster of branches and members. Some used professional organizers who go from community to community, but most asked or encouraged branches in nearby towns to organize their new neighbor. Many associations give annual awards to the local branches which set up the most new groups and enroll the most new members, and the winners obtain increased political strength within the national association. Indeed, a man who wants to be a national or state officer in a service or veterans' club is materially aided in his rise up the hierarchy by getting a reputation as a "starter." This incentive extends to professional organizers as well. Almost two years before Levittown opened, national Boy Scouts headquarters had requested the county office to start tooling up for forming troops in Levittown. A young executive was added to the county staff; he had taken a pay cut to come, knowing full well that he would be able to organize many troops, thereby enhancing his chances for rapid career advancement in the future.

Most organizations waited until the community was settled, but then went into action quickly in the hope of bringing the potential leaders and active participants among the Levittowners into their group before others had a chance to attract them. As a result, the Veterans of Foreign Wars (VFW) arrived on the scene after only three months, when Levittown had barely two hundred families, and the Lions, Kiwanis, and the Junior Chamber of Commerce followed shortly afterwards. Later, O.R.T. (a Jewish women's service organization), 4-H, a B'nai B'rith Lodge for men, a county hospital auxiliary, a civil defense group, the Optimists (a men's service club), B'rith Sholom (a Jewish fraternity), and the American Legion were founded in a similar manner.

The Internal method of organization was used principally by women's groups, with a Levittowner who had been active in the group in the past and had intended to start a new branch doing so as soon as enough potential members seemed to be available. The founders' motives varied. Some were looking for advancement in the national organizational hierarchy; others wanted to be the first president of the new group; but for most, the organization had become integral to their lives. A founder of a Jewish women's group explained her initiative by saying, "I could not conceive of living without Hadassah." Among other groups founded in this fashion were Deborah, a woman's organization supporting a national tuberculosis hospital, a B'nai B'rith Lodge for women, the Federated Women's Club, the League of Women Voters, and Beta Sigma Phi, a sorority for women without college degrees.

Externally and Internally founded organizations were usually national branches, but sometimes people who had been active in local groups in their former communities came with the intention of starting one in Levittown. A Texan imported the Lords and Ladies Club, which held monthly dances at county supper clubs for middle class managerial families who wanted but could not afford a country club. The Emergency Ambulance Squad was initiated by a man who had been an officer of one in his previous community.

Most local groups were Unintended, founded in response to some felt community or individual need. Usually people with similar interests came together, sometimes accidentally, sometimes because they were a minority which needed to be together, and sometimes because they could gain from formal organization. Several ham radio operators met by sheer accident, having heard each other over the air. A Ham Club was started when it became possible to obtain civil defense funds to convert their hobby into a community service.

On the other hand, a number of Unintended groups arose because members individually could not do without them, particularly women who were lonely and could not find compatible neighbors. One woman turned to the national office of Pan-Hellenic, a sorority for college graduates to which she had once belonged. Her decision to form a branch was primarily a function of class difference; she found herself uninterested in block-club card games and gossip. On the other hand, the Levittown Women's Club, a branch of the Federated Women's Clubs of America, was founded without premeditation by a lonely resident who had been active in a branch elsewhere and had simply enjoyed her membership. In many cases, wives whose husbands were frequently out of town became Unintended founders. The organizer of the Women's Club and the two neighbors with whom she worked were married to salesmen or pilots. Subsequently, women whose traveling husbands worked in the same firm or line also started groups. For instance, the local newspaper reported of the "RCA Wives" that "from the first meeting it is evident that a lot of the wives whose husbands are away a great deal are more than eager to constructively fill their time." [3] Similar clubs were organized by the wives of merchant seamen and Air Force pilots.

In other cases, the impetus was culturally based. An All-Nations club of foreign wives, and before that a British Wives club, were organized, as were a dramatic society, a ceramics club, a folk dance group, an art club, and branches of two national groups, the Great Books Club and the Buxom Belles (devoted to group weight reduction). In two neighborhoods the scarcity of baby-sitters encouraged the formation of cooperatives in which women exchanged baby-sitting services for each other. They were popular with Jewish women who wanted to get out for club meetings but whose husbands worked evenings in stores in the Philadelphia area.

Community needs and issues generated a number of spontaneous civic and political groups. Dissatisfaction with Board of Education policies brought about the Citizens' Association for Public Schools; the Levittown Youth Sports Association was founded by the police chief in the hope of keeping adolescents busy to prevent juvenile delinquency; and doctors organized a professional group to protect themselves against the osteopaths who outnumbered them in the area.

As the community matured, a number of Unintended groups arose in opposition to already established ones. A Jewish fraternity sprang up because men wanting social activities were dissatisfied with the existing Jewish men's club, primarily dedicated to fund raising for the synagogue, and civic associations developed in the later neighborhoods to defend their interests before elected officials who came largely from the initially settled areas. The service and veterans' groups stimulated women's auxiliaries, generally Externally, but sometimes on an Unintended basis because the wives wanted to help their husbands, and share a common organizational affiliation. Unintended groups also sprang up in the later neighborhoods because the residents were unwilling to join groups formed by residents from the initial neighborhoods, feeling they would not be welcome by the older residents, or because they thought they had more in common with people who had moved in at the same time. Besides, an ambitious founder could organize a new group more easily than enter an established group and work his way up.

The Organizational Process

Anyone can start an organization, but it can only survive by attracting members, and for this reason the organizational process was often the same. The first step was, of course, to get in touch with potential members. National organizations used mailing lists to find members who had just moved to Levittown or had the school send invitations home via the students. There were newspaper ads and stories and announcements at meetings of other organizations. But perhaps most successful was the practice of enrolling friends and neighbors. People who wanted to start an organization often called on their neighbors for help, exploiting the cohesion developed on the block; people curious enough to come to a first meeting brought a neighbor for company and security. Later interviews showed that of the people who had not intended to join groups, fully 36 per cent had been drawn in by neighbors.[4] This banding together affected the organizational process in two ways. Founders who called on friends to help them quickly developed leadership cliques. This often speeded up the organizing process, but in some cases it led to protests that the group was run by a clique, and then to rival cliques. It also made many groups into virtual neighborhood clubs, and discouraged joiners from other neighborhoods. Thus, new clubs with the same manifest aim, such as service clubs, appeared when new neighborhoods were settled because the previously organized clubs were in effect exclusive.

These consequences were quite unintended, for all groups were open to any person wanting to join. Even those which had membership requirements—for example, service clubs which in other towns took only men in retail business—opened their rolls to anyone who was interested. The opportunity to be a charter member—or an officer—was publicized to get people into the organization and to establish it as quickly as possible on a firm basis. The next step was the election of officers and development of program. Both stages also proceeded with great haste in order to secure the existence of the organization as quickly as possible. Once the group was chartered, the program could be used to attract further members, making available more people and funds to recruit others, expand the organization, and thus guarantee its survival. Officers were usually elected at either the first or second meeting, often before people had a chance to get acquainted. Ambitious leaders could generally get themselves elected and put their friends into office as well, although occasionally attendance was so small that everyone present became an officer willy-nilly. Most of the time, the wish to get the group organized and chartered immediately preempted the selection of the right people for the position. For example, one founder had persuaded the newspaper to run a picture of the elected officers, and the election had to be hurried so that a slate of officers could pose for the photographer when he came. Another meeting was thrown into an uproar by one Levittowner who argued that the norms of democracy demanded the postponement of elections until people knew the candidates and each other, but those in attendance wanted the organization, a neighborhood PTA, established that night, and voted to elect a slate nominated by the founder and her friends.

The Definitional Struggle

The rapidity of the organizing process created a considerable amount of conflict in many organizations. These conflicts were usually ascribed to "personalities", reflecting the inability of people to get along. Some were generated by the newness of the community, for, as one leader put it, "When you don't know each other, it is hard to separate the workers from the talkers." [5] More often, the fights between personalities were actually *definitional struggles* about the purpose, composition, and program of the group, especially in organizations without nationally prescribed activities. Probably the most important source of differences was class. For example, the VFW, the first male organization in Levittown, initially attracted both working class and a smaller number of middle class people. From the start, working class members wanted a primarily social organization; the middle class, a community service group. The confrontation was relatively brief, however; after a few weeks, the middle class leaders left to organize the Catholic church. Where such alternative outlets were not available, factions and bitter struggles developed over the election of the second year's set of officers.

In one women's club, the definitional struggle was over the amount of innovation permissible in club tradition. This involved differences of age and of class. The traditionalists, who were somewhat older and more restrictively lower middle class, wanted a closed group with a statusful program of "culture"; the innovators, more expansive, called for open admission and a program of "community service." The crucial but never stated issue was over the admission of working class women; this came out when the leader of the traditional faction described her opponent as wanting to run the club as if it were a firehouse—a historical preserve for the working class.[6] The adherents of open admission won, and the leader of the traditionalists retired to set up an art club, while the victorious advocate of community service later went into politics.

There was also constant debate over the speed of organization, with "go-slow" factions who wanted the group to establish itself firmly before it indulged in too many activities, and "go-fast" ones which argued—usually successfully—that a rapid pace was needed to advertise the organization in order to enroll new members. A similar conflict was noticeable in leadership struggles. Founders were often dynamic and even charismatic people who attracted publicity and thus members, but then tended to order the more active ones around and alienated them. Whether praised as "starters" or discredited as "pushers," they would eventually be replaced by more diplomatic officers, administrators who were able to get people to work together. Of twelve officers who had succeeded founders, eleven indicated that the one thing they were doing differently was "stabilizing the organization" or "delegating authority to a much greater extent."[7] In some working class groups, the founder sometimes lacked administrative skills and later gave way to a better-educated, lower middle class member who was more able to run meetings and manage relations with other groups.

Most definitional struggles ended with the acquiescence of the losing faction and the gradual departure of its members. Eventually, many organizations achieved a measure of stability, both in number of members and in programs, with occasional innovation in activities, particularly of the community service variety that would publicize the group anew. If membership lagged, there were likely to be periods of organizational revival, sparked by the appearance of a new leader whose dynamism and willingness to work enabled him to move rapidly into the organization's ruling circle. The new arrivals were usually people who had previously belonged to the organization elsewhere.

Not all groups underwent definitional struggles, however. In many national organizations, the leaders had been active in other suburbs and other new branches and thus had a ready answer to the inevitable first question: How should we get started? Indeed, almost all groups tried to find members with past experience in new (or old) groups, hoping that their "ideas" would work in Levittown. Often then, the young organizations relied on traditional solutions, although when definitional struggles developed, the voices of experience were not respected.

The haste with which organizations sought to get started is shown by the chronological pattern of founding. During the first nine months of Levittown's existence, when the population was small and most people were still settling into house and block, 14 groups sprang up (not counting churches and church-related ones), and from September 1959 to June 1960, when the population enlarged and more people were ready to look beyond the block, 36 were founded. The peak had already been reached, however; only 14 additional groups appeared during the 1960–1961 season and just 13 more in the next four years—for a grand total of 77.[8] Only a handful of these failed to survive, although some have carried on with just a few members. When interviewed after two years, about 70 per cent of the respondents reported belonging to at least one of these organizations.

Externally founded groups and branches of national ones were of course able to mobilize more quickly, and regardless of how they were founded, those appealing to ethnic or class minorities were set up earlier than those appealing to the dominant lower middle class population. Among the churches, for example, the Jews and the fundamentalist Baptists were the first, and organizations appealing to lower-status groups preceded those of higher status. Among the men's groups, the order was exactly in terms of status; the VFW arriving first, followed shortly thereafter by the Lions, Kiwanis, and Junior Chamber of Commerce, with the Optimists and Rotarians waiting until the community was two years old. Higher-status organizations can afford to wait because they know that people will join whenever they appear, and such groups even bide their time to see who the highest-status leaders are. Low-status groups benefit from early establishment, for this gives them an opportunity to attract higher-status people who want to become active immediately. Among the women's groups, lower-status groups also preceded higher ones, although those enrolling a large proportion of Jews came before all others. Groups with similar programs and appealing to the same types of people organized almost *en seriatim* so as not to be left behind in the competition for members.

Organizational Origin and Residents' Aspirations

If the aspirations Levittowners volunteered before arrival had guided the founding process, most organizations would have been started Internally by people to whom they were important. Civic groups would have outnumbered social clubs and both would have been surpassed by home-and-family-centered groups such as PTAs, Scouts, and garden clubs.

As it turned out, however, only 24 per cent of the organizations emerging in the first two years were Internal, 31 per cent were External, and the remaining 45 per cent were Unintended. More were social than were civic—28 per cent were purely social and cultural; 28 per cent, mixed social and service; and 16 per cent, civic. Only 14 per cent were family-centered, although that proportion would triple if churches were considered in this category. (The rest included "occupational" groups, such as the Medical Club; an investment club, and, of course, a garden club.)

It is worthwhile asking, therefore, why the groups that sprang up were not those that people wanted before they came, why almost a third could be organized by outsiders who knew nothing about the new community, and whether the large number of Unintended groups, which sprang up on the spur of the moment, represented the impact of community conditions on the origin process.

One answer suffices for all three questions. How organizations were founded was ultimately less relevant than what happened to them once they were founded. No organization, however it started, could exist beyond the initial meeting without responding to some needs among the members it attracted, and these needs were not only more important than founders' or members' preoccupancy aspirations, but they developed largely after people had lived in Levittown for a while. External, Internal, and Unintended groups alike responded to these needs, which turned out to be more social than civic or familial; or to put it another way, civic and familial needs were satisfied by public agencies and political groups, leaving the voluntary associations to fill the social needs.

Aside from the few civic groups, which tried to intervene in municipal affairs, and the men's service clubs, which provided "community-minded" activities for the lawyers, salesmen, realtors, and politicians who needed to advertise themselves in the community, the organizations were primarily *sorting* groups which divided and segregated people by their interests and ultimately, of course, by socio-economic, educational, and religious differences. On the block, people who shared a common space could not really express their diversity; the community sorting groups came into being for this purpose.

Men could divide and segregate themselves on the job, but the women had to do it in the community, and partly for this reason most organizations were sexually separated, with only some of those appealing to upper middle class people providing "coeducational" activities. The total array of women's groups offered the opportunity for extremely fine sorting. Well-educated women would be likely to find compatible people and activities in the American Association for University Women, the League of Women Voters, Great Books, or the Better Schools Committee, and, if they were more socially inclined, the Pan-Hellenic Society; those with less than a college degree could choose from among a dozen groups. Working class women clung to the church—the Altar and Rosary Society was the town's largest club a year after it was started—or joined the auxiliaries of their husbands' groups. Religious sorting was also available, for every church had men's and women's groups, and some secular organizations became predominantly Catholic, others Protestant or Jewish. The Jews had their own secular clubs which sorted by age and class. Occupational specialties were honored; ex-nurses worked in hospital auxiliaries and ex-teachers became active in the PTA. One Levittowner even talked about a Texas club; she too wanted to be "with her own."

Organizational programs reflected these diversities. The organizations of the college-educated stressed cultural activities and local or national political issues; those of the high school graduates scheduled fashion shows and lectures on beauty, home management, and child care. The highly educated shunned "gossip," their own version of it being buried in the discussion of social issues. Games, always major organizational sidelines, were also stratified, ranging from poker, pinochle, and hearts up to canasta, scrabble, and bridge. Municipal services and formal governmental institutions still being in a primitive stage, most groups combined social sorting with a variety of community service activities. The upper middle class groups put on candidates' night and community forums; the working class groups concentrated on sports for the children, fire-fighting, and Fourth of July ceremonies; the lower middle class groups' activities ranged from rolling bandages, running Miss Levittown contests, and collecting books for the library to helping the Superintendent of Schools.

Needless to say, the kinds of sorting groups that Levittown would require could not be determined until after people had lived there for a while and could see how many friends they could find on the block and what charitable and civic activities needed to be supplied. As a result, they could not have anticipated before arrival what kinds of organizations they would actually join.[9] Likewise, the organizations could not anticipate their members' demands and needs in advance, but once they knew them, they adapted to them. This was particularly true of national and Externally founded groups, which developed new functions in Levittown having little to do with the reasons they came or with the aims in their national charters.[10] These groups succeeded only because they were able to bend to local needs when necessary.[11] For example, two Jewish national women's groups became essentially neighborhood clubs for young, managerial upper middle class women and older, lower middle class women, respectively. Most of their members knew little about the national organization but simply wanted Jewish companionship. A 4-H group was rescued after a poorly attended organizational meeting because the county agent chanced on a clique of teenage girls who needed a club to keep the group together, although they were not particularly interested in the 4-H program. The national groups were rarely aware of how their branches changed in Levittown—but then they did not care particularly, so long as they could add to their membership rolls.

The Unintentionally founded clubs were not much different from the others. Although they did not have to alter themselves to succeed, they too functioned primarily as sorting groups. Some were, of course, generated by community conditions, for example, the Sitters clubs, which responded to the shortage of baby-sitters, and a Juvenile Discussion group which met to do something about juvenile delinquency. Sometimes community conditions hastened the arrival of groups that would eventually have developed anyway. The Jewish community organized almost immediately because Jewish women found themselves ill at ease with their neighbors, and an institution was needed to celebrate Chanukah so the children could be discouraged from demanding Christmas trees.

Yet none of the sorting needs and community conditions were so distinctive as to require unique organizations. The ability of national groups to bend to local priorities helped, but even the local associations, 40 per cent of the total, were modeled on similar organizations elsewhere and none was entirely original to Levittown. They were, rather, typical of those found in most other suburbs and communities of young families of similar class. In fact, although they considered themselves community-wide organizations, almost half of thirty-six for which membership addresses were available drew most of their people from one or two neighborhoods. Clearly, people cared less about the nominal purpose and scope of the group than to be with fellow residents who had come to Levittown at about the same time and were compatible in other ways.

THE STRUCTURE OF ORGANIZATIONS

As is usually the case, most organizations consisted of a small group of active people and a large number of members who did little more than attend meetings. Able administrators to do the time-consuming work required by every project—even a seemingly simple affair like a bazaar or bakesale required hundreds of woman-hours and phone calls—were scarce. Women were especially loath to take responsible positions, and pioneers remained in their organizations even after they had served as presidents and could rise no higher. In 1964, many of the same people were still active in—and sometimes in control of—groups that had been founded in 1959. Any person who had shown himself or herself to be effective in one group was asked to help in other organizations. Although some complained about the workload, they found it difficult to turn down these requests.[12] Saying no repeatedly might brand them as "uncooperative" or "lacking community spirit," and unless they wanted to leave community life altogether, the threat was enough to make them cooperative.

As a result, interlocking directorates were created, with the same people or their friends holding leadership positions in several groups. Sometimes, leaders who were friends and worked well together even moved en masse to other groups and eventually became important leadership cliques in them. For example, several middle class Catholics—some managers, others salesmen— came together in the VFW shortly after the community was founded. Then they helped to organize the Catholic parish, the Levittown Youth Sports Association, and subsequently the Holy Name Society. Some also became politically active, later running for the school board and Township Committee. Naturally, they formed alliances between these groups, and eventually they were defined as spokesmen for Levittown's Catholics, politicians and others consulting them on issues affecting their coreligionists.

On the whole, interlocking directorates and alliances developed only among like-minded organizations, "like-minded" being defined primarily by common interests and membership characteristics. The small group of cosmopolitans created alliances between the Citizens' Association for Public Schools, the county Human Relations Council, the League of Women Voters, the American Association of University Women, and even such cultural groups as the Great Books Club, calling on these organizations for help on salient issues. A large number of groups, principally of lower middle class women, including the PTAs and the Federated Women's Club, joined to collect books for the library. Those drawing from working class residents (such as the veterans' groups) cooperated on parades and other ceremonies for national holidays. The Boy Scouts worked with the churches, encouraging them to sponsor troops, in return for which the Scout program, as one Scout executive pointed out, "takes the boy up to the steps of the church and motivates him to enter."

These coalitions were encouraged by the relative internal homogeneity of individual organizations. Being sorting groups, or being nationally affiliated, many Levittown organizations attracted members of common background, and their leaders were thus able to bring them into alliances without creating dissent. For example, the Federated Women's Club attracted mostly Protestant lower middle class women somewhat older than the rest of the community and with more than average interest in community service. This happened quite unintentionally, but since it was a national organization with a set and well-known image, Jews and Catholics stayed out of it; so did women who lacked the social skills they felt were needed and those more interested in political or cultural activities. Groups oriented to children's needs, such as the PTAs and the Scouts, were less stratified by class and religion, although they naturally attracted more middle class members than working class ones.

Joining with other organizations on community projects was considered desirable because it would create favorable publicity for the individual groups, and thus attract more members. One of these joint activities, the erection of a community Christmas tree in 1959, resulted in an abortive attempt to set up a formal structure of organizations, the Levittown Community Council. The Council's founding was stimulated by the desire to prevent any organization garnering more publicity and credit than any other for joint projects, to coordinate organizational activities, and to minimize organizational competition. If community-wide meetings and community-wide fund-raising affairs could be scheduled so as not to coincide, they would be better attended and more profitable; therefore, the first—and last—project of the Council was to set up an overall organizational meeting schedule. The participating organizations were, however, still so eager to maximize their own membership, and therefore, to amass publicity and credit for community service, that they were unwilling to cooperate in the coordinating venture. Under such conditions, there was no incentive for a community leader or politician to step forward and make the Council his own bailiwick, and it disappeared shortly after it was founded. Later, the businessmen in the shopping center formed an association which erected a community Christmas tree every year, staged other national and religious ceremonies, and put on entertainment to bring shoppers into the center.

Some organizations had ties to the political system. The PTAs were committed to defending the school system against opposition, but other organizations had a more voluntary relationship with politics. Leading political figures were also active in a variety of voluntary associations in order to demonstrate their community-mindedness to the voters and to use the organizations as listening posts. Many of them, being lawyers and insurance and real estate salesmen, also had occupational reasons for being active. Then too, it had long been a county tradition for the major fund drives, such as the March of Dimes, cancer and heart funds, and the annual campaigns by local hospitals, to be headed by leading politicians. This not only gave the political parties an opportunity to do a community service, but also helped them to find able party workers. Some organizations had more direct ties to the political parties. For example, several VFW leaders were active Democrats, and many members of the Junior Chamber of Commerce, Kiwanis, and Rotary were Republicans. Although these organizations had no official ties to either party, they gave covert support to party activities, and the parties reciprocated by supporting organizational projects. The political alliances helped to split the total array of organizations even further, so that the emerging structure was actually an aggregate of competing inter-ests and temporary coalitions reflecting the diversity and conflict in the political sphere.

NOTES

1. For descriptions of similar processes in other new developments, see Danhof; Infield; Form (1945 and particularly 1951); Rosenfeld; Whyte (1956), Chaps. 25 and 26; and Gutman.
2. An Unintended organization could, of course, be Externally founded, with outsiders starting a group in the new community in order to protect their own interests. This explains the forma-tion of the Levittown Civic Association, but no other.
3. *Levittown Life,* July 6, 1961.
4. A national study of volunteers for the March of Dimes found that the largest proportion, 52 per cent, joined after being asked by friends. Sills, pp. 102–103.
5. Conversely, a woman who participated in a telephone survey to find mothers for the PTA mentioned that she could tell from the person's voice and the topic of conversation whether that individ-ual was "officer material."
6. When Levittown was racially integrated, this club was one of the few which debated the exclusion of Negroes, but eventually de-cided not to do so.
7. Michelson, p. 91.

8. If the neighborhood PTAs and the men's, women's, youth, and couples' clubs organized by the churches were included, the total would easily reach 100.

9. Later, all belonging to social and civic groups and 73 per cent belonging to the men's service clubs said they had not intended to join these groups before coming to Levittown, as compared to only 31 per cent of those in the PTA, the Scouts, and other child-centered organizations.

10. Although 61 per cent of memberships in national organizations were intended before arrival, as compared to none in local groups, this reflected mainly the willingness of Mobiles and Transients to rejoin groups in which they had been active before.

11. Men's needs seemed more predictable; 73 per cent of their groups were intended, as compared to only 48 per cent of the women's, the latter's founding responding more directly to the sorting needs that developed in the community. Also, middle class founders were more responsive to their fellow residents than working class ones; 56 per cent of organizations with predominantly working class memberships depending on External founders, and only 6 per cent on Internal ones. Among middle class groups, only 9 per cent were founded Externally and 48 per cent Internally.

12. These complaints have become immortalized as the theory of suburban hyperactivity. In Levittown, hyperactivity was limited to a few people, because the majority were reluctant to become involved in strenuous organizational activity.

Chapter Four

THE FOUNDING OF
CHURCHES

IN AMERICA, CHURCHES, WITH THE EXCEPTION OF THE CATHOLIC
Church, are voluntary associations in that people are free to join
or stay away and can choose their denomination. As a result, the
origin of churches differed from that of secular organizations in
only one respect: most were founded Externally. Nineteen
churches (and synagogues) were established in Levittown by
1964, thirteen during the first two years, and of the initial ones,
ten were organized Externally. Most of the churches received
help from Levitt, who gave them free land to hasten the erection
of a building, partly to make the town more attractive to purchasers. Levitt's requirement that the churches build a year after
organization or forfeit the site (although they could get another
later) encouraged External agencies to take over their formation,
although they have also done so in other suburbs where free land
was not available. Moreover, the fundamentalist Protestant sects
in Levittown, which were not given free land, also organized
Externally, and the Jews, who were given land, nevertheless
formed their synagogues Unintentionally. Other explanations
must therefore account for the emphasis on External formation.

Perhaps the principal reason is that churches, like nationwide
voluntary associations, want to add new branches and congregants, and Levittown provided the opportunity—particularly for
a group of "minor" Protestant denominations (the Dutch Re-
formed, the Evangelical United Brethren, and the Church of

Christ) which had long been losing ground to the "major" ones (Methodists, Baptists, Lutherans, Episcopalians, and Presbyterians). They hoped that they could expand in a large new community, especially if they came early to attract the unchurched and those wanting to switch denominations.[1] The builder wanted minor denominations in Levittown, knowing from previous experience that they would offer extra community services as a means of attracting congregants. What the purchasers wanted was difficult to say. None of the pre-occupancy aspirations referred to church activities, although later interviews indicated that 71 per cent then belonging to a church had intended to join before arrival, and most Protestants chose the denomination to which they had belonged before, only 13 per cent switching. The presence of a large number of people committed to membership in a specific denomination probably explains why so many churches could be founded Externally, and the availability of a significant, though smaller, number of unchurched and "switchers" explains why three minor denominations could be started, even though only a handful of Levittowners had previously been members of them.

THE PLANNED CHURCHES: PROTESTANT AND CATHOLIC

Despite organizational and doctrinal differences among the denominations, the formation of new congregations followed a remarkably similar pattern. Before Levittown was occupied, the national or state denominational office began to plan. Most Protestant denominations today have research departments, and these, using figures from other Levittowns and similar new suburban towns, estimated the number of congregants of their denomination likely to purchase in Levittown. Some even projected how much Levittowners could be expected to donate and how soon they would be able to pay for a building. Meanwhile, the denomination selected a minister, often called a "starter," to organize the new congregation. Typically, he arrived in the community shortly after its opening and held services either in his home or at a school until the church building was completed. Concurrently, national church headquarters continued the planning process and, when the building plans were ready, asked the minister to formally organize the congregation, elect officers, and have them review the plans. Once the plans were accepted, the national church made a grant or a loan to the Levittown group to enable it to build a church within the time limit of the builder.

Although the churches were thus essentially preplanned, the preferences of future congregants had to be considered. For example, the National Lutheran Council used data about the religious preferences of young Lutheran suburbanites and chose a liberal branch of German origin which had lost its ethnic character rather than the less Americanized Augustana synod or the theologically conservative Missouri synod. The plans themselves were not implemented until they had been reviewed by the fledgling congregations or their officers, who were often Levittowners with previous church-organizing experience. The work of the External planners was usually accepted, but some congregations questioned the design of the buildings. Many of the laymen and some of the ministers wanted a Colonial church—a white frame building with a steeple—believing that was what a church ought to look like. Since the costs of this design were high, all but one of the churches finally assented to the contemporary style proposed by the denominational architects, frequently adding a small steeple to it, however.

But by far the most important step in planning the new churches was the selection of the minister. Although doctrine holds that people must be attracted by theology and liturgy, the fate of the church depended considerably on the first ministers. They had not only to attract people, but also weld them into a congregation quickly and persuade them to work and contribute funds—and often they were in competition with other ministers. Given the looseness of denominational allegiances among young Protestants, all but the Lutheran and Episcopalian ministers stood the chance of losing potential congregants to other churches. Knowing all this, the denominations selected young men who understood the problems of young families and who themselves wanted to come to Levittown, attracted by the challenge of a new church and a higher salary. The denominations chose well, because all but two of the eight Protestant ministers who came were later named to their posts permanently. The other two were culturally too different from their congregants to be able to bring them into the church.

The Lutherans and Episcopalians organized their churches after Levittowners called the national office, asking them to get

started ahead of the planning schedule, but almost all other denominations began before any demand for them had manifested
itself. Once they had moved in, the ministers began to go from
door to door to enroll members. The "major" ministers had a
difficult time; they had a quota to fill in order to start the church,
and they could recruit the unchurched but not people from
other denominations. On the other hand, the "minor" ministers,
who found only a few from their own denominations, could invite anyone they wished. As a result, the former accused the latter
of "stealing" congregants.

The minor ministers were also more "client-oriented" than
their competitors. They began to build more quickly, knowing
from past experience that many people would not come to services until a building was erected. In one case, the building was
begun when only seventeen families belonged to the church, although the usual lower limit was 100 members. The minister
also persuaded his superiors to build a Colonial church to attract
more people. Minor denominations organized women's and
men's social groups more quickly as well, even though this could
detract attention from the congregational organization or cause
turmoil in the church. The social organizations being more informal than the church, people felt freer to express their dissatisfactions about the church in them. In fact, a congregant revolt
that led to the removal of the Methodist minister had its start in
the couples' club. One minority church started Levittown's first
nursery school to advertise its presence and community spirit—
only to find itself most popular with Jewish residents. Perhaps
the most successful recruitment approach was taken by one minister who immediately immersed himself in civic activity, was the
first to offer counseling services, and by his self-styled ability "to
talk like a truckdriver" attracted working class residents.

The mixture of community service and client-centered recruitment enabled the minor churches to enroll a respectable number
of congregants. In 1961, they each averaged 100 adult members,
compared to 300 each among the major churches. Three fourths
of the members of one minor congregation and half of a second
had crossed denominational lines after coming to Levittown, although, of all church-going Protestants only 13 per cent had done
so. The minor denominations had also become neighborhood
churches, drawing 80 per cent or more of their members from
one neighborhood, whereas the major denominations drew from

all over Levittown. The minor church which had organized the
most social groups had attracted twice as many members as another which had organized none.

Three fundamentalist churches were also founded in Levittown during the first two years, by the same External method and
with only a little less planning. They were not given free
land by Levitt, but because so many of their members tithed,
they needed only a small congregation to start building. One was
collecting $1000 a week from 65 individuals three months after
the church's founding, and was able to build within a year.

The growth of both major and minor churches provided clear
testimony that External planning worked, provided it was done
efficiently. The ministers chosen to carry it out understood their
congregants, and acceded to their wishes on matters of importance to them. The willingness of Externally planned churches to
function thus is nicely illustrated by the Catholic parish, especially since the Catholic Church is often thought to be a centralized and monolithic body in which parishioners are powerless. In
theory the state diocese has complete control over the timing and
development of new parishes. The Trenton diocese, which was
responsible for Levittown, was conservative in starting new parishes and believed in building churches before schools, but the
Catholic Levittowners forced the diocese to alter both the speed
and the character of its planning. Led by a young insurance salesman who went from door to door and registered Catholic
families even while he was trying to sell insurance, a number of
Levittowners pressured the diocese to organize the local parish
ahead of schedule, and eventually it agreed. It also chose as
starter and permanent priest a man who wanted very much to
come to Levittown and who, like his future parishioners, was
more interested in the parochial school than in the church. Because the parish would need more than the three acres Levitt
gave free, the diocese bought its own eleven-acre site, but on that
site built a parochial school which included a "worship area" for
Masses.

Although the diocese gives the parish priest control over parish
activities, in Levittown he had to adjust the organizational process to the Levittowners. An usher's group, functioning as representative of the parishioners, had been formed before he arrived,
and Holy Name and Altar and Rosary societies were set up ahead
of schedule because parishioners wanted them. Financing a new

parish is costly, and both capital and operating expenditures must come from the voluntary donations of the parishioners. Had the pastor not responded to their wishes, their willingness to provide financial support might have been reduced.

Indeed, the only church to run into serious organizational difficulties was the Methodist, which had been in the township for over a hundred years. A new building was put up to make room for the Levittowners, but the previous minister was retained. Although a young man, he was more comfortable with farmers than with suburbanites and sided continuously with the old residents against the newcomers. His failure to allow the Levittowners to assume positions of leadership, his disapproval of dancing and movies, and his overall conservatism led to a definitional struggle, but since the congregation cannot remove the minister and he proved resistant to change, the struggle soon blossomed into an active revolt which lasted for over a year until his superiors eventually transferred him. No other Protestant church experienced a real definitional struggle.

THE UNPLANNED CHURCHES: THE JEWS

Congregation Beth-Torah, the Conservative synagogue, and Temple Emanu-El, the Reform synagogue, were both unplanned.[2] Although all three branches of Judaism are organized into national agencies, and the Reform branch has been active in starting new suburban temples, traditional Jewish practice has been so emphatically congregational that Levittown's Jews never thought of calling on, or waiting for, the External agencies to set up synagogues. And if any resident came to Levittown with the intention of starting a synagogue, he never had an opportunity to act, for community conditions led to the rapid and Unintended formation of both.[3]

Barely three weeks after the first purchasers had arrived in Levittown, a synagogue Sisterhood in nearby Riverside invited one of its past members—now a Levittowner—to a hat show. Believing that this synagogue and another in Burlington might "go after" the Levittown Jews and thus prevent the founding of a local congregation, she concluded that there was no time to spare. Besides, it was almost Christmas, and her children wondered why they should celebrate Chanukah when everyone else was preparing for Christmas. Although neither she nor her husband had originally wanted to start a synagogue in Levittown, they obtained the names of the first twenty-six Jewish families from a Protestant minister and called a meeting early in December 1958.

She was evidently not alone in her feeling of urgency, for at least one person from every Jewish family was in her living room that night. After a brief discussion, which indicated that all three branches of Judaism were represented, it was decided that services would be held the week after and that the organizational discussion would continue at another meeting. At the second meeting, people who had come the first time only to meet other Jews socially did not reappear, but representatives from about fifteen families set up the skeleton of a formal organization, called the Jewish Community Center, and elected the man whose wife had called the first meeting as an unwilling chairman.

For the next six weeks, services were held every Friday night, and after services, as well as between times, there were long debates about the formation of a congregation. Although everyone agreed there were enough people for only one synagogue, they disagreed about which branch of Judaism it should profess. A small group of men, led by a German refugee, wanted a Reform congregation, and another, yet smaller, an Orthodox one. The Orthodox faction was particularly unhappy over the prominence of women in the organizational deliberations and advocated, as is Orthodox custom, a synagogue with separate seating for them. The women had no desire to be either segregated or excluded, however. Most had no intense preference for one branch over another, but were so eager to get Jewish community life under way that they founded a Sisterhood even while the men were still debating about the synagogue. The majority of the participants in the debate were Conservative, and eventually, the choice narrowed down to a Conservative or a Reform congregation.

The conflict centered around religious practices in the synagogue, particularly wearing hats at services, and the observance of dietary laws at synagogue socials. Few people wanted to maintain these practices either at home or in the synagogue, but the Conservatives felt that the synagogue ought to uphold them even if the members' behavior diverged; the Reform group argued that this was hypocrisy. If Jews did not want to keep the Kashrut laws at home or wear hats during prayer, they said, the synagogue should not do so either. "Reform is the religion of the people," one man pointed out. "Each congregation can choose its own form of worship, with or without hats. The Conservatives are boss-run by the rabbis." [4] Much of the argument concerned the children. The Reform group argued that the rabbi should not be allowed to persuade children to follow a tradition their parents were unwilling to maintain in the home. The Conservatives agreed that they did not want their children coming home from Sunday school demanding the keeping of the dietary laws or observance of the Sabbath, but they did want the synagogue to continue *teaching* the tradition. Since the two groups agreed that the synagogue could not compel observance in the home, and since they wanted to establish a single congregation, they continued to look for a formula that would preserve their fragile unity. One man suggested that the group form a community center, the eventual building to have a Conservative and a Reform wing. Every meeting verged on a split and, in near desperation, they invited rabbis from each branch of Judaism to discuss the alternatives before taking a vote on their final choice. Although everyone knew the issues that were causing disagreement, it was hoped that the rabbis would somehow find a way to keep the group together, so the Levittowners insisted that they could not "sell" their own branch of Judaism.

At the time, the Conservative movement was not interested in setting up new synagogues. It had grown so rapidly over the past decade and was so short of rabbis and building funds that the national office was unwilling even to send a rabbi, and someone had to be recruited from a Philadelphia synagogue. The Reform movement, however, was interested in expansion, and had some funds to aid new synagogues. Consequently, it sent an executive from the national office who made what he called a "spirited sales talk" for Reform Judaism, in the course of which he attacked the Conservative movement as well. This was no accident, for he wanted to see a Reform synagogue in Levittown. The Conservatives were enraged, accusing the Reform advocates of violating the agreement. The latter replied angrily, and about 11 P.M. that night they withdrew—with the rabbi at the head—to set up a Reform congregation. Two days later, the Conservatives and the handful of Orthodox residents met to organize a Conservative congregation—then called the Jewish Community Center—and, a week later, the Sisterhood affiliated with it.

After this unintended (though probably inevitable) beginning the two new congregations asked External agencies for help

to obtain rabbis and funds to pay their salaries until the memberships were large enough to pay them. The Reform movement
was able and willing to give both, but the Conservative movement suggested that the Levittowners merge with a synagogue in
Burlington which needed an infusion of new blood. The Levitt-
towners wanted their own synagogue, however, and turned to the
Orthodox movement. Once the largest branch of Judaism in the
country, but now declining in popular support, it had an over-
supply of rabbis and was willing to send one, and even to contribute to his salary, provided the Levittowners would not
affiliate formally with the Conservative movement. Although the
majority of the group was not enthusiastic about having an
Orthodox rabbi, it finally accepted a young man who agreed to
conduct services largely in English, keep his personal religious
practices to himself, and promise not to demand observance from
the children. Later, one of his congregants concluded that "his
orthodoxy gives us no trouble. He lets us do what we want and
we honor his theory. If we had a rabbi who did what we wanted,
we wouldn't respect him."

Once both congregations materialized, enthusiasm for religious activity dimmed; for that matter, attendance at services had
never been very high. Clearly the Jews—Reform and Conservative alike—sought a subcommunity rather than a religious congregation. They wanted to be Jews (and to be with Jews), and
they wanted their children to learn Jewish culture patterns
which parents themselves were neither willing nor able to teach
them at home, but they did not want to attend services, except at
the "High Holidays." Later, when parents with teenagers moved
into Levittown, it became apparent that another function of the
Jewish subcommunity was to prevent intermarriage. Several
Jewish organizations set up teenage groups to engage youngsters
in the Jewish community so that they would not date non-Jewish
Levittowners. There was no restriction on other social relationships with non-Jewish peers, however; only dating them was
taboo.

If the Jews wanted a subcommunity only to maintain the
ethnic tradition and prevent outmarriage, they could presumably
have created a nonreligious body. This alternative was never considered, however, for the tradition was conceived as a religious
one and the synagogue was expected to maintain ethnic cohesion
as well. Besides, no one had yet invented the combination com-

munity-and-social center with a marginal religious program that most people seemed to prefer. A year or so later, after the Conservatives had raised their dues, some parents tried to organize a Hebrew Academy, a school for the children which would also conduct annual High Holiday services for the adults, but not enough families turned out for the organizational meeting to activate it. The failure of the Academy suggests that the synagogue's function was not to represent what Jews did, but what they felt they ought to do: to maintain the tradition whether or not the members observed it. As one Conservative leader put it, "I work on Saturdays and I eat ham, but I want my rabbi to walk to the synagogue and keep kosher. My children are growing up here, and I want a traditional environment for them so that when they are about seventeen, they can choose for themselves." The purpose of the synagogue was to keep the children in the fold to prevent outmarriage, but to leave the adults uninvolved.[5]

Nevertheless, an adult Jewish subcommunity materialized quickly. Although the constant nagging of synagogue leaders for members did not bring them into the congregations, it did create, through social pressure, a feeling of obligation and the recognition that in the case of crisis—such as the emergence of anti-Semitism—the Jews would stand together. Moreover, the mere existence of synagogues could be used by parents as an example to persuade their children to attend the Sunday schools (and among the Conservatives, the afternoon Hebrew school). But most important, Jewish adults were vitally interested in getting together with other Jews, and ultimately, what held the Jewish community together was sociability. Both congregations soon had Sisterhoods with more members than the congregations of which they were nominally subsidiaries. The Sisterhoods were run by people from the first two neighborhoods, and Jews who moved into the later neighborhoods sought organizations of their own; the Reform women tended to join B'nai B'rith; younger Conservative women, O.R.T.; anl older ones, Hadassah. In addition, there was an intricate network of cliques which entertained and partied, formed card clubs, and engaged in a never-ending round of other social activities. Before long, the Jews had more organizations and organizational memberships per capita than all other Levittowners.[6]

The men concentrated on organizing the congregations, although they also had a men's club with poker groups and Sunday

morning softball games. In the fall of 1960, B'rith Sholom, a
Jewish fraternal lodge in Philadelphia, called on five ex-members
who had moved to Levittown, to consider the possibility of setting up a branch. Evidently there had been considerable silent
yearning for such a group, for within three months the lodge had
almost one hundred members, only a few less than the Conservative synagogue had been able to enroll in over a year of strenuous
campaigning. The lodge attracted men who had tired of working
to secure the survival of the synagogue and wanted a purely social
group. As one of the founders of the Center, who had quit to become a charter member of the lodge, put it, "I like it because it's
not a fund-raising thing, it's just social. We use the money only
for social affairs. Each event is run at cost and there are lots of
them. So we get out to dinners this way, and this weekend, there
is a splash party. . . ."

Meanwhile, the development of the congregations proceeded
slowly. The Reform congregation had an easier time of it. Its
membership numbered less than half of that of the Jewish Community Center but it had national guidance and financial support, whereas the Jewish Community Center had to raise almost
all of its own funds and also had to struggle to keep the peace between a predominantly Conservative membership and an Orthodox rabbi.

What attracted adults to the synagogue were the High Holiday
services. Most Jews attended synagogue only twice a year, for
Rosh Hashana and Yom Kippur services. As a result, membership
accelerated just before the High Holidays. In addition, people
with children of Sunday school age became members, for this was
the only way in which they could enroll the children in the
school. One membership chairman said that only perfunctory
pressure was put on Jews with younger children, for they could
not be expected to join until their children were of school age. In
June 1959, the two congregations had enrolled approximately 30
per cent of Levittown's Jews; two years later, the proportion had
risen only 1 per cent—not enough to put the synagogues on a
solid financial footing. Both congregations were caught in a
vicious circle; in order to grow, they needed more programs, full-
time rabbis, and buildings, but these cost money and new members would have to be attracted first. A synagogue building was,
of course, out of the question, but the Reform movement had
bought a Levitt house for its congregation and thereby spurred

the Center to do likewise. Even the upkeep of a house required more members, however, and both groups were searching for dynamic lay leaders able to recruit them. New men were elected to the presidency each year in the hope that they would mount successful membership campaigns.

As early as 1959, some people in each congregation began to feel that lay leadership could not break the circle; the only solution was a charismatic rabbi who could attract members in large numbers, especially among the newer arrivals. The Center began to debate the issue first, but, having to support itself from dues, was also most sharply divided. One group wanted to hire a full-time "go-getter" rabbi, even if it meant deficit financing; another argued for slow growth and a part-time rabbi until more Jews moved to Levittown. The advocates of the full-time rabbi won by a vote in 1960, but at the last minute the only person they could hire was a "scholar" who could not deliver new members.

In 1961, the same factions battled again, but a newcomer to the Center returned to the theme of a lay-centered congregation and ran for the presidency on the platform that the members could support a rapidly growing congregation—provided, however, that they prepared to build, for only "a building" would attract enough recalcitrant Jews to put the congregation on its feet financially. His victory drove out some of the proponents of slow growth, but he brought in a professional fund raiser who collected enough in pledges to initiate a building program. The new president also helped to select a new rabbi who was the "go-getter" the congregation had long been looking for. This rabbi was Orthodox, for Levittown still could not afford a Conservative, but he was an older man with enough experience in Conservative congregations to know that he could not convert them to Orthodoxy. He was not upset by the screening committee's insistence on non-kosher food at synagogue socials—that being cheaper—nor dismayed by poor attendance at Friday night services. He built up attendance somewhat by having children participate in the services, which attracted their parents and friends, and he satisfied his own religious needs by meeting for daily services with a few Orthodox Jews. The rabbi's real interest, however, was in enrolling new members and getting a synagogue erected. With his coming, the Conservative synagogue began to resemble the minister-centered church of the Protestants, and although the laymen still competed for officer posts, they left the running of the synagogue to the rabbi and devoted themselves more fully to social and other activities. The Reform congregation went through roughly the same metamorphosis.

The fund raiser for the Conservative synagogue was an effective practitioner of his craft, who knew how to appeal to what was evidently a widespread desire for a building. A Levittowner and a Catholic, he had previously conducted the fund drive for his own church and had collected an amount that exceeded even his expectations. The synagogue fund drive was aided considerably by $500 pledges from a small group of members, and by a Sisterhood promise to collect $10,000. It was probably aided by the maturing of the Jewish population as well, for as more families had children of Sunday school age, congregational membership increased, reaching 45 per cent of the town's Jewish population by 1962.[7] In 1963, both congregations had begun to erect synagogues, completing them in the sixth of the community's existence. Their co-religionists in Levittown, Pennsylvania, had taken only four years, but then this community had grown much more quickly and the Jewish population was larger.

PLANNED AND UNPLANNED RELIGIOUS GROWTH

The formation of the Jewish subcommunity points up the dilemmas of planned and unplanned formation, and of External and Internal initiative. The Externally planned churches organized quickly and grew systematically about as scheduled, but the development of the Unintended synagogues was slow and turbulent, depending as it did on the varying needs and moods of the membership. Although the synagogues wanted to grow as rapidly and peacefully as the churches, they could not easily agree on growth strategies. For one thing, they lacked studies—and the inclination to conduct them—to determine whether an aggressive rabbi or a building would actually bring in more members, or whether only a larger base population could achieve this aim. In the absence of knowledge, each faction defended what to it was the most comfortable strategy. The merchants and other sales people were inclined toward a rabbinical salesman, the professionals wanted a scholar with whom they could communicate, and the less affluent Jews preferred the cheapest solution. Eventually, the aggressive rabbi and the building did swell membership, but the debates over growth strategy had also postponed their arrival until the total Jewish population had increased.

The definitional struggles had costs other than indecision. The debates that produced the split were carried on by leaders who were extreme partisans of their positions. Each cared deeply about his own view of Judaism—which is what made them leaders—but this partisanship also intensified religious quarrels about which the large majority cared less and prevented the rise of more moderate leaders who could perhaps have achieved a compromise. More important, before the split and after, differences of opinion were frequently taken personally, resulting in personal animosities that were hard to bury. After every debate or election some members left or shifted to the other synagogue, while others refused to work with the people with whom they had argued. Had new leaders who were uninvolved in past animosities not been available from among later arrivals to Levittown, the synagogues would probably have been built still later.

Even so, the intensity of the quarreling stemmed from economic rather than personality factors. The decisions of the Conservatives directly affected their pocketbooks and limited their choices, and the Reform group benefitted more than financially from its subsidy. Not only was it able to hire a full-time rabbi and build as quickly as the Conservatives, even though its membership was much smaller, but its greater freedom from financial worries shortened and tempered the definitional struggles.

If speed and effectiveness of organization are maximal values, then External and planned formation is obviously most desirable; if democracy and lay control are most important, then it is inappropriate. Of course, it is perhaps improper to compare the Protestant and Jewish formation processes, because the Protestant church plays a lesser role than the synagogue in the lives of its members. The church is only a provider of religious services and one of many sources of friends, whereas the synagogue must meet many of the ethnic, emotional, and social needs of an entire subcommunity. Furthermore, only three Jewish religious branches (and two in Levittown) are available to accommodate and sort people differentiated by age, class, and degree of acculturation, and are likely to produce quite heterogeneous congregations. The Protestants, with their many denominations, can sort people into much more homogeneous groups, making it relatively easy for the External planners to anticipate their needs—and therefore, to systematize the church formation. The history of the Methodist church indicates that External planning had to be responsive to membership wishes if definitional struggles were to be minimized—but then, Protestant wishes were much simpler and more obvious than Jewish ones.

Needless to say, lay Levittowners involved in the organizing of their religious bodies did not have a real choice between External and Internal formation. Protestants could, of course, have opposed the prescriptions of the External agencies and their starter ministers, but ministers are viewed both as moral leaders and as experts whose proposals are not easily questioned. Also, most Protestants were not inclined to be critical; neither the structure nor the functions of the church were that vital to them. The Jews had no choice at all, for when they came together, they immediately had to debate far more basic questions, such as the desirability of tradition versus acculturation, and ethnic versus religious identity—questions which few Jews had even thought about before they moved to Levittown. Although some of the people involved in the six-week debate indicated that it had been a significant learning experience, most had considerable difficulty in coping with the conflict and were happy when the split ended the arguments.[8] Had they been able to choose, they would probably have opted for the responsive External planning that created the Protestant and Catholic churches.

CHURCH AND COMMUNITY

By 1961, embryo churches were functioning in Levittown, and some had even achieved that stability one finds among long-established congregations. Most Protestant denominations had either moved into their church or had a building under construction, and Catholics, now running a parochial school, were already envisaging a second parish. Judging from church membership rolls in 1960, about 35 per cent of the nonfundamentalist Protestant families had joined a church, and 40 per cent of this group attended regularly (at least three times a month). Undoubtedly, proportions were higher among Catholics, whereas among the Jews, about 30 per cent had joined a synagogue by 1960, but only about 8 per cent of these attended regularly. All the churches had established Sunday schools, and it seemed that even among Protestants many parents had joined in order to encourage their children to learn the religious and ethical tradition. "I don't quite believe the teachings," said one Levittowner who became active in a church for the first time in his life, "but it's good for the kids to have the background. Also, it's because I bought a house, and for becoming a part of the community." The ratio of attendance to enrollment in the Protestant Sunday schools was 50 per cent higher than in the church itself, but among the Jews, it was 830 per cent higher, for three fourths of the enrolled children were attending Sunday school regularly.

Among Catholics, the church and school had a somewhat different function—to teach children discipline and restraint. Working class Catholics, as well as a number of the Irish middle class, see this as a major purpose of the church, which perhaps helps to explain why Catholic families oversubscribed the school building fund. A few middle class families were restive about the narrowness of the parochial school curriculum, wanting more individual attention, less rote learning, and more emphasis on the arts, but the nuns decided what was to be taught and how. Consequently, these parents sent their children to public schools.

The churches also played a role in the development of social life and in the sorting of residents; about 13 per cent of the interview respondents reported having met their closest friends at church or at the men's, women's, and couples' clubs attached to the church, but the churches did not stress social programs to attract members. The sorting function was further encouraged by providing services in a range of orthodoxy so that people of similarly intensive religious concern would be at church together and no one would feel excluded. Episcopalians held a High service early on Sunday morning and a Low one later, avoiding a decision whether the church should be High or Low; the Conservative synagogue conducted Friday night services with a minimum of Hebrew, added more on Saturday mornings, and offered daily worship for Orthodox Jews; and fundamentalist Protestant churches held Sunday and Wednesday night prayer meetings open only to full members.

Despite normal class differences among denominations, there was no class hierarchy of churches, at least not by 1961. The Presbyterian and Episcopalian churches, which are often high-status denominations in America, did not have this reputation in Levittown. At this stage in the town's history, there was little opportunity to make status judgments about the churches, for they had not yet played a significant role in community life and none had a monopoly, or even a plurality, of community leaders among their members. Indeed, if a church had special prestige, it was based on a large congregation, an attractive building, and the pastor's role in Levittown. By these criteria, the Episcopalian church ranked lower than some others, if only because its minister was older and less active in Levittown affairs than his colleagues. The Methodist church was probably at the bottom of the status hierarchy, for its building was considered ugly, it had permitted Levitt to build a gas station next door, it was known to be undergoing considerable turmoil within the congregation, and its first minister was openly anti-Catholic.[9]

Churches were formally distinct from other community activities, although ministers blessed (and spoke at) community functions.[10] People active in church organizations were frequently busy in secular groups, and vice versa, for someone with a reputation for community activity could hardly escape being asked by his or her minister to take a leading role in church affairs. As a result, there was some relation between the church and the secular community; and, of course, some involvement in town politics—on issues such as opening the township to liquor sales and bingo games and, for the Catholics, on the budget for the public schools.

Relations among individual churches were limited but largely cordial. After the initial competition for recruits, the Protestant ministers formed a Ministerium, held a few joint affairs, exchanged ministers, and celebrated Reformation Sunday together. The Ministerium also played a significant role in the racial integration of the community. Fundamentalist churches stayed out of the Ministerium, however, and relations between major and minor Protestant ministers continued to be somewhat distant because of the early struggle for members. Competition remained rife only among the Jews, where an innovation in one congregation was usually copied by the other shortly afterwards. The ministers and rabbis tried to minimize differences between religions and worked actively to squelch community religious conflict the moment it appeared, fighting charges of anti-Catholicism and anti-Semitism that arose once or twice in political campaigns. They did not have to dwell on religious harmony, however, for it was considered desirable by most residents. Many agreed with one Levittowner who said, "Religious differences aren't important, as long as everyone practices what he preaches." The institutions acted similarly, and the public schools had planned Chanukah celebrations even before the leaders of the Jewish community had asked for them.

NOTES

1. "Unchurched" is religious jargon to describe people who said they had not belonged to a church in their previous residence.
2. The third unplanned and Unintended church was the Unitarian, organized because the nearest congregation was in Philadelphia. The Levittown Unitarian church eventually served all of Burlington County.
3. My study of the origin of the synagogues was more detailed than that of the organization of other churches, because I had previously studied the beginnings of a Jewish subcommunity in another suburban new town and was curious to compare the two. The earlier study is reported in Gans (1951, 1957), and more fully in Gans (1958).
4. A decade earlier the rise of Conservatism was described by Sklare as a congregationally led revolt against the rabbinical domination of Orthodoxy.
5. This followed exactly the pattern I had observed in Park Forest, where I described in detail the change from an adult-oriented to a child-oriented Jewish religion. See Gans (1958), pp. 214–221.
6. Above-average Jewish organizational activity and minimal synagogue attendance were also reported in a study of Levittown, Pennsylvania, in its early years. See Jahoda et al., pp. 95–96.
7. This is close to the national estimate that half of America's Jews belong to synagogues.
8. The researcher has different preferences. I sat in on all of the meetings during the historic six weeks and found them very exciting to study. Indeed, observing the Jewish community was never boring, for meetings of both synagogues and Jewish organizations always produced more participation and argument from the floor than those of Christian and secular nonpolitical groups—where the decisions of leaders were usually accepted without protest and the routine was cut and dried.
9. Although no one paid much attention to them, some of the traditional ethnic differences remained; German names were prominent in the Lutheran church and only slightly less so than Irish ones in the Catholic parish. Italians maintained their traditional lack of interest in church activities except for Mass, although some with non-Italian spouses were involved in church affairs.
10. Levittown unconsciously adopted the tripartite division of American religion, and pains were taken at all community ceremonies to include benedictions by a minister, a priest, and a rabbi. Only at Township Committee meeting benedictions was any effort made to use ministers from all Protestant denominations as well.

Chapter Five

THE NEW SCHOOL SYSTEM

WHEN THE FIRST LEVITTOWNERS MOVED IN THEY KNEW THAT THE
school was ready, but they knew nothing about what their children would be taught or by whom. Questionnaire data collected
before they came indicated that they were not concerned; they
were sure that the new schools would be as satisfactory as their
new neighbors. As I noted in Chapter One, the builder had hired
a national consulting firm to develop the physical plan for the
new school system. This firm, having no parent or student constituency for whom to plan, developed a standard architectural
program adaptable to whatever curriculum would eventually be
created and left the determination of that curriculum up to the
local Board of Education. The board, a group of elected, unpaid
residents then running Willingboro's lone school, was also restrained by the absence of a constituency, and one of its members
later reported that "since we had no Levittowners yet, we tried
to give them a plan for the finest school system in the county."
They decided that this system would be best achieved by giving
the responsibility for course content, teaching methods, and staff
recruitment to the county superintendent of schools.

Since that official was by state law also head of the township
school, the board was familiar with his ideas and methods and
trusted him to design a school system it would find acceptable.
Indeed, its members were pleased that after the Ford Foundation
plan could not be funded, the builder expressed no further desire
to bring in an outsider; they were even more pleased that the
county superintendent was very much interested in establishing

the new system. Shortly before Levittown was opened for occupancy, he became its first Superintendent of Schools. Although
much of the plan was fixed by state and county legislation and
administrative regulations, the superintendent had some leeway
on course content and was free to hire his own staff; most important, he could determine the priorities to be given to bright,
average, and slow students. As a result, the school system was initially shaped by the superintendent's own goals.

The county superintendent had been in office for about ten
years; before that he had headed the schools in one of the larger
towns in the county. The system he developed in Levittown,
however, reflected less his adult experience than his background
and student years. An Irish Catholic of lower middle class origins, he was personally torn between enforcing discipline to
maintain traditional restrictiveness and permitting more freedom to encourage expansiveness and individual development. He
had been taught by rote, and had evidently suffered considerably
at the hands of incompetent and petty teachers who punished for
the slightest infractions of rules. Nothing was more important to
him than to liberate the new generation from these bonds. Like
many Levittowners he wanted the children to grow up under
better conditions than he had experienced. He was not in favor
of progressive education, which struck him as totally permissive,
but sought to combine what he called "the teaching of traditional skills with individual treatment of the children." Hard-
and-fast course outlines would be replaced by projects, and high
school students would be free to choose their own courses, although they would be closely advised by guidance counselors and
held responsible for their choices by a strict grading policy.

Reading was to him the most important of the traditional
skills, and he planned a comprehensive elementary school reading program complementary to other coursework. Its aim was to
teach children to read well, but—equally important—at their own
grade level. When he interviewed a prospective teacher, he asked
what the teacher would do if a child in the second grade had
finished the second-grade reader. Candidates who suggested a
supplementary second-grade reader were considered for a job;
those who suggested a third-grade reader were not. As the reading expert whom he later hired to run the program pointed
out, "A sixth-grade child should not get seventh-grade reading;
that would get him into adolescent reading . . . a child should

not start reading too quickly . . . that would take his childhood away from him."

Because the superintendent had spent his life in rural education, he was intensely concerned with average students, retarded children, and slow learners. Although he realized that many of today's high school graduates would go to college, the colleges he had in mind were not Ivy League types, but state schools and small private colleges in New Jersey and adjoining states—schools like the one he had attended. He determined that, in Levittown, the public school system would devote extra energies and its additional resources to the retarded, with lowest priority given bright students. Not only did he feel that the latter needed little help—much less than retarded students—but he found their motives and their behavior undesirable. In his view they were pushed too hard by their parents, who wanted them to advance beyond grade level, and they were often a burden to teachers, especially if parents demanded too much individual attention "to make sure that they all get college scholarships." An overemphasis on college preparation in the curriculum would ignore, he said, "the great unwashed who can't go to college; the girls who become typists." In line with his own lower middle class outlook, he insisted that Levittown would not copy Brookline and Scarsdale, and rejected such "Brookline ideas" as teaching foreign languages in elementary schools and allowing liberal skipping of grades. He liked to poke fun at a neighboring upper middle class community whose school system prided itself on a high percentage of college scholarships, arguing that it ought to pay more attention to athletics so that average students could obtain scholarships. This justified his advocacy of varsity sports, although he also wanted to bring county athletic leadership to Levittown and end the virtual monopoly of county championships that had been held by a predominantly working class community for many years.

Rather naturally, the superintendent selected assistants who agreed with his basic philosophy. The elementary schools were assigned to a veteran county educator who shared the superintendent's preoccupation with discipline. Known as a "starter," he was an energetic man who thrived on the round-the-clock job of opening new schools. He too said publicly and more than once, "I won't stand for a Brookline education," and reinforced the emphasis on the average student by rejecting IQ tests and academic competition of any kind, whether among parents or children. He also believed that if the school staff took the initiative in shaping the school system, it could set standards which would be observed by students and parents alike. On the first day of school, he welcomed his charges at the front door and laid down his rules. Likewise, he personally initiated the organization of a PTA, choosing it because its bylaws demanded support of school policy and moving quickly to prevent parents from organizing home-and-school groups which could question it. Moreover, he personally recruited the actual PTA founders from people he already knew and trusted, taking strangers only if he could check with their previous communities on their loyalty to the school system. He also demanded that his teachers "belong to the system." Teachers were instructed to pay close attention to parents, for dissatisfied parents would create pressure groups, and these the elementary school official described as "cancers." His self-righteous authoritarianism was overlaid by an expansive idealism, that he or anyone else could do what he wanted provided he wanted it badly enough. This viewpoint not only served as a rationalization for his methods, but also blinded him to the difficulties of his task, making him an efficient starter and encouraging the beginnings of a common "school culture" in all the schools he set up.

For the first year, Levittown's high school students were farmed out to other communities, but in 1959, when it came time to plan a local high school, the superintendent selected a principal who was similarly seeking to balance discipline and freedom. Although he came from a school where 80 per cent of the graduates went on to college, he looked forward to being in Levittown, where preliminary estimates showed that no more than half would continue their education. He too argued that average students were being "robbed" by too much curriculum emphasis on college preparation, and he also resented the demands of "college prep students, who give you a harder time." He wanted to reduce the status hierarchy built into the academic, commercial, and general (a euphemism for vocational) divisions in the country high schools; he hoped that by permitting students to choose courses in all of them, college prep students would come into more contact with the business trainees and the general division students. He had a genuine interest in the last, who he felt were being neglected because of inferior or nonexistent vocational courses and were ostracized by their fellow students. As it turned out, however, not all Levittowners shared the principal's and superintendent's priorities and their belief in compensatory support for the intellectually disadvantaged.

THE DEFINITIONAL STRUGGLES

Voluntary associations and churches, being private agencies with sorting functions, could end definitional struggles by extruding people with divergent views. The school system, however, like all public agencies served the entire community and had to provide for its diverse demands within a single institution. As a result, it was soon embroiled in definitional struggles aimed at revising the superintendent's original goals.

When the Levittowners arrived, they were delighted that the first elementary school was open on schedule, and were pleased with the new, modern facilities and the young, energetic teachers. They seemed satisfied with their children's performance, joined the PTA and crowded its meetings, and even helped the schools by working in a variety of PTA fund raising and other projects. Some Catholics felt that the public school was lax—too much "play" and not enough discipline—and these parents (like most other Catholics) enrolled their children in the parochial school as soon as it opened. Other parents may have been uneasy about one or another aspect of the program, but they decided to be patient with the new system, arguing that "it was too early to heckle." As a result, the administrators and teachers received very little criticism during the first two years—or for that matter, little feedback of any kind. Although the principals maintained an open-door policy so that parents could air complaints at any time, relatively few did so. One man, who had run two Levittown elementary schools, reported that the only curriculum complaint he ever received came from a well-educated mother who wanted more work for her talented daughter. What complaints there were concerned the lunch schedule and overly severe discipline. On one occasion, when a teacher had a near-breakdown in class and upset many children to tears, almost every parent turned out that night at the school board meeting to protest. Beyond that, most parents seemed content to leave education to the school, assuming that the teachers knew best what was good for the children.

Some of the plans made by the superintendent and his associates had to be changed to respond to unexpected conditions. The elementary schools functioned pretty much as their starter intended—but then their students were a captive audience, too young to make choices or to object to adult demands. At first the parents, too, were pleased with him, particularly since he spoke to them idealistically, well, and often, never forgetting to praise their children. Once all the schools had been started, however, and a routine had been established, his flowery speeches began to grate, especially on parents and teachers who disliked his oppressive methods and his way of using rhetoric to avoid confronting disagreement. He resigned before opposition had a chance to become visible and widespread.

When it came to the organization of the high school, the initial plans had to be adapted to the diversity and choice-making ability of the students. Reducing the barriers between the three divisions assumed a fairly equal proportion of choices in each, but 50 per cent of the students opted for the academic track, and general students were a small minority. Consequently, the school had to emphasize "college prep" after all, and even initiated an honors program, but could not mount a vocational program. To prevent the possibility that the general students might become resentful and cause trouble, the principal tried to make them feel part of the school through extracurricular activities and sought, unsuccessfully, to have one elected as a student council officer. Even so, he could not counteract their hostility, and later they ranked high among the dropouts and serious delinquents.

Plans to give all students more freedom of course choice and class attendance were frustrated by the poor marks some had earned while attending neighboring schools the year before. Evidently treated as unwelcome outsiders, one third had to make up work that summer, and their poor records, as well as the initial stirrings of juvenile delinquency just before the high school opened, frightened the school board members. Teenage vandalism and delinquency had been unknown in the township previously, largely because its few adolescents had had to go elsewhere for recreation. Not knowing what to expect from the Levittown youngsters, the board and the administration were reluctant to trust their new charges, and because they were then engaged in a struggle with upper middle class parents on another issue, they were not eager to initiate freedoms that might well engender protests from restrictive parents. Instead, the high school principal sought to instill more "school spirit," particularly by encouraging the immediate formation of a varsity football team. Even though he believed it to be premature, he gave in to the demands of some residents and the wishes of the superintendent, hopeful that it would make for a peaceful and cooperative relationship with the student body. Needless to say, this was too much to expect of a football team, and although students maintained order—except for a rash of bomb scares one spring—the desired feeling of cooperation and trust was not achieved in the early years.

The Revolt of the Upper Middle Class

Highly educated Levittowners with bright children did not take long to realize that the new school was not giving their children high priority. There were relatively few such parents, and those who could afford it transferred their children to nearby private schools, but these did not provide kindergartens. Just as the superintendent had augured, the parents began to "cause trouble" soon after they arrived in Levittown.

In the spring of 1959, the township Board of Education announced that in congruence with state Board of Education policy, it would only admit children into kindergarten if they had reached the age of five by October 1. This policy was at once questioned by a couple of lower middle class parents with children born a few days after the cut-off date, but school officials persuaded them of the wisdom of the policy. At the next school board meeting, however, the issue was reopened by two upper middle class professionals, and before long, they presented the board with a petition signed by 170 parents asking for a change in the cut-off date to December 31. When that petition was rejected, they collected 200 more names, and with it a small but vocal group who kept the issue alive for several months.

The board members had never before been confronted with a petition and reacted with resentment and fear. "If we listened to all the wishes," one said, "there would be government by petition and that is not desirable." Protests would cast aspersions on them and mean longer working hours to deal with the protests as well. They wanted neither, particularly since they knew that they would lose their positions to Levittowners as soon as the latter had fulfilled the two-year residence requirement. A change in the cut-off date would bring more children into schools that were already full, violate state policy as well as the wishes of the super-intendent, and force the board members to support a policy they themselves considered undesirable. The questions now at issue—responsiveness to the constituents, the justification of local inno-vation in county tradition, and the role of the school in the community—would come up again and again in the years to come.

The proponents of the date change were almost all upper mid-dle class people, eager to get their children into school, the sooner to qualify for college competition. The board members and the school staff believed, however, that children should not be asked to sacrifice their childhood or jeopardize their "natural" social adjustment. Indeed, some of them felt that a child should not enter the first grade until he was seven. The older he was at the time of graduation, the more mature he would be, and the more likely to obtain a good job. These were overwhelmingly lower middle class people, concerned only that the children would get good white collar jobs once they finished their school-ing. To them, family came before school; in fact, they accused the proponents of the date change of wanting their children out of the house and of using the school as a baby-sitter. They could not understand that the proponents were already preparing their youngsters for professional careers.

The proponents of change were cosmopolitans and were think-ing in terms of the nationwide competition for admission to "name" universities. The board members and the school staff, on the other hand, had spent all their lives in New Jersey, and their allegiance was to the township, the county, and the local colleges. Finally, the proponents fervently advocated innovation and ar-gued that in a new community a fresh start should be made while conditions were still propitious—at the beginning, with consum-mate speed, and on the basis of expert advice. The board mem-bers retorted that they had no time for innovation, having enough to do just to get the routine established, and besides, as one pointed out, "The community is not like a Cadillac in which everything is finished before it comes out of the factory; it has to develop and the people have to put the finishing touches on it themselves."

In response to the board's call for more facts, the proponents consulted educational psychologists all over the East Coast and

superintendents of school systems with late cut-off dates. Agreeing that age was an arbitrary criterion for cut-off, they recommended a testing program by which children under five before
December 31 would be admitted to the kindergarten upon a
good showing on tests. To their amazement, however, the board
rejected the proposal. It referred to other expert opinion on
which state policy had been based, found studies which claimed
that children's eyes would be damaged permanently if they
started to read before age six or even eight, and sloughed off experience from schools in high-status communities. "We are not
Brookline," said one school official, "and it cannot serve as our
guide." They rejected tests as well, not only because they would
force children to compete against each other but because of their
political consequences. Anger from parents whose child had
failed the test by a percentage point would be more intense than
that generated by a birthday that came a day after the cut-off. But
even as the board members tried to counter facts with other facts
and turn the debate back to opinions which could not be argued
so easily, they recognized a genuine community protest. The
township government had recently rejected petitions on two
issues raised by the newcomers and had roused the ire of many
Levittowners. Even though they were elected on a nonpartisan
basis, the school board members were Republicans, and yet another rebuff could only help the Democratic party. Conversely,
they could not bring themselves to give in to "government by
petition" or to cross professional educators. Indeed, the staff persuaded the board that "they [the proponents] are laymen; they
don't really know what it's all about," but an argument that
might have intimidated most Levittowners did not impress the
proponents, some of whom were better educated and of higher
occupational status than the school administration.

Caught in the middle, the board stalled, hoping that the controversy would abate over the summer. Although this did not
happen, the stalling paid off, for as new purchasers streamed in,
the lack of room for additional kindergartens served as an excuse
to turn the proponents down without passing on the validity of
their demands. Even then, another wave of pressure might have
led to a reversal, particularly after the board met with the Levitt
officials to seek their advice—and learned that they had no objection to the change—but also because all along the board had
assumed that all Levittowners agreed with the proponents and

might decide to petition en masse. Now, one board member who was active in the community and sat on other township boards, decided to sample Levittown opinion. To his surprise, he found that many Levittowners shared his own feeling that children should be kept at home as long as possible and that the proponents were most likely only a small minority. Once he communicated this to the board, it felt strong enough to resist further pressure.

The long struggle had unified the protesting parents and, a week after their defeat, they organized a Citizens' Committee for Better Schools, later renamed the Citizens' Association for Public Schools (C.A.P.S.), because some members felt the reference to "better schools" might cast aspersions on the Levittown system that would cost the group community support. Once organized, C.A.P.S. did not have to wait long for a new issue on which to oppose the school board: overcrowding and class size.

The schools had been planned on the basis of population data collected in Levittown, Pennsylvania, to permit classes of 25–30 pupils. But the new Levittown had attracted a higher proportion of larger families with school-age children, and the parochial school would not take as many Catholic students as had originally been expected. As a result, classes in the second neighborhood elementary school grew to 35 or more. Levitt altered his construction plans to build more four-bedroom and fewer three-bedroom houses in newer "parks," but he was unwilling to plan more classrooms in the schools for these neighborhoods, arguing that the overcrowding would be temporary and assuming that there would be no objection to bigger classes in the meantime. C.A.P.S., supported by the neighborhood PTA, asked that classes be restored to their original size by busing the overflow to the first school (which served a smaller neighborhood). However, the superintendent, suspecting that the two organizations did not reflect majority opinion, conducted an attitude survey, asking parents whether they preferred busing or larger classes.[1] Three fourths of parents responding favored larger classes, and the C.A.P.S. proposal was rejected.[2]

The Attack on the School Budget

After this defeat, C.A.P.S., expecting to be permanently at loggerheads with the school system, started to draft what it considered to be a more desirable curriculum. The superintendent sought to reduce its antagonism, however, and asked several members to assist him on school board work, partly to coopt them, partly to take advantage of their research and their planning skills lacking in his own small staff. In working together, the antagonists discovered some shared goals. The superintendent actually supported the C.A.P.S.' desire for small classes, and a year later, he implemented a busing plan based on its original proposal. He also set up a testing system to enable children to enter kindergarten before the age of five if their parents requested it.

The sudden compatibility was, however, primarily a response to the development of a new and much stronger set of opponents to the school system: Levittowners who demanded less expensive schools devoted to little more than basic teaching functions, and who sought to prevent the establishment of additional educational services which both the administration and C.A.P.S took for granted as absolutely necessary. By 1960, the rising school population and the hiring of auxiliary staff—for example, varsity coaches and a school psychologist—required a significant increase in the school budget. In Levittown, as in most other small New Jersey communities, this budget had to be approved by the voters, and in February 1960, the first election in which a sizeable number of Levittowners were eligible to vote, it was badly beaten. Even though the budget was then slightly cut, and even though Levitt was then paying about 40 per cent of all municipal operating expenditures, the tax rate rose 15 per cent, or about $25 a year.

When the new tax bills went out in the summer of 1960, widespread grumbling developed about school expenditures, too much expansion and innovation, and the high salaries of the school administration. To add fuel to the fire, a consultant hired by the Township Committee to help reorganize municipal government predicted that taxes in Levittown would eventually rise from about $275 per house to $645. Opposition to the rise in school taxes—which accounted for about three quarters of the total tax bill—came from families without school-age children and from less affluent Levittowners who were finding the cost of home ownership higher than expected. The most vocal attacks seemed to come from Catholics, who not only had lower incomes and more children than Protestant and Jewish Levittowners, but who were at that time also being asked to fund the building of a parochial school.

In the fall of 1960 the first Levittowners became eligible to run for the Board of Education, and leading Catholics in the Democratic party—whose leadership was largely Catholic to begin with—began to look for candidates for the 1961 board election who would vote for lower school budgets. As a result, C.A.P.S. rallied behind the school board and superintendent and, by the beginning of 1961, it had emerged as their principal defender in the community. The proposed budget for the 1961–1962 school year was again higher than the previous one, and because Levitt could no longer afford to subsidize school operations, except in new neighborhoods not yet on the tax rolls, another tax increase was threatening. Eventually, it came to about $100 per house, a 33 per cent increase over the previous year's tax bill.

By county tradition, school board elections were "above politics" and enough Levittowners agreed, thus discouraging the Democrats from forming a slate. Shortly before the mandatory public hearing on the budget and the election, however, three anti-tax candidates, two of them leaders of the Holy Name Society, were being talked up by many Levittowners as a so-called "Catholic slate." The year before, the public hearing had attracted only a handful of people, but in February 1961, more than 600, the largest crowd of Levittowners ever to meet together, jammed the auditorium in an angry mood to protest the proposed budget. The complaints of the previous year were repeated, and there was violent criticism of the superintendent's $18,000 salary and a newly suggested administrative post for curriculum planning. A group of engineers, constituting a Committee for Efficient Schools, argued that all the school really needed was teachers and that volunteers from the community could administer and plan. Others in attendance attacked the classroom size policy, pointing out that the parochial school was providing adequate education with 60 children per class; and a few people even objected to teachers' salaries, the highest of which—for ten years' experience—were then approaching the community's median income of $7500. The opposition to teachers' salaries came largely from a handful of working class Levittowners who had never before encountered teachers earning more than they. Most Levittowners were careful not to object to teachers' pay, however, and reserved their disapproval for "administrators."

The meeting was extremely bitter, with angry charges and

exaggerated claims freely traded. The conflict was clearly between the haves and the have-nots, for when one lone budget
supporter ended his speech, he was asked how much he was earning. There was also conflict, as in the voluntary associations, between the (few) advocates of rapid growth who wanted a fully
staffed school system *now,* and the (many) proponents of
gradual maturation, although they were only rationalizing their
demand for tax reduction.

The protesting Levittowners resented particularly what they
considered to be taxation without representation. Despite
C.A.P.S. suggestions that the school board improve its "public relations," the budget was printed only in the classified advertising
pages of the two county newspapers, as required by law—where,
of course, few people saw it. Since attendance at board meetings
had been minimal and the school board still had not become acquainted with many Levittowners, they did not know how to
communicate with or represent their new constituents. At the
public hearing itself, the board again objected to government by
protest and petition, reinforcing the Levittowners' feeling that
they lacked control over their own elected officials. As a result,
the budget was voted down overwhelmingly at the election,
and the so-called Catholic slate replaced three of the old residents
on the nine-man school board. Subsequent interviews showed
that blue collar and lowest income respondents rejected the
budget in largest numbers. Unexpectedly, the most poorly educated parents were more favorable than high school and college
graduates, as were mothers—not fathers—of school-age children,
and 90 per cent of the Catholics turned down the budget as compared to 67 per cent of the Jews.

Once Levittowners had achieved even minority representation
on the school board, the community's anger abated. In 1962, the
school budget rose again, and the voters again rejected it, but
they did not complain when the school board refused to cut it
afterwards and levied another 15 per cent tax increase. Moreover,
the voters elected to the board two C.A.P.S. leaders who had
campaigned strenuously as a pro-budget slate, although they did
poorly in the first neighborhoods and obtained their winning
margin from the more recently settled ones. Thanks to rising
house prices, the newer arrivals were somewhat more affluent;
also, having come to Levittown after the initial tax hikes, they

were not faced with so precipitous an increase in monthly payments.

After public concern over the budget had died down, the C.A.P.S.-administration alliance disintegrated. The main source of conflict now was the superintendent's unwillingness to plan for the future and to find some way of dealing with the growth needs of the system and the annual budget rejections by the voters. Indeed, the superintendent was too sluggish even for the remaining old residents on the school board who had originally appointed him, and in the fall of 1962, they joined forces with the two C.A.P.S. members in asking him to resign. Old differences with C.A.P.S. about what made for a good school, and the priorities for serving bright, average, and slow students also contributed to the superintendent's downfall, as did his reluctance to improve "public relations." Yet these factors were only symptomatic of a more basic problem—his inability to adapt his previously rural experience to the wishes of the suburbanites. He could, perhaps, not have avoided antagonizing the minority who wanted an upper middle class school system or the less affluent Levittowners who demanded economy above all and asked him to provide what he considered inferior education, but he did not really understand even the majority of his constituents. In a speech to the National Education Association, he mischaracterized Levittowners as "descendants of second or third generation immigrants whose national customs and mores are very slowly discarded," and compared them to his previous rural constituents, whom he eulogized as "descendants of early Colonial stock or the solid conservative descendants of the European farmer. . . . As our farms grow into neighborhoods, we [must] provide American, not foreign, education," he said, as if his role was to Americanize the Levittowners.

Ironically, and despite his ethnic misinterpretation, he differed little from the lower middle class majority in Levittown, and it agreed with most of his teaching policies. Indeed, the overall consensus between him and most parents about what class culture was to be transmitted by the school system had enabled him to implement his substantive educational ideas without much opposition. Conversely, if the Ford Foundation scheme for an upper middle class school system had been put into practice, and the school had consequently required what lower middle class

students would consider excessive learning demands, they probably would have protested to their parents, who in turn might
have forced the school board to transform the system into a lower
middle class institution.

The superintendent's departure, and the ability of the two
C.A.P.S.-affiliated board members to organize a coalition that
outvoted the advocates of economy, now encouraged the twosome
to believe that it could reorganize the school system closer to its
wishes, but this hope was short-lived. The victory of the C.A.P.S.
members appeared certain when a liberal Pennsylvania educator,
who shared many of their standards, was found to replace the superintendent. Shortly before he was to take office, however, Democrats on the Township Council told him they would fight any policies that would result in higher taxes. He decided that it would
be foolhardy to come to Levittown to face a continuous political
battle, and resigned. The search for a new man took several
months but, eventually, a more compatible New Jersey administrator was hired. Meanwhile, the Democrats then in control of
the Township Council had decided that the traditional taboo
against political party involvement in school politics was less
sacred to their constituents than lower taxes, and put pressure on
the school board for budget cuts. In this atmosphere, C.A.P.S.'s
short-lived influence came to an end at the next school election.
After one of the C.A.P.S.-affiliated board members had left Levittown for a better job in another state, the remaining member became the sole target for attacks on "better schools" and higher
taxes. Although the newer neighborhoods provided some support, she trailed behind the other candidates and the brief reign
of the cosmopolitans was over.

THE EVOLUTION OF THE SCHOOL SYSTEM

Recurring struggles over the amount and allocation of school
funds did not prevent the rapid development of a functioning
school system in Levittown. By September 1965, more than 8000
students were attending five elementary schools, two junior (or
middle) ones, and a high school, the latter built entirely from
public funds. These schools included all the curricular and extracurricular accouterments one would expect in a modern
middle (but not upper middle) class suburb; the education they
provided would prepare the students for about the same white

collar, technical, and subprofessional jobs held by their parents and for the lower middle class culture that dominated the community. Perhaps the schools favored the restrictive subculture more than the expansive; the course offerings were quite traditional, and there was none of the "life adjustment" and "learning to get along with the group" approach that Whyte had found in Park Forest.[3] The teachers gave their students individual attention and demanded neither superior intellectual achievement nor oppressive memorizing. As a result, the dropout rate was infinitesimal, and about 50 per cent of the graduates enrolled in college, although in 1963 a third of them chose junior colleges and teachers' colleges, and only 5 per cent went to "name" schools. It was, as one unhappy C.A.P.S. member put it, "the school system the community deserved." Interviews conducted in 1961 suggested, however, that the majority was pleased. Seventy-five per cent of all parents and 87 per cent of non-Catholic ones felt their children were either learning better or about as well as in their previous community, and 75 per cent of the parents considered the Levittown system superior to the one they had come from, praising it for better teachers and higher performance requirements from the children.[4]

A minority Catholic bloc had seemingly settled into the school board and opposed many majority decisions, but the conflict never reached the intensity or the longevity that had developed in Levittown, New York, where a large, predominantly Catholic group fought the budget and also accused the system of Communist leaning for many years.[5] Levittown, New Jersey still struggled with an increasing school population and rising budgets, requiring a 6 per cent tax increase in 1964 and a 16 per cent increase in 1965. In addition, insufficient classroom space continued to be a problem, possibly requiring an eventual enlargement of the elementary schools. However, it seemed as if the Levittowners preferred larger classes to rising taxes.

Actually, school expenditures could not have been considered unreasonable; in 1965, they amounted to $465 per student, less than in all but two of the seven townships surrounding Levittown. Even taxes were not exorbitant, amounting in 1965 to $425–$530, depending on the house type. The actual tax rate was only about 8 per cent higher than in 1959, and what had caused the precipitous tax rise, a total of 122 per cent since that year, was the withdrawal of the Levitt subsidies which paid for almost half of all municipal expenditures during the first two years.[6] Some Levittowners were undoubtedly hard pressed to pay the higher taxes, especially on top of increases in the cost of living and the rising expenses of maintaining their houses. For many, however, it was not so much the money as the idea of having to pay for a school their children did not attend—and then to have to fund the parochial school as well, and for others, of having to support a system with more "frills" than they wanted for their children. These parents were essentially objecting to a school that taught the culture of their more affluent and higher-status neighbors, a culture which they neither wanted to finance nor to have their children adopt. Since education is supposedly not only above politics but also classless, the class conflict—for that is what it was—never came to the surface, but it pervaded the definitional struggle nevertheless.

Even so, the less affluent Catholic population was not quite as threatened either financially or in terms of status as its equivalent on Long Island—where half the people were blue collar workers and the cosmopolitan opposition, as well, was larger. This probably explains why the panic, the anti-Communist hysteria, and the witch-hunting never developed.[7] In 1963, a Birchite group did attack the school board for Communist sympathies but it received no support from other Levittowners and quickly faded out of the picture. Dobriner describes Levittown, Long Island, as "bimodal" in class, and Catholic blue collar anger there may have been heightened by relative deprivation vis-à-vis a single class enemy, whereas Levittown, New Jersey, was more "trimodal," and on some issues, working class residents found allies among lower middle class ones. The Long Island community was almost ten years old when the conflict reached its peak, and it may also be that the relative newness and the concurrent reservoir of residents' patience muted it in the New Jersey community.

NOTES

1. Despite the principal's careful screening of prospective PTA officers, this PTA regularly criticized school policy and, at one point, even proposed secession from the national PTA to enable it to fight the school system. The proposal was beaten by pressure from

county and state PTA leaders and the lack of sufficient support from the neighborhood membership.

2. My reanalysis of the survey suggested that parents who liked their children's teachers opposed busing; those who disliked them favored it, and class size was of lesser importance to them.

3. Whyte (1956), pp. 387–392.

4. Among Catholic parents with children in public school, 25 per cent reported improvement in school performance; 22 per cent, deterioration; and 53 per cent, no change. Among non-Catholics, the figures were 29 per cent, 13 per cent, and 58 per cent, respectively.

5. Dobriner (1963), pp. 113–118. See also Wattel, pp. 306–311, and Orzack and Sanders.

6. Altogether, the builder contributed about two million dollars between 1959 and 1963. See League of Women Voters, Willingboro, New Jersey, p. 14.

7. Dobriner (1963), p. 100. Also, the tax rate in Levittown, Long Island, rose a full 784 per cent between 1947 and 1962.

Chapter Six

THE EMERGENCE OF
PARTY POLITICS

EVEN THOUGH THE FORMATION OF THE SCHOOL SYSTEM WAS MARKED
by recurring conflict, the students were for all practical purposes a
captive constituency, which limited the extent of the definitional
struggles. Municipal government represented all Levittowners,
however, and had to cope with all their diversities. Nowhere was
the origin process more chaotic than among and within the political parties.

When Levitt first purchased the land, Willingboro was governed by a three-man Township Committee, each member
elected for three years, and by an appointed township solicitor
who drafted—and often suggested—legislation and supervised
the Committee's few administrative and executive tasks. Levitt's
arrival did not immediately change this pattern. He built roads
and other municipal facilities, the Township Committee's major
function being to review the firm's plans.

Until the Levittowners moved in, the township was a one-
party community, having been Republican since its inception,
and as everybody knew everyone else, there was no need for election campaigns or even for an active local party. After Levitt arrived, the community and the party split into pro- and anti-
Levitt factions, the former headed by the old elite, the latter by a
conservative ex-New Yorker who belonged to the opposing faction in the county Republican party. An Episcopalian of Catholic birth and a public relations man by trade, he disagreed on

almost every issue with the Methodist and Presbyterian farmers on the other side, particularly on the question of liquor, he favoring a wet community, they a dry one. The newcomer soon came to support Levitt, but his other differences with the old elite remained, and were to affect Levittown politics for the next two years, especially after he was chosen Mayor.

By the time the Levittowners came, everyone knew that change was just around the corner, for the first ones would be eligible to vote in the April 1959 primary. They would outnumber the old residents by 1960, at the latest; and eventually they might, as residents of the largest community in the county, dominate its politics as well. No one realized this more clearly than four young Democratic hopefuls, all previously active in county politics—two as Republicans—who were among the first purchasers in Levittown. Having known each other before, they caucused quickly, constituted themselves a steering committee, and in December organized the township's first Democratic club. Shortly thereafter, they began a house-to-house survey to look for Democratic voters and workers.[1] In March the Republicans, spurred on by a lone Levittowner, buried the factional hatchets long enough to organize a formal Republican club. Both clubs immediately started to look for candidates for the November Township Committee election, but neither party knew what kind of a candidate might appeal to the new voters. The Democrats used survey results, and judging from the enthusiastic responses among working class residents (middle class ones were likely to call themselves independents), they concluded he ought to be a "working man." The Republicans knew almost nothing about the Levittowners, but the Mayor's faction, also considering them to be working class, selected a Catholic salesman, whereas the old elite guessed high and picked a Protestant Harvard Law School graduate. Eventually, both these prospective candidates withdrew to avoid a primary fight and the nomination went to a lower middle class Catholic insurance salesman.

While the parties were readying their nominees for the November election, the Township Committee labored in near-anonymity. It passed a variety of uncontroversial ordinances, partly for the newcomers but also to protect the old residents against possible "undesirables" among the Levittowners. For example, a Police Department had been established just before they arrived, and a year later an ordinance was passed requiring

the registration of residents with prison records. Shortly thereafter, some county people considered the establishment of a
mental health clinic, reportedly for the newcomers. Few Levittowners went to Township Committee meetings, but then few
had expressed civic or political aspirations on the mail questionnaire before they arrived. More questionnaire respondents
had wanted "a voice in community affairs," however, and the opportunity to raise it soon arrived.

Two seemingly innocuous issues, both generated by the builder
and both arousing political and status fears among the newcomers, suddenly placed the Township Committee in the fore-
front of public attention. First, Levitt acted to eliminate a deed
restriction which forbade nonresident doctors from purchasing
houses solely for office use. When he sought to have the Township Committee amend the zoning ordinance—as he generally
tried to do for all restrictions that could be legitimized and thus
strengthened by municipal action—the already resident doctors
protested. Since there was at that time still a shortage of patients,
they feared competition from nonresidents, many of whom
would be specialists. They were joined by homeowners, many of
them working class, who felt that nonresident doctors would take
only their money, whereas residents of the community would respect them.[2] But their major concern was that if houses were
bought by nonresident professionals, their blocks would soon be
semicommercial and the community would suffer the same status
deterioration that had taken place—for other reasons—in Levittown, Pennsylvania.[3] Distrustful of the builder and the old residents on the Township Committee, they claimed that the ordinance might let in barbers, beauticians, and other low-status
quasi-professionals as well. "I make $7000 a year," said one. "I
came here for a residential community; don't cheapen this area
by bringing doctors in to practice. All we want for our own class
is a residential area."

There was considerable validity in the homeowners' expectation that the Committee would be unresponsive, for rumors to
this effect had already circulated. When they came to the public
hearing 150 persons strong, with 450 signatures on a petition and
20 people to testify against the amendment, the Committeemen
listened in silence and then summarily rejected their demands.
Like the school board, the Committee was opposed to government by petition and was so fearful about its first confrontation

with the newcomers that the police were ordered out in full force, ringing the meeting room to forestall possible violence. The Mayor favored the zoning amendment (to attract specialists), and besides, the Committee intended, as it had in the past, to satisfy the builder's wishes whenever it could, feeling that as he was the largest landowner and the determiner of the township's future, blocking him would only hurt the community. The Committee did not give final approval to the amendment that night, for the Mayor saw an opportunity to embarrass the leader of the old elite, then Chairman of the Planning Board and the Mayor's bitter political enemy, by passing the buck to his board for action.

What 150 people could not achieve at the Township Committee meeting a smaller group was able to do at the Planning Board a month later. The planning consultant suggested that the matter be postponed until the zoning ordinance could be rewritten entirely to conform with a preliminary master plan that had just been approved. The board moved to accept his suggestion, but the opponents suspected a stall that would lead to the eventual admission of nonresident doctors and angrily demanded that the board take immediate action. Momentarily intimidated, the board gave in and voted against nonresident doctors. When the issue was then returned to the Township Committee, the nonresident doctors came with 1200 signatures, and a compromise was passed, allowing only doctors to purchase houses and no more than two to a house. Both political parties refused to take a stand on the controversial issue, not knowing how the Levittowners felt; instead, they asked the Levittown Civic Association to hold a "nonpartisan debate" to find out. Still run entirely by old residents, the Association too was fearful of controversy, and when Levittowners refused to come out for noncontroversial meetings, it expired.

No sooner had the "doctor issue" been resolved than another arose—on the sale of liquor in the township—and the same pattern was repeated. Again, the Levitt organization provided the impetus. Willingboro had been dry since its inception, but the builder wanted to include a restaurant-bar and a package store in his shopping center. He requested an ordinance to that effect, and once again, the Township Committee acquiesced after a stormy public hearing. The opposition consisted primarily of "drys" from the Methodist church and many Levittowners who had objected to nonresident doctors and now envisioned bars and liquor stores on every corner. Again they feared a status decline, using Levittown, Pennsylvania, as an example, and again they exaggerated the consequences of the ordinance. Angered by the last meeting and by the wild charges leveled at them from an audience of "cranks and Democrats," the Committeemen made it clear that they had not paid attention to the protesting witnesses, for after the public hearing was ended they voted unanimously for the ordinance without even a preliminary caucus.

Again, both political parties stayed out of the issue because of its controversial nature, but they could not avoid internal splits over it. Most Democrats were wet, and the leaders expected campaign contributions from liquor dealers. Many of the opponents to both nonresident doctors and liquor dealers were also Democrats, however. Led by an old resident who was angry over being denied the Township Committee candidacy after many years as the lone township Democrat, they set up a separate faction in the Democratic camp. The Republican factions had been divided on this issue previously, and two leaders who opposed the Mayor organized a referendum to overturn the Township Committee's decision. Funded by liquor dealers outside the township who wanted no competition, and drawing workers from the Methodist church, they campaigned for a dry town, and at the November election, won by a 6 to 4 margin.[4] That election also produced a resounding Democratic victory, with a 90 per cent turnout giving the party 60 per cent of the vote.

The outcome was less a victory for the Democratic party than a protest against the Mayor's and the Township Committee's lack of responsiveness to the new community and the Republican party's domination by the old residents. It was also, of course, a vote against any governmental action to reduce the community's status. However, not all Levittowners felt threatened, for another referendum, initiated by both parties at the request of the builder, changed the legal name of the township from Willingboro to Levittown. Many middle class residents preferred the old name because of Levittown's national image as a low-prestige community, but enough of them joined working class Levittowners who felt Levitt deserved recognition for having built a town in which they could afford to live, and the name change passed by a small margin.

THE REORGANIZATION OF TOWNSHIP GOVERNMENT

Once the voters had expressed their disapproval of the old regime, and had placed one Levittowner in its midst, they lost immediate interest in the affairs of government. Over the next two years the Township Committee saw to its own internal problems by setting up a civil service structure; passed ordinances to protect the residents from traffic dangers, garbage dumps, and the like; and approved Levitt's plans for future subdivisions—matters which people took for granted or which affected only a small number or only future purchasers. Of the 65 ordinances passed between October 1958 and May 1960, just 9 per cent were in direct response to citizens' requests, principally to approve church and associational activities regulated by municipal ordinances and to change the building code to permit the construction of patios.[5] Few were controversial, and ordinances which could not be passed unanimously were either tabled or rewritten until unanimity was achieved.

The only significant innovation was the reorganization of the Township Committee. From the time Levittown was occupied, incumbent Committeemen and leading politicians realized that the Committee had to be expanded, for otherwise there would be too much work for individual members and it would be difficult to get candidates for the office. There was, however, no agreement over one detail: who would direct day-to-day governmental activities. Both parties favored a strong-mayor form of government, for the new town required leadership, the parties needed symbolic and real leaders, and a strong mayor could generate patronage. It had already become clear that neither party could attract enough volunteer manpower for election campaigns; both looked forward to a mayor who could provide them with loyal workers. But the politicians could not come out for a strong mayor. Even before the first election, old residents had talked of a city manager, mostly to forestall a Democratic takeover.[6] When the Democrats promised, as part of their 1959 election campaign, to set up a Study Group to consider reorganization of the government, many people already favored a city manager, for what with rising taxes, his professional skill would lead to efficient and inexpensive government. As one man, who himself had ambitions for becoming mayor, admitted, "A city manager is a good thing; we need a college man, a specialist in there to do the job. We have to get someone from outside."

Even so, the Township Committee was to pick the members of the Study Group and could, presumably, have packed it with advocates of a strong mayor. In the spring of 1960, however, both parties were so disorganized that none of the six chosen had close party ties. Also, the title "Study Group" made it almost mandatory to name well-educated men, and neither party could afford to appoint professional politicians. The Republicans chose two businessmen, as well as a banker and an accountant; the Democrats, a lawyer who had just become a judge and a social worker; and four of the six had already decided privately to recommend a city manager, each on his own, before the Study Group ever met. Nevertheless, a conscientious survey of all possible alternatives preceded the unanimous vote for city-manager government. The Group also recommended a five-man Township Council to be elected on a partisan basis. Most Study Group members would as soon have recommended a nonpartisan Council, but as businessmen and professionals they found it difficult to think through the issue and acquiesced in the social worker's opposition to nonpartisan elections. In effect, then, one man determined the continued existence of national parties in Levittown.

At this point, neither the Study Group nor the politicians knew whether the voters would approve the city manager, and expecting opposition, the Study Group decided that it would be necessary to "sell" its recommendation to the voters. A hired consultant wrote a strongly worded document which argued that a city manager was essential because, by his calculations, the annual tax bill might well rise to $645 a house. Although working class Levittowners were doubtful about a city manager—as they were about all experts and outsiders—they and everyone else at once turned their attention to the tax estimate. Coming just after new and higher tax bills had been mailed out, this estimate created a furor and later, in February 1961, provided a rallying point for opponents to the school budget. If any popular controversy existed about the desirability of a city manager, it now faded into the background. Just before the election, the dissident Democrats tried unsuccessfully to organize against the Study Group's recommendation. The Republicans pointed out that they had been for a city manager before the Study Group ever met, the Democrats said unenthusiastically that governmental reorganization was the will of the people, and it carried by more than 4 to 1 in the November 1960 election. The Study Group had no advance idea of what people wanted, but a fortuitous combination of circumstances, aided by the inability of the political parties either to carry out or to oppose the wishes of their constituents, had brought about the type of government most Levittowners undoubtedly favored, and a year later the new Township Council and the City Manager took office.

THE UPS AND DOWNS OF PARTY POLITICS

Even though the three Township Committeemen were not talking to each other in the spring of 1960, they had to suppress their personal and political hostilities in order to run the government. The political parties had no routine and continuing function, however; their job was to find the constituencies, candidates, workers, and issues that would produce election victories and a viable party organization. This they failed to do, for the 1959 Democratic victory was followed by a Republican landslide in 1960, a Democratic landslide in 1961, a Republican victory in 1963, and a standoff in 1965; and after each election, the party organization was sure to suffer, particularly among the Republicans.[7]

The constant political flux was caused partly by the parties' relationship to the county organization—traditionally the determining one in New Jersey politics—and the resulting involvement in county issues and factions which had nothing to do with Levittown but from which the local groups could not disentangle themselves. Nonpartisan elections would have helped, although they would also have deprived local candidates of county and state assistance. They would not, however, have eliminated the flux, for many Levittowners considered themselves independents who decided each November for whom they would vote, depending on the choice of candidates and the then salient issues. Local politics thus became a never ending attempt to develop stable constituencies and organizations among a population which regularly changed its political allegiances in response to the conditions of the moment.

The Democrats were more successful than the Republicans in building a stable party organization. Being almost entirely Levittowners, they were able to avoid conflict with the old residents, at least at the local level, and being Democrats they had an easier time finding party workers. Such people seem to be recruited principally from working class or ethnic backgrounds, groups which gravitate more often to the Democrats than to the Republicans. The Levittown Democrats had attracted a number of men who had either been active in politics previously or were interested in becoming active; many of them were of Irish and Italian working class or Jewish middle class origins, who had no other organizational interests and were ready to devote time and energy to the party. A permanent cadre encouraged permanent leadership, enabling one of the four party founders to wrest control from his companions after the 1959 victory. An experienced politician, he weathered attempts to depose him after each election defeat, and he remains the party leader to this day.

The Republicans attracted some of the same sort of people: a handful of Protestant working class Levittowners and some Irish Catholic middle class ones who moved out of the Democratic party as they left the city. But many of the Republican workers were temporary "volunteers." These were lower middle and upper middle class managers and salesmen, who were active in service clubs and other voluntary associations but had little taste for party politics, coming in only to help a particular candidate and then returning to their nonpolitical groups. The resulting conflict between the volunteers and the regular workers prevented the development of permanent party leadership, and it changed hands after almost every election, win or lose.

Stable party leadership alone could neither produce election victories nor prevent factionalism, however. Without loyal constituencies and a set of issues on which to build a persuasive party image, the parties were forced in each election to fight internal battles as well as their opponents, and most of these struggles represented attempts by various class blocs to obtain power and to shape the party, the government, and the community in their own image.

In the spring of 1960, both parties were split. The Democratic party leader, who stood for a wet community and cooperation with Levitt, was opposed by the group who had attacked the non-resident doctor and liquor ordinances and who wanted to fight the government and the builder in order to make certain that Levittown would assure them the lower middle class status they thought they had purchased with their houses. The Republicans, still largely old residents, were split by county factional fights and lacked both a leader and a candidate for the November election. At the last minute, the regular Republican party workers, then in control of the organization, found a candidate, but the opposing faction thought he could not win and persuaded a Junior Chamber of Commerce leader to run against him. In the primary, both organization candidates won. Shortly thereafter, they both resigned; the Republican, for business reasons; the Democrat, a tough young Italian businessman, because he threatened the party leader's control, was unpopular with the workers, and had allegedly misrepresented his educational background. If it came out in the open, the Republicans could expose him and his party to charges of dishonesty.

Until then, neither party had an issue to catch the interest of the electorate. Although the community was concerned about the first increase in taxes, municipal expenditures were of minor importance, and the parties realized, as did the Levittowners, that the tax rate depended on the actions of the school board. The new Democratic candidate gave the Republicans the issue they needed. The Democrats knew after the 1959 victory that they would have to offer middle class candidates, but these were in short supply and, at the last minute, they picked one who was also a veteran county politician. The Republicans named the J.C.C. leader, who lacked political experience of any kind. Borrowing the issue of "bossism," which had been raised against the Democratic party leader by his party's dissidents, the Republicans campaigned on the theme that their candidate would be above politics and would prevent the emergence of an urban political machine in Levittown.[8] This plank, the personal attractiveness of the candidate and his running mate (an officer in the Holy Name Society), attracted a number of volunteers—most of them associational colleagues of the candidates—who took charge of the campaign. The campaign manager, also a young Catholic, rented a bookmobile, renamed it a "bandwagon," and rode it through the streets of Levittown offering coffee, doughnuts, and a chance to meet the candidates in an informal, almost neighborly encounter. The Democrats could not fight the image of bossism, and although John F. Kennedy visited Levittown just before the election, his gesture did not impress the voters. The Republicans took all election districts and 55 per cent of the total vote. The independents, who were decisive, had rejected alleged machine politics for what many called "a young Eisenhower."

In 1961, the situation was reversed. Government reorganization had been approved at the 1960 election, and with the City Manager there to do most of the administrative work and the old residents safely out of the picture, neither party lacked candidates for the new five-man Township Council. This time, the Democratic leader sensed what the electorate wanted. Taxes had become *the* issue, and he selected a slate described as qualified to work with the City Manager in the overriding task of keeping taxes low, including an accountant, a cost engineer, and two other white collar workers. He also made sure that the slate included a Protestant, a Jew, and a man from the most recently settled neighborhoods. The Republicans fared less well. Once the 1960 election was won, the volunteers had departed, and the small band of working class party workers took over. They forced out the victorious campaign manager and put up a slate consisting largely of their own people. Feeling that this slate lacked both the skill and the status to win, the ex-campaign manager organized an opposing ticket of "quality" candidates, several of them Catholics and almost all with high-level white collar or professional jobs. If the independents among the Levittowners had voted in the primaries, the "quality slate" might have won, but they did not, and the organization candidates of both parties were victorious.[9] The Democrats hammered on the need for tax reduction and the qualifications of their candidates for achieving it, keeping the party leader behind the scenes to forestall further charges of "bossism." They easily beat the Republican ticket in a lackluster election.

With no election scheduled for the next two years the Democrats consolidated their hold over township government with municipal appointees, and also strengthened their image as the party of low taxes by forcing a cut in the school budget after the February 1963 school election.[10] It seemed as if Levittown might become permanently Democratic, but now it was that party's turn to misjudge the electorate. Shortly before the 1963 election the Township Council approved a zoning amendment permitting Levitt to build garden apartments in the community. Many Levittowners felt that these would bring in more transient, lower-status families with many children, which would require yet higher school taxes. They also objected to the Council's policy of helping the builder out of sales difficulties. Most important, they resented the Council's failure to listen to their protest against the amendment at a public hearing. Once again Levittown politicians were punished by the voters for the same unresponsiveness to status fears that had defeated the old residents in 1959, and the Republicans were swept into office, taking control of the Township Council.

Prior to this victory, the Republican party had been virtually moribund. The old workers had left and, for a time, were replaced by the Birchites who had attacked the school board for Communist sympathies. In 1962, they led an energetic campaign against fluoridation of the town's water supply, but when the voters rejected their appeals by a considerable margin they disappeared, and a new group of more liberal Republicans came into the party.

The 1963 election ballot also included a referendum to change the township's name back to Willingboro. Initiated by C.A.P.S. leaders who had also led the fight against garden apartments, the referendum was supported by middle class people who felt the old name was more prestigious and would repair the damage to the community's reputation generated by the tax disputes. The vote was close, but the name change carried by 100 votes out of 6000. The referendum was significant also in that both parties took stands on a controversial issue, the Republicans favoring the name change and the Democrats opposing it.

It would appear, then, that separate constituencies were developing and the two parties were lining up as they do on the national scene. Middle class voters seeking to maintain the community's status were now siding with the Republicans, joined by some cosmopolitans who had despaired of "reforming" the Democrats. Working class Catholics and less affluent white collar workers who, pressed financially, either could no longer worry about status or were less concerned about what outsiders thought of Levittown, were voting for Democrats. In the 1965 election, a Republican candidate spoke of "the failure to project a desirable image of the community. . . . Outsiders sneer 'Kookstown' when Willingboro is mentioned." The Democrats attacked a Republican plan for a "million-dollar municipal complex" when "hundreds of families are on the brink of economic survival," arguing for belt-tightening on taxes instead.

As in prior years, both parties continued to hope that industry could be attracted into the township to relieve the tax burden, but by this time, neither was confident that it would happen. The election was extremely close, the voters choosing one Republican and one Democrat, with only 25 votes separating the winning and losing candidates. The community seemed almost evenly divided between those fearful of lowered status and those fearful of higher taxes, but an unexpected event or a new issue could change the political complexion at once, reversing the fortunes of the two parties or of their internal factions at the next election.

THE ORIGIN OF MUNICIPAL SERVICES

Before the Levittowners came, the township had obtained fire protection and ambulance services from an adjacent community, and its residents used the county library. Once the newcomers had arrived, the Township Committee set up a Police Department and a Board of Health, took over the operation of the Levitt-built water and sewage treatment plant, and regulated garbage removal (which was privately contracted), but it was too busy to consider other services. These were left to the initiative of External and Internal founders, and although they started like voluntary associations, they soon requested municipal subsidies and eventually became governmental appendages. Their founding illustrates the close relationship between organizational and political party politics and the impact of class on both.

The Township Library and the Volunteer Fire Company

After an abortive attempt by the county librarian to persuade the builder and the Township Committee to start a library in Levittown, two women, needing a library for themselves and their children, proposed its establishment at a Civic Association meeting in September 1959. Unskilled at the finer points of organizing, however, they soon gave way to a lawyer who had been forced out of the Republican party leadership during the hassle over liquor sales. Aided by the county librarian, he set up a Levittown Library Association later that month and, in November, persuaded the builder to donate a three-acre site to celebrate the community's first anniversary. Then, with the help of women's clubs and the PTAs, the Association organized a book collection drive; after Levittowners had contributed 2000 books, the Township Committee provided a vacant room in the township building. Because most of the donated books were old bestsellers and book club selections, discards of little interest to adults and not suitable for children, the lawyer asked the Township Committee for municipal funds and, having engineered support from women's clubs, PTAs, and service clubs, he was able to get them.

The two women had wanted only a modest library, and one of them, who later became active in the Democratic party, was fearful that too large a municipal subsidy would result in a tax increase or retard the development of a fire company and a hospital. Although she said that "The first thing I look for in a community is my church and a library," she qualified: "As much as I want a library, it is second to fire protection and a hospital." Her attitude reflected Democratic and particularly working class sentiment, which held, in the words of one Levittowner, that "Body comes before mind."

The Republican lawyer and his colleagues were interested in getting an impressive library—and as quickly as possible—to develop a community service that would bring them political support and perhaps even make the library a Republican satellite. Most of their initial support came from organizations in which Republicans were especially active, and many hoped the library could thus be a symbol of Republican strength and achievement. At that time, the Veterans of Foreign Wars, predominantly Democratic, had organized a volunteer fire company and were asking for public funds to build the company and a firehouse. Indeed, their plans were so far advanced that they had just asked Levitt to give the site originally donated for a library to the fire company. The founder of the library also wanted an impressive structure to provide the community with a cultural and therefore unmistakably middle class institution to compete with and counteract the fire company, which demonstrated working class strength. There was merit in establishing both a library and a fire company in Levittown, for using the county library and the fire companies of nearby towns was inconvenient, but questions of merit were forgotten as the two facilities became symbols in the struggle between two classes over their ability to commandeer public funds, to show class power, and to determine the class image of the community.

The Township Committee pared the initial demand for library funds to $5000, sufficient to buy more useful and respectable books and to hire a part-time librarian. By 1960, almost two thirds of the families held library cards (although the main book borrowers were children) and there was enough public interest in the library to pass a referendum making it a municipal agency. There was not enough demand, however, for a building, and the library was located first in the Town Hall and later in the main shopping center.

The initial competition between the library and the fire company had developed because, after the Library Association was safely established, its founder, who had meanwhile been frustrated in his attempt to return to power in the Republican party, set out to organize a fire company as well. He first proposed the idea at a Kiwanis meeting, suggesting it become a club project. This galvanized another Kiwanis member, the Democratic party leader, into action, and before the Kiwanis could meet again to consider the matter he encouraged one of his precinct captains, a founder of the VFW, to recruit sufficient members from that organization to form the company. The reasons for their urgency and their success are not hard to find. The Democratic party leader wanted to bring the fire company into the Democratic fold both as community service advertising for the party and as a possible future source of patronage. If the firemen were predominantly VFW members, that organization would benefit in community stature and, perhaps, would also attract more veterans. It was essential, therefore, that the two Democrats beat the Republican lawyer and the Kiwanis—also predominantly Republican in outlook—to the punch. The service club unwittingly played into their hands; at the last minute, it postponed the meeting on the fire company for what it considered a more urgent issue.

Proud of his working class origins and quite hostile toward the middle class elements of the community, the Democratic precinct captain felt that the fire company provided an opportunity for "working men" to do their part for the community and to obtain their share of municipal funds, particularly since the township had just funded the library. He also knew how to sell the fire company to his VFW members. It would enhance local pride, end the drain of Levittown tax monies to other communities, and reduce fire insurance rates for the homeowners. Soon it would build a firehouse which would become a social center for working class men, particularly since the defeat of the liquor referendum had decreased the attractiveness of the VFW clubhouse as a gathering place.

The VFW leader probably knew also that a number of his members craved the excitement of fire fighting, enjoyed maintaining the fire truck, and above all, wanted to get out of the house. The fire company would give them a proper excuse. Finally, for the leader himself there was, aside from the political triumph, the chance to upstage the middle class by showing that it depended on working class people for the protection of life and property. He was fond of telling everyone that "schools and libraries are fine, but they don't put out the fire or stop the enemy." (The enemy was the Russians, who would presumably be stopped by Levittown's civil defense program which he had also just helped to organize.)

Once the fire company was safely organized, the VFW leader decided that fire protection was too crucial to be left to laymen and looked for an expert. The Kiwanis club had contacted a resident fire insurance underwriter, but when their meeting was postponed, the VFW approached him, promising not only the top job but enough men to staff a company. In addition, they told him that some civil defense money could legitimately be diverted to help the fire company get started and the Township Committee was willing to provide municipal funds to buy the first engine. The Democrats' choice was not random; the underwriter had been one of the first active Republicans among the Levittowners and was then being wooed by the Democratic party. He was also of working class origin and, whether his pursuers knew it or not, felt uncomfortable in Republican and Kiwanis circles. After he took over the fire company, he joined the Democrats.

Like other predominantly working class groups, the fire company included some middle class people, in order to obtain political support from organizations with which they were affiliated and to get legal and medical services. Doctors vied for the unpaid position of medical director, for it offered splendid advertising among a working class population they could not easily reach otherwise. A fire company auxiliary was initiated by the wives of company officers. At its founding, one of the men joked about its purpose: "It's to train the women to let the husbands out of

the house to fight fires." There was some justification for his sar-
casm, for aside from community service and a chance to help
their husbands, the auxiliary gave the wives an opportunity to
discourage the men from holding stag smokers and drinking
parties. The company soon asked Levitt for a building site; a firehouse was put up in 1961, and from then on, many members
spent a great deal of time there, most of it polishing the fire
engines. Subsequently, the VFW and some Democrats helped
start an Emergency Ambulance Squad and an auxiliary, again
made up predominantly of working class residents. But with a
hospital in the community, its services were not in as much demand, and the squad never grew large enough to obtain its own
building, housing its ambulance in a gas station.

Public Recreation

Class conflict also pervaded the development of public recreation in Levittown, but this conflict paled alongside political and
jurisdictional struggles between the school board and the Township Committee, which have so far prevented the development of
a municipal recreation agency. Levitt had located playgrounds
around the elementary schools with the intention that they, like
the pools, would be used by the community after school hours.
He provided no money to develop them, however, and the
schools, beset by budget cuts, never had the funds, so they have
remained little more than baseball fields.

Two months after the first Levittowners arrived, the newly appointed police chief appealed to the newcomers to set up a Levittown Youth Sports Association (L.Y.S.A.) to forestall the juvenile delinquency he expected to develop the next summer. His
appeal turned up a dozen men, some previously active in local
juvenile athletic programs, others in Little Leagues. Soon they
were embroiled in a bitter definitional struggle, one group seeking strictly local leagues in which everyone could play, the other,
eventual affiliation with the national Little League, a baseball
program modeled on the major leagues which favored athlet-
ically inclined youngsters. During the first year the advocates of
local programs, most of them middle class Protestants who only
wanted to enable their children to play softball, were in control,
but even then the team coaches and managers, who were predominantly working class Catholics, favored the heightened competition of Little League ball.[11] The latter also scheduled dances

for teenagers, outvoting the middle class men who did not share their concern with keeping the youngsters from "getting into trouble."

After the first year of baseball, the predominantly working class group ejected the middle class officers and elected as president of the Sports Association a professional youth worker (a leader of the Catholic parish), and other leading Catholics as directors. As the second year's program was getting underway, the parish priest wanted to set up a branch of the Catholic Youth Organization, but the new Catholic officers persuaded him to postpone his plans in order to prevent a mass exodus of adults and children from L.Y.S.A. He was eager to cooperate in order to avoid religious strife, but the remaining Protestants were not pacified and they became more dismayed as the baseball program moved closer to the Little League model. That winter, their dissatisfaction and a small-scale rebellion by teenagers who resented the Catholics' close supervision over them at L.Y.S.A. dances sparked the mass resignation of the Catholic officers; they were replaced by a new group of anti-Little League Protestants. Even so, an ex-minor league ballplayer now took over the baseball program and brought it yet closer to Little League standards, although he also made sure that less skillful youngsters would play. This in turn upset the managers, who, wanting urgently to win, began to question the decisions of the umpires. The officers rebuked the managers for poor sportsmanship and setting a bad example for the children, and at the end of the season the managers forced the incumbents out of office.[12] After another year of skirmishing, the last opponents of Little League were gone and L.Y.S.A. affiliated itself with the national Little League. In 1964, a Willingboro team nearly won a world championship.

The youth worker who had been elected by the managers in the winter of 1959 had proposed that L.Y.S.A. be taken over by the municipality to solve its financial problems and to become the spearhead of a municipal recreation program (which, the story went, he hoped to run). Instead, the Township Committee provided L.Y.S.A. with a small subsidy and set up a Recreation Study Group to look into the community's overall recreation needs. After his election to the school board as part of the so-called "Catholic slate," he urged the board to provide more money for recreation, and when this failed, to transfer all recreation functions to the Township Committee. Some board members agreed, for with the opposition to higher school budgets, recreation would always receive a low priority, but the playgrounds did belong to the school system and the first superintendent, an athletic enthusiast, would not surrender them.

The Study Group met for almost a year, but could not agree on a plan, for some members wanted to support L.Y.S.A., some wanted a parks program, and yet others viewed recreation only as a means of delinquency prevention. Also hampered by the unwillingness of the school board to let anyone plan for its playgrounds and by the builder's reluctance to provide alternative recreational sites, the Study Group disbanded without a report. As long as the Township Committee and the successor Council were under Democratic control, however, these bodies continued to talk about municipal recreation, and in 1961, paid for bleachers in the high school stadium and for uniforms for the high school band when the school board had to cut its budget. Aware of the interest in recreation of working class and Catholic Levittowners, Democratic politicans also became boosters of the varsity teams and campaigned for municipal support of teenage facilities. For a variety of reasons, however—to be described in Chapter Nine—no such program has yet been established, although parks are planned under a state and federally funded "Green Acres" program.

NOTES

1. This was part of a county- and state-wide survey then being made as a test for the 1960 Presidential campaign by a pro-Kennedy New Jersey Congressman.
2. This was pure fantasy on their part, for the resident doctors were already looking forward to the day when they could buy $25,000 houses Levitt was proposing to build in a separate neighborhood.
3. Levittown, Long Island residents had also tried to eliminate non-resident doctors. Orzack and Sanders, p. 6.
4. This combination was a county tradition, for other townships had voted to remain dry in earlier years, campaign funds being supplied by liquor dealers from adjacent wet townships. Five years later, the earliest election at which the question could be raised again in referendum, Levittowners voted once again to keep the community dry.
5. Thirty per cent concerned internal governmental affairs; 45 per cent, citizen protection; and 16 per cent, the legitimation of build-

ing programs, either Levitt's or those of other developers con-
structing small shopping centers and individual stores on land
not owned by Levitt.

6. Republicans traditionally favor the city manager because he is
   viewed as using business techniques to run the government. Banfield and Wilson, Chap. 13.

7. In state and national elections the Levittowners voted more consistently, usually going Democratic by a small margin.

8. Ironically, while the Republicans were publicly attacking the
   Democrats for bossism, they were privately searching for a leader
   to unify the party.

9. There was also an Independent ticket, set up by a Republican who
   wanted to establish a following that would force the party to take
   him in its inner circle. When he left to join the "quality" Republican group, the others, most of them professionals and liberals,
   filed anyway to see if they could attract the independent vote.
   Their platform, a municipal equivalent of C.A.P.S., sought to
   substitute planning for partisan politics and patronage, but their
   brand of upper middle class cosmopolitanism—they even opposed
   ward organization—drew less than 10 per cent of the primary
   vote.

10. Earlier, the accountant had used his professional skill to uncover
    a small surplus in the school budget, enabling the Democrats to
    demonstrate the qualifications of their candidates for the job of
    tax reduction and allowing the accountant to become Mayor.

11. Paradoxically, in this instance, cosmopolitans favored a local pro-
    gram, whereas the locals wanted a national one—partly to put
    Levittown, then still without high school varsity athletics, "on
    the map."

12. This conflict is endemic to Little League, and many professional
    recreationists oppose it, considering competition harmful to chil-
    dren. Some of the Levittown managers had played professional
    ball and wanted badly to win, but their desire was shared by the
    children. Although they could have been restrained, there is no
    evidence that the children were hurt by the competition, except,
    of course, the poorer players who were shunted aside. The case
    against the Little League is stated in *Recreation* (1952); a study
    showing no harmful effects is reported in *Recreation* (1951), p. 490.

Chapter Seven

THE ORIGIN OF
A COMMUNITY

IN OCTOBER 1961, LEVITTOWN WAS THREE YEARS OLD. AS OF THAT
July 4200 homes had been built and occupied; the shopping
center was half completed; most of the churches were either in
their buildings or about to move in; new schools were still going
up and a six-grade parochial school was in operation. Nearly a
hundred organizations were functioning; government reorganization was about to take effect and a city manager was being hired.
Levittown had become a community. It resembled the other
Levittowns in its daily routine, its array of voluntary associations,
and its politics, and it was probably typical as well of many other
settlements of young middle-income families who had chosen to
live outside the city limits.[1]

In becoming a community, Levittown had also gone through
what seemed a typical origin process.[2] The residents had at first
associated almost exclusively with their neighbors, but some had
then sought more compatible people and activities outside the
block and had thereby set in motion the founding of community-
wide groups. These groups were started by founders who either
came to Levittown with the intent of setting them up or were
stimulated by outsiders, or they began spontaneously in reaction
to momentary community and individual needs. Yet even when
founders were individuals, they usually did not start groups without some assurance that others were interested, either because
they might be "in the same boat"—for example, a lonely house-

wife—or because they suspected people of similar interests and backgrounds were available. Until such people were found the organization could not really begin to function. Once it had begun to function, the need to survive in the midst of competing organizations with the same need required numerical strength (so that pre-existing membership requirements were abrogated) and haste (so that officers were elected quickly and activities gotten underway).

Relaxation of membership requirements and speed of organization were sure to generate definitional struggles over the future of the organization. The manifest struggles were usually about the content of the organizational program and the speed of growth. Those advocating a specific program usually favored slow growth; those less dedicated to a program and more concerned with organizational survival (and victory in the interorganization competition) demanded rapid growth. The advocates of rapid growth generally won out in the voluntary associations and the churches, whereas in the public agencies—particularly in the school system and the government—the victory went to the advocates of slow growth. In this instance, their victory did not signify public support of governmental programs, however, but reflected the demand of the "members" for minimal expenditures (and taxes). That victory also signified the absence of competing groups in the public sphere, which eliminated the most urgent organizational incentive for speed.

At a more latent level, organizational struggles were reflections of class differences, intertwined with religious ones and the ever present split between the locals and the cosmopolitans. In the voluntary associations, the proponents of rapid growth were usually lower middle class people who sought to put their organizations on the map in the community; the advocates of slow growth were often upper middle class cosmopolitans, less concerned with organizational status than with substantive programmatic goals. In the public agencies, the positions were reversed; the cosmopolitans wanted rapid growth so that these agencies would get to the programs they demanded. The majority of locals favored slow growth, except for athletic and other activities which would aid Levittown in the county's intercommunity competition.

The cross-cutting of class and cosmopolitan-local considerations is illustrated by the behavior of two township officials, both also active in the Jewish community, who took diametrically different positions in their synagogue and municipal roles. One was an upper middle class professional and, as president of the school board, he urged rapid expansion of the curriculum and guidance programs to benefit bright children; whereas the other, a lower middle class manager and then Mayor of Levittown, feared further tax increases and urged minimal expansion. In the Conservative synagogue, their positions were reversed. The professional wanted a congregation dedicated to Jewish education; the manager wanted a rapidly growing congregation with a building and a full-time rabbi. The professional, a cosmopolitan, saw both institutions in terms of program; the manager, a local, was most concerned with assuring their survival. The government and the school would survive regardless of financial problems, but the synagogue might not, and so the manager favored low taxes in the former, but deficit financing for the latter. The two men also split on who should make the decisions; the cosmopolitan argued that a qualified professional should guide both school and synagogue; the local believed that these should be responsive to their constituents, a majority of whom favored his own priorities.

The definitional struggles, when added to interorganizational competition, produced considerable insecurity, which in turn led to the speedy rejection of dissidents. The first to be extruded were individuals whose backgrounds differed sharply from those of the majority, "loners" who did not get along with their colleagues, and "idealists," people with unusual but acceptable ideas that were too expensive. The bitterest hostility was reserved for "radicals," people with unusual and unacceptable ideas who refused to compromise.[3] The term did not refer to political views, and in the commonsense usage of the word, Levittown had few radicals (none of the left and only a handful of the right). It was, rather, a relative term, applied to powerless dissidents. One Levittowner, who was forced to leave several organizations during his first year because of his unwillingness to compromise, soon acquired a reputation as a man "with axes to grind" and a "radical." When he ran for the school board as a member of the Catholic slate, however, he had support for his point of view, and though as irascible and uncompromising as ever, was no longer described as a radical. Once anger over the school budget had died down, his brief popularity ended, and when he had difficulties in working with his fellow board members, he resigned. Soon afterward he left Levittown.

In many organizations, people of higher or lower status than the majority of members were also extruded eventually, although more gradually and less acrimoniously than radicals. For example, an upper middle class program chairman in a lower middle class group learned quickly that her "educational" aims for the organization were not welcome. As she described it, "There's been criticism that the programming is too high, that there aren't enough laughs. I think the girls want a lecture from a beautician or a program about hats, but this is a waste of time for me. . . . I have invited the Anti-Defamation League for next month's program. That should generate some criticism, but I don't care." Actually, she was never criticized openly, but the group picked a culturally more congruent program chairman the following year. The most systematic extrusion, though not planned, was of the cosmopolitans, who soon found themselves in a minority in most of the organizations they entered and in constant conflict with the local orientation of their leaders. Eventually, they resigned from the groups in which they had been active, limiting themselves to organizations with cosmopolitan aims or surfacing sporadically to head protest movements against particular school and township policies.[4]

As organizations matured, conflicts over the speed of growth became irrelevant, and after losers in the definitional struggle had left or had given up the fight, the groups achieved a measure of stability. Major organizational crises were replaced by the everyday mixture of cooperation and petty conflict that marks any organization; membership size became constant; attendance, habitual; and programs, routine. There was still a constant search for "ideas" that would attract new members or bring back laggard ones, and occasionally new activities were started or organizational revivals held for this purpose. The continuing development of new neighborhoods always provided additional members and an occasional new leader, although, as I noted earlier, the later arrivals tended to prefer their own organizations. Even so, most of the organizations now functioning in Levittown were founded during the first two or three years; later, new ones came slowly. External founders were no longer interested, and besides, almost all the national groups that might appeal to people like the Levittowners were already present. In addition, I suspect, the later arrivals had less need for new organizations, for the sorting function could be taken care of by existing ones and moving into an established community is not quite the same as moving into a brand new one. The pioneering impulse to participate in a new group simply because such a group was needed to make Levittown into a community had died out— it was never very strong even among the first arrivals—and the later purchasers probably even more than the first came for the house rather than for the community.[5] They were no longer "in the same boat," for the original boat that had arrived in the unknown and possibly hostile seas of Burlington County had become firmly anchored.

The process of community origin I have described fits most closely that of the voluntary associations and the churches. Properly speaking, neither the school system nor the government was founded anew in Levittown; they were taken over from the old residents and altered. Of course, the school system—as distinguished from the school board—was new, and it went through the same definitional struggles as a voluntary organization. The superintendent-founder had to bend his ideas to residents who had different conceptions of the school, but ultimately was replaced—like many an organizational founder—because he could not get along with his "members" and was unable to achieve the growth speed those in power wanted from him. Also, the school and the municipal government were, like voluntary associations, involved in a daily routine from which they could not diverge significantly, so that they too described a path from origin (or rebirth) through definitional struggle to uneasy stability.

Their political arms could not follow such a path, however; indeed, it is difficult to talk of an origin process in politics at all, for political institutions must always respond to changing community conditions, sometimes almost at a moment's notice, and have little opportunity to build stable organizations. School politicians could protect themselves somewhat against constant ups and downs, for the school was endowed with enough civic sacredness to be "above politics." The political parties could not so protect themselves, however, and had to bear the brunt of the community-formation conflicts. Unlike voluntary associations or even the schools, which extracted some loyalty from the parents, the political parties had no loyal members to speak of, for the party workers gave their allegiance more to victorious candidates than to the party and too few voters considered themselves partisans. They shifted their votes to whatever party—or more often, to whatever candidate—promised to meet their current needs. The parties could not easily adapt to this flux, however, for being connected to county, state, and national bodies, they also had to pay attention to outside requirements. In most suburbs, the Democrats represent working class and ethnic populations; the Republicans, the middle class and Protestant ones. In Levittown, however, both had to appeal to the lower middle class in order to have a chance of victory, and this group included not only the independents but also a large number of mobile Catholics, once Democrats, who were now quite undecided as to which party would best meet their needs. As a result, both parties had to develop flexible local programs and images without totally surrendering their county and national programs, and this ambivalence added to the constant factional battles.

The parties' problems were compounded by the Levittowners' distrust of politics and politicians. Among ex-city dwellers, the distrust had been learned in childhood, but became stronger when they were able, for the first time, to see politicians and the political process up close. Levittowners from other suburbs had perhaps become accustomed to this view, but their suspicion was also heightened at first by the failure of the old residents to respond to their new constituents. As a result, when Levittown was less than a year old many people believed that the community was run by a corrupt political clique which would be difficult to remove. Later events disproved this assessment, of course, but the distrust was transferred to Levittowners who became politicians, particularly because of the ambivalence the voters imposed on them. The politicians were also confronted with insoluble problems for which, like American politicians everywhere, they had to promise solutions during election campaigns. Without an industrial tax base, Levittown was condemned to ever rising taxes, and many voters were sophisticated enough to know that the candidates' best intentions, their earnest campaign promises, and even their energetic efforts once in office could not really snip more than a few dollars off either school or municipal budgets. This increased the voters' distrust and heightened their demand for someone above politics, a city manager or a politician who sought to be nonpartisan. Nonpartisanship was not enough, however, for the voters rejected the upper middle class Independent slate which ran on an antipolitical platform in 1961. They wanted nonpartisans of their own class, who reflected their desire to limit the expansion of municipal services.

In the end, they resigned themselves to the continued existence of party politics; and, being neither cosmopolitan nor upper middle class, they were even willing to live with a party boss (at least in the Democratic party) provided he continued to press for lower taxes and remained in the background, perhaps only to serve as a convenient scapegoat if and when another political crisis arose.[6] Of course, they could always point to the city manager and the school superintendent as professionals who would provide nonpolitical services, but in the last analysis the Levittowners settled for party politics because what they wanted from the political process was ultimately more important to them than who would oversee it.

Individual associations, churches, and even political parties did not function in isolation, and though they competed against each other for members, they were also thrown together for common tasks. These tasks and the shortage of leaders had produced the interlocking directorates, temporary alliances, and political ties I described among voluntary associations in Chapter Three; and the cooperative ventures among ministers, as well as their coopting of secular leaders and their activities in school and government affairs I described in Chapter Four. Intergroup competition was too strong in the first years to provide much incentive for joint ventures, but one could predict that, eventually, the entire array of formal organizations and institutions would become a structure of sorts, an uneasy network of occasional relationships and a few more permanent alliances that would bind some of them together against each other in coalitions of likeminded people and, perhaps, bring many of them together if Levittown faced a threat from an outside enemy.

Although the voluntary associations and churches were ostensibly nonpolitical, they could not really stay out of politics. Since the primary issues debated in the community—taxes, status, and schools—involved almost everyone and were often more important than the organizational agenda, few of the organizational leaders could avoid taking sides on them—although, of course, they never did so officially. As early as 1960, when a civic group was holding a candidate's night for school board hopefuls, it could not find a single community leader, in either secular associations or churches, who could be considered neutral on the issues then facing the schools. Ultimately, it had to invite some-one from outside the community to chair the meeting.

THE EVOLUTION OF CLASS AND POWER STRUCTURES

The youthfulness of the community also affected the development of class and power structures, although they were shaped by distinctive qualities of Levittown as well. Despite the overriding importance of class in the origins and the definitional struggles of the community's groups, no clearly visible class structure had evolved in the first three years of Levittown's existence. National distinctions and judgments regarding class and prestige pervaded its everyday life, of course, and the organizations sorted residents by their socioeconomic level. Even so, traditional class distinctions had to be altered somewhat. People did not know each other well enough to have information about their parentage, and those who came for upward social mobility carefully avoided reference to their past histories. Without knowledge about people's income, with the absence of very poor and very rich neighbors, and with the ever present fact that everyone lived in virtually the same house, it was difficult to base judgments on income. People in the $12,000 houses might be less well off than those in the $14,000 houses, but no one could be sure, particularly since the cheapest house, at first the only one with four bedrooms, could have been chosen on the basis of family size.[7] Needless to say, people who had part-time maids or two new cars were suspected of greater affluence, but they were also criticized for "showing off" or "trying to keep up with the Joneses," and on the block, their status was lower than that of the less affluent neighbor trying hard to make ends meet.

Occupation and education were more reliable indices of class position, and the professional received more deference than the factory worker, but many people had obtained some college education and the majority were white collar workers. Also, many were working in new and unfamiliar technical jobs, for example, as computer programmers, whose status could not easily be judged by traditional indices. There were also new and obfuscating labels for old jobs, and not many people could guess that a "supply specialist" was really only a high-grade stock clerk, particularly if he worked for a large and well-known corporation.

Finally, and perhaps most important, the intense need for community leaders and organizational participants in the early years temporarily set aside traditional class distinctions and allowed people of low status to become prestigious community figures.[8] Once the need for the services of leaders had decreased, people were more ready to notice that they lacked the education, job, speech habits, and other refinements that went with high status. Then, more typical class judgments could be made about them.

Eventually, when the supply of leaders with sufficient status catches up to the demand, national class distinctions will probably become more important in Levittown, and churches and associations may be ranked by the same criteria that obtain in other American communities. This process might have been hastened if Levitt had been able to build the $20,000–$25,000 houses he had intended, but because of Levittown's image as a low-status community, sales were slow and construction was halted after 80 such houses had been sold.[9]

One likely deviation from the standard class hierarchy was already apparent. In many suburbs the professional upper middle class is, by virtue of its income, education, and occupation, the highest-ranking group, but this is not likely to happen in Levittown. For one thing, the professionals are a small minority, and many are Jewish. Although there is almost no overt or even covert anti-Semitism in Levittown, a predominantly Protestant and Catholic town in a predominantly Protestant county is not likely to award highest status to a Jewish group. More important, the professional group has generally taken unpopular stands, and many of its members are known to be in Levittown only temporarily and will, like other Mobiles, eventually depart for higher-priced suburbs. This group is, therefore, a deviant minority. If any single population is likely to have the highest prestige in the community in the future, it is the managerial upper middle class, whose political stance is more locally oriented and whose way of life is more in line with what most Levittowners would like to achieve.

The class structure most likely to develop in Levittown is what might be called a multinucleated one, consisting of fairly separate working class, lower middle class, and upper middle class sectors, each of which will consider itself to be of most worth, if perhaps not of highest status, in the community, and each of which will award top prestige to its own organizational, political, and social leaders. In a bedroom community, in which few people are economically dependent on fellow residents, there is less need to feel inferior to neighbors of higher income and education, particularly if one's own group is politically and symbolically stronger in the community by sheer weight of numbers. Of course, working class people know that they have less education and income than professionals and will express hostility toward the community activities of the latter, but as long as they can outvote them, class difference is less likely to be felt as status inferiority. If changes in the national or metropolitan economy hurt the working class and leave its more affluent neighbors untouched, however, feelings of status inferiority will surely develop, accompanied by demands for retribution through local political actions.

The multinucleated structure may also become subdivided by religion, separating a fundamentalist Protestant working class segment from the Catholic one, and creating Protestant, Catholic, and Jewish segments in each of the other classes. Religious segregation and conflict have been present in Levittown from the start, but these had nothing to do with doctrinal or even denominational differences and often represented class variations that correlate with religion. Some were gross variations: Catholics, particularly the less affluent working class ones, who had to support both public and parochial schools, were obviously against higher taxes. Some differences were more subtle, as when restrictive lower middle class people in conservative Protestant denominations objected to the sale of liquor and the holding of bingo games, which were favored by expansive lower middle class residents and Catholics; or when liberal upper middle class Levittowners, mostly Jewish, were more enthusiastic over the teaching of foreign languages in elementary schools than the largely Protestant managerial upper middle class or, for that matter, than lower middle class Jews who had fewer academic ambitions for their children. The correlation between religion and class also complicated the alignment of the political parties. The Democrats traditionally favor patronage and the rapid expansion of municipal services which appeal to working class voters, but in Levittown, this conflicted with the need of their Catholic working class constituents to keep taxes minimal. The Republicans, traditionally the party of low taxes, were more inclined to defend public school budgets for their Protestant constituents, particularly in a community in which Catholics were in a plurality, and thus the party had to support higher school taxes. Since school elections were nonpartisan, these conflicts never became visible, but they complicated internal party definitional struggles. For a time, the Republicans advocated lower municipal taxes while keeping quiet about the school budget, whereas the Democrats supported lower taxes across the board, but always suggested the need to expand municipal services as well.

In a community without sources of employment, the political power of residents is a major determinant of their position in the local class hierarchy, and Levittown's power structure may, therefore, coincide even more than elsewhere with the class structure. So far, political fortunes have shifted too often from election to election to suggest which group, if any, will eventually have the most power. Moreover, until now, the most powerful bloc has been the Levitt organization. As the largest single landowner in the township, its contribution to the tax rolls, the influence of its building program on the future of the community, and its very real interest in the activities of the municipal government in connection with its building program have made it the most persistent petitioner for action by the government, and an ever present interest group whose wishes need to be considered. As the building program comes to an end, the builder's involvement in the community and his power will decrease and perhaps disappear entirely, but given the constant arrival of new purchasers and the high proportion of Transients and Mobiles in the present population, it is too early to tell which population group will ultimately be most numerous and thus most influential.

As yet, no definable and stable voter blocs have emerged in Levittown, except perhaps a Catholic bloc which has solidified around the issue of school taxes. Although politicians have sometimes acted (particularly when they slated candidates for township office) as if there were other religious blocs, blocs of earlier and later arrivals, and "working men," white collar, and professional blocs as well, these assumed blocs have rarely voted as such.[10] Nor has a stable set of leaders developed around specific issues, because of the turnover of office holders, and because most issues generate somewhat distinctive constituencies and decision-makers. There have been alliances among Catholic and less affluent non-Catholic Levittowners, and anti-Levitt coalitions have developed among low-status and cosmopolitan residents, but these have not yet become stable enough to become solid interest groups. Consequently, it is probably premature to identify a power structure in Levittown. For the time being, the builder's influence, the existence of the Catholic bloc, and the Democratic party leader's ability to retain his hold on the party have generated a somewhat more monolithic local power structure, less varied from issue to issue than in most American communities.

Since the people who described themselves as Settlers are the only ones who can be expected to remain in Levittown in the years to come, and may develop a more stable voting pattern over time, they are likely to be the most influential group in the future. Because Settlers include an undue proportion of working class and less affluent lower middle class people, who are for the most part Catholics as well, a Catholic bloc may well become the single most powerful group in the community. Since it contains many of the least affluent residents who are particularly sensitive to status decrease inside the community and are most threatened by downward mobility, it may also become the most vocal political constituency. The balance of power will probably always be held by the non-Catholic lower middle class, but because its party loyalty is weaker and because it includes both Transients and Settlers, it may not be as politically cohesive as the Catholic population. The absence of industry, the relatively small number of store owners, and the endemic conflict of interest between the various shopping centers are likely to mean that businessmen will be less influential than they are in other communities, and that on issues affecting them as well as residents, the latter will always win out. On issues that concern the businessmen alone, however, their ability to organize and to provide campaign funds will provide them with sufficient power to achieve their ends.

CRUCIAL DECISIONS AND FACTORS IN THE ORIGIN OF THE COMMUNITY

Of all the decisions and factors that made a community out of the strangers who purchased Levitt houses, the most important were, of course, the builder's. His decision to build another Levittown near Philadelphia, with houses in a $12,000–$15,000 price range, determined the age, class, and religious characteristics of the population, and these in turn influenced—perhaps determined—

the informal and formal groups and institutions that developed in the community. Had he decided to build more expensive houses, a different kind of community would have resulted. Of course, his decision was not made in a vacuum; it was based on the firm's previous success in building for young middle-income people and its belief that there were enough of them in the Philadelphia area to justify another Levittown. The specific location of the community outside what was then Philadelphia's commuting area at first attracted fewer Philadelphians than had been expected, resulting perhaps in a smaller Catholic population, and its proximity to an Air Force base and the research laboratories near Camden brought in more Transients. On the whole, however, the population that came to Levittown was not much different from those in the earlier Levittowns.

A second important decision was to buy enough land to build 12,000 homes and to announce this publicly, which in turn decided a significant number of External agencies to start churches and voluntary associations. This resulted in the immediate founding of many groups, speeded up their formation, and reduced false starts and mistakes, thus assuring their survival more quickly than would otherwise have been the case. It may also have increased the number of national branches in the new community.

Another significant Levitt decision was to concentrate on the building and marketing of houses and to leave the planning of local institutions and facilities to the residents. This enabled the old residents to build county values into Levittown's school system, government, and party politics; integrated Levittown into the county social structure more quickly than would otherwise have been the case; led directly to the early definitional struggles between the old residents and the newcomers, but also encouraged alliances against the common cosmopolitan foe; and of course, limited possible sources of resident hostility toward the builder.

A fourth, perhaps more important, decision was to subsidize the operating expenditures of the schools, which artificially reduced the tax rate for several years and thus enabled less affluent Levittowners to buy. When the Levitt subsidy was withdrawn, these less affluent homeowners were among the most insistent supporters of the tax-reduction forces that played such a determining influence in Levittown politics.

A fifth decision, to mix house types on the block, undoubtedly affected the organizational and political life of the new community. If each neighborhood had consisted of a single house type, three different types of neighborhoods would have developed, each with slightly different social and political interests. For example, a neighborhood of three-bedroom houses would have concentrated childless and older couples, least interested in school matters, and might have encouraged more organized protest against school budgets. More neighborhood-based voluntary associations would have been formed and party politics might have been more organized on the neighborhood level, with conflicts developing between groups of similar ones.

Of course, other builder (and township) decisions played some role in the development of the community, but none were as material. Indeed, most developmental processes were predictable and almost inevitable consequences of the very establishment of a new community. For example, the inrush of External agencies could have been predicted after Levitt's announcement that he would build 12,000 houses, for national associations everywhere are expanding their membership rolls. Limited social choices on the block inevitably created a need for community sorting organizations, and one could have expected that minorities and the lonely would be the first to start them. Similarly, once organizations had been started, their need to survive amidst competition could only lead to the hurried selection of officers, the relaxation of membership requirements, definitional struggles, and the arrival of similar organizations which could not lag behind in the competition for members and leaders. It is not surprising, therefore, that most of the associations and churches now in the community were organized during the first couple of years, drawing on the initial purchasers to man them and awarding them positions of power and status that they held on to in later years. The end result may have looked like the much discussed suburban hyperactivity, but it was hyperactivity on the part of organizations rather than on the part of residents. Properly speaking, it was not hyperactivity at all, but simply the rapid development of organizational structures in order to assure their survival.

Pre-Occupancy Aspirations and Community Origin

One of my initial hypotheses, that the origin of the community and the formation of particular groups and institutions would reflect the aspirations Levittowners expressed before arrival, was clearly not supported by what actually happened. Only a few residents aspired to community activities before they came, and Levittown's organizations were started instead by whatever External agencies were interested in the new community and by residents who had personal loyalties to a specific group. This would suggest that the aspirations and wishes of the mass of residents are irrelevant, and that a new community can be organized by individuals and even nonresidents who are determined to realize their own preferences, provided only that they have enough organizational know-how and persistence to put them over to the population.

It is true that almost anyone could start an organization in Levittown, but it is also true, and in the long run more important, that the organization's survival could only be assured by adapting it to the needs and wishes of its members, so that Levittowners could determine the fate of organizations by transforming what was started for them to their own preferences. This transformation process began even before Levittowners moved into their houses, for the builder acted in their behalf by using experience collected in previous Levittowns to design the community and to select the churches to which he would give free land. The churches themselves used data from these earlier Levittowns to determine which denominations would attract enough members to make it worthwhile to build, and they were careful to select "starters" who, wanting to work in Levittown, would be responsive to their future congregants.

The national associations which were founded Externally always began by finding a Levittowner who would do the actual organizing, and limited their role to getting the group safely under way. They left the local leaders free to determine membership qualifications and programs, which in turn enabled these leaders to adapt themselves to the needs of people who wanted *an* organization without having to follow the official purposes of the group. Usually, the process was almost automatic, for given the shortage of active participants, any resident who proposed a program idea was immediately named chairman of a committee to carry it out, and old army jokes were revived warning people to keep their mouths shut at meetings if they did not want to "volunteer" for leadership. Leaders who were not responsive to group demands or could not persuade members to carry out their proposals were extruded at the earliest opportunity.

Organizational responsiveness was also encouraged by the availability of *general* or instrumental leaders, individuals who wanted to lead but had no strong preferences for a specific organization or program and were thus flexible enough to provide leadership to any group or cause willing to put them in office. Three types of general leaders played an important role in the community's origin.

Some people were motivated by such strong personal needs for being leaders that, given the early shortage of leaders, they were willing to become general leaders instead of waiting for the specific organizations they preferred. One woman explained her transformation from a specific to a general leader as follows: "I wanted to be active when I first came here; I have a need for it in spurts and this was the year I needed it. I had been cooped up with three children for a whole year before and had a desperate need to be active. The Sisterhood happened to be the first thing I was asked to be active in and so I became active in it. Now I'm a little sorry because I want to organize a nursery school more, but I have an obligation to the Sisterhood."

The most frequent and most reliable source of general leadership came from occupationally motivated individuals, however. The lawyers, salesmen, realtors, and local retailers who needed to advertise their presence in the community, and had to do so at once, provided the community with leadership talent at a time when other residents were still settling down in their houses or exploring the block for friends. Since their livelihood depended on it, they were ready to move into any organization which needed them, to encourage its growth so as to obtain more personal publicity, community stature, and new business contacts, and to lead it in whatever directions the members preferred or accepted. Most of these general leaders enjoyed their organizational activity, for it required many of the same social skills they used in their jobs. "I like to join and it's good for business," one salesman pointed out. "I feel bad every time I go past the school and see a meeting I hadn't known about. But I'm not involved in any of the organizations . . . the only organization I really care about is the church." This man switched jobs several times until he found a company which encouraged his joining, and as he put it, "They said the more groups I joined, the better, as long as they're not political."

A third type of general leader functioned in interstitial capacities. He was usually a man looking for a better job, and was interested in organizational activities that would publicize him in the community. He provided leadership in the interstices of the community, wherever there were "holes" not being filled by others or activities that had to be done quickly. Interstitial leaders gravitated particularly to the political parties and were, of course, hoping for political jobs as a reward for their work. Lawyers also functioned as interstitial leaders, making themselves available to organizations as negotiators, arbitrators, and brokers. Bound by codes of ethics that guaranteed clients secrecy, they were particularly useful as go-betweens and "fixers" to resolve conflicts among community groups and between petitioners and government.

Unintended organizations were, by definition, responsive to some sudden community need. These brought forth *unintended* leaders, people who had not thought about being active before coming to Levittown and who often became leaders because they felt they had to, not because they wanted to. Occasionally, such people discovered hidden leadership needs and skills in the process. One woman, who had not belonged to an organization since high school, began by starting a neighborhood club to relieve her loneliness, and before long, she was named president of Levittown's largest church women's club. "I didn't want it and I didn't campaign for it," she later explained, "but some women asked me and I said yes. Now I love it. Before Levittown, I always kept things inside." She was exceptional, however, and most founders who lacked leadership needs or talents soon passed the responsibility to more suitable colleagues.

Politicians had to be particularly responsive, not only to get themselves elected, but at first also to recruit workers into the party. The fate of the old residents on the Township Committee and the Board of Education had demonstrated clearly how the voters would react to government unresponsiveness. Even the builder, who had the most power in the community and was not accountable to anyone except prospective purchasers, was responsive to resident demands when they did not conflict with higher priorities. He eliminated plans for a small shopping center and several gas stations upon resident protest, and in 1960, decided not to build an $11,000 house because he felt his earlier customers would resent his attempt to attract lower-income purchasers to the community. When resident demands did conflict with higher priorities, the builder was apt to be less responsive—as in the case of expanding the schools to reduce classroom size—but when enough Levittowners cared, they could force him into responsiveness by voting against government officials who had supported his requests.

What brought a community into being in Levittown, then, was not the pre-occupancy aspirations of the residents, but rather a complex process of external initiative and subsequent internal transformation that produced organizations and institutions which reflected the backgrounds and interests of the majority of the population. The new Levittowners had not thought much about their future community life before they arrived, but once they had settled down, they chose to enter the community being founded for them and then to alter it to meet their requirements. These choices were based less on explicit individual wishes than on requirements themselves generated by the community; that is, people went into and reshaped the organizations *on the basis of needs that had developed in the situation in which they found themselves in Levittown. The principal situation was the presence of the kinds of people with whom they lived, for insofar as Levittowners used organizations for sorting purposes and sorted themselves as they did, they were reacting to the population mix that had come about in Levittown.* Ultimately, then, the community evolved as it did because of the kinds of people who had decided, each on his own, to buy a house in Levittown, organizational and political life uniting them for cooperative ventures, segregating them for competitive ones, and bringing about class and other conflicts to determine which elements of the population mix would have power over the whole.

As a result, it would be absurd to argue that Levittown evolved out of a conspiracy, either on the part of a profit-seeking builder to entice buyers into his development or on the part of national organizations intent on adding to their membership rolls among an essentially captive audience. Indeed, few Levittowners objected that many of their organizations were national ones initiated from outside, and I am not sure that very many even noticed it. Not everyone was happy with what Levitt had wrought, and many were unhappy over the conflict generated by definitional struggles and by township politics, yet the events that made them unhappy were rarely conspiratorial or dictatorial measures, but almost always the outcomes of organizational and political compromises required by the need to establish a community quickly and to cope with the diverse requirements of that community. In the end, the community was an expression of the lower middle class culture of the majority, altered somewhat to accede to the demands of insistent minorities.

Prerequisites for Community Origin

Although it is dangerous to generalize from one new community, at least seven prerequisites seem to be necessary, or at least helpful, for the formation of new communities like Levittown. *First,* the new population must be culturally and emotionally "open," receptive to interaction with strangers, even from a somewhat different background, and trusting enough to participate with them in joint enterprises. At the same time, sufficient social and cultural homogeneity is required to enable strangers to talk to each other without immediate conflict over values, and equally important, they must face a common situation that places them all in the same boat. *Second,* the population must have some needs that cannot be met in the home and on the block. *Third,* group formation is enhanced if there is sufficient population heterogeneity to create minorities or socially isolated groups who need organizations and who are socially skilled enough to participate in them in order to eliminate their isolation.

Fourth, there must be residents with some incentive to undertake founding and leadership tasks. In a heterogeneous community, these must include general leaders who are willing to carry out membership demands that may conflict with their own preferences. Community prestige is usually a sufficient incentive for recruitment of needed leaders, particularly if the class structure is open enough to allow low-status people to achieve upward mobility through leadership. A most effective second incentive is occupational, and if there are sufficient lawyers, insurance salesmen, and merchants in the population, they will perform many of the needed general leadership roles. *Fifth,* leaders with previous experience can reduce organizational floundering, and may prevent the dissolution of groups during the early interorganizational competition.

Sixth, organizational formation and community activity generally are enhanced by conflict and crisis. Participation in political and civic affairs is assured if there is disagreement, especially if the most important goals people bring with them into the community are threatened. If a population is homogeneous and its political institutions are responsive to its needs, it is unlikely to participate except to vote, and even then may do so in limited number, leaving the decision-making task to a small elite. If a population is heterogeneous, however, and the demands of a significant proportion are downgraded or ignored, these are likely to form pressure groups and political factions.

Seventh, community participation requires physical facilities for meetings and some organs of communication to publicize the existence of organizations. The latter can be created as part of the origin process, but meeting rooms and small auditoriums must be available to facilitate the creation of organizations with more members than can fit into a living room.

THE NATURE OF A NEW COMMUNITY

Whether or not the outcomes of the diverse processes described above result in a community depends in part on one's definition of the term. Strictly speaking, what emerged in Levittown was the typical array of municipal bodies and individual associations which worked together when common interests were at stake, but competed most of the time. Many associations also had ties to county, state, and national bodies that were more important than their ties to other Levittown organizations.[11]

These groups, taken together, were commonly thought to be "the community," mainly because their activities took place within the township limits and their jurisdictions began and ended there. Their influence was limited to the population living within those limits, but they could act on this population, make rules regulating its behavior, and even speak in its behalf to people who lived outside. For example, an outsider curious about the ideas and attitudes of Levittown women would probably ask the Women's Club, and its leaders would feel that they could speak for all Levittown women. In reality, they did not even represent all who belonged to their own or the other women's clubs, but neither did any other visible community group, and thus each felt itself free to speak for the community, and—more important—make demands on the community which were claimed to benefit it. Residents tended to accept the formal organizations as representing the community, for when I interviewed leaders of less formal clubs, explaining that I was making a study of the community, they were often reluctant to talk about their groups, because they did not consider them to be a part of that body *they* defined as "the community." [12]

Since most Levittowners did not participate actively in the so-called community organizations, the community that had been originated in their names was of minor importance in their lives. What involved them deeply was their house and the lot on which it stood, the adjacent neighbors and perhaps the block, friends elsewhere in Levittown, and the particular church or organization in which they were active.[13] If one could measure "sense of community," it embraced only these, but not the community or even the neighborhood in which they had bought. Neighborhood boundaries had little meaning, for units of 1200 families were too large for face-to-face relations, and even the so-called neighborhood clubs usually recruited from only a block or two. Children who attended neighborhood schools may have felt neighborhood loyalty, based on a childish belief that their school was better than others, but since some students were bused in from other neighborhoods, not even the schools were pure neighborhood organizations. Some adults described their neighborhood as the best and friendliest in town, but further probing indicated that they were really talking about their own block, although some insisted that other neighborhoods were inferior because the houses were built closer together or were of poorer construction.

The feelings about the block, neighbors, friends, and favorite organizations were sometimes translated into a more general identification with Levittown as the best possible place to live, and some people took pride in a winning football team or an organizational achievement that lent distinction to Levittown. These feelings were neither intense nor of long duration; they were generated less by intrinsic qualities of the community than by the desire to put Levittown "on the map" in the unending competition with other communities. "The map" was usually Burlington County, but when L.Y.S.A. asked the Township Committee to finance a local team to play in the county baseball league, it pointed out that this league was regularly scouted by the majors, so that a $1000 municipal subsidy might one day enable a Levittowner to represent the community in the American or National League. Even the name change that transformed Levittown into Willingboro was justified largely by the negative headlines about the town in the Philadelphia area press, and reflected less a concern about the community than the belief that the name created a community image (and a *persona* for its residents) which they wanted the outside world to respect.

There were, of course, attempts to instill "community spirit" by merchants, party leaders, club presidents, municipal officials, and other boosters hoping to motivate their constituents to greater effort for their particular agency. Some residents believed deeply in community spirit and praised Levittowners for having more of it than their previous neighbors, but what they meant by it was a willingness to act unselfishly toward other Levittowners. For example, a man who missed a night's work and pay in order to coach his Little League team was described as having community spirit, and so were the people who sent donations and cards to a just-widowed Levittowner and prayed for a little girl, new in the community, who would be dead of cancer in six months. This kind of community spirit reflected mutual help patterns among neighbors more than an attitude toward the community, and developed only in personal or organizational crises and disasters. It could not have been generated—and would not have been expected—for events and political issues which might deprive some Levittowners and benefit others. Perhaps if the community were threatened by powerful outside forces which would hurt the community as a whole or deprive every Levittowner, an intense identification with the community might be created, but most people hoped such a threat would never develop. Even if it did, the resulting cohesion would be only transitory, disappearing once the threat was removed or leading to disaffection with the community and eventual departure if it could not be removed.

By any traditional criteria, then, Levittown could not be considered a community. It was not an economic unit whose members were dependent on each other for their livelihood, and it was not a social unit for there was no reason or incentive for people to relate to each other as Levittowners on any regular or recurring basis. And Levittown was clearly not a symbolic unit, for the sense of community was weak. If Levittown was a community, and of course it was, it could best be defined as an administrative-political unit plus an aggregate of community-wide associations within a space that had been legally established by William Penn and his associates as a township some three hundred years before.[14] As such, it provided residents with a variety of services and required them to act in a limited number of community roles—for example, as voters, taxpayers, and organizational participants—but these roles encouraged division rather than cohesion.

Indeed, just because Levittown was only a loose network of groups and institutions it was possible for these to develop quickly and in large numbers. Had the community been a cohesive social body, there would have been fewer groups, for the founding of additional ones would have signified an intrusion into a tight-knit social body. Conversely, not being a social body, Levittown needed to find groups, people, and symbols to make it appear as a body to other communities—which were equally busy persuading Levittowners that *they* were social bodies. The attempts of the builder and, later, the township fathers to require stores and gas stations to adopt a uniform pseudo-Colonial façade for their buildings was, likewise, an architectural means for creating a unity and cohesion that did not exist in the social system.

I do not mean to downgrade Levittown as a community, for my observations apply equally to all other communities, urban and suburban, and probably even to most communities of the past, including those now celebrated as cohesive units.[15] Moreover, Levittown probably displayed a greater sense of community, social cohesion, and symbolic (as well as spatial) unity than established and more typical settlements, if only because it was new and because it was atypical in its architectural homogeneity and the youthfulness of its population. It also had a stronger self-image as a community than Levittown, Long Island, which, being spread over many municipalities, has had to debate with itself whether it was a community or not.[16] My argument here is not with Levittown, then, but with critics who seek to find a social unit in the community where none exists, and with romantic city planners, abetted by nostalgic social critics, who want to "revive" a sense of community that never was save in their imagination, instead of planning for the effective functioning of and improved living conditions in those aggregates to which we give the name "community."

Newness and Deliberate Innovation

City planners usually reserve the term "new town" for a community that contains enough employment opportunities to provide jobs for about half of its residents. In this sense, Levittown was not a new town, for even if it had been able to attract industry, not enough land was reserved for this purpose to employ more than a fraction of all Levittowners. Physically Levittown was, of course, new, yet in many ways it was not a new community. The people who moved there wanted a new house but not a new life, and the community they established was not particularly novel. None of its organizations, institutions, and public agencies were distinctive, or different from those one might find in a community of other young families of similar socioeconomic level. Indeed, many factors in its origin discouraged novelty and innovation. Both External and Internal founding encouraged the establishment of previously existing organizations and churches in Levittown, and once started, these as well as Unintended groups looked desperately for people with "experience." As a result, new organizations adopted old structural and programmatic ideas that had worked elsewhere. In fact, the need to assure the survival of the group and develop a routine discouraged innovation and experimentation, which took place either because there was no other alternative or because only a new solution would fit the needs of the moment. For example, the Republican invention of the "bandwagon" resulted from the lack of experienced campaigners and speechmakers and the need for an alternative method of reaching the voters. When proposals were advanced as deliberate innovations and experiments they were likely to be rejected, because people resented being used as guinea pigs, particularly when the call for innovation and experimentation came from the cosmopolitans. Levittowners were perfectly willing to innovate and experiment in their own homes, but not at the community level.

The fact remains, however, that Levittown was planned from scratch by the builder and the consultants who worked with him, and by the External agencies who came in to found organizations before Levittown was even six months old. It is, therefore, worth while asking whether deliberate planning could have gone one step further and introduced innovations prior to the opening of the community, presenting the arriving Levittowners with a *fait accompli*. Would early initiative combined with organizational know-how have enabled school, church, and organizational planners to lay out a novel community structure which would have been so appropriate to the Levittowners' needs that they would have accepted it and thus made Levittown a really new community?

Much of the know-how was available; from information on the price range and the number of houses to be built in Levittown, an organizational planner could have used (as did the research departments of the Protestant denominations) data from previous Levittowns to predict fairly accurately the array and range of organizations and institutions that would be relevant to the new population. He might even have been able to start them, for once Levittown was occupied, anyone who decided to set up a specific organization thereby generated processes which encouraged its survival. That the planner could also have programmed the memberships and activities of these groups is, however, doubtful. Unless he could have accurately predicted what minorities would find themselves at a loss on the block and what sorting criteria would eventually have emerged out of the population mix, his plans would surely have been diverted once the Levittowners arrived, and the organizations would have been changed to meet the needs that developed after their arrival. Prior planning might even have increased the diversion, for the new residents would have been suspicious that organizations already in existence were set up for some ulterior purpose on the part of the builder or the old residents, and might therefore have stayed away from them altogether.

Perhaps Levitt's consultants and the old residents were right in their unwillingness to plan without constituents, to schedule only the institutional shells and let the Levittowners fill in the details once they arrived. In fact, more attention should have been paid to these shells. For example, more accurate population estimates might have ensured elementary schools with enough classrooms to keep class size at the intended level. An organizational planner might also have been helpful to small organizations which lacked the communications skills to find enough eligible or interested people among the mass of Levittowners, and he might have been able to bring organizations into being to provide activities and viewpoints not available in the community. As of 1961, there were no mental health clinics or counseling centers, almost no recreation opportunities for girls, no high-culture organizations, no local and national political groups that offered the community alternative points of view—for example, the Americans for Democratic Action or a local citizens' planning group. Given the small number of residents with the requisite interests, however, it is not certain whether such groups could have survived even if they had been started by a professional organizer.

Ultimately, any attempt at significant organizational innovation would probably have foundered because Levittowners came not to build a new community but to move into a new house in which they could carry on old ways of family life, neighbor relations, and civic activity. Perhaps the only new communities are utopian ones formed deliberately by people who have decided to alter their life according to a common plan, and such people would not have considered buying in Levittown. A few Levittowners came to start a new life or make significant changes in the old one, and some came with a fragile hope that, somehow, a virginal community would avoid the problems and conflicts of an established one. This hope was soon dashed by the necessities of the origin process. As one of the first arrivals recalled later: "I was so naive before I moved here. I didn't think there would be any juvenile delinquency; I thought only angels were moving in. It never occurred to me that people are people no matter where you live." She put it well, for people being people, they brought their cultures with them and the community they established thus only re-created old life styles and institutions on new soil.

NOTES

1. Clark has called these "packaged" suburbs because their builders provided at least some of the community facilities that go with the house. The term is apt, but it underemphasizes the extent to which the population, once arrived, shapes the contents of the package to suit its own needs. See Clark, pp. 6–7.
2. Form (1951), pp. 127–130.
3. Similar people in Levittown, Long Island were described as "Communists," perhaps because the community conflict took place during the McCarthy era. See Liell (1952), pp. 273ff.
4. Similar departures have been observed in Greenbelt, Maryland, by Form (1944), pp. 283ff; and in Park Forest, Illinois, by Gans (1953), p. 7.
5. On the role of pioneers in Levittown, New York, and Park Forest, Illinois, see Liell (1952), p. 258; and Whyte (1956), pp. 310–311.
6. Upper middle class suburbs have, however, rejected political bosses. Wood (1959), pp. 166–175.
7. Soon after the community opened, Levitt built a four-bedroom version of the $14,000 model, but it was often in short supply, so

that family size remained a significant determinant of house choice.

8. On the block, where leaders were ordinary residents and behaved more in line with their backgrounds, the usual status judgments could be made; indeed, neighbors often wondered how people who acted as if they were of low status could be so successful outside the block.

9. Since the houses were neither visibly more statusful nor functionally much better than the cheaper models, few Levittowners were interested in exchanging them for what they had, although in Levittown, Pennsylvania, a neighborhood of more expensive houses did attract more affluent and higher-status people who had become dissatisfied with their cheaper models. By 1966, Levitt began to build higher-priced houses again, locating them (as planned earlier) on the Rancocas River at the extreme edge of the community.

10. The politicians, of course, prefer voting blocs, since these can be reached more easily during election campaigns. However, not even the Catholic bloc leaders could control the vote of their coreligionists. The small neighborhood of higher-priced houses and the larger neighborhoods that were settled later immediately organized civic associations to defend their interests against a government then controlled by the first arrivals, and new areas have sometimes voted differently from older ones on some issues.

11. A study of a Scottish new town described its social organization as "a host of small internally interacting groups between which there are no connecting links." Hole, p. 171.

12. In Levittown, Pennsylvania, people active in formal organizations considered themselves as belonging to the community and perceived it more accurately than the inactive. Jahoda et al., p. 145.

13. Hole, p. 168.

14. For a similar analysis of the suburban community, see Greer (1960), pp. 519–520.

15. An insightful analysis of the absence of "community" in the revered Athenian *polis,* and of the same divisive class conflicts associated with the modern city, is to be found in Gouldner, Chap. 4.

16. Orzack and Sanders, pp. 3–11; and Dobriner (1963), pp. 118–125.

Part 2 · THE QUALITY OF SUBURBAN LIFE

Chapter Eight

SOCIAL LIFE: SUBURBAN HOMOGENEITY AND CONFORMITY

IN PART TWO, MY FOCUS SHIFTS FROM LEVITTOWN TO THE LEVIT-towners, and from a historical to a cross-sectional perspective—from the community to the people and the way they live at a specific point in time. Some critics charge that suburban life is socially, culturally, and emotionally destructive, and that the causes are to be found in the nature of suburbia and the move from the city. Testing their charges requires evaluation of the quality of Levittown life and measurement of Levittown's impact on its residents to determine what changes in behavior and attitudes have actually resulted from the move.

Many of the findings on Levittown's impact are based on interviews with two sets of Levittowners, one a nearly *random sample* of 45 buyers in Somerset Park, the first neighborhood to be settled, and the second, of 55 others in that neighborhood who had moved there from Philadelphia, here called the *Philadelphia* or *city sample*. The two samples were interviewed during 1960 and 1961, after they had lived in Levittown two to three years, and this determines the period on which the cross-sectional analysis is reporting. (The random sample was also interviewed just after its arrival in Levittown, thus providing data on the immediate impact of the move as well.) Both samples are small and not entirely random, so that the statistics cannot supply the final scientific proof that statistics often imply, but they do illustrate what happened to people as a result of moving to Levittown.

THE QUALITY OF SOCIAL LIFE

Perhaps the most frequent indictment of suburban life has been leveled against the quality of social relationships. The critics charge that the suburbs are socially hyperactive and have made people so outgoing that they have little time or inclination for the development of personal autonomy. The pervasive homogeneity of the population has depressed the vitality of social life, and the absence of more heterogeneous neighbors and friends has imposed a conformity which further reduces the suburbanite's individuality. Indeed, studies showing the importance of physical propinquity in the choice of friends have been interpreted to suggest that physical layout, rather than people, determines the choice of friends. Because many suburbanites are Transients or Mobiles, they have been accused of wanting social companions only for the duration of their stay, disabling them for more intimate friendship.[1]

Evidence from Levittown suggests quite the opposite. People report an accelerated social life, and in fact looked forward to it before moving to Levittown. The major reason for the upswing is indeed homogeneity, but an equally appropriate term might be "compatibility." Propinquity may initiate social contact but it does not determine friendship. Many relationships are indeed transient, but this is no reflection on their intensity. Finally, conformity prevails, although less as malicious or passive copying than as sharing of useful ideas. In short, many of the *phenomena* identified by the critics occur in Levittown but their alleged *consequences* do not follow. Levittowners have not become outgoing, mindless conformers; they remain individuals, fulfilling the social aspirations with which they came. To be sure, social life in Levittown has its costs, but these seem minor compared to its rewards.

Neighboring [2]

About half the Levittowners interviewed said that they were visiting more with neighbors than in their former residence; about a quarter said less, and the remaining quarter reported no change.[3] The greatest increase was reported by the people who said they had wanted to do more visiting, particularly those who had had little opportunity for it in their previous residence. As one Philadelphian said, "We used to be with the in-laws and with my mother; we didn't bother with the neighbors before." Others had lacked compatible neighbors; people living in apartments had found few opportunities to get acquainted, and those in older or transitional areas had found their fellow residents unsuitable. This was as true of former suburbanites and small-town residents as of those from cities, and affected owners as well as renters. One homeowner explained, "Here in Levittown I have more in common; where we lived before, the neighbors were all my mother's age."

In addition to the desire to do more neighboring, the increase resulted initially from the newness of the community and the lack of shopping facilities and other places for daytime activities. But these reasons were mentioned far less often than the "friendliness" of the neighbors, and this in turn was a function of population homogeneity. One Levittowner, describing her next-door neighbor, said, "We see eye to eye on things, about raising kids, doing things together with your husband, living the same way; we have practically the same identical background." Conversely, the people who reported less neighboring were those who could not find compatible people on the block: older ones, some (but not all) people of highest and lowest status, and those who had difficulties in relating to neighbors, particularly second generation Jewish women from Philadelphia who were used to living among Jewish neighbors.[4] A handful wanted to continue spending their social life with relatives or preferred to have nothing to do with neighbors.

Of course, some friendliness was built into the neighbor relationship, for people needed each other for mutual aid. In a community far from the city, women are cut off from relatives and old friends—as well as from commuting husbands—so that readiness to provide mutual aid is the first criterion of being a good neighbor. This includes not only helping out in emergencies, but ameliorating periodic loneliness by being available for occasional coffee-klatsching and offering informal therapy by being willing to listen to another's troubles when necessary. Helping out also offers an opportunity—rare in everyday life—to practice the dictates of the Judeo-Christian ethic, and brings appropriate emotional rewards. The reciprocity engendered by mutual aid en-

courages—and allows—neighbors to keep a constant watch on
each other, as they do in established neighborhoods everywhere.
One night I drove out of my driveway at a slightly higher than
usual speed, and my next-door neighbor came over to find out if
anything was wrong, although later he wondered whether in his
desire to be a good neighbor he had violated the norms of privacy
and was being too nosy. The mutual observation that makes the
block a goldfish bowl goes on mainly among adjacent neighbors,
for with houses only ten feet apart, they see each other frequently
and have to maintain friendly relations if that is at all possible.
More distant neighbors could be ignored, however. Indeed, a
Levittowner who had moved from a cohesive working class district said, "It's not like Philadelphia here. There you might
know someone four blocks down the road as well as your next-
door neighbor. Here you don't know people down the road."
The block was a social unit only to assure a modicum of house
and lawn care, beyond which there was no obligation for neighbors to associate.

Even propinquity did not require visiting. Although a number
of studies have shown that social relationships are influenced and
even determined by the site plan, this was not the case in Levittown.[5] Since Levittown was laid out with curved blocks, houses
facing each other across front and back, there were relatively few
neighbors with whom one had constant and involuntary visual
contact. Sometimes, even relationships with directly adjacent
neighbors could be restricted to an exchange of hellos. For example, it took more than a year for me to meet the occupants of a
house diagonally across the street from mine, even though we had
been saying hello since the first weeks of occupancy. Another person told me he had never even met his next-door neighbor. Thus,
despite a fairly high building density—five to six houses to the
acre—there was no pressure to be sociable. Neighboring rarely
extended more than three or four houses away in each direction,
so that the "functional neighborhood" usually consisted of about
ten to twelve houses at the most, although people did say hello to
everyone on the block.[6] The boundaries of the functional neighborhood were delimited either by physical barriers or by social
isolates who interrupted the flow of social relations.[7]

A more systematic test of the propinquity theory was made by
asking interview respondents to rank the amount of visiting with
their six most adjacent neighbors. If propinquity alone had

TABLE 4
VISITING AMONG ADJACENT NEIGHBORS, BY AMOUNT OF VISITING

LOCATION OF NEIGHBOR	PERCENT REPORTING Ranked Amount of Visiting					
	First	Second	Third	Fourth	All	Not Visited
Next door, right side	31	31	15	14	24	24
Next door, left side	24	38	20	14	26	15
Across the street	36	22	23	23	26	4
Across the backyard	7	7	32	27	17	57
Other*	2	2	10	23	7	N.A.**
N	(45)	(42)	(40)	(22)	(149)	(26)

* This included other neighbors across the street or the backyard when a house faced or backed on two others.
** Not asked.

determined visiting, one or two of the most adjacent neighbors, those on the right and left sides, should have been visited most often. As Table 4 indicates, however, about three quarters of *all* visiting was equally distributed between these two and the neighbor across the street, who was a little farther away, and the latter was actually visited most often. If people's first and second choices are combined, the data show that 31 per cent chose right-hand neighbors, an equal number left-hand ones, 29 per cent those across the street, and the rest other adjacent ones. Thus, distance does not affect choice of the closest neighbors, although it does discourage visiting the less adjacent ones, and particularly backyard neighbors. Because of the 100-foot depths of the lots and the heat of the New Jersey summer, people made little use of the backyards, and the 200 feet between houses reduced visiting considerably.[8]

Some propinquity studies have found that visiting is affected by the location of the front door, and, among women, of the kitchen window from which they can see their neighbors while doing housework. This was not the case in Levittown. If the front door had been significant, owners of the Cape Cod and ranch houses should have chosen their right-hand and across-the-street neighbors most often; those of the Colonial houses should have chosen their left-hand and across-the-street neighbors. The data show that Cape Cod owners visited most often across the street, but equally between right- and left-hand neighbors; the ranch owners chose the left-hand neighbors twice as often as their other neighbors; and the Colonial owners showed a slight preference for left-hand neighbors.[9] In the "kitchen window test," the expected pattern was found only among Cape Cod house owners, but not the other two.[10] Had location been the prime determinant of friendship choice, neighbors should also have been mentioned as friends more than other Levittowners. Respondents said, however, that only 35 per cent of the five couples they visited most frequently lived on their street, and 31 per cent said that none of these favorite couples lived on their street.[11] Moreover, propinquity affected some types of social gatherings but not others; baby showers, cookouts, and barbecues drew only nearby neighbors; more formal parties involved mainly guests from other streets and neighborhoods.[12]

Since most of the interview questions were about adjacent neighbors, the findings are only a partial test of the propinquity theory. They suggest that a sizeable functional distance discourages visiting, but that among adjacent neighbors, people choose not the closest or the ones they see most often, but the ones they consider most compatible. Indeed, fully 82 per cent of the respondents mentioned compatibility as the reason for choosing the neighbor they visited most frequently. If the site plan had forced some neighbors into constant visual contact—as do court or cul-de-sac schemes—they might have reacted by increased visiting (or intense enmity if they were incompatible), but the block layout gave Levittowners the opportunity for choice.

Neighbor relations among adults were also affected by the children, for children are neighbors too, and their mingling was determined almost entirely by age and propinquity.[13] The relatively traffic-free streets and the large supply of young children enabled mothers to limit their supervision of the children's outdoor play; and the overall compatibility, to give youngsters a free choice of playmates. But children were likely to quarrel, and when this led to fights and childish violence, their quarrels involved the parents. Half the random sample had heard of quarrels among neighbors on their block, and 81 per cent of these were over the children. Adults quarreled most often when childish misbehavior required punishment and parents disagreed about methods. If the parents of fighting children agreed on discipline, each punished his child the same way and the incident was soon forgotten. If they disagreed, however, the parent who believed in harsh punishment often felt that the more permissive parent, not having punished "enough," was accusing the other child of having been at fault. A single parental disagreement might be forgiven, but if it happened repeatedly, an open break between neighbors could result. Of seventeen quarrels about which interview respondents were knowledgeable, nine had been concluded peacefully, but in the other eight cases, parents were still not talking to each other. In one case, two neighbors finally came to blows and had to be placed on a peace bond by the municipal court.

Another type of adult quarrel involved physical disciplining of children by neighbors. Some people believe that only parents should spank their children; others, that neighbors have the right to do so if the child misbehaves out of sight of the parents. When a neighbor punishes another's child, he not only takes on a quasi-parental role but, by implication, accuses the parents of not raising and watching their children properly. In one such case, where a neighbor punished a little boy for sexual exhibitionism, the parent never spoke to him again.

Basically, differences over discipline reflect class differences in child-rearing. Middle class parents tend to be somewhat more permissive than working class ones, and when two children play together, the middle class child may be allowed to act in ways not permitted to the working class one. Also, working class parents administer physical punishment more freely, since this is not interpreted as a withdrawal of affection, whereas middle class families reserve spankings for extreme misbehavior. Then, as children get older, practices change. The working class child is given more freedom, and by comparison, the middle class child is given much less. He is expected to do his homework while his working class peers may be playing on the streets. Middle class people who observe this freedom, as well as the working class parents' tolerance of childish profanity, interpret it as neglect.

In some cases, middle class families even prohibit their children from playing with working class children. Prohibition is feasible if children are old enough to respect it or if parents supervise the children's play. Younger children cannot be prevented from playing with each other, however, and parental quarrels may result. If the working class children are older and in a minority, as they often are on the block, they may become outcasts, and since they are mobile, may look around for other, similarly discredited companions. Out of this may come a gang that vandalizes hostile middle class society.[14] People of low status experienced (or saw) the most quarrels, for 72 per cent of blue collar respondents reported quarrels in their neighborhood, as compared to only 41 per cent of the middle class.

The repetition of parental conflict over children's quarrels can lead to increasing estrangement, because other values and behavior patterns also differ between the classes. For example, in one case, what began as a series of minor disagreements about child-rearing was soon reinforced by critical comments on the part of the middle class people about the working class neighbor's laxity toward his lawn and his taste for expensive automobiles. All of these disagreements spiraled into considerable hostility over a year's time. Eventually, one of the feuding neighbors may move out—usually the middle class family which has greater resources to go elsewhere.

If the overall social climate of the block is good, other neighbors will try to patch up conflicts between parents. On one block, a child hit another with a toy, drawing blood and requiring a doctor. The mother of the injured youngster admitted it was his fault and suggested to the other mother that the two children be kept apart for a few days. However, she did not punish her child at once, and this was resented by the other mother (of working class background). She, in turn, forbade her child to see the guilty one, and both she and her husband broke off with his parents as well. After about a week, however, the feud ended. Each mother told other neighbors of what had happened, and the woman whose child had provoked the incident finally learned that the other mother thought he had not been properly punished. She thereupon let it be known among her neighbors that the child had in fact been punished on the day of the incident. In a few days the message reached its intended destination, whereupon the mother whose child had been hit invited her neighbor and another, neutral, neighbor to coffee. The coffee-klatsch resolved the differences, but only because the block's friendly climate had provided for the prior and circuitous communication that allowed the one mother to learn that the guilty child had indeed been punished. Had communication been poorer, other differences between the two neighbors might have been invoked to increase the conflict. Indeed, when the block's social climate is poor, the struggle will be limited to the involved parents, for no one wants to take sides. If a family becomes enmeshed in battles with a number of neighbors, however, that family is likely to be quickly ostracized, regardless of the social climate.

The importance of compatibility is extended also to relationships that do not involve children, and is underscored by the problems encountered by neighbors who differ significantly. One potential trouble spot was age. Although some elderly Levittowners were able to assume quasi-grandparental roles toward the street's children, others were lonely and uncomfortable among the young families, and enthusiastic gardeners were upset when children romped over flowerbeds and carefully tended lawns. The difficulty was exacerbated by the builder's prohibition of fences, a clause in the deed restriction that was later violated on a number of blocks and actually taken to court.

Class differences also expressed themselves in areas other than child-rearing.[15] Upper middle class women—whose concept of after-housework activity did not include coffee-klatsching, conversation about husbands, homes, and children, or gossiping about the neighbors—rejected and were rejected by the neighbors. So were women who were especially active in organizational life. Perhaps the major problems were faced by working class people who had been used to spending their free time with relatives or childhood friends and found it hard to become friendly with strangers (especially middle class ones). The change was particularly distressing to those who had spent all their lives in the neighborhood in which they grew up. If, when they moved to Levittown, they were sufficiently "open" to respond to friendly neighbors and found others of working class background nearby, they could adapt; if not, they were virtually isolated in their houses. For the latter, a small minority to be sure, life in Levittown was hard.[16] Ethnic differences were also a barrier between neighbors. Groups without a strong subcommunity were isolated, notably a handful of Japanese, Chinese, and Greek families. Some neighbors came with ethnic and racial prejudice, and anti-Semitism, though rare, could be justified by the old charge of Jewish clannishness [17] and by class differences resulting from generally higher incomes among Jews.[18]

A final barrier was sexual, and this affected the women whose husbands worked irregular schedules and might be home during the day. A woman neighbor did not visit another when her husband was home, partly because of the belief that a husband has first call on his wife's companionship, partly to prevent suspicion that her visit might be interpreted as a sexual interest in the husband. This practice is strongest among working class women, reflecting the traditional class norm that people of the opposite sex come together only for sexual reasons, and becomes weaker at higher class levels; in the upper middle class there are enough shared interests between men and women to discourage suspicion.[19] The sexual barrier sometimes inhibited neighbor relations among women whose husbands traveled as salesmen, pilots, or seamen, forcing their wives to associate with each other.

Couple Visiting [20]

Although 40 per cent of the Levittowners reported more couple visiting than in their former residences, the change was not quite as great as for neighboring, requiring as it does the compatibility of four rather than two and more of a commitment toward friendship as well.[21] Like neighboring, the increase in couple visiting resulted principally from the supply of compatible people, although it was also encouraged significantly by organizational activity; members of voluntary associations and of the highly organized Jewish subcommunity reported the greatest increase.[22] Even the people who had not wanted to do more visiting before they moved to Levittown found themselves doing more if they were in organizations. Whether organizational membership encourages more visiting or vice versa is not clear; most likely, the same gregariousness that induces visiting also makes "joiners," for the latter have more friends in Levittown than the unaffiliated.

Couple visiting is governed by narrower criteria of compatibility than neighboring, for religiously mixed marriage partners reported more neighboring, but found themselves doing less couple visiting in Levittown.[23] Older people and people of lower status also reported decreases. Evidently, friendship choices were affected by religion, and people who straddled two had trouble finding friends. So did people who straddled the classes, for some Jewish women who had found Jewish organizations not to their liking, wanting more "cultural" activities but not being quite up to the civic programs of the cosmopolitans, reported that their social life suffered.

The patterns of couple visiting in Levittown question two features of the suburban critique—the superficiality of friendships and social hyperactivity. According to many critics of suburban life, the transience of the population induces transient relationships which end with departure from the community. Transient relationships undoubtedly exist; one Levittowner, who had gone back to visit old friends in her former community, returned to report that she no longer had much in common with them and that they had been, as she put it, "development friends." Other Transients established close friendships, however, and one family, temporarily transferred, returned to the block to be close to friends even though they would have preferred to move into one of Levitt's newer houses.

The criticism of "development" friendship harbors an implicit comparison with "bosom" friendship, assumed to have existed in the past, but there is no evidence that the comparison is empirically valid. Close friendships, I suspect, typically develop in childhood and adolescent peer groups, and can continue in a static society where people have as much in common in adult-hood as in childhood. But in American society, and especially in the middle class, geographical and social mobility often separates people who have grown up together, so that shared interests among childhood friends are rare. Often, only nostalgia keeps the relationship going. Many Levittowners talk about close friends "at home," but they see them so rarely that the current strength of the friendship is never properly tested. Instead, they develop new friends at each stage of the life cycle or as they move up occupationally and develop new social and leisure interests. Closeness is not replaced by superficiality, but permanent friendships give way to new and perhaps shorter ones of similar closeness.[24]

Whether or not this relationship is desirable depends on one's values. People today, particularly the middle classes, are more gregarious than those of the past. The working class, restricted in social skills or content to range within a smaller, perhaps closer, network of relatives and childhood friends, comes nearest to retaining the traditional "bosom" friendship. But these people, in my research as in many other studies, report difficulties in making new friends as their life conditions change.[25]

The critics' charge that suburbanites indulge in hyperactive visiting to counteract boredom and loneliness brought on by the lack of urbanity in their communities is equally mistaken. Coming from academia where the weekend brought parties, and having just lived in an Italian working class neighborhood in Boston where people maintained an almost continual "open house," I was surprised at how little entertaining took place among Levittowners.[26] Although people often had visitors on Sunday afternoons, weekend evenings were not differentiated from the rest, a fact that should be obvious from the high ratings of television programs on the air at that time. I would guess that, on the average, Levittowners gathered informally not more than two or three times a month and gave formal parties about once a year, not counting those around Christmas and New Year's Eve. Social life in Levittown was not hyperactive by any stretch of the imagination, except perhaps in the first few months of putting out feelers. I suspect that the critics either confuse the early hyperactivity with the normal pattern once life had settled down, or they generalize from observations in upper middle class suburbs, where partying is a major leisure activity.

Admittedly, the critics could question my assumption that an increase in social life is equivalent to an improvement in its quality, and argue that it represents instead an escape from pervasive boredom. If the Levittowners had found their social life boring, however, they would either have cut it down or complained about greater boredom. The data indicate just the opposite, for those visiting more were less bored (and vice versa), and besides, if social life had been as dull as the critics claim, why would the interview respondents have been so enthusiastic about the friendliness of their fellow residents?

THE PROS AND CONS OF
POPULATION HOMOGENEITY [27]

The suburban critique is quite emphatic on the subject of demographic homogeneity. For one thing, homogeneity violates the American Dream of a "balanced" community where people of diverse age, class, race, and religion live together. Allegedly, it creates dullness through sameness. In addition, age homogeneity deprives children—and adults—of the wisdom of their elders, while class, racial, and religious homogeneity prevent children from learning how to live in our pluralistic society. Homogeneity is said to make people callous to the poor, intolerant of Negroes, and scornful of the aged. Finally, heterogeneity is said to allow upward mobility, encouraging working and lower class people to learn middle class ways from their more advantaged neighbors.[28]

There is no question that Levittown is quite homogeneous in age and income as compared to established cities and small towns, but such comparisons are in many ways irrelevant. People do not live in the political units we call "cities" or "small towns"; often their social life takes place in areas even smaller than a census tract. Many such areas in the city are about as homogeneous in class as Levittown, and slum and high-income areas, whether urban or suburban, are even more so. Small towns are notoriously rigid in their separation of rich and poor, and only appear to be more heterogeneous because individual neighborhoods are so small. All these considerations effectively question the belief that before the advent of modern suburbs Americans of all classes lived together. Admittedly, statistics compiled for cities and suburbs as a whole show that residential segregation by class and by race are on the increase, but these trends also reflect the breakdown of rigid class and caste systems in which low-status people "knew their place," and which made residential segregation unnecessary.

By ethnic and religious criteria, Levittown is much less homogeneous than these other areas because people move in as individuals rather than as groups, and the enclaves found in some recently built urban neighborhoods, where 40 to 60 per cent of the population comes from one ethnic or religious group, are absent. Nor is Levittown atypically homogeneous in age; new communities and subdivisions always attract young people, but over time, their populations "age" until the distribution resembles that of established communities.[29]

Finally, even class homogeneity is not as great as communitywide statistics would indicate. Of three families earning $7000 a year, one might be a skilled worker at the peak of his earning power and dependent on union activity for further raises; another, a white collar worker with some hope for a higher income; and the third, a young executive or professional at the start of his career. Their occupational and educational differences express themselves in many variations in life style, and if they are neighbors, each is likely to look elsewhere for companionship. Perhaps the best way to demonstrate that Levittown's homogeneity is more statistical than real is to describe my own nearby neighbors. Two were Anglo-Saxon Protestant couples from small towns, the breadwinners employed as engineers; one an agnostic and a golf buff, the other a skeptical Methodist who wanted to be a teacher. Across the backyard lived a Baptist white collar worker from Philadelphia and his Polish-American wife, who had brought her foreign-born mother with her to Levittown; and an Italian-American tractor operator (whose ambition was to own a junkyard) and his upwardly mobile wife, who restricted their social life to a brother down the street and a host of relatives who came regularly every Sunday in a fleet of Cadillacs. One of my next-door neighbors was a religious fundamentalist couple from the Deep South whose life revolved around the church; another was an equally religious Catholic blue collar worker and his wife, he originally a Viennese Jew, she a rural Protestant, who were politically liberal and as skeptical about middle class ways as any intellectual. Across the street, there was another Polish-American couple, highly mobile and conflicted over their obligations to the extended family; another engineer; and a retired Army officer.

No wonder Levittowners were puzzled when a nationally known housing expert addressed them on the "pervasive homogeneity of suburban life."

Most Levittowners were pleased with the diversity they found among their neighbors, primarily because regional, ethnic, and religious differences are today almost innocuous and provide variety to spice the flow of conversation and the exchange of ideas. For example, my Southern neighbor discovered pizza at the home of the Italian-American neighbor and developed a passion for it, and I learned much about the personal rewards of Catholicism from my Catholic convert neighbors. At the same time, however, Levittowners wanted homogeneity of age and income —or rather, they wanted neighbors and friends with common interests and sufficient consensus of values to make for informal and uninhibited relations. Their reasons were motivated neither by antidemocratic feelings nor by an interest in conformity. Children need playmates of the same age, and because child-rearing problems vary with age, mothers like to be near women who have children of similar age. And because these problems also fluctuate with class, they want some similarity of that factor—not homogeneity of occupation and education so much as agreement on the ends and means of caring for child, husband, and home.

Income similarity is valued by the less affluent, not as an end in itself, but because people who must watch every penny cannot long be comfortable with more affluent neighbors, particularly when children come home demanding toys or clothes they have seen next door. Indeed, objective measures of class are not taken into account in people's associations at all, partly because they do not identify each other in these terms, but also because class differences are not the only criterion for association.[30] Sometimes neighbors of different backgrounds but with similar temperaments find themselves getting along nicely, especially if they learn to avoid activities and topics about which they disagree. For example, two women of diverse origins became good friends because they were both perfectionist housekeepers married to easygoing men, although they once quarreled bitterly over child-rearing values.

But Levittowners also want some homogeneity for themselves. As I noted before, cosmopolitans are impatient with locals, and vice versa; women who want to talk about cultural and civic matters are bored by conversations about home and family—and, again, vice versa; working class women who are used to the informal flow of talk with relatives need to find substitutes among neighbors with similar experience. Likewise, young people have little in common with older ones, and unless they want surrogate parents, prefer to socialize with neighbors and friends of similar age. Some Levittowners sought ethnic and religious homogeneity as well. Aside from the Jews and some of the Greeks, Japanese, and the foreign-born women of other nations, observant Catholics and fundamentalist Protestants sought "their own," the former because they were not entirely at ease with non-Catholic neighbors, the latter because their time-consuming church activity and their ascetic life styles set them apart from most other Levittowners. They mixed with their neighbors, of course, but their couple visiting was limited principally to the like-minded. Because of the diversity of ethnic and religious backgrounds, the Philadelphia sample was asked whether there had been any change in the amount of visiting with people of similar "national descent or religious preference"; 30 per cent reported a decrease, but 20 per cent reported an increase.[31] Those doing less such visiting in Levittown also said they were lonelier than in Philadelphia.

Most people had no difficulty finding the homogeneity they wanted in Levittown. Affluent and well-educated people could move into organizations or look for friends all over Levittown, but older people and people of lower income or poorly educated women were less able to move around either physically or socially. Women from these groups often did not have a car or did not know how to drive; many were reluctant to use baby-sitters for their children, only partly for financial reasons. Heterogeneity, then, may be a mixed blessing, particularly on the block, and something can be said for class and age homogeneity.

The alleged costs of homogeneity were also more unreal than the critics claim. It is probably true that Levittowners had less contact with old people than some urbanites (now rather rare) who still live in three-generation households. It is doubtful, however, that they had less contact with the older generation than urban and suburban residents of similar age and class, with the exception of the occupational Transients, who are far from home and may return only once a year. Whether or not this lack of contact with grandparents affects children negatively can only be discovered by systematic studies among them. My observations of children's relations with grandparents suggest that the older generation is strange to them and vice versa, less as a result of lack of contact than of the vastness of generational change.

This is also more or less true of adult relationships with the older generation. Social change in America has been so rapid that the ideas and experiences of the elderly are often anachronistic, especially so for young mobile Levittowners whose parents are first or second generation Americans. Philadelphia women who lived with their parents before they moved to Levittown complained at length about the difficulties of raising children and running a household under those conditions, even though some missed their mothers sorely after moving to Levittown. A few found surrogate mothers among friends or neighbors, but chose women only slightly older than themselves and rarely consulted elderly neighbors. As for the husbands, they were, to a man, glad they had moved away from parents and in-laws.

That suburban homogeneity deprives children of contact with urban pluralism and "reality" is also dubious. Critics assume that urban children experience heterogeneity, but middle class parents—and working class ones, too—try hard to shield them from contact with conditions and people of lower status. Upper middle class children may be taken on tours of the city, but to museums and shopping districts rather than to slums. Indeed, slum children, who are freer of parental supervision, probably see more of urban diversity than anyone else, although they do not often get into middle class areas.

The homogeneity of Levittown is not so pervasive that children are shielded from such unpleasant realities as alcoholism, mental illness, family strife, sexual aberration, or juvenile delinquency which exist everywhere. The one element missing on most Levittown blocks—though, of course, in many city neighborhoods too—is the presence of Negro families. Although young Negro women came from nearby Burlington to work as maids, there were only two Negro families in the three neighborhoods built before Levittown's integration, and about fifty in the three built since then. Most Levittown children are unlikely to see any Negroes around them and will not have real contact with them until they enter junior high school. But it is not at all certain that mere visual exposure—to Negroes or anyone else—encourages learning of pluralism and tolerance. Children pick up many of their attitudes from parents and peers, and these are not neces-

sarily pluralistic. If visual exposure had the positive effects attributed to it, city children, who see more Negroes than suburban children do, should exhibit greater racial tolerance. In
reality they do not; indeed, the middle class child growing up in
a white suburb may be more opposed to segregation than one
raised in an integrated city. This is not a justification for segregation, but a suggestion that visual exposure is no sure means to integration.

A generation of social research has demonstrated that racial
and other forms of integration occur when diverse people can in-
teract frequently in equal and noncompetitive situations.[32] Here
the suburbs are at an advantage when it comes to religious and
ethnic integration, but at a disadvantage for racial and class integration, for aside from residential segregation, suburban high
schools bring together students from a narrower variety of residential areas than do urban ones. Again, mere diversity does not
assure the kind of interaction that encourages integration, and a
school with great diversity but sharp internal segregation may
not be as desirable as one with less diversity but without internal
segregation. Judging by life on the block in Levittown, maximal
diversity and extreme heterogeneity encourage more conflict
than integration, and while conflict can be desirable and even
didactic, this is only true if it can be resolved in some way. People
so different from each other in age or class that they cannot agree
on anything are unlikely to derive much enrichment from heterogeneity.

A corollary of the belief in diversity as a stimulant to enrichment holds that working class and lower class people will benefit—and be improved—by living among middle class neighbors.
Even if one overlooks the patronizing class bias implicit in this
view, it is not at all certain that residential propinquity will produce the intended cultural change. In Levittown, working class
families living alongside middle class ones went their own way
most of the time. For mobile ones, heterogeneity is obviously desirable, provided middle class people are willing to teach them,
but nonmobile ones will react negatively to force feedings of
middle class culture. Neighbors are expected to treat each other
as equals, and working class residents have enough difficulty paying the higher cost of living among middle class people, without
being viewed as culturally deprived. When working class organizations used middle class Levittowners for technical and admin-

istrative services, they rejected those who looked down on them and constantly tested the others to make sure they measured up to the norms of working class culture. For example, at a VFW softball game, two middle class members were razzed unmercifully for their lack of athletic skill. Children are not yet fully aware of class, so that they can be with (and learn from) peers of other classes, and there is some evidence that in schools with a majority of middle class children, working class children will adopt the formers' standards of school performance, and vice versa.[33]

By its very nature, demographic homogeneity is said to be incompatible with democracy, and advocates of diversity have emphasized that a democracy requires a heterogeneous community. However, as the description of Levittown's school and political conflict should indicate, bringing people with different interests together does not automatically result in the use of democratic procedures. Instead, it causes conflict, difficulties in decision-making, and attempts to sidestep democratic norms. If one group is threatened by another's demands, intolerance may even increase. Indeed, democratic procedure is often so fragile that it falls by the wayside under such stress, causing hysteria on the part of residents and the sort of panic on the part of the officials that I described. The fact is that the democratic process probably works more smoothly in a homogeneous population. Absence of conflict is of course a spurious goal, particularly in a pluralistic society, and cannot be used as an argument for homogeneity. On the other hand, unless conflict becomes an end in itself, heterogeneity is not a viable argument for greater democracy.

Critics of the suburbs also inveigh against physical homogeneity and mass-produced housing. Like much of the rest of the critique, this charge is a thinly veiled attack on the culture of working and lower middle class people, implying that mass-produced housing leads to mass-produced lives. The critics seem to forget that the town houses of the upper class in the nineteenth century were also physically homogeneous; that everyone, poor and rich alike, drives mass-produced, homogeneous cars without damage to their personalities; and that today, only the rich can afford custom-built housing. I heard no objection among the Levittowners about the similarity of their homes, nor the popular jokes about being unable to locate one's own house.[34] Esthetic diversity is preferred, however, and people talked about moving to a custom-built house in the future when they could afford it. Meanwhile, they made internal and external alterations in their Levitt house to reduce sameness and to place a personal stamp on their property.[35]

Block Homogeneity and Community Heterogeneity

Putting together all the arguments for and against homogeneity suggests that the optimum solution, at least in communities of homeowners who are raising small children, is *selective homogeneity at the block level* and *heterogeneity at the community level*. Whereas a mixture of population types, and especially of rich and poor, is desirable in the community as a whole, heterogeneity on the block will not produce the intended tolerance, but will lead to conflict that is undesirable because it is essentially insoluble and thus becomes chronic. Selective homogeneity on the block will improve the tenor of neighbor relations, and will thus make it easier—although not easy—to realize heterogeneity at the community level.

By "block" I mean here an area in which frequent face-to-face relations take place, in most cases a *sub-block* of perhaps ten to twelve houses. Selective homogeneity requires enough consensus among neighbors to prevent insoluble conflict, to encourage positive although not necessarily intensive relationships between them, and to make visiting possible for those who want it in the immediate vicinity. If Levittown is at all typical, the crucial factors in homogeneity are age and class. The range of ages and classes that can live together is not so limited, however, as to require tenant selection programs. The voluntary selection pattern that now occurs on the basis of house price is more than sufficient, and as the ghettoization of the poor in public housing suggests, formal and involuntary selection has many serious disadvantages. Besides, it is questionable whether planners have the knowledge to go about planning other people's social relations, and even if they had the knowledge, it is doubtful that they have the right to do so.[36] Of course, selection through house price is also a form of planning, but since it is not directly related to tenants' specific characteristics, it leaves more room for choice.

The emphasis on voluntary selection also copes with another objection to homogeneity, that it crystallizes class divisions and makes people more aware of class differences. Implicit in this objection is the assumption that awareness of class differences is wrong, and that any attempt to use class as a separating criterion is undesirable. This assumption would be defensible if it were part of a larger program to eliminate or at least reduce economic inequities, but it is generally put forth by people who are uncomfortable about the existence of classes and want to solve the problem by avoiding it.

These observations have a number of implications for site planning. Given the boundaries within which neighboring takes place, the significant social unit in the community (at least, in one like Levittown) is the sub-block—which is not a physical unit. Conversely, the neighborhood of several hundred families which city planners have traditionally advocated is socially irrelevant, whatever virtues it may have in defining a catchment area for the elementary school or the neighborhood shopping center. In fact, in order to maximize community heterogeneity, it might be desirable to eliminate the neighborhood unit and plan for a heterogeneous array of homogeneous blocks, each block separated from the next by enough of a real or symbolic barrier to reassure those concerned with property values. This would encourage more heterogeneity in the elementary school and other neighborhood facilities, and would thus contribute significantly to community heterogeneity.[87]

Communities should be heterogeneous because they must reflect the pluralism of American society. Moreover, as long as local taxation is the main source of funds for community services, community homogeneity encourages undesirable inequalities. The high-income community can build modern schools and other high-quality facilities; the low-income community, which needs these facilities more urgently, lacks the tax base to support them. As a result, poor communities elect local governments which neglect public services and restrict the democratic process in the need to keep taxes minimal. Both financial inequity and its political consequences are eliminated more effectively by federal and state subsidy than by community heterogeneity, but so long as municipal services are financed locally, communities must include all income groups.

The criteria on which the advocacy of block homogeneity and community heterogeneity is based cannot justify racial homogeneity at either level. Experience with residential integration in many communities, including Levittown, indicates that it can be achieved without problems when the two races are similar in socioeconomic level and in the visible cultural aspects of class—provided, however, the whites are not beset by status fears. Indeed, the major barrier to effective integration is fear of status deprivation, especially among white working class homeowners. The whites base their fears on the stereotype that nonwhite people are lower class, and make a hasty exodus that reduces not property values but the selling prices that can be obtained by the departing whites. When class differences between the races are great, the exodus is probably unavoidable, but where Negroes and whites have been of equal status, it can be prevented, at least in middle class areas. Yet even if this were not the case, homogeneity is only one value among many, and if any person chooses to move among people who differ in race—or age, income, religion, or any other background characteristic—he has the right to do so and the right to governmental support in his behalf. That such a move might wreak havoc with a block's social life or the community's consensus is of lower priority than the maintenance of such values as freedom of choice and equality. The advantages of residential homogeneity are not important enough to justify depriving anyone of access to housing and to educational and other opportunities.

CONFORMITY AND COMPETITION

The suburban critique is especially strident on the prevalence of conformity. It argues that relationships between neighbors and friends are regulated by the desire to copy each other to achieve uniformity. At the same time, the critics also see suburbanites as competitive, trying to keep up or down with the Joneses to satisfy the desire for status. Conforming (or copying) and competing are not the same—indeed, they are contradictory—but they are lumped together in the critique because they are based on the common assumption that, in the suburbs, behavior and opinion are determined by what the neighbors do and think, and individualism is found only in the city. Both competition and copying exist in Levittown, but not for the reasons suggested by the critics. They are ways of coping with heterogeneity and of retaining individuality while being part of the group. They exist in every group, but are more prevalent among homeowners and, because of the fascination with suburbia, more visible there. But this does not make them suburban phenomena.

Enough of the suburban critique has seeped into the reading matter of Levittowners to make "conformity" a pejorative term, and interview questions about it would have produced only denials. Competition is talked about in Levittown, however, and 60 per cent of the random sample reported competition among their neighbors.[38] The examples they gave, however, not only included copying, but half the respondents described it positively. "I don't know what competition is," said one man. "Perhaps when we see the neighbors repairing the house, and we figure our own repairs would be a good idea." Another put it more enthusiastically: "Friends and neighbors ask me what I've done, and by our visiting different neighbors we get different ideas about fixing up the house—how we are going to paint. Instead of both of us buying an extension ladder, we go half and half."

In effect, diverging or deviant behavior can be seen as competition, conformity, or the chance to learn new ideas, depending on the observer. One who dislikes behavior common to several neighbors may accuse them of copying each other. If the behavior is dissimilar, it must be a result of competition: "keeping up with the Joneses" or "spending beyond one's means." When the behavior is approved, however, it is interpreted as sharing ideas. The observer's perspective is shaped principally by his relative class position, or by his estimate of his position. If the observer is of *higher* status than the observed, he will interpret the latter's attempt to share higher-status ideas as competing, and his sharing of lower status ways as copying. If the observer is of *lower* status than the observed, his ideas will not be shared, of course, but he will consider the more affluent life style of the higher-status neighbor as motivated by status-striving or "keeping up with the Joneses." [39] As one blue collar man put it, "There are some who act so darned important, as if they have so much, and I can't figure out what they are doing in Levittown when they have so much." Another blue collar man who had taught his neighbors about lawn care, and felt himself to be their equal, was not threatened: "One or two try to keep up with the Joneses, but generally people are not worried. If one gets ahead and another copies him, we laugh. Our attitude is, all the more power to him. When we can afford it, we make improvements too." In other words, when the observer feels he is equal to the observed, he will see competing and copying either as sharing or as friendly games. And socially mobile people tend to judge the ways of higher-status people positively, for they can look to their neighbors for guidance about how to live in the suburbs. "Everyone has fixed up their houses, but not to compete," a former city dweller reported. "At first none of us had anything and maybe you saw what others did and you copied it." Needless to say, those who are being copied may consider the mobile neighbor a competing upstart.

Status-striving is generally ascribed to people with more money, more education, and a different life style by those who cannot afford the style or prefer a different one. The same motive is inferred about social relations. Cliques of higher-status people are seen by lower-status observers as groups that coalesce for prestige reasons, and lower-status cliques are viewed by higher-status observers as groups that come together to conform. When relations among neighbors of unequal status deteriorate, the higher-status person explains it in terms of culturally or morally undesirable actions by the lower-status neighbor; the lower-status person ascribes the break to his neighbor's desire to be with more prestigious people. In reality, instances of overt status-striving, carried out to show up the lower status of neighbors, are rare. "Keeping up" takes place, but mainly out of the need to maintain self-respect, to "put the best face forward" or not to be considered inferior and "fall behind." Serious status-striving is usually a desperate attempt by a socially isolated neighbor to salvage self-respect through material or symbolic displays of status, and is dismissed or scorned. One such neighbor was described as "trying to be the Joneses, and hoping people will follow him, but we don't pay any attention to him." Indeed, the social control norms of block life encourage "keeping down with the Joneses," and criticize display of unusual affluence, so that people who can afford a higher standard of living than the rest and who show it publically are unpopular and are sometimes ostracized.[40]

Conforming and copying occur more frequently than competition, mostly to secure the proper appearance of the block to impress strangers. A pervasive system of social control develops to enforce standards of appearance on the block, mainly concerning lawn care.[41] Copying and some competition take place in this process, but neither the Levittowners nor the suburban critics would describe it in these terms. Everyone knows it is social control and accepts the need for it, although one year some of my neighbors and I wished we could pave our front lawns with green concrete to eliminate the endless watering and mowing and to forestall criticism of poor lawns.

The primary technique for social control is humor. Wisecracks are made to show up deviant behavior, and overt criticism surfaces only when the message behind the wisecracks does not get across. Humor is used to keep relations friendly and because people feel that demands for conformity are not entirely proper; they realize that such demands sometimes require a difficult compromise between individual and group standards. When it comes to lawn care, however, most people either have no hard-and-fast personal standards, or they value friendly relations more. Since the block norms and the compromises they require are usually worked out soon after the block is occupied—when everyone is striving to prove he will be a good neighbor—they are taken for granted by the time the block has settled down.

The demand for compromise is also reduced by limiting block standards to the exterior appearance of the front of the house and the front yard, the back being less visible to outsiders. Interiors, which involve the owner's ego more, are not subjected to criticism. People are praised for a nice-looking home, but there are no wisecracks about deviant taste in furnishings—at least, not to the owner. The same limitation holds for cars and other consumer goods purchased. Although I drove a 1952 Chevrolet, by far the oldest car on the block, no one ever joked with me about it,[42] but Levittowners who used trucks in their work and parked them on their streets at night, giving the block the image of a working class district, were criticized by middle class neighbors. The criticism was made behind their backs, however, because it affected the neighbors' source of livelihood. In this case, as in some others, social control was passed on to the township government, and eventually, it voted an ordinance prohibiting truck-parking on residential streets.

What people do inside their houses is considered their own affair, but loud parties, drunkenness, and any other noticeable activities that would give the block a bad reputation are criticized. So are parents who let their children run loose at all hours of the evening, not only because they publicly violate norms of good parenthood, but also because they make it harder for neighbors to put their own children to bed. Private deviant behavior is, of course, gossiped about with gusto, but only when it becomes visible, and repeatedly so, is gossip translated into overt criticism.

Even visible deviance that affects block appearance is tolerated if it is minor and if the individual believes firmly in what he is doing. One Levittowner decided that he would buy a wooden screen door, rather than the popular but more expensive aluminum one. He decided, however, to maintain block uniformity by painting it with aluminum color. "People will think I'm cheap," he told me, "but I don't mind that. I know I'm thrifty." I do not know what people thought, but he was not criticized.

Copying also takes place without being impelled by conformity, and then becomes a group phenomenon that occurs in spurts. When one neighbor builds a patio or repaints his house, others are likely to follow his lead, but not automatically. On my block, for instance, one homeowner repainted his house in 1959 but no one imitated him. When another began to do it the next year, however, a rash of repainting occurred. If this had been simply a copying phenomenon, the painting should have started in 1959, especially since the first painter was a popular community leader. What happened in 1960 is easily explained. By that time, houses built in 1958 needed repainting, and when one man, who had an early vacation, devoted his two weeks to it, other men followed his example when they went on vacation.[43]

People also buy household items and plants they have seen at their neighbors', but only when the item is either widely desired or clearly useful. For example, early in Levittown's history, a rumor spread that the willow trees the builder had planted would eventually root into and crack the sewer pipes, and one man promptly took out his tree. Neighbors who were friends of his followed suit, but others refused to accept the rumor and kept their trees. On my block, the rumor was initiated by a Catholic leader, and within a week, the Catholics had taken out their willow trees, but the others had not followed suit. My own innovation, inexpensive bamboo shades to keep out the blazing sun, was not copied; people said they looked good, but no one imitated me.

COMPETITION, CONFORMITY, AND HETEROGENEITY

Both competition and conformity are ways of coping with heterogeneity, principally of class. When lower-status people are accused of copying and higher-status ones of living beyond their means to impress the neighbors, disapproval is put in terms of negative motives rather than class differences, for accusations of deviant behavior which blame individuals make it more difficult for the deviant to appeal to his group norms. Such accusations also enable people to ignore the existence of class differences. Class is a taboo subject, and the taboo is so pervasive, and so unconscious, that people rarely think in class terms.

Competition and conformity exist also because people are dependent on their neighbors. In working class or ethnic enclaves, where social life is concentrated among relatives, their criticism is feared more than the neighbors'. Upper middle class people, having less to do with neighbors, conform most closely to the demands of their friends. In Levittown, neighbors are an important reference group, not only for lower middle class people but for working class ones cut off from relatives. Even so, the prime cause of both competition and conformity is home ownership and the mutual need to preserve property and status values. Only 11 per cent of former renters but 70 per cent of former homeowners reported noticing competition in their former residence, but both observed it equally in Levittown. Moreover, whether they came from urban or suburban neighborhoods, they reported no more competition in Levittown than in the former residence. Consequently, competition is not distinctive either to Levittown or to the suburbs.

What, then, accounts for the critics' preoccupation with suburban conformity, and their tendency to see status competition as a dominant theme in suburban life? For one thing, many of these critics live in city apartments, where the concern for block status preservation is minimal. Also, they are largely upper middle class professionals, dedicated to cosmopolitan values and urban life and disdainful of the local and antiurban values of lower middle class and working class people. Believing in the universality of these values, the critics refuse to acknowledge the existence of lower middle class or working class ways of living. Instead, they describe people as mindless conformers who would be cosmopolitans if they were not weak and allowed themselves to be swayed by builders, the mass media, and their neighbors.

The ascription of competitive behavior to the suburbs stems from another source. The upper middle class world, stressing as it does individuality, is a highly competitive one. In typically upper middle class occupations such as advertising, publishing, university teaching, law, and the arts, individual achievement is the main key to success, status, and security. The upper middle class is for this reason more competitive and more status-conscious than the other classes. Popular writers studying upper middle class suburbs have observed this competition and some have mistakenly ascribed it to suburbia, rather than to the criteria for success in the professions held by these particular suburbanites.[44] Those writing about lower-status suburbs have either drawn their information from upper middle class friends who have moved to lower middle class suburbs for financial reasons and found themselves a dissatisfied minority, or they have, like upper middle class people generally, viewed the lower-status people about whom they were writing as trying to compete with their betters.

Finally, the new suburbs, being more visible than other lower middle and working class residential areas, have become newsworthy, and during the 1950s they replaced "mass culture" as the scapegoat and most convenient target for the fear and distaste that upper middle class people feel for the rest of the population. Affluent suburbs have become false targets of dissatisfaction with the upper middle class's own status-consciousness and competition, the "rat-race" it experiences in career and social striving having been projected on life beyond the city limits.

The inaccuracy of the critique does not, of course, exclude the possibility that conforming and competing are undesirable or dangerous, or that too much of both take place in Levittown. I do not believe either to be the case. If one distinguishes between *wanted* conformity, as when neighbors learn from each other or share ideas; *tolerated* conformity, when they adjust their own standards in order to maintain friendly relations; and *unwanted* conformity, when they bow to pressure and give up their individuality, only the last is clearly undesirable, and in Levittown it is rare. Tolerated conformity requires some surrender of autonomy, but I can see why Levittowners feel it is more important to be friendly with one's neighbors than to insist on individual but unpopular ways of fixing up the outside of the house. The amount of copying and conformity is hardly excessive, considering the heterogeneity on the block. Indeed, given the random way in which Levittowners become neighbors, it is amazing that neighbor relations were so friendly and tolerant of individual differences. Of course, the working class and upper middle class minorities experience pressure for unwanted conformity, but the latter can get away from the block for social activities, and ultimately, only some of the former suffer. Ironically, their exposure to pressures for conformity is a result of the heterogeneity that the critics want to increase even further.

NOTES

1. These charges can be found, for example, in Henderson, Allen, Keats, and Whyte (1956), Chaps. 25, 26.
2. Neighboring, or visiting with neighbors, was defined in the interview as "having coffee together, spending evenings together, or frequent conversations in or out of the house; anything more than saying hello or polite chatting about the weather." It was further defined as taking place among individuals rather than couples, and people were asked, "Are you, yourself, doing more visiting with neighbors than where you lived before, or less?"
3. Fifty-four per cent of the random sample was neighboring more than in the previous residence; 16 per cent, less; and 30 per cent, the same. Among Philadelphians, the percentages were 48, 19, and 33, respectively.
4. Thus, one third of the least educated in the random sample, and two thirds of the college-educated in the Philadelphia sample reported less neighboring. Jews from smaller towns who had already learned to live with non-Jewish neighbors, and third generation Jewish Philadelphians did not report less neighboring.
5. The principal post-World War II studies are Merton (1947a); Caplow and Foreman; Festinger, Schachter, and Back; Festinger; Dean (1953); Haeberle; Blake et al.; Whyte (1956), Chap. 25; and Willmott (1963), Chap. 7. Critical analyses of these studies can be found in Gans (1961a), pp. 135–137 and Schorr, Chap. 1; of earlier ones, in Rosow.
6. Similar observations were reported in English new towns by Hole, pp. 164–167, and Willmott (1962), pp. 124–126. See also Willmott (1963), pp. 74–82.
7. The initial report on this phenomenon was by Whyte (1956), Chap. 25.
8. On narrower blocks, there was more interaction between backyard neighbors, however.
9. Among Cape Cod owners, 22 per cent visited most often with the right- and left-hand neighbor, and 43 per cent, with the across-the-street neighbor. Among the ranch owners, the percentages were 46, 23, and 23, respectively; and among the Colonial ones, 30, 35, 30. The remaining visits were with yet other neighbors across the street or backyard.
10. If the location of the kitchen window had been significant, women

in Cape Cod houses should have visited most often across the street, and 50 per cent did, as compared to 17 and 25 per cent with the right- and left-hand neighbor, respectively. Those in ranch houses should have visited most with the right-hand and backyard neighbors, but none chose the former, 17 per cent the latter, 33 per cent the left-hand neighbor, and 50 per cent the one across the street. Those in Colonial houses should also have chosen the backyard neighbor, but only 11 per cent did; 44 per cent preferred the right-hand one, and 22 per cent each the left-hand and the across-the-street neighbor.

11. Thirty-one per cent said more than two favorite couples lived on their street, and the remaining 38 per cent, less than two. As might be expected, college-educated respondents chose even fewer friends from their own street. Using street addresses actually overstated the role of propinquity, for not all people on the same street—especially if it was a long one—are neighbors, and several first met such couples in church or in a club. A study of an Irish new town reported 31 per cent of the best friends were neighbors, See Field and Desmond, p. 54.

12. Southworth.

13. This relationship varies with age, of course, and older children do not choose propinquitous playmates as often. Olsen's study of children's birthday parties reported in the Levittown newspaper showed that among three-year-olds, guests came from a median distance of 364 feet; 775 feet among four-year-olds, 1130 feet among seven-year-olds. The distance then remained fairly stable until it rose to about 2000 feet among twelve- and thirteen-year-olds.

14. A study of newcomers in an old suburb suggests that teenagers may even react to class conflict that is limited to parents. "If a family is scapegoated, the youngsters will soon turn up in some mischief or as delinquents." Thoma and Lindemann, p. 193.

15. Class conflicts among neighbors in Levittown, New York, are described by Dobriner (1963), pp. 107–108; in English new towns by Young and Willmott, Chap. 10, and by Willmott (1963), p. 114.

16. The social isolation of suburban working class women and better-educated ones with distinctive tastes is also reported by Gutman, pp. 174, 181–182. See also Haeberle, Chap. 7.

17. Although only 20 per cent of the random sample reported cliques on their blocks, all were Jewish ones, with one exception.

18. Jews often move into communities where the median income is lower than their own, partly because some prefer to spend a lower share of their income on housing, partly because they fear rejection from non-Jewish neighbors of similar income and education.

19. The sexual overtones did not affect my interviewing, because strangers were exempt. Women are permitted to have latent sexual interest in casual encounters—giving rise to jokes about the iceman and the milkman—and only neighbors' husbands are taboo.

20. People were asked about "the visiting you and your husband (wife) do with other couples, either among neighbors or anywhere else in Levittown.

21. Forty-four per cent of the random sample reported more couple visiting; 21 per cent, less; and 35 per cent, no change. Among the Philadelphians, the percentages were almost the same: 39, 22, and 39, respectively. In a new working class suburb, 38 per cent said "they entertain friends at home" more often than before, but 27 per cent reported less. See Berger (1960), p. 65.

22. Fifty per cent of organizational members and 27 per cent of non-members reported more couple visiting. So did 83 per cent of the Jews in the random sample, and 53 per cent in the city sample, as compared to 30 per cent and 17 per cent of the Protestants. The association between visiting and organizational activity was also found in Levittown, Pennsylvania by Jahoda et al., p. 107.

23. Among Philadelphians of mixed marriage, only 20 per cent reported an increase, and 60 per cent a decrease in couple visiting after leaving the city. Sixteen per cent in both samples were intermarriages, usually of Catholics with Protestants.

24. See, e.g., Whyte (1956), Chap. 21.

25. Low-status respondents have as many friends as middle- and high-status ones, but the former do less couple visiting than in the previous residence.

26. The neighbors I knew best in the West End of Boston had open house every Tuesday night, visited the open house of relatives every Friday night, and visited with yet other relatives and friends on Sundays.

27. Much of this section is taken from Gans (1961b).

28. For an incisive critique of the balanced community ideal, see Orlans, pp. 88–94.

29. For a description of this trend in the first Levittown, see Liell (1963). See also Willmott (1963), p. 23.

30. For similar findings in Fairless Hills, Pennsylvania, see Haeberle, p. 75.

31. Forty-four per cent said they had done "much" visiting with ethnic or religious peers in Philadelphia, and 52 per cent, "some." In Levittown, the percentages shifted slightly, to 37 and 66, respectively. Respondents were free to define what they considered "much" or "some." Jews and low-status people reported the most ethnic-religious visiting; Irish Catholics, the greatest increase after moving to Levittown.

32. See, e.g., Williams, pp. 437–447.

33. See, e.g., Wilson, but also the study by Sewell and Armer which questioned the impact of "neighborhood context" on educational aspirations. Of course, in school students are a captive audience, and school contacts among working and middle class students may evaporate after school hours.

34. A study of a Scottish new town reported that "only one-fifth of

the tenants said they would prefer more variety and intermixture of house-types, while two-fifths regarded the row of identical buildings as a desirable feature," and that "a house which is one of many in a street can become personalized without much aid from the architect." See Hole, p. 169.

35. It is illuminating to compare the early popular writing about Levittown, New York, to more recent reports. Initially, the Long Island community was widely described (and decried) as a hideous example of mass-produced housing which would soon turn into a slum; twenty years later, journalists report the diversity produced by the alteration of houses, and the charm created by the maturing of trees and shrubbery—and, of course, the demand for the houses, which now sell for about twice their original price.

36. Orlans, pp. 95–104, and Whyte (1956), pp. 348–349.

37. A similar solution has been proposed in England by Willmott (1963), pp. 117–118. See also Dean (1958).

38. People were asked, "What kind of competition have you noticed between the neighbors about such things as getting things for the house, fixing up the yard, or repainting the house?"

39. Forty-four per cent of the blue collar respondents reported "keeping up with the Joneses" among their neighbors, but only 31 per cent of the white collar and professional ones did so. In an English working class new town, 26 per cent made similar complaints, principally lower-income people about those with higher incomes. Willmott (1963), p. 98.

40. Whyte (1956), Chap. 24.

41. Meyersohn and Jackson, p. 281.

42. In fact, I was more often praised for having taken good care of the car, for my thrift, and for my good luck in possessing a better car than the more recent models.

43. Copying took place only when someone decided to paint his house another color. Since this violated a deed-restriction, people waited for someone to break the rules and then followed suit quickly—but they did not copy the initiator's color scheme.

44. See, e.g., Spectorsky.

Chapter Nine

THE VITALITY OF COMMUNITY CULTURE

LEADING WITH THEIR ASSUMPTION OF HOMOGENEITY AND CONFORM-
ity, many critics see the culture of communities like Levittown—
those features transcending social life—as marked by sameness,
dullness, and blandness. The image of sameness derives from the
mass-produced housing, and also from the prevalence of a national and equally mass-produced culture of consumer goods which is
extended to characterize the consumers themselves. Part of the
critique is tinged with political fear that the national culture
and the deleterious effects of conformity may sap the strength
of local organizations, which will in turn break down the community social structures that act as barriers between the individual and the state. According to theorists of the mass society, the
individual then becomes submissive and subject to demagoguery
that can incite mass hysteria and mob action, destroying the
checks and balances of a democratic society. This hypothesis, developed originally by Ortega y Gasset, the Spanish conservative
philosopher who feared popular democracy, gained prominence
during the 1930s when Hitler and Stalin systematically eliminated local organizations to forestall opposition to their plans.
In America, this analysis has flowered with the increasing central-
ization of the federal government, but suburbia is considered
particularly susceptible to the dangers of mass society because of
the rootlessness and absence of community strength supposedly
induced by the large number of Transients.[1] Other observers,

less fearful of mass society, stress and blandness of suburban life, which, they fear, is producing dull and apathetic individuals.[2]

These charges are serious and, if accurate, would suggest that suburbia is a danger to American democracy and culture. Most of them, however, are either inaccurate or, when accurate, without the negative consequences attributed to them. Levittown is very much a local community; if anything, it neglects its ties to the larger society more than it should. It is not rootless, even with its Transients, and it is not dull, except to its teenagers. The critics' conclusions stem in part from the previously mentioned class and cultural differences between them and the suburbanites. What they see as blandness and apathy is really a result of the invisibility and home-centeredness of lower middle class culture, and what they consider dullness derives from their cosmopolitan standard for judging communities, which condemns those lacking urban facilities—ranging from museums to ethnic districts—that are favored by the upper middle class.

They also look at suburbia as outsiders, who approach the community with a "tourist" perspective. The tourist wants visual interest, cultural diversity, entertainment, esthetic pleasure, variety (preferably exotic), and emotional stimulation. The resident, on the other hand, wants a comfortable, convenient, and socially satisfying place to live—esthetically pleasing, to be sure, but first and foremost functional for his daily needs. Much of the critique of suburbia as community reflects the critics' disappointment that the new suburbs do not satisfy their particular tourist requirements; that they are not places for wandering, that they lack the charm of a medieval village, the excitement of a metropolis, or the architectural variety of an upper-income suburb. Even so, tourism cuts across all classes. A neighbor, returning from a trip to Niagara Falls, complained bitterly about commercialization, using much the same language as the critics do about suburbia. What he felt about the Falls, however, he did not feel about Levittown.

We are all tourists at one time or another, but most communities can serve both tourist and residential functions only with difficulty. For example, the crowding and nightlife that attract the tourist to Greenwich Village make it uncomfortable for the resident. Although the tourist perspective is understandable, and even justifiable, it is not by itself a proper criterion for evaluating a community, especially a purely residential one like Levittown. It must be judged first by the quality of community life and culture it offers its residents; the needs of the tourist are secondary.

THE NATIONAL CULTURE AND THE COMMUNITY

To the outside observer, Levittown appears to be a community on which the national American culture has been imprinted so totally as to leave little room for local individuality. The houses express the current national residential style: pseudo-Colonial fronts borrowed from the eighteenth century glued on a variety of single-family house styles developed between the eighteenth and twentieth centuries, and hiding twentieth century interiors. Schools are contemporary, modular, one-story buildings that look like all other new schools. The shopping center is typical too, although the interior is more tastefully designed than most. It consists mainly of branches of large national chains, whose inventory is dominated by prepackaged national brands, and the small centers are no different. The old "Mom and Pop" grocery has been replaced by the "7 to 11" chain, which, as its name indicates, opens early and closes late, but sells only prepackaged goods so that each store can be serviced by a single cashier-clerk. Even the Jewish and Italian foods sold at the "delis" are cut from the loaf of a "pan-ethnic" culture that is now nationally distributed.

A large, partially preplanned residential development must almost inevitably depend on national organizations, since these are the only ones that can afford the initial capital investment and the unprofitable hiatus before the community is large enough to support them properly. This is as true of stores in a new shopping center—which sometimes wait years before they show a profit—as it is of churches and voluntary organizations. In addition, Levittown itself is in some ways a national brand, for the size of Levitt's operation in an industry of small entrepreneurs has made his communities a national symbol of low-price suburbia. This has helped to attract national organizations, as well as Transients who work for large national corporations. When they move into a new metropolitan area, they usually do not know where to find housing, and having heard of Levittown, are likely to look there first. The brand name "Levittown" makes the housing more trustworthy than a small subdivision constructed by an unknown local builder.

Although Levittown would thus seem to be, as much as any community in America, an example of Big Culture, this is only superficially true, for the quality of life in Levittown retains a strictly local and often antinational flavor, exploiting national bodies and resources for strictly local purposes whenever possible. To the visitor, the Levittown houses may look like all other pseudo-Colonial ones in South Jersey, but Levittowners can catalog the features that distinguish their houses from those in nearby subdivisions. The stores may be chains selling brand-name goods, but the managers become involved in local activities and enable local groups to hold bazaars and other fund-raising affairs, including bakesales which compete with store merchandise. The same patterns obtain in voluntary associations and churches. For example, the Boy Scouts are run by an intricate national bureaucracy which sets detailed rules for the activities of local troops. Since the organization must attract children, however, what actually goes on at troop meetings bears little resemblance to the rules, and the less the national office knows, the better for it and the troop leader.

The priority of local concerns is even more emphatic in government, for federal agencies and national party headquarters are viewed mainly as sources of funds and power to be used for local needs. A civil defense agency was set up in Levittown, not to satisfy national regulations, but because the county civil defense director was running for political office. The national program provided him an opportunity to distribute some funds to local communities, which in turn enhanced his political fortunes. Federal funds which came to Levittown for civil defense were used for local police and fire needs as much as possible within the limits of the law. Similarly, when the Township Committee in 1960 invited both Nixon and Kennedy to campaign in Levittown, its purpose was not to support the national candidates of the two parties but to gain publicity for Levittown.

Many Levittowners work in branch offices or factories of national corporations, and their reports about their work and their employers suggest that national directives are often viewed as outlandish and unreasonable, to be sabotaged in favor of local priorities. However much a national corporation may give the appearance of a well-run and thoroughly centralized monolith, in actual fact it is often a shaky aggregate of local baronies. The result is considerable skepticism among Levittowners about the effectiveness and power of national corporations, a skepticism easily extended to all national agencies.

Generally speaking, Levittowners do not take much interest in the national society, and rarely even see its influence on their lives. As long as they are employed, healthy, and able to achieve a reasonable proportion of their personal goals, they have no need for the federal government or any other national agency, and being locals, they do not concern themselves with the world outside their community. Indeed, they might better be described as *sublocals,* for they are home-oriented rather than community-oriented. Although the lower middle class is sometimes said to reject bigness, the Levittowners do not share this feeling. They do not scorn big supermarkets and national brands as do the critics, and although they do not see the big society very clearly, it appears to them as an inept octopus which can only cope with the community through force or bribery. It is opposed not because of its size, but because it is an outsider. When a national service club organized a branch in Levittown, one of the Levittowners said, "They are big and they can help us, but we don't have to follow national policy. . . . National headquarters is only a racket that takes your money." The cultural orientation toward localism is supported by more pressing sociological factors; if a local branch of a national association is to succeed, it must adapt itself to local priorities in order to attract members, and national headquarters must be opposed if it refuses to go along. The most disliked outsider is not the national society, however, but the cosmopolitan with his "Brookline values."

All this does not, of course, imply that the national society and culture are powerless in Levittown. When industrial giants set administered prices for consumer goods sold in the local shopping center, or when Detroit engineers the annual style change in its automobiles, the individual purchaser can only express his discontent by refusal to buy, and when it comes to necessities, he lacks even that choice. In Levittown, however, the discontent and the lack of choice are minimized, for most people have enough money to pay administered prices and enough freedom to choose among products. In fact, they find themselves well served by the corporations who sell them their housing, food, furnishings, and transportation. However, Levittowners are less concerned with "consumption" than the critics. They care less about the things they buy and are less interested in asserting individuality through consumer behavior, for they do not use consumption to express class values as much as the upper middle class does. They may not like mass-produced bread as well as the local bakery product they perhaps ate in childhood, but they do not make an issue of it, and do not feel themselves to be mass men simply because they buy a mass-produced item. Goods are just not important enough. Only when they become tourists are they "materialistic"—and traditional. One of my neighbors who was once stationed in Japan was not at all concerned about the national prepackaged brands sold in Levittown, but talked frequently about the commercialization of Japanese culture and the unattractive goods he found in the souvenir shops.

The Mass Media

For Levittowners, probably the most enduring—and certainly the most frequent—tie to the national culture is through the mass media. Yet even this is filtered through a variety of personal predispositions so that not many messages reach the receiver intact. Few people are dominated by the mass media; they provide escape from boredom, fill up brief intervals, and (perhaps most important) occupy the children while the adults go about their business.

The most frequently used mass medium is television, with newspapers, magazines, and paperback novels following in that order. In working class homes in Levittown as elsewhere, the TV set is likely to be on all the time, even when company comes, for as one Levittowner explained, "If conversation lags, people can watch or it gives you something to talk about." This statement suggests more the fears that working class people have about their social skills than their practice, for conversation does not often lag, at least among friends.

Middle class people, surer of their social skills, use television more selectively. The children watch when they have come in from play; after they are put to bed the adults may turn on the set, for television fills the hours between 9 P.M. and bedtime, when there is not enough of a block of time for other activities. A few favorite programs may get rapt attention, but I doubt that television supplanted conversation among either middle or working class Levittowners. There is no indication that television-viewing increased after people moved to Levittown, for no one mentioned it when interviewed about changes in spare-time activities. I suspect that viewing had actually decreased somewhat, at least during the time of my study, when gardening was still a time-consuming novelty for many people.

Television viewing is also a much less passive activity than the critics of the mass media suspect.[3] Routine serials and situation comedies evoke little response, although Levittowners are sensitive to anachronisms in the plots and skeptical of advertising claims.[4] Dramatic programs may provoke spirited—and quite personal—reactions. For example, one evening my neighbors and I watched an hour-long drama which depicted the tragic career of an introverted girl who wanted desperately to become a serious actress but was forced to work as a rock-and-roll dancer, and finally decided to give up show business. One neighbor missed the tragedy altogether, and thought the girl should have kept on trying to become an actress. The other neighbor fastened on— and approved of—the ending (in which the actress returned to her husband and to the family restaurant in which she had been "discovered") and wondered, rightly, whether it was possible to go back to a mundane life after the glamor of the entertainment world.

People do not necessarily know what they want from the media, but they know what they do not want and trust their ability to choose correctly. A discussion of television critics one night revealed that Levittowners read their judgments, but do not necessarily accept them. "The critics see so much that they cannot give us much advice," said one. "They are too different in their interests from the audience, and cannot be reviewers for it," said another.

Forty per cent of the people interviewed said they were reading new magazines since moving to Levittown; general-interest periodicals—*Life, Look, Reader's Digest, Time,* and the *Saturday Evening Post*—led the list. Only 9 of the 52 magazines were house-and-garden types such as *American Home* and *Better Homes and Gardens,* but then 88 per cent of the people were already reading these, at least in the year they moved to Levittown. Although not a single person said these magazines had helped in the decision to buy a home in Levittown, 57 per cent reported that they had gotten ideas from the magazines to try out in their houses, primarily on the use of space, furniture, and shrubbery arrangements, what to do about pictures and drapes, and how to build shelves and patios. The magazines provided help on functional rather than esthetic problems of fixing up the new house. People rarely copied something directly from the magazines, however. Most often, their reading gave them ideas which they then altered for their own use, sometimes after talking them over with the neighbors. Similarly, people who adopted new furniture styles after moving to Levittown got their inspiration from their neighbors rather than from magazines, although all who changed styles (but only 53 per cent who did not) said they had obtained some hints for the house from the home and garden magazines.

The media also provide "ideas" for community activities, but these are altered by local considerations and priorities. For example, a few days after the Nixon-Kennedy television debates in 1960, candidates for township offices were asked to participate in a similar debate in Levittown. Everyone liked the idea, but after a few innocuous questions by out-of-town reporters, the debate turned into the traditional candidates' night, in which politicians from both parties baited their opponents from the audience with prepared questions. Sometimes, local organizations put on versions of TV quiz games, and honored retiring officers with a "This Is Your Life" presentation. A few clubs, especially Jewish ones, held "beatnik" parties, but since most Levittowners had never seen a beatnik, the inspiration for their costumes came from the mass media.

The impact of the media is most apparent among children; they are easily impressed by television commercials, and mothers must often fight off their demands on shopping trips. But the adults are seldom touched deeply; media content is always secondary to more personal experience. For example, people talked about articles on child-rearing they had seen in popular magazines, but treated them as topics of conversation rather than as possible guides for their own behavior. A neighbor who had read that "permissive" child-rearing was going out of style after thirty years had never even heard of it before, even though she had gone to college. I remember discussing Cuba with another neighbor, an Air Force officer, shortly after Castro confiscated American property there. Although he had been telling me endless and angry stories about being exploited by his superiors and about corruption among high-ranking officers, he could not see the similarity between his position and that of the Cuban peasant under Batista, and argued strenuously that Castro should be overthrown. His opinions reflected those of the media, but their content did not interest him enough to relate it to his own experiences. He did, however, feel that Castro had insulted the United States—and him personally—and the media helped him belong to the national society in this way. Indeed, the media are a message from that society, which, like all others, remains separate from the more immediate realities of self, family, home, and friends. These messages really touch only the people who feel isolated from local groups or who, like the cosmopolitans, pay close attention to the printed word and the screen image.

Levittown and the Mass Society

The Levittowners' local orientation will not prevent them from becoming submissive tools of totalitarian demagogues if, according to the critics of mass society, the community is too weak to defy the power of the state. Social scientists concerned about the danger of dictatorship have often claimed, with De Toqueville, that the voluntary association is the prime bulwark against it. For example, Wilensky writes: "In the absence of effective mediating ties, of meaningful participation in voluntary associations, the population becomes vulnerable to mass behavior, more susceptible to personality appeals in politics, more ready for the demagogues who exploit fanatical faiths of nation and race." [5]

If Wilensky is correct, Levittowners should be invulnerable to mass behavior, for they have started about a hundred voluntary associations and 73 per cent of the two interview samples belong to at least one. Levittown should also be more immune than other communities, for about half of both interview samples reported more organizational participation than in the former residence.[6] The way they participate, however, has little consequence for their relation to the national society. The handful of leaders and really active people become familiar with the mechanics of organizational and municipal politics, but the rank-and-file members, coming to meetings mainly for social and service reasons, are rarely involved in these matters. Yet not even the active participants are exposed to national issues and questions, and they learn little about the ways of coping with the manipulatory techniques feared by the critics of mass society.

Nor does participation necessarily provide democratic experience. Organizations with active membership are likely to have democratic politics, but when the membership is passive, they are

often run by an individual or a clique and there is little demand
for democratic procedure. Nothing in the nature of the voluntary association would, however, preclude mob behavior and
mass hysteria when the members demand it. The ad hoc groups
that arose during the school budget fight and in the controversies
over liquor, nonresident doctors, and fluoridation, often acted in
near-hysterical ways. Admittedly, these were temporary organizations; permanent ones, conscious of their image, are more likely
to refrain from such behavior and, like political parties, often
avoid taking stands on controversial issues. They do inhibit mob
action—or, rather, they refuse to be associated with it, forcing it
into temporary organizations. Yet if the majority of a permanent
group's membership is angry about an issue, it can act out that
anger and even put its organizational strength behind hysteria.
At the time of racial integration, a sizeable faction in one of the
men's groups was contemplating quasi-violent protest, and was
restrained as much by pressure from the churches, the builder,
and some government officials as by cooler heads within the
group.

Mob action and mass hysteria are usually produced by intense
clashes of interest between citizens and government agencies, especially if government is not responsive to citizens' demands. If
an issue is especially threatening and other avenues for coping
with it are blocked, irrational action is often the only solution.
Under such conditions, voluntary associations can do little to
quell it, partly because they have no direct role in the government, but mainly because their impact on their membership is,
in Wilensky's terms, not meaningful enough to divert members
from affiliating with violent protest groups. Even national officers
of voluntary associations can rarely control irrational actions by
local branches, especially since these rarely come to "national's"
attention.

The other relationships of the individual Levittowner vis-à-vis
the national society are so indirect that it would be hard to pin-
point where and how the two confront each other. It would be
harder still to convince the average Levittowner, locally oriented
as he is, to change his stance. Unlike the aristocrat or the intellectual, who was once able as an individual to influence the national society and still attempts to do so, the Levittowners come
from a tradition—and from ancestors—too poor or too European
even to conceive the possibility that they could affect their na-

tion. And unlike the cosmopolitans of today, they have not yet learned that they ought to try. As a result, the Levittowner is not likely to act unless and until national issues impinge directly on his life. When this does happen, he is as frustrated as the cosmopolitan about how to be effective. All he can really do is voice his opinion at the ballot box, write letters to his congressman, or join protest groups. In times of crisis, none of these can change the situation quickly enough, and this of course exacerbates threat, hysteria, and the urge toward mob action or scapegoating.

The national society and the state have not impinged negatively on the average Levittowner, however; indeed, they have served him well, making him generally content with the status quo. The Congress is dominated by the localistic and other values of the white lower middle and working class population, and since the goods and services provided by the influential national corporations are designed largely for people like the Levittowners, they have little reason to question corporate behavior. The considerable similarity of interests between Levittowners and the nationally powerful agencies, private and public, makes it unnecessary for the Levittowners to concern themselves with the national society or to delude themselves about the sovereignty of the local community.[7]

What appears as apathy to the critics of suburban life is satisfaction with the way things are going, and what is interpreted as a "retreat" into localism and familism is just ahistorical thinking. Most lower middle and working class people have always been localistic and familistic; even during the Depression they joined unions only when personal economic difficulties gave them no other alternative, becoming inactive once these were resolved or when it was clear that political activity was fruitless.[8] Indeed, the alleged retreat is actually an advance, for the present generation, especially among working class people, is less isolated from the larger society than its parents, less suspicious, and more willing to believe that it can participate in the community and the larger society. The belief is fragile and rarely exercised, but people like the Levittowners confront the national society more rationally than their ancestors did, and if the signs of progress are few, progress has nevertheless taken place. Whether there has been enough progress to prevent the emergence of dictatorship in a severe national crisis is hard to tell, but certainly the Levit-

towners and their community fit few of the prerequisites that
would make them willing tools of totalitarian leaders today.

TRANSIENCE AND ROOTLESSNESS

Part of the fear of mass society theorists and suburban critics
alike is the transience of the new suburban communities and the
feelings of rootlessness that allegedly result. About 20 per cent of
Levittown's first purchasers were Transients, who knew even
when they came that their employers—national corporations or
the armed services—would require them to move elsewhere some
years hence. Their impermanency is reflected in residential turnover figures which showed that in 1964, 10 percent of the houses
were resold and another 5 per cent rented, and that annual turnover was likely to reach 20 per cent in the future.[9] Not all houses
change hands that often, of course; a small proportion are
sold and rented over and over again.[10] Much of the initial turnover resulted from job transfers—55 per cent in 1960, with another 10 per cent from job changes.[11]

Whether or not the 15 per cent turnover figure is "normal" is
difficult to say. National estimates of mobility suggest that 20 per
cent of the population moves annually, but this figure includes
renters. Levittown's rate is probably high in comparison to older
communities of home owners, fairly typical of newer ones, and
low in comparison to apartment areas.[12] Conventional standards
of "normal" turnover are so old and communities like Levittown
still so new on the American scene that it is impossible to determine a normal turnover rate. Indeed, the need to judge turnover
stems from the assumption that it is undesirable; once there are
sufficient data to test this assumption, the concept of normal
turnover can perhaps be dismissed.

The crucial element in turnover is not its extent but the
change in population composition and its consequences. If the
departing Transients and Mobiles are replaced by Settlers, then
turnover will of course be reduced. Early in the 1960s, the second
buyers were, however, also Transients, who needed a house more
quickly than the builder could supply it, as well as people of
lower income (probably Settlers) who could not afford the down
payment on a new house. If more of the latter come to Levittown
over the years, the proportion of lower-status people in the community will increase, and there may be fears of status loss among

those of higher status. Although such fears were rare during my time in the community, they existed on a few blocks and may account in part for the strong reactions to status-depriving governmental actions that I described earlier.

Despite the belief that Transients do not participate in community life, in Levittown they belonged to community organizations in considerably larger numbers than Settlers did, partly because of their higher status.[13] More of them also reported increased participation after moving to Levittown than did Settlers.[14] They were, however, likely to list fewer people with whom they visited frequently.[15] Their organizational activity is not surprising, for being used to transience, they are socially quite stable, usually gravitating to the same kinds of communities and joining the same kinds of organizations in them. In fact, their mobility has provided them with more organizational experience than other Levittowners have, enabling them to help found several groups in the community.

It has often been charged that modern transience and mobility deprive people of "roots." Because of the botanical analogy, the social conception of the word is difficult to define, but it generally refers to a variety of stable roles and relationships which are recognized by other residents. Traditionally, these roles were often defined by one's ancestors as well. Such roots are hard to maintain today and few people can resist the temptation of social or occupational mobility that requires a physical move. This does not mean, however, that the feeling of rootedness has disappeared. One way in which Transients maintain it is to preserve the term "home" for the place in which they grew up. When Levittowners talk of "going home," they mean trips to visit parents. People whose parents have left the community in which they grew up may, however, feel homeless. I remember a discussion with a Levittowner who explained that he was going "home to Ohio" to visit his mother, and his wife said somewhat sadly, "My parents no longer live where I grew up, and I never lived with them where they live now. So I have only Sudberry Street in Levittown; I have no other home." Because they were Transients, she could not think of Levittown as home and, like many others, looked forward to the day when her husband's occupational transience would come to an end and they would settle down.

Such Transients obviously lack roots in an objective sense and may also have feelings of rootlessness. My impression is that these feelings are not intense or frequent. One way they are coped with is by moving to similar communities and putting down temporary roots; another, by joining organizations made up of fellow Transients.[16] Professionals who are transient often develop roots in their profession and its social groups. As Melvin Webber and others have argued, occupational or functional roots are replacing spatial roots for an ever increasing proportion of the population.[17] This kind of rootedness is easier for men to establish than for women, and wives, especially the wives of professionals, often suffer more from transience than their husbands. Some become attached to national voluntary associations—as men in nonprofessional occupations do—and develop roots within them. This is not entirely satisfactory, however, for it provides feelings of rootedness in only a single role, whereas spatial rootedness cuts across all roles, and rewards one for what one is rather than for what one does.

New communities like Levittown make it possible for residents, even Transients, to put down roots almost at once. People active in organizations become known quickly; thus they are able to feel part of the community. Despite Levittown's size, shopkeepers and local officials get to know people they see regularly, offering the feeling of being recognized to many. The ministers take special care to extend such recognition, and the churches appoint themselves to provide roots—and deliberately, for it attracts people to the church. Protestant denominations sought to define themselves as small-town churches with Colonial style buildings because these have been endowed with an image of rootedness.

Intergenerational rootedness is seldom found today in any suburban or urban community—or, for that matter, in most small towns—for it requires the kind of economic stability (and even stagnancy) characteristic only of depressed areas of the country. Moreover, the romanticizing of this type of rootedness ignores the fact that for many people it blocked progress, especially for low-status persons who were, by reason of residence and ancestry, permanently defined as "shiftless" or "good for nothing." Roots can strangle growth as well as encourage it.

Transience and mobility are something new in middle class American life, and like other innovations, they have been greeted by predictions of undesirable consequences, on family life, school performance, and mental health, for example. Interviews with school officials, doctors, and policemen indicated, however, that Transients appeared no more often as patients and police or school problems and delinquents than other Levittowners. Transience *can* create problems, but it has different effects for different people. For young men, a transfer usually includes a promotion or a raise; for older ones it may mean only another physical move or a transfer to a corporate "Siberia." If a Transient is attached to his home, but is asked to move by his company, he can say "no" only once or twice before being asked to resign or face relegation to the list of those who will not be promoted further. The move from one place to another is a pleasure for few families, but the emotional costs can easily be overestimated.[18] Because Transients move to and from similar types of communities, they have little difficulty adapting themselves to their new homes. In large corporations, they generally receive advice about where to look for housing, often going to areas already settled by colleagues who help them make the residential transition.

Frequent moving usually hurts other family members more than the breadwinner. Wives who had made good friends in Levittown were especially sad to go, and adolescents object strenuously to leaving their peers, so that parents generally try to settle down before their children enter high school. For wives and adolescents transience is essentially an involuntary move, which, like the forced relocation of slum dwellers under urban renewal, may result in depression and other deleterious effects.[19] Transience may also engender difficulties when problems of social mobility antedate or accompany it, as in the case of older corporate employees who must transfer without promotion, or suburbanites who move as a result of downward or extremely rapid upward social mobility.[20] Studies among children of Army personnel, who move more often than corporation Transients, have found that geographical mobility per se did not result in emotional disturbance,[21] except among children whose fathers had risen from working class origins to become officers.[22]

These findings would suggest that transience has its most serious effects on people with identity problems. The individual who lacks a fairly firm sense of his identity will have difficulties in coping with the new experiences he encounters in moving. He will also suffer most severely from rootlessness, for he will be hindered in developing the relationships and reference groups that strengthen one's identity. This might explain why adolescents find moving so difficult. Transients without roots in their community of origin or their jobs must rely on their family members in moments of stress. Sometimes, the family becomes more cohesive as a result, but since stresses on one family member are likely to affect all others, the family is not always a reliable source of support. If identity problems are also present, the individual may have no place to turn, and then transience can produce the *anomie* that critics have found rampant in the suburbs. But such people are a small minority in Levittown.

THE VITALITY OF LEVITTOWN: THE ADULT VIEW

When the Levittowners were asked whether they considered their community dull, just 20 per cent of the random sample said yes, and of Philadelphians (who might have been expected to find it dull after living in a big city), only 14 per cent.[23] Many respondents were surprised at the very question, for they thought there was a great deal to do in the community, and all that was needed was a desire to participate. "It's up to you," was a common reaction. "If a person is not the friendly type or does not become active, it's their own fault." "I don't think it's dull here," explained another, "there are so many organizations to join." Some people noted that Levittown was short of urban amusements, but it did not bother them. A former Philadelphian pointed out: "If Levittown is compared to city living, there are no taverns or teenage hangout places. Then it is dull. But we never had any of this in our own neighborhood and it's even better here. . . . We are perfectly content here, I'm afraid. Social life is enough for us; we are becoming fuddy-duddy." Nostalgia for urban places was not common; most people felt like the one who said, "We like quiet things . . . visiting, sitting out front in summer, having people dropping by." And if Levittown seemed quiet to some, it did not to others. "This is the wildest place I've ever been. Every weekend a party, barbecues, picnics, and things like that. I really enjoy it."[24] The only people who thought Levittown was indeed dull were the socially isolated, and upper middle class people who had tasted the town's organizational life and found it wanting.

What Levittowners who enjoy their community are saying

is that they find vitality in other people and organizational activities; the community is less important. That community may be dull by conventional standards (which define vitality by urban social mixture and cultural riches) but Levittowners reject these standards; they do not want or need that kind of vitality or excitement. Mothers get their share of it from the daily adventures of their children and the men get it at work. The threshold for excitement is low, and for many, excitement is identified with conflict, crisis, and deprivation. Most Levittowners grew up in the Depression, and remembering the hard times of their childhood, they want to protect themselves and their children from stress.

Another difference in values between critics and Levittowners is at play here. The Italians who lived in the center city working class neighborhood I studied before Levittown were bored by "the country"—in which they included the suburbs—and so are critics of suburbia, albeit for different reasons. Many working class city dwellers enjoy street life and urban eating or drinking places; upper middle class critics like crowds and cosmopolitanism. The lower middle class and the kinds of working class people that came to Levittown had no interest in either. Even previous urbanites had made little if any use of the cultural facilities valued by the cosmopolitan, and had no need for them in the suburbs. And as the struggles over the liquor issue suggest, they want none of the vitality sought by the working class urbanite, for they are just escaping corner bars and the disadvantages of aging urban areas. What they do want is a kind of interpersonal vitality along with privacy and peace and quiet.[25] Vicarious excitement is something else again. Television provides programmed and highly predictable excitement, but it can get boring. A fire or accident, a fight at a municipal or school board meeting, and marital strife or minor misbehavior among neighbors involve real people and known ones. The excitement they provide is also vicarious, but it is not programmed and is therefore more rewarding.

The Blandness of Lower Middle Class Culture

Levittown's criteria for vitality may spell dullness to the critic and the visitor, partly because much of community life is invisible. Lower middle class life does not take place either on the street or in meetings and parties; it is home-centered and private.

Once one penetrates behind the door, however, as does the participant-observer, people emerge as personalities and few are
either dull or bland. But when all is said and done, something is
different: less exuberance than is found in the working class, a
more provincial outlook than in the upper middle class, and a
somewhat greater concern with respectability than in either. In
part, this is a function of religious background: being largely
Protestant, the lower middle class is still affected by the Puritan
ethos. It lacks the regular opportunity for confession that allows
some Catholics to live somewhat more spiritedly, and has not
adopted the sharp division into sacred and secular culture that
reduces Jewish religiosity to observance of the High Holidays and
permits Jews to express exuberance in their organizational, social, and cultural activities. But the difference is not entirely due
to Puritanism, for "restrictive" lower middle class culture appears also among Catholics who have moved "up," especially
German and Irish ones, and even among Italians and among
some Jews who have risen from working class origins.

If "blandness" is the word for this quality, it stems from the
transition in which the lower middle class finds itself between the
familial life of the working class and the cosmopolitanism of the
upper middle class. The working class person need conform only
within the family circle and the peer group, but these are tolerant of his other activities. Believing that the outside world is un-
alterably hostile and that little is to be gained from its approval,
he can indulge in boisterousness that provides catharsis from the
tensions generated in the family and peer circles. The upper
middle class person, on the other hand, is lodged firmly in the
world outside the home. At times he may have trouble reconciling the demands of home and outside world, but he has a secure
footing in both.

Lower middle class people seem to me to be caught in the middle. Those whose origins were in the working class are no longer
tied so strongly to the extended family, but although they have
gone out into the larger society, they are by no means at ease in
it. They do not share the norms of the cosmopolitans, but, unlike
the working class, they cannot ignore them. As a result, they find
themselves in a situation in which every neighbor is a potential
friend or enemy and every community issue a source of conflict,
producing a restraining and even inhibiting influence on them.
Others, lower middle class for generations, have had to move

from a rural or small-town social structure. They too are caught in the middle, for now they must cope with a larger and more heterogeneous society, for which their cultural and religious traditions have not equipped them.

If left to themselves, lower middle class people do what they have always done: put their energies into home and family, seeking to make life as comfortable as possible, and supporting, broadening, and varying it with friends, neighbors, church, and a voluntary association. Because this way of life is much like that of the small-town society or the urban neighborhood in which they grew up, they are able to maintain their optimistic belief that Judeo-Christian morality is a reliable guide to behavior. This world view (if one can endow it with so philosophical a name) is best seen in the pictures that amateur painters exhibited at PTA meetings in Levittown: bright, cheerful landscapes, or portraits of children and pets painted in primary colors, reflecting the wish that the world be hopeful, humorous, and above all, simple. Most important, their paintings insisted that life can be happy.

Of course, life is not really like this, for almost everyone must live with some disappointment: an unruly child, a poor student, an unsatisfied husband, a bored wife, a bad job, a chronic illness, or financial worry. These realities are accepted because they cannot be avoided; it is the norms of the larger society which frustrate. Partly desired and partly rejected, they produce an ambivalence which appears to the outsider as the blandness of lower middle class life. This ambivalence can be illustrated by the way Levittown women reacted to my wife's paintings. Since her studio was at home, they had an opportunity to see her work and talk to her about being a painter. The working class Italians with whom we had lived in Boston previously knew, by and large, how to deal with her activity. Unacquainted with "art," they could shrug off her activity and her abstract expressionist style to admire colors they liked or forms that reminded them of something in their own experience. Not knowing what it all meant, and not having to know, they concluded that painting was a good thing because it kept her out of trouble, preventing boredom and potentially troublesome consequences such as drinking or extramarital affairs.

The lower middle class Levittowners could not cope with her paintings as easily. They did not like her abstract expressionist style any more than the working class women, but they knew it was "art" and so could not ignore it. They responded with anxiety, some hostility, and particularly with envy of her ability to be "creative." But even this response was overlaid with ambivalence. As teenagers they had learned that creativity was desirable, and many had had some cursory training in drawing, piano, or needlework. Once they had learned to be wives and mothers and had enough sociability, the urge for creativity returned—but not the opportunity.

For working class women, keeping the family together and the bills paid is a full-time job. Upper middle class women are convinced that life ought to be more than raising a family, but lower middle class ones are not that sure. They want to venture into nonfamilial roles, but not so intensively as to engender role conflict and anxiety. As a result, they search for easy creativity, activities that do not require, as Levittowners put it, "upsetting the family and household." Serious artistic activity is difficult under such conditions, yet a compromise solution such as needlework or painting-by-numbers is not entirely satisfactory either, because, however rewarding, people know it is not really art. One Levittowner I met expressed the ambivalence between the familial role and artistic aspirations in an especially tortured way. She explained that she was very sensitive to paintings, but confessed that whenever she visited museums, she would begin to think about her family. She resolved the ambivalence by rejecting paintings that made her "think too much about art." For most people, however, the ambivalence is less intense.

A similarly ambivalent pattern is evident in governmental involvement. Many lower middle class people believe that the moral framework which governs their personal lives, the sort of relations they have with family members and friends, ought to govern organizational life and society as well. Any other type of behavior they call "politics," in and out of political life, and they try to avoid it as immoral. Working class people have the same perspective, but they are also realists and will exploit politics for their own ends, and upper middle class people believe in moral (reform) politics, but its norms are not borrowed from the family. Lower middle class citizens are once again caught between the standards of home and of the outside world, however, and the result is often political inaction. It is for them that politicians put on performances to show that their decisions are based on the standards of home and family and run election campaigns demonstrating the personal honesty of their candidates and the opposition candidates' immorality.

Of course, these are cultural propensities to act, and when personal interests are threatened, lower middle class people defend them as heartily as anyone else. Then, they identify their actions with morality—so much so that they lose sight of their self-interest and are easily hurt when others point out to them that they are selfishly motivated. Whereas working class people then become cynical, lower middle class people become hypocritical, often without being conscious of it. Blandness turns easily to bitterness, anger, and blind conflict—blind because every act of offense or self-defense is clothed in the terminology of personal morality.

What appears as blandness, then, to the outside observer is the outcome of conflict between self and society, and between what ought to be and what is. When and if a lower middle class person is secure, he appears bland, because he is not really willing to act within the larger society; when he is threatened, he is extremely angry, because his moral view of the world is upset. One target of his anger is the working class people who are less bothered by the moral dilemmas of the larger society; another is the upper middle class activists who keep pressuring him to translate morality into action and to take a stand on community issues.

Many of these cultural predispositions seem to occur more among lower middle class women than among their husbands. If the men are employed in a bureaucracy, as most are, their work involves them not only in the larger society but also in office or factory political struggles which leave them little time to think about the ambivalence between the standards of home and outside world. The women, however, caught in a role that keeps them at home, are forever trying to break out of its confines, only to confront ambivalent situations. They respond with inhibiting blandness; it is they who are most concerned with respectability. Indeed, living with neighbors employed in large bureaucracies, I was struck over and over again by the feeling that if the men were "organization men," they were so only by necessity, not by inclination, and that if they were left alone, they would gravitate toward untrammeled creativity and individualism. Their wives, on the other hand, defended what Whyte called the Social Ethic, rejecting extreme actions and skeptical opinions, and tried to get their men to toe the line of lower middle class morality. If anything, their inclinations drove them toward being "organization women." But then, they had the job of maintaining the family's status image on the block, and they spent their days in the near-anarchy created by small children. Perhaps they were simply escaping *into* the order of lower middle class norms, while the men were escaping *from* the order imposed by their bureaucratic work.

LEVITTOWN IS "ENDSVILLE": THE ADOLESCENT VIEW

The adult conception of Levittown's vitality is not shared by its adolescents. Many consider it a dull place to which they have been brought involuntarily by their parents. Often there is no place to go and nothing to do after school. Although most adolescents have no trouble in their student role, many are bored after school and some are angry, expressing that anger through thinly veiled hostility to adults and vandalism against adult property. Their relationship to the adults is fraught with tension, which discourages community attempts to solve what is defined as their recreational problem.

Essays which students in grades 6–12 wrote for me early in 1961 suggest that most children are satisfied with Levittown until adolescence.[26] Sixty-eight per cent of the sixth-graders liked Levittown, but only 45 per cent of the eighth-graders, 37 per cent of the tenth-graders, and 39 per cent of the twelfth-graders did. In comparison, 85 per cent of the adults responded positively to a similar question.[27] Likes and dislikes reflect the state of recreational and social opportunities. Girls make little use of recreational facilities until they become adolescents, and before the tenth grade, they like Levittown better than the boys. Dislikes revolve around "nothing to do." The sixth- and eighth-grade boys say there are not enough gyms, playing fields, or hills, and no transportation for getting to existing facilities. Both sexes complain about the lack of neighborhood stores and that the houses are too small, lack privacy, and are poorly built. By the twelfth grade, disenchantment with the existing facilities has set in; those who like Levittown stress the newness and friendliness of the community, but references to the pool, the shopping center, and the bowling alley are negative.[28] As one twelfth-grader pointed out, "Either you have to pay a lot of money to go to the movies or the bowling alley, or you go to too many parties and that gets boring." Lack of facilities is reported most often by the older girls, for the boys at least have athletic programs put on by civic groups.[29]

But the commonest gripe is the shortage of ready transportation, which makes not only facilities but, more important, other teenagers inaccessible. One girl complained, "After school hours, you walk into an entirely different world. Everyone goes his own separate way, to start his homework, take a nap, or watch TV. That is the life of a vegetable, not a human being." A car, then, becomes in a way as essential to teenagers as to adults. Moreover, many small-town teenagers like to meet outside the community, for it is easier to "have fun" where one's parents and other known adults cannot disapprove. A high school senior who took a job to buy a car put it dramatically:

> I had no choice, it was either going to work or cracking up. I have another week of boring habits, then (when I get the car) I'll start living. I can get out of Levittown and go to other towns where I have many friends. . . . In plain words, a boy shouldn't live here if he is between the ages of 14–17. At this age he is using his adult mind, and that doesn't mean riding a bike or smoking his first cigarette. He wants to be big and popular and go out and live it up. I am just starting the life I want. I couldn't ask for more than being a senior in a brand new high school, with the best of students and teachers, and my car on its way.

Girls are less likely to have access to a car, and one explained, "We have to walk, and the streets wind, and cause you to walk two miles instead of one as the crow flies."

The adults have provided some facilities for teenage activities, but not always successfully. One problem is that "teenage" is an adult tag; adolescents grade themselves by age. Older ones refused to attend dances with the younger set, considering forced association with their juniors insulting.[30] Some adolescents also found the adult chaperones oppressive. At first, the chaperones interfered openly by urging strangers to dance with each other in order to get everyone on the floor and to discourage intimate dancing among couples. When the teenagers protested, they stopped, but hovered uneasily in the background.[31]

Specifically, adolescent malcontent stems from two sources: Levittown was not designed for them, and adults are reluctant to provide the recreational facilities and gathering places they want.

Like most suburban communities, Levittown was planned for families with young children. The bedrooms are too small to permit an adolescent to do anything but study or sleep; they lack the privacy and soundproofing to allow him to invite his friends over. Unfortunately, the community is equally inhospitable. Shopping centers are intended for car-owning adults, and in accord with the desire of property owners, are kept away from residential areas. Being new, Levittown lacks low-rent shopping areas which can afford to subsist on the marginal purchases made by adolescents. In 1961, a few luncheonettes in neighborhood shopping centers and a candy store and a bowling alley in the big center were the only places for adolescents to congregate.[32] Coming in droves, they overwhelmed those places and upset the merchants. Not only do teenagers occupy space without making significant purchases, but they also discourage adult customers. Merchants faced with high rent cannot subsist on teenage spending and complain to the police if teenagers "hang out" at their places. Street corners are off limits, too, for a clump of adolescents soon becomes noisy enough to provoke a call to the police. Eventually they feel hounded and even defined as juvenile delinquents. Said one twelfth-grade girl, "I feel like a hood to be getting chased by the police for absolutely nothing."

The schools were not designed for after-hours use, except for adults and for student activities which entertain adults, such as varsity athletics. The auditoriums were made available for dances, although when these began, the school administration promptly complained about scuffed floors and damaged fixtures. Only at the swimming pool are teenagers not in the way of adult priorities, and during the day, when adults are not using it, it is their major gathering place. But even here, smoking and noisy activities are prohibited.

The design deficiencies cannot be altered, and should not be if they are a problem only for teenagers, but there is no inherent reason why teenage facilities cannot be provided. However, adults disagree on what is needed and, indeed, on the desirability of facilities, for reasons partly political, but fundamentally social and psychological. For one thing, adults are uncertain about how to treat teenagers; for another, they harbor a deep hostility toward them which is cultural and, at bottom, sexual in nature. There are two adult views of the teenager, one permissive, the other restrictive. The former argues that a teenager is a responsible individual who should be allowed to run his own affairs with some adult help. The latter, subscribed to by the majority, considers him still a child who needs adult supervision and whose activities ought to be conducted by adult rules to integrate him into adult society. For example, when one of the community organizations set up teenage dances, there was some discussion about whether teenagers should run them. Not only was this idea rejected, but the adults then ran the dances on the basis of the "highest" standards.[33] Boys were required to wear ties and jackets, girls, dresses, on the assumption that this would encourage good behavior, whereas blue jeans, tee shirts, and sweaters somehow would not. The adults could not resist imposing their own norms of dress in exchange for providing dances.

The advocates of restriction also rejected the permissive point of view because they felt it wrong to give teenagers what they wanted. Believing that teenagers had it "too easy," they argued that "if you make them work for programs, they appreciate them more." Logically, they should, therefore, have let the teenagers set up their own activities, but their arguments were not guided by logic; they were, rather, rationalizations for their fear of teenagers. Although the "permissives" pointed out that teenagers might well set up stricter rules than adults, the "restrictives" feared catastrophes: fights, the "wrong crowd" taking over, pregnancies, and contraceptives found in or near the teenage facility. These fears accounted for the rules governing dances and inhibited the establishment of an adult-run teenage center, for the voluntary associations and the politicians were afraid that if violence or sexual activity occurred, they would be blamed for it.

The problem is twofold: restrictive adults want adolescents to be children preparing for adulthood, and are threatened by the teenage or youth culture they see around them. By now, adolescents are a cultural minority like any other, but whereas no Levittowners expect Italians to behave like Jews, most still expect teenagers to behave like children. They are supposed to participate in the family more than they do and, legally still under age, to subsume their own wishes to the adults'. The failure of teenagers to go along is blamed on the parents as well. If parents would only take more interest in their adolescent children, spend more time with them, be "pals" with them, and so on, then misbehavior—and even youth culture—would not develop. This argument is supported by the claim that delinquency is caused by broken homes or by both parents' holding full-time jobs.

Such views are espoused particularly by Catholics, who share traditional working class attitudes; the parochial school, with its emphasis on discipline to keep children out of trouble, is their embodiment. Even adult-devised programs are considered undesirable, for, as one Catholic working class father put it, "In summer, children should either work or be at home. Summer arts and crafts programs are a waste of time. My kid brought home dozens of pictures. What's he going to do with so many pictures?" The adolescents' social choices are also restricted. Adults active in youth programs frequently try to break up their groups, damning them as cliques or gangs, and even separating friends when athletic teams are chosen. Some teenagers react by minimizing contact with adults, pursuing their activities privately and becoming remarkably uncommunicative. In essence, they lead a separate life which frees them from undue parental control and gives an air of mystery to the teenager and his culture.

Among restrictive adults, the image of the teenager is of an irresponsible, parasitic individual, who attends school without studying, hangs out with his peers looking for fun and adventure, and gets into trouble—above all, over sex. There were rumors of teenage orgies in Levittown's school playgrounds, in shopping center parking lots, and on the remaining rural roads of the township. The most fantastic rumor had 44 girls in the senior class pregnant, with one boy singlehandedly responsible for six of them. Some inquiry on my part turned up the facts: two senior girls were pregnant and one of them was about to be married.

If the essays the students wrote for me have any validity, the gap between adult fantasy and adolescent reality is astonishing. Most teenagers do not even date; their social life takes place in groups. Judging by their comments about the friendliness of adult neighbors, they are quiet youngsters who get along well with adults and spend most of their time preparing themselves for adulthood. Needless to say, these essays would not have revealed delinquent activities or sex play. However, I doubt that more than 5 per cent of the older teenagers live up to anything like the adult image of them.

What, then, accounts for the discrepancy? For one thing, adults take little interest in their children's education; they want to be assured that their children are getting along in school, but not much more. The bond that might exist here is thus absent. Changes in education during the last two decades have been so great that even interested parents can do little to help their children with their school work. Consequently, adults focus on teenagers in their nonstudent roles, noting their absence from home, the intensity of their tie to friends and cliques, and their rebelliousness.

Second, there is the normal gap between the generations, enlarged by the recent flowering of youth culture, much of which is incomprehensible or unesthetic to adults. Despite the parents' belief that they should be responsible for their adolescents' behavior, they cannot participate in many joint activities or talk meaningfully with them about the experiences and problems of teenage life. This gap is exacerbated by a strange parental amnesia about their own—not so distant—adolescence. I recall a letter written by a twenty-one-year-old mother who wanted to help the Township Committee set up a delinquency prevention council because she was concerned about teenage misbehavior.

Third, there is enough teenage vandalism and delinquency to provide raw material for the adult image, although not enough to justify it. According to the police and the school superintendent, serious delinquency in Levittown was minimal; in 1961, about 50 adolescents accounted for most of it. Many were children from working class backgrounds who did poorly in school, or from disturbed middle class families. From 1959 to 1961, only 12 cases were serious enough to go to the county juvenile court, and some were repeaters. Vandalism is more prevalent. The first victim was the old Willingboro YMCA, which was wrecked twice before it was torn down. Schools have been defaced, windows broken, garbage thrown into the pools, flowerbeds destroyed, and bicycles "borrowed." The perpetrators are rarely caught, but those who are caught are teenagers, thus making it possible for adults to suspect all adolescents and maintain their image.

Finally, some adults seem to project their own desires for excitement and adventures onto the youngsters. For them, teenagers function locally as movie stars and beatniks do on the national scene—as exotic creatures reputed to live for sex and adventure. Manifestly, teenagers act as more prosaic entertainers: in varsity athletics, high school dramatic societies, and bands, but the girls are also expected to provide glamor. One of the first activities of the Junior Chamber of Commerce was a Miss Levit-town contest, in which teenage girls competed for honors in evening gown, bathing suit, and talent contests—the "talent" usually involving love songs or covertly erotic dances. At such contests unattainable maidens show off their sexuality—often unconsciously—in order to win the nomination. Men in the audience comment *sotto voce* about the girls' attractiveness, wishing to sleep with them and speculating whether that privilege is available to the contest judges and boyfriends. From here, it is only a short step to the conviction that girls are promiscuous with their teenage friends, which heightens adult envy, fear, and the justification for restrictive measures. The sexual function of the teenager became apparent when the popularity of the Miss Levittown contest led to plans for a Mrs. Levittown contest. This plan was quickly dropped, however, for the idea of married women parading in bathing suits was thought to be in bad taste, especially by the women. Presumably, young mothers are potential sexual objects, whereas the teenagers are, like movie stars, unattainable, and can therefore serve as voyeuristic objects.

Although suburbia is often described as a hotbed of adultery in popular fiction, this is an urban fantasy. Levittown is quite monogamous, and I am convinced that most suburbs are more so than most cities.[34] The desire for sexual relations with attractive neighbors may be ever present, but when life is lived in a goldfish bowl, adultery is impossible to hide from the neighbors—even if there were motels in Levittown and baby-sitters could be found for both parties. Occasionally such episodes do take place, after which the people involved often run off together or leave the community. There are also periodic stories of more bizarre sexual escapades, usually about community leaders. In one such story, a local politician was driving down the dark roads of the township in a sports car with a naked young woman while his wife thought he was at a political meeting. If there was any roadside adultery, however, it remained unreported, for no cases ever appeared on the police blotters during the two years I saw them.[35] Similar stories made the rounds in Park Forest, the new town I studied in 1949, and one of them, which began after a party where some extramarital necking had taken place, soon reported the gathering as a wife-swapping orgy.

"The Juvenile Problem" and Its Solutions

The cultural differences between adults and adolescents have precipitated an undeclared and subconscious war between them, as pervasive as the class struggle, which prevents the adults from solving what they call "the juvenile problem." Indeed, putting it that way is part of the trouble, for much of the adult effort has been aimed at discouraging delinquency, providing recreational activities in the irrational belief that these could prevent it. Sports programs were supposed to exhaust the teenagers so that they would be too tired to get into trouble (harking back to the Victorian myth that a regimen of cold showers and sports would dampen sexual urges, although ironically, varsity athletes were also suspected of being stellar sexual performers); dances were to keep them off the street. When delinquency did not abate, a Youth Guidance Commission to deal with "the problem," and a Teenage Panel to punish delinquencies too minor for court actions, were set up. The police chief asked for a curfew to keep youngsters off the street at night, hoping to put pressure on parents to act as enforcing agents and to get his department out of the cross fire between teenagers, merchants, and home owners. Chasing the teenagers from shopping centers and street corners was useless, for having no other place to go they always returned the next night, particularly since they knew people would not swear out complaints against their neighbors' (or customers') children. The police chief also did not want "the kids to feel they are being bugged," for they would come to hate his men and create more trouble for them.[36] If he cracked down on them, they would retaliate; if he did not, the adults would accuse him of laxity. Although the curfew was strongly supported by parents who could not control their children, it was rejected as unenforceable.

Adult solutions to the juvenile problem were generally shaped by other institutional goals which took priority over adolescent needs. The organizations which scheduled dances wanted to advertise themselves and their community service inclinations, even competing for the right to hold them, and the churches set up youth groups to bring the teenagers into the church. Indeed, those who decide on adolescent programs either have vested interests in keeping teenagers in a childlike status (parents and educators, for example) or are charged with the protection of adult

interests (police and politicians). The primacy of adult priorities
was brought out by a 1961 PTA panel on "How Is Our Community Meeting the Needs of the Adolescents?" With one exception the panelists (chosen to represent the various adults responsible for teenagers) ignored these needs, talking only about what
teenagers should do for *them*. For example, the parent on the
panel said, "The needs of adolescents should first be met in the
home and young energies should be guided into the proper normal channels." The teacher suggested that "parents should never
undermine the authority of the teacher. Parents should help
maintain the authority of the school over the child, and the
school will in turn help maintain the authority of the parent over
the child." The minister urged parents to "encourage youth
leadership responsibilities within the church," and the police
chief explained "the importance of teaching adolescents their
proper relationship to the law and officers of the law." [37]

Political incentives for a municipal or even a semipublic recreation program were also absent. Not only were prospective sponsors afraid they would be held responsible for teenage misbehavior occurring under their auspices, but in 1961 not many Levitt-
towners had adolescent children and not all of them favored a
public program. Middle class parents either had no problems with
their youngsters or objected to the working class advocacy of
municipal recreation, and some working class parents felt that
once children had reached adolescence they were on their own.
The eventual clients of the program, the adolescents, had no political influence whatsoever. They were too young to vote, and although they might have persuaded their parents to demand facilities for them, they probably suspected that what their parents
wanted for them was more of what had already been provided.

In the end, then, the adults got used to the little delinquency
and vandalism that took place, and the teenagers became sullen
and unhappy, complaining, "This place in Endsville," and wishing their parents would move back to communities which had facilities for them or pressuring them for cars to go to neighboring
towns.

The best summary of what is wrong—and what should be
done—was stated concisely by a twelfth-grade essayist: "I think
the adults should spend less time watching for us to do something
wrong and help us raise money for a community center. We're
not asking for it, we only want their help." If one begins with the

assumption that adolescents are rational and responsible human beings whose major "problem" is that they have become a distinctive minority subculture, it is not too difficult to suggest programs. What else the teenagers want in the way of recreation can be readily inferred from their essays: besides the center, a range of inexpensive coffeehouses and soda shops and other meeting places, bowling alleys, amusement arcades, places for dancing, ice and roller skating rinks, garages for mechanically inclined car owners (all within walking or bicycling distance or accessible by public transportation), and enough of each so that the various age groups and separate cliques have facilities they can call their own. Since adolescents are well supplied with spending money, many of these facilities can be set up commercially. Others may need public support. It would, for example, be possible to provide some municipal subsidies to luncheonette operators who are willing to make their businesses into teenage social centers.[38]

Recreational and social facilities are not enough, however. Part of the adolescents' dissatisfaction with the community—as with adult society in general—is their functionlessness outside of school. American society really has no use for them other than as students, and condemns them to spend most of their spare time in recreational pursuits. They are trying to learn to be adults, but since the community and the larger society want them to be children, they learn adulthood only at school—and there imperfectly. Yet many tasks in the community now go unfilled because of lack of public funds, for example, clerical, data-gathering, and other functions at city hall; and tutoring children, coaching their sports, and leading their recreational programs. These are meaningful duties, and I suspect many adolescents could fill them, either on a voluntary or a nominal wage basis. Finally, teenagers want to learn to be themselves and do for themselves. It should be possible to give them facilities of their own—or even land on which they could build—and let them organize, construct, and run their own centers and work places.

Needless to say, such autonomy would come up against the very real political difficulties that faced the more modest programs suggested in Levittown, and would surely be rejected by the community.[39] The ideal solution, therefore, is to plan for teenage needs outside the local adult decision-making structure, and perhaps even outside the community. It might be possible to establish Teenage Authorities that would play the same interstitial role in the governmental structure as other authorities set up in connection with intercommunity and regional planning functions. Perhaps the most feasible approach is to develop commercially profitable facilities, to be set up either by teenagers or by a private entrepreneur who would need to be less sensitive to political considerations than a public agency. If and when the "juvenile problem" becomes more serious in the suburbs, federal funds may become available for facilities and for programs to create jobs, like those now being developed for urban teenagers. Most likely, this will only happen when "trouble" begins to mount.

NOTES

1. See, e.g., Fromm, pp. 154–163; and Stein, Chaps. 9 and 12.
2. This charge is made by Keats and, in more qualified and muted tones, by Riesman (1957).
3. This cannot be surmised either from inferences about media content or from sociological surveys, but becomes quite evident when one watchès TV with other people, as I did with my neighbors.
4. I had observed the same reactions among the working class Bostonians I studied previously, although they were more interested in the performers than the Levittowners. Gans (1962a), Chap. 9.
5. Wilensky, p. 237. See also Kornhauser, Chap. 3, and Lipset, pp. 66–67.
6. Fifty-six per cent of the random sample and 44 per cent of the city sample reported more participation than previously.
7. In this respect, the Levittowners differed significantly from the residents of Springdale, a rural community in New York State, who developed a set of illusions to hide their dependence on state and national political and economic forces. See Vidich and Bensman.
8. Part of the difficulty is that critics compare the present generation to the previous generation, that of the Depression, which was an unusual period in American history and no baseline for historical comparisons of any kind.
9. There is no secular trend in turnover, however, for between 1961 and 1964 the rate in the first neighborhood increased from 12 per cent to only 14 per cent, but the third and fourth neighborhoods both showed turnover rates of 19 per cent in 1964. Renting occurs primarily because the softness of the housing market makes it difficult for people to sell their houses without a considerable loss; they find it more profitable to rent them, with management turned over to the local realtors.

10. According to a story in the October 21, 1957 issue of Long Island's *Newsday*, 27 per cent of the first 1800 families in Levittown, New York, were still living there ten years later.

11. Another 10 per cent left because they were unhappy in the community; 7 per cent, for financial reasons; 5 per cent, because of an excessive journey to work; and 4 per cent, because of death, divorce, or other changes in the family. These figures were collected from real estate men and people selling their homes privately and may not be entirely reliable. Real estate men may not be told the real reasons for selling and private sellers may have been reluctant to mention financial problems. However, only about 1 per cent of the houses were foreclosed annually.

12. In the mid-1950s, when Park Forest was seven years old, annual turnover of homes was 20 per cent. See Whyte (1956), p. 303. In Levittown, New York, a 1961 study reported an average annual rate of about 15 per cent. See Orzack and Sanders, p. 13. In Levittown, Pennsylvania, the rate varied from 12 to 15 per cent between 1952 and 1960. See Anderson and Settani. A study of a forty-year-old English new town reported an annual rate of 10 per cent the first ten years, which has now dropped to 1 per cent. See Willmott (1963), p. 20. A study of 30,000 apartments in 519 buildings all over the country, conducted by the Institute of Real Estate Management and reported in the *New York Times* of November 10, 1963, showed an annual turnover of 28 per cent, and 35 per cent for garden apartments.

13. Eighty-four per cent of the Transients reported organizational membership at the time of the second interview, as compared to 86 per cent of the Mobiles and only 44 per cent of the Settlers. Sixty-two per cent of the Transients belonged to organizations other than the church, compared to only 25 per cent of the Settlers.

14. Seventy-five per cent of the Transients were more active than in their former residence, as compared to 60 per cent of the Settlers, and none of the Transients but 20 per cent of the Settlers said they were less active than before.

15. The mean number of couples named by Transients was 2.75; by Mobiles, 3.25; and by Settlers, 3.3. Nineteen per cent of the Transients said they had no friends in Levittown, as compared to 8 per cent of the Settlers.

16. Whyte (1956), p. 289.

17. Webber.

18. Gutman, p. 180.

19. See, e.g., Fried.

20. Gordon, Gordon, and Gunther. This study did not distinguish between residential and social mobility, but its case studies of disturbed suburbanites suggest the deleterious effects of the latter.

21. Pederson and Sullivan.

22. This study—by Gabower—came to other conclusions, but a close

reading of her data shows that the strains of the long and arduous climb required of an enlisted man in the Navy who becomes an officer were passed on to the children. Conversely, children from middle class homes, whose fathers had graduated from Annapolis, rarely suffered emotionally from geographical mobility. Teenagers of both groups suffered from moving, however.

23. The question read: "Some people have said that communities like Levittown are pretty dull, without any excitement or interesting things to do. How do you feel about that? Do you agree or disagree?"

24. This respondent was describing the extremely active social life of the Jewish community. Even so, Jews (particularly the better educated) were more likely than non-Jews to agree that Levittown was dull. Jews also seem to be more interested in city amusements.

25. Cosmopolitan friends often asked me if I did not find Levittown dull. As a participant-observer, I could not answer the question, for I was immersed in community life and strife and saw all of their vitality and excitement. Even the most routine event was interesting because I was trying to fit it into an overall picture of the community. As a resident, I enjoyed being with Levittowners, and the proportion of dull ones was certainly no higher than in academic or any other circles. Of course, Levittown lacked some of the urban facilities that I, as a city-lover, like to patronize. It was not dull, however—but then I would not make a public judgment about any community simply because it could not satisfy some of my personal preferences, particularly when the community seemed to satisfy the preferences of the majority of residents so well.

26. The students were asked what they liked and disliked about living in Levittown, and what they missed from their former residence. Since they were not asked to sign their names, and the questions were general, I believe the essays were honest responses. I purposely included no questions about the schools, and teachers were instructed not to give any guidance about how the questions should be answered. (One teacher did tell the children what to write, and these essays were not analyzed.) The data presented here are based on a sample of one sixth- and one eighth-grade class from each of the three elementary schools, and of all tenth- and twelfth-grade classes.

27. The data are not strictly comparable, for the adults were asked outright whether they liked or disliked living in Levittown, whereas the teenagers' attitudes were inferred from the tone of the essays.

28. Twenty-eight per cent of the boys liked the community's newness; 18 per cent, the friendly people. Among the girls, 34 per cent liked the people; 20 per cent, Levittown's newness.

29. Twenty-five per cent of the tenth-graders and 50 per cent of the

twelfth-graders say there is nothing to do, and 25 per cent and 46 per cent, respectively, mention the lack of recreational facilities. Among the twelfth-grade girls, 56 per cent mention it.

30. Similarly in the elementary schools, seventh- and eighth-graders complained about having to go to school with "immature" and "childish" students; when they were moved to the high school, the older students objected to their presence in the same terms.

31. There was also a dispute over programming: the adults wanted slow music and the traditional dances they knew best; the teenagers wanted the latest best-selling records and the newest dances. They signed petitions for the ouster of the man who chose the records, but the adults refused to accept the petitions, arguing that they would be followed by petitions to oust the school superintendent.

32. Indeed, the existing teenage hangouts in little luncheonettes resulted from the lucky accident that the builder and the township planner were unable to regulate and limit the number of small shopping centers which sprang up on the edge of the community.

33. At one point adult-run dances failed to attract teenagers, and a group of teenage leaders was delegated to run the dances themselves. This foundered because other teenagers disagreed with the rules and program set up by these leaders, and since only one opportunity for dancing was provided, they could express their disagreement only by nonattendance.

34. A comparison of urban and suburban marriages indicated that extramarital affairs occur principally in older and well-educated populations, and that place of residence is irrelevant. Ubell. For another observer's skepticism about suburban adultery, see Whyte (1956), pp. 355–357.

35. Since the blotter listed adolescent promiscuity, adult suicide attempts, and even drunkenness and family quarrels among community leaders, I assume it was not censored to exclude adultery.

36. Actually, since the police usually sided with the merchants against the teenagers, the latter did feel "bugged."

37. "Panel Features Junior High P.T.A. Meeting," *Levittown Herald,* January 26, 1961.

38. A combination neighborhood store and social center has been proposed in the plan for the new town of Columbia, Maryland.

39. In 1966, no teenage centers had yet been established in Levittown, and campaigning politicians were still arguing about the wisdom of doing so.

Chapter Ten

FAMILY AND INDIVIDUAL ADAPTATION

THE SUBURBAN CRITIQUE CONSIDERS LIFE BEYOND THE CITY LIMITS harmful both to family life and to the happiness and mental health of the individual. The critics have argued that long commutation by the father is helping to create a suburban matriarchy with deleterious effects on the children, and that homogeneity, social hyperactivity, and the absence of urban stimuli create depression, boredom, loneliness, and ultimately, mental illness.[1] The findings from Levittown suggest just the opposite—that suburban life has produced more family cohesion and a significant boost in morale through the reduction of boredom and loneliness. Some problems remain, and since this study is not intended as a eulogy for suburban living, I will emphasize them. Even so, most Levittowners have adapted positively to their new community.

By "adaptation," I mean simply how people respond to Levittown; I use the term neither normatively nor negatively, but descriptively. I assume that people sometimes adjust to the situations they face and sometimes react against them, but whether or not they ought to do either is up to them. Similarly, I take it for granted that people know when they are bored and, if properly asked, can report their feelings. Of course, they cannot tell about subconscious maladaptation and boredom, but when it surfaced in their answers or was apparent from my observations, I have reported it here. I do not want, however, to impute boredom simply because some critics' standards dictate that Levittowners ought to have been bored by activities they actually enjoyed. Finally, respondents may have underreported undesirable changes and overreported desirable ones, and the percentages that follow should be read with this in mind.[2] Because women, who report undesirable changes more often than men, were over-represented in my interview samples, however, this discrepancy may cancel out.

THE QUALITY OF FAMILY LIFE

Since people move to the suburbs as families, it is difficult to separate individual from family adaptation, and maladaptation often affects people in their family roles. Obviously, many Levittowners came partly to facilitate family life: to have more space in the house and a yard so that young children could play without supervision, while parents spent more time with other children and adults. Forty per cent of the wives and 65 per cent of the husbands wanted to spend more time with their children in Levittown, and interestingly enough, all of the former city dwellers, as compared to half of the previous suburbanites and none of the small-towners, expressed this wish. Evidently, life in the suburbs deprives parents of time with their children less than that in the city. Because of the charge that suburbia encourages matriarchy, I was curious whether wives wanted their husbands to spend more time with the children; 45 per cent did, but almost the same number wished to be with their children more themselves. Again, former urban wives felt this need most often.[3]

Levittown made it possible for these particular parents to achieve their wishes, for 85 per cent of the wives and 71 per cent of the husbands wanting more time with the children now had it. For the sample as a whole, about 40 per cent were with the children more frequently, but the remaining 60 per cent reported no change. And all of the wives who wanted their husbands to devote themselves more to the children got what they wished.[4] The new house was the cause, for children and adults were around the house more, and they often worked together on the yard.

Moving to Levittown did not cut into the time available for family activities, for the journey to work, often alleged to have this effect, did not change significantly. It changed even less for former city dwellers, who previously commuted longer than suburbanites, than for the random sample. The Philadelphians' median trip increased from 35 minutes each way to 37 after the move, with 11 per cent now reporting a short trip (0–19 minutes); 47 per cent a medium one (20–39 minutes); 31 per cent a long one (40–59 minutes); and 11 per cent a very long one (60 minutes or more).[5] Twenty-five per cent reported a lengthier commute than before, but 30 per cent a shorter one, and 45 per cent reported no change. The median increase was 30 minutes; the median decrease, 22.[6] People with lengthier commutes now traveled a median 45 minutes, although 33 per cent had a long trip and 25 per cent a very long one.[7]

Levittowners did not share the critics' and the planners' distaste for commuting. Most said they like or do not mind a trip up to 40 minutes; only a longer one garnered a significant number of dislikes.[8] One third of the Philadelphians said their commute was "wearing," and what made it so was not trip length but mode of travel, two thirds of those taking the bus, 37 per cent of those driving, and only 20 per cent of car pool members reporting weariness after their journey.[9] Indeed, for some people, the drive to and from work is one of the few moments of total privacy and may thus be a relaxing transition between the social demands of the job and the family.[10] Conversely, the car pool is a social experience, and in a community like Levittown, it becomes a substitute-on-wheels for all male social clubs and neighborhood taverns. It is thus no surprise that even car pool trips of more than 40 minutes were not found wearing. Indeed, women seem to be more affected by their husbands' journey to work than the men themselves, partly because the men cannot be with the children during the preparation of dinner and perhaps because the men take the strain of a long trip out on their wives.[11]

Commutation played a minor role in the parental time budget, however. Two thirds of the men with short work trips had more time for the children, while those with longer trips were unaffected, and wives reported that men with trips over 40 minutes had more time with their children than those with shorter ones. Actually, longer hours on the job (often required by the promotion which financed the purchase of the new house) was a more significant factor in preventing the 29 per cent of husbands who wanted more time with their children from finding it.

Fifty-seven per cent of the husbands—mainly the younger ones —sought more time with their wives and all but one got it. Only 37 per cent of the wives wanted to be with their husbands more, but all got their wish. Age made no difference, but once again, the former city residents felt a greater need for more time with their men. In the random sample as a whole, about 40 per cent said they had more time with each other in Levittown.[12] Short work trips seem to give spouses more time with each other, but long ones do not deprive them of time, for there was no statistical association between people who reported long trips and those who reported less time with their spouses.[13]

Levittown also provided more opportunity for parents and children to do things together; nearly half the random sample respondents reported increased joint family activity [14] in both the first and second interviews.[15] In the first interview, 72 per cent explained that fixing up the house and the yard were responsible; by the second, 40 per cent pointed to new social and recreational opportunities. When children were old enough to join in shopping, recreation, and visiting, joint family activity rose; when they became old enough to prefer peers, it decreased, and as the effects of the house and community wear off, age is likely to be the more important determinant of family cohesion.

Because the random sample had interpreted joint family activity as referring to parents and children, the Philadelphians were asked, "Do you and your husband do more things together in Levittown than where you lived before, or fewer things?" Although 40 per cent reported more "joint couple activity," 20 per cent mentioned a decrease. House and community activities are again significant reasons for the increase, while the reduction is explained by age. Newlyweds find children distracting to their own relationship—fully 55 per cent of couples under twenty-five report a decrease in joint activity in Levittown. And when older children join their peers, a cleavage is created between their parents. Husbands who are now working longer hours and traveling longer to work also mention fewer shared activities, as do professionals, the well educated, and Jews.

Levittown seemed to have no effect on marital happiness, however. Only about 20 per cent reported an improvement in the marital relationship; [16] as might be expected, few were ready to admit a poorer marriage, and most just indicated it had remained about the same. Older couples reported the least change, and among the Philadelphians, low-status ones the most deterioration, but otherwise class differences were negligible. The happier couples credited the house, particularly additional space which reduced getting in each other's way, and home ownership, which encouraged "maturity," reduced petty bickering, and increased contentment. One woman pointed out, "The house keeps me so busy, I don't have time to nag him, but I'm more content here too." But the initial lift to the marital relationship produced by the house and ownership lasted only until the novelty wore off. Indeed, in the second interview, the woman just quoted said the marriage had returned to the status quo before Levittown: "He has become so wrapped up in community activities and his work that he has forgotten his family." Commuting seems to influence the marital relationship, particularly for wives; both joint couple activity and marital happiness are affected negatively when the wives consider their husband's commute wearing. The men do not agree, however, getting along with their wives as well when the trip is wearing as when it is not.

Thus the interviews suggest that the suburban critique is wrong; family life has changed relatively little for the majority, and the changes are mainly improvements. These data, the minimal impact of the journey to work, and my observations also cast doubt on the fear of an incipient suburban matriarchy. Although Philadelphians had had a sizeable journey to work even when they lived in the city and studies of urban neighborhoods indicate that men are away from the house during working hours as much as in Levittown, no critic has yet begun to worry about urban matriarchy. Among middle class families in Levittown, some household roles that were once the woman's monopoly are now shared, but among the working class families, suburban husbands were as reluctant to wash the dishes or look after the children as they had been in the city. In some cases, they even left lawn-mowing to the women, or tried to, but were quickly discouraged by block social pressure.

Much of the popular talk about an emerging matriarchy strikes me as a misreading of the trend toward greater equality between the sexes—a middle class value which is also being adopted by many working class women these days—and the development of more shared interests, owing to increased (and increasingly coeducational) schooling for women. Yet even among highly educated Levittowners, the husbands still made the decisions, and women still threatened errant children with "wait till your father comes home." There were some domineering wives and henpecked husbands, but they were considered as deviant in Levittown as elsewhere. Public concern about matriarchy is natural—at least among men, for they are undoubtedly losing some of the power they held in the past, and those who must relinquish power usually phrase their complaints as social criticism.

Family life in Levittown also impressed me as being no different from that in other communities. A few marriages were very happy, and a few very unhappy.[17] The latter were of course more visible; during my three years of research, 14 suicide attempts took place, all but one by women and only one successful.[18] In most instances, women took sleeping pills and then called the police, their doctor, or their minister immediately, reversing what was surely an impulsive and pathetic cry for attention. Two women accounted for four of the unsuccessful attempts. About a hundred cases of serious domestic conflict made the police blotter, usually when a wife called for protection against a violent husband. Seventy families contributed to this figure, but 15 accounted for fully half of it, and 55 called the police only once. Conflicts on record were usually among working class families, for the middle class uses techniques of fighting that are not noisy or violent enough to merit official intervention. Conversely, I suspect that the suicide attempts were more often a middle class method of coping with an unhappy marriage, and the one woman who killed herself left a tragic note to this effect.

These are extreme situations, however. Another assessment of marital life comes from a survey taken in 1961 among a random sample of 100 Levittowners regarding a family service agency. Twenty-six per cent said one was needed, 51 per cent were sure it was not, and 23 per cent were uncertain. If one assumes that people were really talking about their own marriages, a quarter expressed the desire for help. Undoubtedly class enters the picture; one would not expect working class families to resort to an agency. On the other hand, young middle class families might seek an agency without being desperate. Survey data tell little about married life in Levittown, however, and observation suggests that the majority of marriages combine that mixture of bliss and bickering to be found everywhere.

PATTERNS OF INDIVIDUAL ADAPTATION: SUBURBAN HAPPINESS AND FEMALE MALAISE

The literature of suburban criticism abounds with references to suburban malaise and *anomie,* but however colorful, these terms are not quite accurate. In fact, it would be more correct to speak of suburban happiness, for most Levittowners experienced less depression, boredom, and loneliness after the move. Even so, a minority, sometimes up to a third, report the opposite, particularly among the Philadelphians. Occasionally these feelings stem from being isolated in the community, but usually they reflect more general problems of working and lower middle class women in contemporary society. If there is malaise in Levittown, it is female but not suburban.

Morale and Health

Thirty-six per cent of the random sample spoke of improved morale after coming to Levittown and all but 6 per cent of the remainder reported no change.[19] Among the Philadelphians, however, only 22 per cent reported a better disposition, and 31 per cent a poorer one (among the women, the percentages were 19 and 38)—one of the few instances in which change was more negative than positive.[20] High- and low-status urbanites and people under twenty-five were unhappier now, and only those over forty-five raised their morale significantly.[21] In both samples, the improvement in morale could be traced mainly to the new house and yard, and the greater ease in rearing children, producing a feeling most often described as "relaxation." A Philadelphian said, "In the city, I'd have all that tension being out with my son. Here I can let him go, and if I want to do something I can putter in the garden. It is so quiet and serene here, it just makes you relax."

The people with poorer dispositions fall into four types. Young women who have become mothers in Levittown, particularly those who worked before, find it difficult to be full-time housekeepers and to cope with the children, and this is compounded by the feeling of being "stuck." Without a car or compatible neighbors, there is no respite or escape.

A second group, primarily working class women, miss family and friends in the city and find it difficult to cut their ties to them. Among the random sample, more neighbor and couple visiting results in better morale, but among unhappy Philadelphians it does not help, even for women who have found a close friend in Levittown. The problem is summed up well by one young working class ex-Philadelphian: "It's too quiet here, nothing to do. In the city you can go downtown shopping, see all the people, or go visit mother. If there were more friendly people here it would be better. I knew more people the first year, but also I didn't have any kids—I was only carrying the first—so I could go downtown and see mother, and the days would go by fast."

Third, some Jewish women, either more or less educated than the majority or with non-Jewish husbands, were now more unhappy. One, a working class woman married to a Catholic, said, "Here you meet people only through organizations, churches, and clubs, but we are not organizational types and I don't care for organizational life." A better-educated one had the opposite problem: "I'd feel better if I could make friends with people, if the women here were more sincere. A lot of them here like to play cards and I don't, and there are a lot of gossip-mongers and I don't believe in that. Several organizations are bothering you to join, a constant annoyance of activities, and if you don't join, they say you are a grouch, you lack community spirit."

Last, women with poor marriages and with husbands on the road or with long commutes suffer from poorer morale, although their prime reaction is loneliness.[22] One woman pointed out, "If you are alone here, you are alone. In an apartment, you can walk out the door. It's OK though, when my husband is home. But when he's not, then I feel isolated."

Changes in physical health were minor, and reflected those in morale. Eighteen per cent of the random sample reported better health; the same proportion, poorer health. Among the Philadelphians, the percentages were 9 and 17, respectively.[23] The healthier people said they were now less tense, the more relaxed way of living having alleviated colds and allergies. For random sample respondents, more sickness was usually a recurrence of old ailments, but the Philadelphians reported new complaints, mainly colds, allergies, nervous tension, and increased weight. Their illnesses were probably emotionally caused; half in poorer health also reported poorer morale, but in the random sample, even sicker people had improved dispositions.[24] High- and low-status Philadelphians and the very young felt their health had deteriorated most; the older people, that it had improved the most—the same groups who also reported poorer and better morale. Some Philadelphians, especially men, said they became sick over financial worries; for others, particularly lower-status and Jewish respondents, loneliness and distaste for suburban living were involved.

Boredom

The amount of boredom in Levittown is shown in Table 5. Although people may underreport, 40 per cent (about a third of the women and more than half the men) are never bored and only a few women are constantly so. Boredom does not seem to be a serious problem in Levittown. Younger people experienced somewhat more boredom than older ones, but there was no pattern by class.[25] Since former city dwellers reported as much boredom in their prior residence as suburban ones, the common idea that suburbanites are more bored than city dwellers is inaccurate.

TABLE 5
AMOUNT OF BOREDOM IN LEVITTOWN *

	PER CENT REPORTING								
	Random Sample						Philadelphia Sample		
AMOUNT OF BOREDOM	*First Interview*			*Second Interview*					
	W	M	All	W	M	All	W	M	All
"Almost every day"	4	0	2	4	0	2	8	0	5
"A few times a month"	21	6	14	15	22	18	27	17	24
"About once a month"	21	28	24	27	6	18	27	11	22
"Less often than that"	21	11	17	23	17	21	11	5	9
Never	33	55	43	31	55	41	27	67	40
N	(24)	(18)	(42)	(26)	(18)	(44)	(37)	(18)	(55)

* People were asked, "We all get bored every so often. How often do you find yourself feeling bored, having nothing to do, or nothing you want to do especially? Do you feel this way: almost every day, a few times a month, about once a month, or less often than that?" The never category was not read to the respondents.

About a third of the bored women attributed it to the menstrual period, poor health, or a periodic bad mood. But two other reasons are mentioned more often: housework and being "stuck." Some women complain about the monotony of housework, especially ironing, yet what invites boredom most often is simply "doing the same thing over and over again." This reaction is voiced by women impatient with being only housewives, but not yet able to see themselves in other roles, for example, in voluntary associations.

The move to Levittown has improved matters, principally for the random sample, for 51 per cent said their boredom had decreased or disappeared, 33 per cent reported no change, and 16 per cent, that it had increased or appeared for the first time.[26] Among the Philadelphians, 51 per cent report no change; 27 per cent (a third of the women) report an increase; 22 per cent, a reduction.[27]

The reduction in boredom is explained by the activities around the house and yard and the increased social life. Interestingly enough, the house's impact on boredom does not disappear even after its novelty has worn off. Joint family activity drops off, but the house offers diversion even after three years. As one person put it, "You start trimming the lawn or pull one weed, and then you go on to do the job right because you want it to look right, and the time goes. There's less time to be bored."

Increased boredom was concentrated largely in the Philadelphia sample, with people of low status, those under twenty-five and over forty-five, and Jews reporting considerably higher increases and smaller decreases than others. For example, 70 per cent without a high school diploma felt more boredom, as compared to 20 per cent of the college-educated. There is little pattern to the increase. Sometimes it is caused by being kept in the house by weather or children's illnesses; sometimes it is a more permanent feeling of isolation, either because there is not enough housework or because the role change from worker to mother has proved restrictive and less interesting. The major complaint, however, was "nothing to do." Philadelphians who find Levittown dull report boredom more often, as do those who do not belong to organizations or who are less active than they had been in the city. Born-and-bred city people are bored more than those who moved to Philadelphia in adulthood, and so are people who lived with their parents or in-laws or miss relatives and close friends. Those who became organizationally active and some who increased their visiting were less likely to become bored; for others new friends do not seem to be enough, people who felt close to someone in Levittown reporting as much increase in boredom as those who had not found anyone.[28] Their problem is mainly separation from their Philadelphia companions, but also the loss of what one might call the "urban safety valve." As one Philadelphian pointed out, "In the city I was able to go into town every once in a while, but here I can't. I get restless at times, fed up. Then I need a change, have to get out. Being with the kids all the time builds up tension and you get rid of it by going out and away from them." Of course, this was accentuated by the shortage of shopping and window-shopping facilities in Levittown at the time of the interviewing.

If life in Levittown really produced boredom, one would expect an increase over time, but most respondents who had been bored when they first came to Levittown reported a decrease two years later, and only 5 and 8 per cent in the two samples an increase. Of the Philadelphians initially *not* bored, however, 73 per cent say they are now bored. They found Levittown very exciting at the start but now lack activities and friends to keep them busy. Once the novelty wore off, they became disenchanted. Two thirds of these women had been bored in Philadelphia, however, and the early months in Levittown were only a temporary respite. The move initiated boredom for the remaining third and for 17 per cent of the men. The trend to less boredom with length of residence is supported by a study in Levittown, Pennsylvania. Fifty-four per cent with two years' residence were bored, but only 29 per cent with four, and 22 per cent with seven. Of course, the really bored may have left the community, but of those who stayed, only 18 per cent say they are bored more often now than when they first arrived.[29]

Loneliness

Loneliness is as rare in Levittown as boredom.[30] Table 6 shows that only about 20 per cent of the women are lonely at least a few times a month, and taking underreporting into account, these can be thought "really lonely." Loneliness is roughly similar in amount to boredom, and the two also overlap, mainly because being stuck in the house can produce both feelings.[31] Unlike boredom, however, loneliness strikes all kinds of Levittowners and does not vary with age, class, religion, or other characteristics. For example, 20 per cent of blue collar Philadelphians reported being lonely at least a few times a month, but so did 25 per cent of professional ones.[32]

The reason for this unexpected finding is that there are three types of loneliness: *social,* which develops from lack of friends;

familial, which, at least in Levittown, is felt by women cut off from their parents and, more important, from husbands whose jobs require traveling, long hours, or such preoccupation with work that they have little time for their wives; and *chronic,* a personal alienation above and beyond social and familial causes. The three types can strike the same person; indeed, when familial loneliness is not compensated for by social life, it may lead to the chronic variety.

TABLE 6

AMOUNT OF LONELINESS IN LEVITTOWN, WOMEN ONLY *

AMOUNT OF LONELINESS	PER CENT REPORTING	
	Random Sample † *Second Interview*	Philadelphia Sample
"Almost every day"	0	3
"A few times a week"	4	5
"A few times a month"	15	16
"About once a month"	22	14
"Less often than that"	15	19
Never	44	43
N	(27)	(37)

* Respondents were asked, "In a new community, people sometimes feel lonely. How often would you say you feel lonely here?" All categories with the exception of never were read to them.

† In the first interview, the random sample respondents were asked only if they were lonely or not. Nineteen per cent said they were lonely.

Of the small number of really lonely in both samples, 38 per cent gave reasons which suggested social loneliness and 54 per cent, familial. As might be expected, no one admitted chronic loneliness, but I would guess that not more than 10 per cent of Levittown's women were in this condition.[33] Fifty-seven per cent of Philadelphians who had lived with parents or in-laws report being really lonely in Levittown; so do half the wives of salesmen and pilots, but only 12 per cent of those married to office and factory workers.[34] Since 67 per cent of wives with traveling husbands and only 35 per cent of the others were lonely before the move, and since loneliness does not vary with length of trip to work, occupational absence is clearly at fault. (I should note that not all salesmen were travelers, and more subtle psychodynamic factors may be at play in salesmen's marriages.) Improved social life does not reduce this type of familial loneliness, for the proportion lonely is as high among those visiting more as among those visiting less.

Almost half the random sample and 22 per cent of the Philadelphians had been lonely in their former residence, and most seemed to have suffered from social loneliness. Levittown was a godsend for them, for 70 per cent of the former and all of the latter reported less loneliness after the move. One Philadelphian said, "In the city, if I was alone, I stayed home. Here a neighbor comes over to talk. In the city, everyone worked and people didn't come out and talk." In other instances, husbands are no longer away so much, or work shorter hours. For the random sample as a whole, about a third reported that loneliness had set in or increased, a third that it had decreased or disappeared, and a third that nothing had changed. Among the Philadelphians, however, only 22 per cent reported less, and 43 per cent more.[35] The women in the random sample are not seriously bothered; none are really lonely, but in the Philadelphia group more than half are, most of them with familial loneliness. Some who report being lonely in Levittown for the first time are Jews who do not fit into the Jewish subcommunity, being more or less educated than their peers or married to non-Jews. Most of the newly lonely are, however, low-status people (of all religions) who not only miss their families in Philadelphia but also have trouble finding friends in Levittown. Even so, judging from the reasons given for changes in loneliness, the husband's absence and separation from relatives are more frequent causes of loneliness than is social isolation.

Because so much loneliness is familial, it does not decrease with length of residence and, in fact, only becomes apparent after some time in Levittown. For example, of those not lonely after six months in Levittown, 18 per cent of the random sample and 55 per cent of the Philadelphia sample were lonely by the second interview. Some had been seeing their families in the city or were busy venturing into new relationships in Levittown at first. Others were Jewish women, initially quite active, who realized after the organizational tasks had been taken care of and sociability became more important that they did not share prevailing group interests. Conversely, those whose initial loneliness was due to lack of social life reported that it had been dispelled after two years in the community.[36]

Because so many lonely Philadelphians mentioned missing people from the city, this sample was asked an additional question about it.[37] Altogether, 68 per cent of the women and half the men had "close family" in Philadelphia, particularly the wives of blue collar workers, Catholics, Italians, Jews, and previous homeowners. Two thirds saw these relatives less often since they had moved; 15 per cent saw them more, especially recently married women who needed their mothers once they themselves had children. Of those who visit family less often, 35 per cent of the women, but none of the men, feel badly about it. (Whether or not they visit, none of the men, but 53 per cent of the women, miss someone in the city—mainly, of course, their families. Although low-status wives do so most often, higher ones are not far behind.[38]) Religion and ethnic background make no difference, but 80 per cent of the women under twenty-five and the same proportion of mixed marriage partners say they miss their families.

Over time, the physical distance from the family becomes an emotional one, at least for some, 46 per cent missing their families less after two years in Levittown.[39] Eighty-five per cent of these women have met someone else to whom they feel close, 72 per cent having found neighbors and the rest friends. These "family substitutes" do not decrease loneliness for, in this group, people who still miss their families are lonelier than those who do not, but only occasionally so, about once a month.[40] Just 25 per cent of the women who miss their mothers or parents want to move closer to them, but to other suburbs, and none wants to return to the city just to be near them. Undoubtedly, the unanimous failure of husbands to miss their relatives or in-laws is partly responsible.

My definition of real loneliness (a few times a month or more) may be exaggerated, and the resulting data may overestimate the extent of traumatic aloneness. In any case, they hardly demonstrate the alienation which the critics ascribe to suburbia. Indeed, suburbia clearly reduces alienation, its abundant social life even ameliorating the pains of chronic and familial loneliness. But there is also that third of the population for whom one woman spoke when she said, "I'd never feel lonely no matter where I was. There are always nice people close by whom you can visit. And then there's the TV and radio. And besides, I'm always busy and never have time to be lonely." It may be that cosmopolitans project the alienation they experience in American society onto suburbanites.

Problems and Worries

Another way of shedding light on family and individual adaptation in Levittown is through the problems raised and eliminated by the move. The random sample was asked to describe new and old problems; since some respondents seemed hesitant to talk about them, the interview schedule for former Philadelphians added a question about old and new worries, which elicited a better response.[41] Problems and worries are universal, about 60 per cent reporting the former and 93 per cent the latter. Because of the stigma attached to problems, the proportion of worries is probably more accurate. As expected, low-status people reported more problems than higher-status ones, although all classes worried in equal numbers. About 70 per cent of the problems and 62 per cent of the worries could be related to Levittown. The principal irritant was family finances, second was child-rearing, and third was illness.[42]

Seventy-two per cent of the Philadelphians and half the random sample suggested finances as the major trouble spot, with furnishings, heat bills, and the added wear and tear on the automobile mentioned as specifics. Worries about taxes were voiced also, but less often. Obviously, low-status and low-income people (earning under $6500) worried most over finances, but high-income ones (earning over $9000) reported financial problems as often as the rest—they just did not worry so much about them. Families whose income decreased or remained stable after the move worried too, regardless of how much they earned, and poor Levittowners in large numbers said they had not had financial worries before the move.[43] Budgetary troubles create other problems, particularly marital ones. As one blue collar wife explained, "It's money that causes all the other problems. When my husband and I quarrel, it's because of not being able to do things and have things." For most Levittowners, however, increases in the cost of living created inconveniences and occasional arguments rather than serious difficulties. One comment is typical: "Living around here is a little higher than we expected, and we don't have quite so much money to flash around."

Children, too, cause problems and worries, mostly over discipline and school performance. Of fourteen discipline problems reported in the interviews, half could clearly be traced and, of these, five to Levittown. They stem from the attempt to maintain standards in the face of different ones among neighbors. As one mother put it, "In a community like this, they have lots of children who run wild, stay up late at night. When I call my daughter home to bed or supper, she does not want to come because her friends are out late." Middle class families with discipline problems complain about bad influences from neighbors; working class ones, that their children become "smart-alecks" as they grow up. Two Jewish respondents reported difficulties resulting from the pace of Jewish life. "The children are oversocialized here, and there are discipline problems—this is new to Levittown," one said. The other said, "It takes more time to raise children. They belong to more clubs and we have to take them from place to place." School problems result mainly from changing schools, especially when a child moves from a city parochial school to a more permissive public school. Parental roles have an impact on the child as well. In the case of a socially isolated Jewish family, the child seems to be lonely too, which in turn affects his school performance. Of the seven school problems reported, however, only two have developed since the move.

Illness is mentioned third, but all cases were carryovers, not a result of the move, as were three cases of emotional difficulties. The two cases of marital difficulty also existed prior to Levittown, but one marriage broke up after previous economic troubles were augmented by the move. Some respondents were concerned about job problems, and ex-servicemen or Transients who wanted to stay in the community worried about finding work in the area.

While Levittown created new problems and worries, it also reduced or eliminated some old ones. For about a third of the people in each sample, old problems and worries disappeared or were tamed, while only 7 per cent of the random sample and 17

per cent of the Philadelphians reported that old problems had
been exacerbated. The latter difficulties were financial, whereas
improvements were primarily in health and family relationships.
One respondent claimed that his children's asthma had "improved 90 per cent." Better family relationships were credited
largely to the increased space in the house. One mother pointed
out, "We were terribly crowded; now I don't have to sit on the
boys anymore." Another woman said, "I was a golf widow before.
My husband hasn't lost interest in golf, but there are other things
to do. We used to argue a lot. Now he works around the house
and we don't argue." Philadelphians felt they had escaped from
undesirable conditions in the city. One mother summarized it, "I
worry less about the traffic, and kids running in the street. I don't
fear that the kids will be picked up by strangers any more; there
is better police protection here." Others were relieved of traffic
noises, dirt, and living next to factories.

Emotional Disturbance and Mental Illness

Suburbia is purported to breed mental illness, but relevant
data are hard to come by, especially in a new community without
a hospital or a local psychiatrist.[44] Although I talked regularly
with doctors and ministers about the number of nervous breakdowns and people referred to psychiatrists, checked police records for instances of repeated marital conflict and suicide attempts, and tried to learn prior histories, most of the resulting
data are only estimates. During the first two years of Levittown's
existence, while 3000 families were arriving, I counted 14 suicide
attempts, 15 families who appeared more than once before the
police on domestic conflict charges, an estimated 50 nervous
breakdowns, an estimated 100 psychiatric referrals by doctors, a
similar number of cases of pastoral counseling judged by the
ministers to involve "serious" problems, and an estimated 50
juvenile delinquents in repeated difficulties with the police or
the school. Comparisons to other communities are impossible because of the nature of the data and because of the difficulty of
computing rates in a town just being occupied, but the figures do
not seem alarming. I would judge there is no more mental illness, at least of the kind that surfaces into statistics, in Levittown
than in other communities, and certainly less than in the cities.[45]

More important, of 16 case histories gathered from doctors,
ministers, and the police, 13 indicated similar emotional dis-

turbances in former residences, and in no case was there any evidence that the problem had developed in or worsened in Levittown. Indeed, most of these people had come with the hope that a change of scenery might resolve their emotional problems. For example, two women, one married to an alcoholic, the other to a compulsive gambler, persuaded their husbands to move to Levittown, but once the novelty of the house and of home ownership wore off, the old problems returned, and eventually both families moved out. Needless to say, emotional problems resolved by the move did not come to public attention, but I doubt that the move could have solved serious disturbances. Conversely, it could—and did—alleviate emotional problems created by social isolation in the previous residence.

Almost all emotional difficulties that came to light were experienced by women, and among these, two familiar types stand out: the working class woman cut off from her parents and the wife whose husband is occupationally on the road. Among them, the ones who are also socially isolated tend to express their emotional problems visibly and publicly. Nevertheless, in most instances marital conflict is also present, and indeed, the women most beset by breakdowns, even the wives of salesmen, are those with unhappy marriages. A happy marriage does not assure emotional equilibrium and marital difficulties are not necessarily the cause of the trouble, but individual problems often vent themselves in marital tension. Nor does the preponderance of female cases mean that the women are the source of the difficulties, but only that they express family tensions more frequently or more visibly.[46] For a man, the job is often supportive, rewarding him even if he is emotionally disturbed, whereas for a woman, household and maternal functions provide fewer tangible rewards and more minute-to-minute tension. Being alone with small children seems to result in a kind of sensory deprivation for mothers, causing them to lose touch with their adult selves, particularly when they are unduly isolated from the husband or other adults. When serious marital conflict develops, the man may be more disturbed than the woman and may resort to violence, but she calls the police, and it takes a while to discover who is actually the more troubled party.

The suggestion that mental illness has nothing to do with the suburbs may be surprising. It contradicts not only the critics but some English studies which found unexpectedly high rates of treated and untreated mental illness, of all degrees of seriousness, in new towns,[47] and American research in suburbs and rapidly growing communities.[48] These rates are sometimes attributed to the nature of suburban life—falsely, I think. The suburbs—like the English new towns—attract young, relatively sophisticated, and comparatively better-educated people than established communities. As a result, they are physically healthier, and routine anxieties may express themselves through functional illnesses more often than organic ones. A sophisticated population is more aware of emotional problems and able to articulate them, and a new-town population will undoubtedly include disturbed people who came to the town to cure their problems or at least escape from the scene of previous disturbances. As a result, statistics of treated and untreated cases are likely to be higher than in established communities.[49]

New suburbs also attract an unusually large number of socially mobile people. Downwardly mobile people have been shown by many studies to be troubled emotionally, and if they come to a new community with the false hope of improving their lot and find a majority of their neighbors upwardly mobile, their difficulties may only increase. Upwardly mobile people are occasionally beset by problems, too, and it is perhaps no coincidence that the more troubled Levittowners included working class women who had married into the middle class or had left a cohesive ethnic enclave. Mobile people make considerable demands on community institutions which these cannot always satisfy; conversely, hyperactivity or social isolation may drive troubled people to the breaking point.

But the notion that suburban life is inherently stressful and dangerous for all its residents is simply inaccurate. The testimony of people who found Levittown more relaxing than their previous residence, and my own observations about the relatively slow pace of community life, suggest that, if anything, stress is reduced by the move to suburbia. If the stress of organizational life is as great as claimed, it touches only the few who are really active, but most such Levittowners were already active in their former communities, so that Levittown did not create a new strain. The preplanned founding of organizations may even have reduced the pressure of newness on active people. Obviously, stress existed and continues to exist—as it does in all human encounters—but this does not make it inherently pathological.

The American study which found increased mental illness in suburbia was done in an upper middle class area; quite possibly, upper middle class life is more nerve-racking than that of other groups, particularly for people newly arrived at that status.[50] This would explain the high stress among a suburban Jewish population in Toronto so well described by Seeley and his associates.[51] Such people could be found in Levittown as well, putting inordinate pressure on their children to perform well in school and running themselves ragged in community activities. Yet they are not typical of suburbia nor is their behavior inherently suburban.

Indeed, my findings suggest that the major sources of stress are not to be found in the community, but in being left out of it, excluded from activities and relationships of crucial personal importance. *Social isolation is the main source of stress,* be it from spouse, neighbors, friends, or organizations. Even among upper middle class and Jewish Levittowners, those who suffered were not the hyperactive ones but those excluded from activity, and especially those who, not fitting in, were extruded by their groups. Conversely, initially isolated people who became active in Levittown were less troubled than before, even when their activity was hectic and seemingly full of potential stress.

Social isolation can affect anyone, all classes and ages, and can be found in any community. It probably strikes newcomers and mobile persons more often, because they are moving from an old to a new way of life and may not fit in. Levittown, where everybody was a newcomer, reduced this kind of isolation, but the smallness and homogeneity of the population made it difficult for the culturally and socially deviant to find companions. Levittown benefitted the majority but punished a minority with exclusion, what Whyte called the "misery of the deviate." But if Levittown increased their chances of mental illness, it had the opposite effect on a much larger number.

I have purposely concentrated on mental illness rather than mental health in Levittown, because most current definitions of the latter include, overtly or covertly, a conception of the good life which usually equates mental health with an idealized upper middle class cosmopolitan culture and implies that other ways of living are potentially illness-producing. This bias fails to distinguish what is different from what is pathological in other subcultures; and until research shows, for example, that the restrictiveness and localism of some kinds of working class and lower middle class culture are pathological, it is impossible to accept most current definitions of mental health.

The tendency to identify the different as pathological is at the heart of the suburban critique and helps to account for the critics' belief that suburban life is undesirable. Although the move to the suburbs has brought about many positive changes, the critics argue that these are spurious and the suburbanites' contentment self-deceptive. Because the suburban way of life strikes them as intrinsically dull, its sociability unsatisfying, and its activities boring, they believe it will inevitably generate considerable ennui and mental illness in the future.

There is no evidence to back up these predictions, however, and I doubt that they will come to pass, because the critics are not speaking of suburban conditions, but are, again, making negative judgments about lower middle and working class cultures based on their deviation from cosmopolitan values. Levittowners, not sharing these, are not deprived of the urban pleasures of the cultured cosmopolitan since they did not indulge in these pleasures even when they lived in the city. Indeed, none who were bored in Levittown suggested that they missed what cosmopolitans value about the city. On the other hand, alienation from community life reported by some highly educated Levittowners indicates that they share the critics' values. As it turns out, then, the critics are right about members of their own culture, but wrong when they presume to judge and speak for the majority of Levittowners.

References to suburban malaise also express the critics' reaction to novelty. Suburbs first sprang up around American cities about a century ago, but the talk about "suburban malaise" dates only from the development of the postwar housing developments. Class difference intrudes here too, for at first suburbia (another new term) was accessible only to the upper middle class. The critics' fears arose only when lower-status groups were able to move beyond the city limits. The critics seem to be most threatened by communities like Levittowns which are a new social invention. In other countries, similar and equally inaccurate critiques are specifically directed at new settlements; the English worry about "new-town blues," and the Japanese, about "Danchi-byo," an ailment ascribed to brand new suburban projects called *Danchi*.[52] Of course, the critics are not the only ones threatened by newness. For example, Canadian journalists and government officials told hair-raising stories of social disorganization and mental illness among Eskimos in an Arctic new town, but systematic anthropological research concluded they were untrue.[53]

SOME SOLUTIONS TO PROBLEMS OF ADAPTATION

Although only a minority of Levittowners encountered problems and although few of these were distinctive to suburbia, they still need to be solved. One is the women's feeling of being "stuck" in the house. One solution would be separating mothers and children during part of the day through community-wide nursery schools or day-care centers. However, these are most often used by well-educated women, who suffer least from being "stuck." The failure of such schools to reach the women who need them most is only partly one of cost (which could be dealt with), for many lower middle and working class mothers are reluctant to give up their children because it implies that they are poor mothers. If nursery schools were attached to the public school system, they might be less reluctant, but they would still need to find activities of enough significance to justify leaving their children in someone's care. Women with these feelings are often also ill at ease in organizations, but they would respond favorably to work opportunities. However, jobs for women, except as teachers, are as rare in Levittown as in other suburbs. Still, many unfilled community posts exist. The schools could use teachers' aides: the hospitals, nurses' aides; and libraries, government offices, and other public agencies could improve services with auxiliary workers. Levittowners might accept tax increases that would result in employment for women, especially in the form of four- to six-hour jobs, but most likely jobs will have to be created through federal programs like those now being instituted to hire and train "nonprofessionals" to work with the city's poor.[54]

For many women, downtown shopping and window-shopping opportunities are sufficient to overcome physical isolation, but quick and easy access to the city is now not available, and some even have trouble getting to the Levittown shopping center. At the time of my research, the demand for public transportation was too low to encourage private enterprise to provide full service, and the only solution is a system subsidized either by merchants or by a federal mass transit program.[55] Stores within walking distance that can function as informal meeting centers for adults as well as teenagers would also help, but these would have to be located so as to preclude fears of homeowners about decline in property values, which accompany the entrance of commercial facilities into the hearts of residential areas.

The second and more serious problem is social isolation. Adequate public transportation to the city would ameliorate the separation from parents for former Philadelphians, and so would reduced telephone charges. A call from Levittown to the city is now a long-distance one, and people who want to be in daily touch with their families run up monthly phone bills of $20 or more, which they cannot afford. For some, the only solution is either a return to the city or a parental move to the suburbs. The dislike of urban living and the husband's opposition to being near in-laws prevents the former; the high cost of suburban housing for older people who own their homes in the city or pay low rent discourages the latter. Suburban low-rent housing for the elderly might attract some parents, but many want to maintain social ties in the city or need a central location that puts them close to children living in different suburbs. Some Philadelphians might not have moved to Levittown had they known the emotional cost of leaving parents, but there is now no agency to make people aware of this possibility. One cannot expect builders to do it, but discussion of the problem in the mass media might help.

Coping with the husband's absence for occupational reasons is more difficult, although when automation begins to make inroads into white collar jobs, it should be possible to decentralize offices to minimize extended traveling or to reduce the salesman's territory to an area that can be covered in a day or two. Sometimes, occupational absence is only a symptom, however, for men who are uncomfortable in the marital relationship may choose a job that requires traveling. This is part of the more general problem of marital strain. Difficulties caused by financial worries can be reduced by long-term, low-interest loans for the period when the costs of raising a family are greatest, or better still, by adoption of the European system of family allowance grants. It would be possible to set higher income thresholds to discourage potential buyers who cannot really afford home ownership or suburbia, but neither builders nor banks can be expected to do so. Higher FHA thresholds could be required, but preventing young families from realizing the living standards which their culture is constantly preaching would be difficult as well as undesirable. It would be, after all, tantamount to restricting aspirations and arguing that a low-income family is not good enough for the suburbs. Extending the recently established federal rent-supplement program to the purchase of suburban homes would be better.

Other causes of marital difficulty are more difficult to resolve. Despite the social isolation of partners of mixed marriages, it would be facile to discourage marriage across religious or class lines, and wrong as well. Nor can a return to the extended family be proposed or expected. Even if some problems that face young couples (and the nuclear family generally) were reduced by the presence of a parent or other relative in the household, new problems would arise. The Levittowners who previously lived with their parents all reported considerable conflict with the older generation, and none wanted to move back with them. One must accept the reality of nuclear family living, find new institutions and functionaries to replace the parental generation, and help people learn to cope with the strains inevitable to the nuclear family. Some Levittowners have found substitutes among older neighbors, but this assumes an intimacy in the neighbor relationship that is not often possible.

Some pressures on the family can be reduced by counseling, and several suburbs have developed highly successful family counseling agencies.[56] They generally attract only better-educated families; people like the Levittowners more often take their problems to doctors and ministers. Unfortunately, both professions now treat counseling only as a sideline, and are often ill-trained to do it in any case. Levittown patients undoubtedly came to doctors with more functional and "psychosomatic" illnesses than purely organic ones, but most general practitioners had taken only introductory courses in psychiatry. If these doctors were better trained, they could function more adequately as counselors, and if more were available, they could spend more time with each patient. Cost is a fundamental problem, however, and until Medicare is extended to young families and to those with emotional problems as well, people will not get the counseling or the systematic psychotherapy they need. Ministers do not charge fees, and pastoral counseling is likely to become a more significant ministerial role in the near future. The churches must place more stress on this function, and a builder like Levitt, who gives free land to churches, could insist that, in exchange, they appoint ministers who are properly trained in pastoral counseling.

Nevertheless, family counseling agencies should attempt to reach working and lower middle class clients. They need Medicare or other public support to extend their activities, enlarge their staffs, and make their services less expensive, but they must also reorient themselves away from upper middle class culture. I recall a visit to an agency in another Levittown; it was furnished in Danish Modern, with *The New Yorker* and *Time* magazines as reading materials, and classical music on the hi-fi system—thus effectively telling potential clients it was an upper middle class agency before they even got in to see a counselor. Counseling techniques need redesign as well, to provide the kinds of help acceptable to working and lower middle class clients. Psychotherapy may be useful, but when marital conflicts result from financial difficulties, the best solution is a loan; when the problems are social, it is to help clients find compatible people. Psychoanalytic methods need revamping to make them relevant to clients less trained in self-awareness than the upper middle class, and agencies must place less stress on professionalism, instead using the kinds of people and techniques that neighbors do when they provide therapy to each other across a morning cup of coffee. More counselors should share the clients' culture, and more use should be made of the nonprofessional, trained in professional techniques but able to combine these with traditional nonprofessional solutions familiar to the client and relevant to his situation.[57] Until people stop treating marital problems as shameful and counseling as a sign of defeat, agencies will have to be located outside the communities they serve. A greater emphasis on children's problems would also help, not only because many families have them, but also because parents are more willing to bring children in for treatment and can be persuaded to accept help themselves once they realize their own role in the children's difficulties.

The final source of problems is social isolation from compatible people. Meeting people is easier in a new community than in an established one, yet it remains difficult for people who cannot find the right ones, are unable to join organizations, or suffer from a shortage of compatibles in the community. The first group and perhaps the third can be helped by developing local publications which describe organizations not just by their activities but also by the kinds of people who belong—thus institutionalizing a function often performed by the grapevine. The second group might be aided by the formation of small social clubs, modeled on the coffee-klatsch or the fellowship groups of fundamentalist Protestants, both of which serve people with culturally based difficulties in making new friends. The third group must be aided in finding compatible people outside the community; they might also be encouraged to help old friends from the city to move to their suburb, possibly with financial incentives provided by the builder. Some builders have employed social workers and community organizers to function in what Gutman calls "integrator" roles, and these could be helpful in reducing social isolation provided they do not act as front men for the builder to stifle complaints about the houses.[58]

None of these proposals will help people who define compatibility by ethnic or religious criteria or those who suffer from a real shortage of compatible people that cannot be ameliorated by communications devices. Here, perhaps the only solutions are negative or positive methods of tenant selection. The former would discourage purchasers whose social life and emotional support depend on people not now living in the community, by telling them that they can expect to be lonely. The latter would make sure that cultural and social minorities come in sufficient numbers to assure them of social ties. One way of doing this is to announce in advance that ethnic and religious facilities will be available; Levitt did this in order to attract Jewish buyers.[59] A builder could even encourage such minorities to buy as a group by advertising his development in their publications and giving discounts to groups of significant size, without, however, either helping or preventing them from living next door to each other.

These proposals would even increase the diversity of the community and achieve the planner's aim for balance, not to duplicate urban cross sections based on statistical artifact but to promote happier lives. For the people concerned, however, homogeneity would be increased and ethnic assimilation inhibited, but I would argue that involuntary heterogeneity and assimilation policies are rarely effective, and in a community like Levittown, many opportunities exist for those who want diversity and freedom from ethnic tradition.

NOTES

1. On matriarchy see Duhl; on mental illness, Gordon, Gordon, and Gunther. Yet another critic, Wyden, eschews matriarchy, but blames the suburbs for producing children that dominate their parents.
2. The interview questions assumed that boredom, loneliness, etc., existed, and asked respondents to estimate their own, requiring them to volunteer if they were never bored. Comparisons with the former residence similarly asked whether there was more or less boredom, etc., in Levittown, forcing them to volunteer if it had remained the same. They did not hesitate to do so, and probably did not underestimate seriously the amount or increase of boredom.
3. Eighty-three per cent of them, but only 20 per cent of the suburban and small-town respondents, wished husbands to be with children more often.
4. For the sample as a whole, 52 per cent of the wives said their husbands were spending more time with the children, 11 per cent less, and 37 per cent the same.
5. For the random sample, the median trip decreased from 36 minutes to 35. Twenty-nine per cent reported a short trip; 34 per cent a medium one; 26 per cent a long one; and 11 per cent a very long one.
6. Among the random sample, 42 per cent experienced an increased commute, 45 per cent a decreased one. The median increase was 15 minutes; the median decrease, 28.
7. Random sample respondents with an increased work trip also traveled a median 45 minutes now, but 44 per cent traveled 40–59 minutes, and 19 per cent an hour or longer.
8. Among men with medium-length trips, 17 per cent liked it, 12 per cent disliked it, 55 per cent "don't mind" it, and 16 per cent "don't care one way or the other." For those reporting long trips, however, only 3 per cent liked it, 30 per cent disliked it, 47 per cent "don't mind," and 20 per cent "don't care." For men with very long trips, the percentages were 3, 44, 42, and 11 respectively. The proportion of dislikes rose from 15 per cent among people with 30–39-minute trips to 32 per cent with 40–45-minute trips.
9. However, 75 per cent of the Philadelphians drove their own car, and only 20 per cent belonged to a car pool. Six per cent used the bus, but many employed women, whose response was not studied, used it to get to work.
10. Professionals and intellectuals who work in solitude have more privacy, and since time is their scarcest resource, probably find driving to work a boring and unnecessary expenditure of time.

Among the Levittowners, half the professionals and white collar workers, but only 29 per cent of the blue collar workers, found driving 40 minutes or more to work wearing. Moreover, professionals and white collar workers reported longer commutes, both before and in Levittown, than blue collar ones. These findings suggest why planners have been more anxious about the suburban journey to work than many of the people for whom they are planning.

11. For a similar finding see Blood and Wolfe, p. 172.

12. Thirty-seven per cent of the wives had more time with their husbands, 13 per cent, less, and half, the same. For the husbands, the percentages were 4, 6, and 50 respectively.

13. Eighty per cent of the wives whose husbands have short work trips report spending more time with them, as compared to 20 per cent and 33 per cent of those whose husbands have medium and long trips. The husbands who report more time with their wives have shorter work trips since the move.

14. The question was worded, "Does your family do more things together in Levittown than where you lived before, or fewer things?" Although the interviewer did not suggest that more joint family activity was desirable, respondents answered as if it were.

15. In the first interview 43 per cent reported more, 2 per cent less, and 55 per cent the same. In the second, the percentages were 45, 10, and 45.

16. The interview question read, "How do you and your husband (or wife) get along in Levittown, better than where you lived before or not as well?" In the random sample, 23 per cent reported improvement, 3 per cent deterioration, and 74 per cent no change; in the Philadelphia one, the figures were 20, 11, and 69 per cent respectively.

17. Comparative studies of urban and suburban marriages surveyed by Ubell found little difference in marital happiness when social and economic variations between suburbanites and city dwellers were controlled.

18. Since suicide is a crime in New Jersey, attempts must be reported to the police, and the number appearing on the police blotter is probably accurate.

19. People were asked whether their "disposition or state of mind had gotten better, worse or stayed the same since they moved to Levittown."

20. Among the random sample, 34 per cent of the women reported better morale, 11 per cent, worse, and 55 per cent, no change. For the men, the percentages were 39, 0, and 61 per cent respectively. Among the Philadelphia men, 28 per cent said their morale was better, 17 per cent, worse, and 55 per cent, no change.

21. Twenty per cent of working class Philadelphians were happier, but 40 per cent were unhappier. In a predominantly working class English new town, 19 per cent reported better "general fitness,"

12 per cent, worse, and 68 per cent, no change. About the same proportions obtained for ability to sleep, but 30 per cent had a better appetite and only 6 per cent a poorer one. Taylor and Chave, p. 39.

22. The men's disposition is not affected by a longer work trip.

23. In the working class English new town, 26 per cent were now in better health, 14 per cent in poorer. Taylor and Chave, p. 38. Among Philadelphia working class respondents in Levittown, the proportions reporting change were about the same, 21 per cent reporting better health and the same number poorer.

24. "Nervous" English new-town residents also reported poorer health than the rest. Taylor and Chave, pp. 55–56.

25. Among the Philadelphians, 45 per cent of the well educated and 57 per cent of the least educated, and 60 per cent of the blue collar workers reported some boredom; 16, 36, and 20 per cent were bored at least a few times a month. The English working class new-town survey distinguished only between the absence and presence of boredom, and found 38 per cent were bored, with no difference between the sexes. Taylor and Chave, computed from Table 33, p. 66.

26. The group reporting no change includes 31 per cent who were never bored, either in Philadelphia or Levittown; among the random sample, the percentage is 23.

27. In the random sample, 19 per cent of the women and 12 per cent of the men report new or increased boredom; for 57 and 41 per cent, respectively, it has decreased or disappeared. Among the Philadelphians, 32 per cent of the women and 17 per cent of the men say they are more or newly bored; 30 per cent and 5 per cent, respectively, say they are less or no longer bored.

28. Although 60 per cent in this group who do less couple visiting are more bored now, so are 38 per cent of those doing more, and 44 per cent of those doing more neighbor visiting. However, a quarter of those who found someone spoke of less boredom, but none of those unable to find someone.

29. Pierson's study showed that 80 per cent reported no change, and the general pattern did not vary with length of residence. The kinds of people who are bored and the reasons they give are the same as in the newer Levittown. Only well-educated women complain about boredom more than in Levittown, New Jersey, perhaps because they are more isolated in a community with a larger working class population.

30. Only women were asked about loneliness, since the first interview had shown that none of the men felt lonely. I do not know whether they were reporting accurately or refusing to admit to a feeling associated with women.

31. The question on loneliness appeared in a different part of the interview schedule from the one on boredom to prevent overlap.

In the random sample, 60 per cent of those lonely a few times a month or more are also bored that often, and vice versa. Only 38 per cent of bored Philadelphians are lonely, and 70 per cent of the "never bored" are at least occasionally lonely.

32. The English new-town survey found 26 per cent of the women lonely, boredom also overlapping with loneliness. Men were as often bored as women, but reported little loneliness. Taylor and Chave, computed from Table 33 and pp. 66–67.

33. This is purely a guess, but of the nine women in the random sample lonely before Levittown and still lonely now, one was lonely a few times a week, and four more a few times a month. The first would represent 3 per cent of the total sample, the latter 15 per cent, but it is questionable whether people who are lonely that infrequently can be called chronic cases.

34. In the random sample, 44 per cent of salesmen's and pilots' wives and none of office and factory workers' said they were lonely.

35. In both samples, the 35 per cent reporting no change said they had never been lonely in either residence.

36. Fifty-eight per cent of the random sample and 41 per cent of the city one said they had been lonely the first six months, but they all reported less loneliness after two years. Interestingly enough, when they were first interviewed, only 19 per cent of the former said they were lonely, although after two years, 58 per cent remembered being lonely at the start. Evidently, loneliness was felt less while it was actually being endured, perhaps because many people shared it, perhaps because standards for loneliness had risen in the meantime.

37. The question was, "Did you have any close family, I mean relatives you were really close to, where you lived before?"

38. Sixty per cent of the least educated and 67 per cent of the blue collar wives miss someone, but so do 53 per cent of the better educated, and 57 per cent of the white collar wives. Wives of professionals do not miss their families, however.

39. Thirty-nine per cent miss them as much, and 15 per cent, more.

40. Sixty-eight per cent of the women with close relatives in the city are lonely in Levittown, as compared to 34 per cent without them, but those who miss relatives are no lonelier than those who do not miss them. People who now miss their families more than they did at the start are lonelier than those who now miss them less or no more than before.

41. People were asked, "Making a home and raising a family sometimes brings problems such as illnesses, discipline problems, school problems, marriage problems, job or money problems, and the like. What problems have you and your family experienced since you moved to Levittown?" The Philadelphians were also asked, "What things have you worried about more since you moved to Levittown?"

42. In the English new town, only 33 per cent reported problems, financial ones being mentioned most often and illness second. Taylor and Chave, computed from Table 38 and pp. 77–78.

43. A quarter of Philadelphians with rising incomes, but two thirds of those with decreasing and 55 per cent of those with stable incomes, worried over finances.

44. The most explicit statement of this charge is in Gordon, Gordon, and Gunther.

45. In the English new town, 33 per cent of the adults reported "subclinical neurotic symptoms," and 14 per cent more were treated by general practitioners and psychiatrists. Taylor and Chave, p. 166. These rates are lower than reported for cities; a New York survey, for example, found almost 80 per cent of the population beset with psychiatric symptoms ranging from mild to serious. See Srole et al.

46. English studies also report more emotional difficulties among women than men. See Martin, Brotherston, and Chave; Taylor and Chave, p. 125.

47. Martin, Brotherston, and Chave. A later study concluded, however, that there were no differences in the number reporting "nervous symptoms" in an old town, a new town, and a new dormitory suburb. See Taylor and Chave, p. 49.

48. The Gordons found a higher incidence of emotional disorders in newly suburbanizing counties than in nearby rural areas. Gordon and Gordon; and Gordon, Gordon, and Gunther. A study of fifty Massachusetts communities by Wechsler found that rapid growth resulted in significantly higher rates of hospitalized depressive disorders and suicide.

49. Martin, Brotherston, and Chave found mental illness and psychoneurotic symptoms highest among newly arrived residents and the old people. Taylor and Chave (p. 125) found them highest among the latter. Psychologists active in American suburbs have also observed "post-occupancy depression," e.g., in Urban Studies Center, pp. 13–14, but I saw little of it in Levittown. If it had occurred, one would expect the random sample to have reported lower morale in the first interview than in the second, but it did not.

50. The Gordons contrasted the suburbs with an agricultural community which seemed more ideal than real, and their findings may show only that suburbs for the upwardly mobile are more stressful than static but affluent rural areas. This critique is detailed in Gans (1962c).

51. Seeley, Sim, and Loosley, Part II passim.

52. The "new-town blues" are analyzed critically by Thomas. For a study of the *Danchi*, see Hoshino.

53. See Honigmann.

54. See, e.g., Pearl and Riessman.

55. Levittown's internal public transportation is better than most,

thanks to a "jitney" system which goes to the main shopping center every half hour.

56. Urban Studies Center, pp. 16–27.
57. This role is described in detail in Reiff and Riessman.
58. The emotional difficulties of the move and prospects for reducing them are discussed in Urban Studies Center, and by Gutman.
59. He identified a site for a synagogue on the community map before the community was occupied and before any plans for a Jewish congregation had been made. Jewish buyers were thus told that the Jewish population would be large enough for a temple, and it became a self-fulfilling prophecy. Of course, Levittown also attracted Jews because the builder is Jewish, for many seem to choose houses built by their coreligionists when they can.

Chapter Eleven

THE IMPACT OF
THE COMMUNITY

CRITICS OF SUBURBAN LIFE ASSUME THAT THE UNDESIRABLE FEA-
tures of life beyond the city limits are produced by behavior and
attitude changes people undergo when they move out there, and
thus they conclude that it is necessary to do away with or transform the suburbs if American civilization is to be preserved. City
planners assume similarly that the community creates a negative
impact on people, and propose policies for a "well-planned"
community that will produce more desirable behavior. By "community" the planner means the "physical" community; the architecture, site layout, transportation system, and array of community facilities must, he argues, be altered through a master
plan that will then improve the social environment.

A number of sociological studies have effectively questioned
the amount of change that results from the suburban move.[1]
Consequently, I have tried to go one step further: to find out *who*
is actually changed by the move and *how,* and which *sources* and
agents within that complex mixture of physical, economic, social,
and political components we call "the community" create the
change and therefore its impact.[2] By sources, I mean such causal
factors as the move from apartment to house or from city to suburb, as well as Levittown's social structure. Unless the real
sources can be isolated, effective policies for altering and improving the community cannot be formulated. In this connection, I
proposed in the Introduction that change could be either *in-*

tended or *unintended,* the former resulting from the reasons and aspirations for moving to the suburbs, the latter developing after people move out, and therefore traceable to the community itself. Intended changes can be satisfied or frustrated in the community, but since their origin lies elsewhere, their elimination—if that is desired—can come only by altering people's aspirations or creating better solutions for existing aspirations. Unintended changes can be dealt with by intervention in the community, however, provided their sources are in the community and are not outside ones such as the national economy, or extraneous ones such as the impact of children's ages on family cohesion.

I must repeat that the data are based on small samples and cannot be considered statistically significant. Nevertheless, the findings are valid, because they often fit into a pattern. Levittown has created similar changes for similar kinds of people, and these can be attributed to a limited number of sources, some related to the community, many unrelated.

GENERAL BEHAVIOR CHANGE

The overall amount of change after the move to Levittown can be estimated from the fact that three fourths of both samples mentioned one or more changes in their lives.[3] Many changes were intended: 62 per cent of those reported in the first interview with the random sample, 51 per cent in the second. Preoccupancy aspirations were realized as well, since 86 per cent of the random sample achieved the changes it had desired. However, 48 per cent of those not wanting any change also experienced some, suggesting the emergence of unintended effect.

In the first interview the most change, as well as the highest proportion of intended change, was reported by previous city dwellers, apartment dwellers, and renters. Suburbanites, small-town residents, and owners encountered not only less change but less intended change. This finding can be explained by the kinds of changes people reported. Early intended ones were mainly the increased morale stemming from home ownership and the satisfactions from increased visiting, which were of course principal moving reasons for urbanites, but already familiar experiences for former suburbanites. The latter therefore reported more unintended change.[4] High-status people reported change and intended change more often than low-status people; the latter had perhaps thought less specifically about the future and were surprised by unexpected effects. As one working class Levittowner put it:

> We didn't know before we moved here that we would entertain more, go out less. Not that we were boozehounds before, though. Not that we can't afford to go out; we just don't want to. We have a new house and want to keep it up nice; this is not work but enjoyment. I've never been more content. In the city, we looked forward to going to the shore; here my mind is occupied all the time. Over there, if she asked me to wash, paint, I'd throw my things at her; here I do it . . . I even gave up fishing here. Working in the yard is just like fishing, so relaxing. I have more pep here than in Philadelphia.

By the second interview former city residents report the most unintended change, class differences have vanished, and even the people who had thought a lot about their life in Levittown before arrival now report more unintended than intended change. The major unintended effects are increased organizational activity and more visiting (half the respondents mentioning the former, 14 per cent the latter), but 25 per cent are now negative ones—not having enough friends or missing parents back home. The principal intended changes were, as before, the satisfaction of the house and more visiting. Even so, when it comes to the source of change, 67 per cent is now attributable to the social structure of the new community and only 25 per cent to the house.

Women reported more change, and more of the intended variety than men did, in both interviews, probably because they were more interested in the house to begin with. The men were more surprised by the pleasures of their house and the new social life. Among the Philadelphians, there was less sexual difference, men reporting as much change as women, indicating the impact of the move from city to suburb.

A second way of estimating the overall impact of the community is through a summary of changes reported for individual types of behavior. As Table 7 indicates, the move typically resulted in change for only about half the respondents. Since none experienced a consistent pattern of change across *all* types of behavior, however, people could not be divided simply into changers and nonchangers.

SPECIFIC BEHAVIOR CHANGES

Levittown's impact and the reasons for its impact are best described through specific behavior changes and their sources. Some of the data reported in previous chapters (on individual adaptation, family life, and visiting) are reanalyzed briefly to identify the sources which produced the changes already reported. (All of the data, old and new, are brought together in Table 7.)

Individual Adaptation

The sources of change in morale, boredom, loneliness, and worries are often similar, and can be traced to the house, home ownership, social life (these being the major sources of improvement), social isolation, and separation from relatives. The major non-Levittown sources (aside from those causing chronic depression and loneliness) are probably age and the husband's absence from the home. Higher morale can be traced to the house, since apartment dwellers experienced the greatest increase, although among former urbanites the role of the yard in decreasing adult supervision of children was also mentioned.[5] Estimating roughly, about half the reduction in boredom could be traced to work around the house and yard, a quarter to social and organizational activities, and the rest to a combination of the two.

Since the Philadelphia sample—particularly the women—showed less improvement and more deterioration for all types of adaptation, it would seem not only that the move from city to suburb resulted in undesirable emotional effects but also that the move causes change in individual adaptation. A more detailed analysis indicates otherwise, however. For one thing, half the Philadelphians were bored before coming to Levittown, suggesting that city life can bring on ennui too. (The source was lack of compatible neighbors, particularly among apartment dwellers.) Since the same people reported higher morale, less boredom, and less loneliness in Levittown, the move and the population mix that created Levittown's social life had a positive impact. Nevertheless, both the lower morale and the greater boredom experienced by some Philadelphians stem from community-related sources in Levittown: physical and social isolation and separation from relatives. Former Philadelphians were stuck in the house without the access to downtown stores that had previously

TABLE 7

CHANGES OF BEHAVIOR AND ATTITUDES IN LEVITTOWN [a]

| | Random Sample | | | | | | Philadelphia Sample | | |
| | 1st Interview | | | PER CENT REPORTING 2nd Interview | | | | | |
ITEM: Change after moving to Levittown.	More	Less	Same	More	Less	Same	More	Less	Same
Disposition *	46	5	49	36	6	58	22	31	47
Health *	N.A.	N.A.		18	18	64	9	17	74
Boredom	N.A.	N.A.		16	51	33	27	22	51
Boredom: those bored in previous residence only	4	38	58	10	70	20	20	52	28
Boredom: since first six months in Levittown	N.A.	N.A.		5	57	38	8	77	15
Loneliness	N.A.	N.A.		30	35	35	43	22	35
Loneliness: those lonely in previous residence only	N.A.	N.A.		23	70	7	0	100	0
Loneliness: since first six months in Levittown	N.A.	N.A.		7	93	0	0	100	0
Problems: new ones in Levittown **	N.A.	N.A.		81	19	0	71	29	0
Problems: fate of old ones in Levittown * b	N.A.	N.A.		39	7	N.A.	34	17	N.A.
Worries: new ones in Levittown **	N.A.	N.A.		N.A.	N.A.	N.A.	63	37	N.A.
Worries: fate of old ones in Levittown * c	N.A.	N.A.		N.A.	N.A.	N.A.	37	N.A.	N.A.
Children's school performance *	N.A.	N.A.		24	21	55	27	17	56
Parents: time spent with children	38	3	59	N.A.	N.A.	N.A.	N.A.	N.A.	N.A.
Wives: husbands' time spent with children	52	11	37	N.A.	N.A.	N.A.	N.A.	N.A.	N.A.
Husbands: time spent with wives	43	6	51	N.A.	N.A.	N.A.	N.A.	N.A.	N.A.
Wives: time spent with husbands	37	13	50	N.A.	N.A.	N.A.	N.A.	N.A.	N.A.

Joint family activity: parents and children	43, 2, 55	45, 10, 45	N.A. / N.A.
Joint family activity: since first six months in Levittown	N.A.	40, 3, 57	N.A. / N.A.
Joint couple activity			40, 20, 40
Quality of marital relationship *	29, 3, 68	23, 3, 74	20, 11, 69 / N.A.
Visiting family in Philadelphia	N.A.	N.A.	15, 68, 17
Visiting with neighbors	52, 24, 24	54, 16, 30	48, 19, 33
Visiting with neighbors: since first six months in Levittown	N.A.	30, 23, 47	N.A. / N.A.
Visiting with couples	39, 19, 44	44, 21, 35	39, 22, 39
Visiting with couples: since first six months in Levittown	N.A.	43, 23, 34	N.A. / N.A.
Visiting with those of similar ethnic–religious background			19, 30, 51
Organizational activity	N.A.	53, 7, 40	44, 11, 45
Church attendance	N.A.	33, 9, 58	29, 15, 56
Political party preference ***	N.A.	N.A.	19 / 81
Spare time	N.A.	35, 56, 9	N.A.
Spare time activities ***	N.A.	71, 29	N.A. / N.A.
Furniture style preference ***	N.A.	30, 70	25 / 75
Length of journey to work #	42, 45, 13	30, N.A., 70	25, 30 / 25, 45

* Read: better—worse—same   # Read: longer—shorter—same
*** Read: change—no change   ** Read: yes—no
N.A.: not asked

a The number of persons responding for the random sample is usually 44, for the Philadelphia one, 55. In the former, N for women only was 26; in the latter, 37.
b These data are only for improvement or deterioration; lack of change was not studied.
c These data are only for improvement.

assuaged boredom. Among them, those who found friends and organizations suffered less, but socially isolated working class people suffered more. Depression, boredom, and loneliness were most serious among people who had formerly been close to parents and childhood friends, however, so that it was not the move from city to suburb, but from a particular kind of city life—that of the working class or ethnic "urban village"—which produced deleterious effects. Only 28 per cent of the overall increase in boredom could be attributed to Levittown, suggesting that much boredom was prior or chronic.

The sources of impact can also be seen through long-run change. Levittown's social life reduced boredom for the previously isolated, but its newness provided only temporary respite for many Philadelphians, their boredom returning as physical and social isolation and familial loneliness beset them. Yet Levittown's permanent role was minor; two thirds of these women had been bored in Philadelphia too. For about a quarter of the total sample of city women, and about 10 per cent of men, Levittown meant new boredom, however, social isolation being the major source and the role change from worker to mother the second.

Loneliness existed among 48 per cent of the random sample women and 22 per cent of the Philadelphians before they ever came to Levittown; even then it was due to the same factors that caused it in Levittown—the husband's traveling, separation from relatives, and social isolation. The random sample proportion is high because of Transients who are far away from their parents; the Philadelphia one is low because they were still close. The new opportunities for visiting ended social loneliness for all those previously isolated, and even reduced it for Transients missing their parents. But 43 per cent of the Philadelphians found themselves newly lonely, because of the absence of husband, of relatives, and because of social isolation—in that order. Loneliness also increased over time, familial as well as social loneliness having been held back at first by the newness of the community.

Levittown's quantitative impact on loneliness was as follows: 12 per cent of the random sample (and 8 per cent of the Philadelphia one) found that loneliness had disappeared or decreased after the move; 4 per cent (and 11 per cent), that it rose during the early months in Levittown but then disappeared; another 4 per cent (and 5 per cent), that it disappeared at first and then returned; and 19 per cent (and 43 per cent), that it was created by the move. A significant proportion was not affected by Levittown at all, however; 35 per cent of the random sample (and 8 per cent of the Philadelphia one) had been lonely at least once a month before and remained so in Levittown, and 26 per cent (and 25 per cent) said they had never been and were not lonely now.

Problems and worries, which also contributed to lower morale, could be traced to Levittown in about two thirds of the cases. These resulted principally from financial problems due to the higher cost of living, the sources being both home ownership and such community-related features as greater car expenses and taxes. Sixty-three per cent of the Philadelphians reported new worries after coming to Levittown. Of all their worries, about a third were old ones, 55 per cent were new and related to Levittown, and 15 per cent were new but unrelated. Once more, financial worries were uppermost among new ones, but a quarter stemmed from the impact of heterogeneity on children's behavior at home and at school. Conversely, over a third of both samples found problems and worries reduced or disappearing, the space provided by the house giving people more privacy and making family life less discordant, and the lack of traffic in the streets eliminating fear for the children's safety.

Family Life

Levittown's impact on family life represented the achievement of an intended change for most people, the new house playing a major role. Family members who wanted more time together had it, partly because commuting did not increase, but mainly because they wanted it. More time was diverted to the family by increased opportunity to do things together, at first in fixing up the house and yard.[6] The role of the house is demonstrated further by the sharp increase in joint family activity among former apartment dwellers, whether they came from cities or suburbs. Part of the impact of the house was the result of novelty, for after two years people cited patio and community recreational opportunities as more important than the house. These interests may also wear off over time, although 40 per cent of the respondents reported more joint activity at the time of the second interview than at the first, and only 3 per cent reported less. For former city dwellers, the long-term impact of house and community is even greater, for 62 per cent found more joint family activity than at arrival, as compared to only 30 per cent of former suburbanites. A second source of family cohesion, perhaps most important in the long run, was the age of children, which was extraneous to Levittown, and suggests that suburbia per se plays only a minor role in familial change.

The sources of increased cohesion among spouses are also house and community, but after two years the former has not yet lost its novelty value for former city dwellers, suggesting that the move to a house is more important than that to the suburb. The Philadelphians also reported some decrease, largely as a result of babies' taking time away from the parents, older children separating them when they leave the family to be with other youngsters, and men's longer work hours.

Three quarters of the random sample attributed what little change took place in the quality of married life to joint activity around the house, greater privacy gained by additional space, and "maturity" associated with home ownership.[7] Two years later, the impact of the house had begun to wear off, but again, not among the Philadelphians, who still give it as the prime reason for getting along better with their spouses.[8] Even so, the group reporting better marital relations most often are men who have moved away from parents and in-laws, 50 per cent saying their marriages had improved. Only 14 per cent of the women felt this way, but neither they nor the men reported poorer marriages as a result of leaving parents. The suburban separation from relatives thus has some family benefits to counteract the emotional costs to the individual. But suburbia had marital costs too; almost all Philadelphians who reported a poorer marriage blamed financial problems contracted in Levittown.

Although English new-town studies have reported that nuclear family cohesion increases after separation from the extended family in the city, this was not the case among Levittowners.[9] People having close relatives in Philadelphia, those who missed them, and even those who had lived with them before all reported doing fewer things with their spouse in Levittown than people without relatives in the city. Marital life, however, improved among couples who did not miss close relatives.[10]

Because arrival in Levittown was followed by a rash of pregnancies (and much joking about it as well), people were asked whether "living here had anything to do with your wanting another child." The jokes had children being conceived because entertainment facilities were scarce, and later, because pregnancy was fashionable—the "suburbia as rabbit hutch" myth. Forty-three per cent of the random sample and 62 per cent of the Philadelphia sample had children after moving, but 71 per cent of the former and 53 per cent of the latter said they had intended to enlarge their families. None of the remainder ascribed the new babies to Levittown; [11] they explained that they either did not practice birth control or that the children were "accidental." [12] Perhaps the latter came as an unintended result—or expectation —of greater contentment in Levittown, for one woman said blithely, "It just happened when we were moving."

Neighbor and Couple Visiting

The sizeable increases in visiting were largely intended, 40 per cent of the random sample saying they came to Levittown with the idea of doing more visiting of both kinds. Levittown enabled them to achieve their wish, for the greatest increase was reported by those intending it.[13] Yet there were also unintended changes, mostly in the direction of more visiting.[14] The sources of change are the newness of the community and the population mix; the friendliness of the people and the availability of compatible ones even persuading some to do more visiting than they had intended. Decreases, largely unintended, were explained by the lack of compatible people.[15]

If suburbia had a significant impact on social life, one would expect former city dwellers to report a greater increase in visiting than former suburbanites, and this occurred in neighboring, but not in couple visiting. However, even the increase in neighboring is more a result of the move from apartment to house than from city to suburb, and from transitional areas, urban and suburban, where compatible neighbors were scarcer.[16] Compatibility in Levittown is more influential than the move, for not all former city residents reported the same changes. Moreover, being integrated into the community played a major role. In both samples, organizationally active people and Jews, who were so well organized as an ethnic group, reported the greatest increases in couple visiting, whereas partners in mixed marriages reported significant decreases. The lesser increase in couple visiting as compared to neighboring among Philadelphians is explained by their continued association with old friends in the city, although those lacking compatible people in Levittown preferred old friends more than the rest.[17]

Changes over time again identify the primary sources of change. If the initial increase in visiting had been due to the community's newness, decreases should have taken place after two years, but 30 per cent of the random sample reported more neighboring then than after six months (when most said they had settled down), 43 per cent reported more couple visiting, and only 23 per cent reported decreases for both types of visiting. The changes go hand in hand; those who visited neighbors more also visited couples more, and vice versa. In some instances, the reduction was due to the fading of novelty and the departure of favorite neighbors, but the greatest reductions between interviews, in both kinds of visiting, took place among low-status people and mixed-marriage partners; the greatest increases, among people of middle status and organization members. Compatibility or lack of it is still the significant source of change.

Compatibility and the population mix which creates it are usually found in the suburbs, but are not uniquely suburban; they occur in all new settlements, even in the city, because they bring together homogeneous young people.[18] Consequently, the increase in social life cannot be ascribed as much to suburbia as to newness and to the desire for sociability among residents.[19] Nevertheless, neither friendliness nor the population mix are a result of newness per se, for as long as people remain compatible, and compatible people remain in the community, visiting will not be reduced by the mere aging of the community, but only by the development of population turnover—and incompatibility— over time.[20]

Organizational Participation

I turn now to behavior changes not discussed previously, and will describe both the changes and their sources. One of the most frequently reported changes was an increase in organizational activity: 53 per cent of the random sample and 44 per cent of the Philadelphia sample considered themselves more active in secular and church-related organizations (not including churches) than in the former residence. Altogether, 73 per cent in both samples belonged to local groups, though almost three fifths of all memberships were in churches and church-related ones only, and just 30 per cent (in both samples) belonged to a secular organization. The rise in activity was as high among people who described themselves as particularly active in their former residence as among the rest.[21] True to expectations, high-status people reported increased activity most often, but half of the low-status respondents were more active than before, particularly in religious groups. The desire to meet people, the availability of more spare time, and the need to join PTA or the church because children were old enough to be in school or Sunday school were the prime reasons for stepped-up membership, although a fifth of the more active also said they wanted "to be a part of the community" or were persuaded by friends and neighbors to help out by joining.

A slight majority of the random sample, 58 per cent, was intended joiners, but the proportions varied by type of organization.[22] Intended memberships reflected personal or family needs, leading people into church, PTA, or Scout groups; unintended ones implied a greater involvement in community affairs. Seventy per cent of memberships in churches or church-related groups were intended, but only 22 per cent of those in civic and service clubs, and none in social, political, and cultural groups. Indeed, unintended activity was usually stimulated from outside the home, 58 per cent of the respondents indicating they had been asked to join by a neighbor or a canvasser, and 14 per cent, because they had seen the group's announcement in the paper.[23] Unintended members had also been less active in their former communities.

The high proportion of intended joining suggests that Levittown's impact on organizational activity was hardly universal.[24] The intended joiners were most interested in meeting new people or providing for their children, neither of which factors could be considered specific to Levittown, but the unintended joiners came also because they were asked, responding to the community's newness, to the need of organizations to enroll members, and to people's desire to belong to the community in some way. If suburbia per se encouraged organizational activity, however, one would have expected former city residents to be more active than former suburbanites (which was not the case) and also that there would be an increase in activity over time. The latter did take place, because of the scarcity of groups at the time of the first interview; even so, 30 per cent who had been members at the time of that interview had dropped out by the second interview.[25] A quarter of the dropouts could not get along with their fellow members; the rest left because family obligations of one kind or another were more important to them.

Religious Attendance

Although suburbia has allegedly brought about a religious revival, only a third of the Levittowners reported increased church or synagogue attendance after the move, and close to 60 per cent said no change had taken place.[26] If suburbia were responsible for the rise, former city dwellers should have reported more attendance, but as Table 7 indicates, increased attendance was about the same for both samples, and the Philadelphians actually experienced a greater decrease in attendance than the random sample. Although this could mean that the move to the suburbs discourages religiosity, it is actually a result of relaxed parental ties, for Philadelphians who had lived with parents or in-laws report considerably more decrease than others.[27]

If suburbia were the source of change, it should have been uniform for all religions, but in both samples, Jews increased their attendance most often and Catholics the least. In the random sample, 14 per cent of the Catholics and all of the Jews now worshipped more often, and none of them worshipped less often. Twenty-nine per cent of the Protestants also worshipped more often, but 17 per cent, less often.[28] Catholic stability is explained by the compulsory nature of attendance, but among other religious groups, changes reflect the impact of the community—particularly the intensity of church organization. Jews responded less to religion than to the ethnic subcommunity, and Jewish women, who were more active in it, reported a higher increase in attendance than men.[29] On the other hand, Catholic men were more active than women in their church, and their Mass attendance rose more than their wives'. The previously noted marginality of mixed-marriage partners manifests itself again; they reported the smallest increase and the largest decrease in church attendance.[30]

The role of the community comes through clearly in the reasons Jews and Protestants give for increasing worship. Among the former, the search for friends, the need to have the children educated in Jewish ways, and the adult desire to be part of the Jewish subcommunity were mentioned in equal numbers. As one respondent summarized it, "To be honest, it's partly social. There is a moral responsibility to make a good synagogue and to have a Sunday school for the children, but it's also for affairs and activities." "Belonging" was most important to former city dwellers, and in the words of one, "In New York, [religious observance] was only for the very old and the very religious. Here you get an identity and you flock to your own kind." While most Jews would eventually have joined a synagogue to educate their children, living among non-Jews hurried the process and produced an unintended effect of the move to Levittown. That the search is for ethnic cohesion rather than religiosity is brought out by the fact that none of the Jews with Christian spouses reported increased synagogue attendance.

Protestants stressed even more that "it's for the children's sake," and "to be a part of the community." They do not see the community as a group of fellow religionists, however, but as a place in which to settle down. One pointed out, "We are active in the community, so we should be active in church too." A former tenant explained his failure to go to church before he moved to Levittown by saying, "Apartment living is not conducive to churchgoing; you are withdrawn into yourself, you don't do as many things." In fact, former apartment-dwelling Protestants in both samples increased their church attendance more than row house or single-family home occupants, and former city dwellers more than suburbanites.[31] Among Philadelphia Protestants, but no others, higher church attendance was also associated with increased visiting, suggesting that the church helped integrate them into social life—or vice versa.[32] Purely social motives for church attendance were rare, however, only 20 per cent of Protestant friendships being made in church, as compared to 42 per cent among Jews.[33] My hunch is that Protestants who felt themselves part of the community were more active religiously and socially, whereas those left out of it were less active.

For these Protestants and almost all Jews, the suburban move brought about greater religious participation, but it had different meanings and sources for each. Both attended partly for their children's sake and for social reasons, but the Protestants were impelled principally by home ownership, the Jews by ethnic needs heightened by the population mix. In neither case was there any evidence of a religious revival, however. Nor do people attend more often for social than for theological reasons since they moved to the suburbs, although I doubt that they were as theologically inclined in the city and in the fabled past as is sometimes claimed.

Political Party Shifts

Suburbs are often reputed to turn Democrats into Republicans, but in Levittown, only about a fifth of the voters have changed parties, many of them Democrats who became independents, "voting for the man, not the party." Among the Philadelphians, 21 per cent of former Democrats, 10 per cent of former Republicans, and 22 per cent of former independents reported changing their party preference after moving to Levittown.[34] The changers were more often high-status people (none of the low-status respondents gave up their prior party allegiance) and of all religions; however, Irish Catholics—in political transition all over the country—changed parties twice as often as all other ethnic groups. Four of the six previous Democrats became independents and two became Republicans; two previous independents and a Republican were now voting Democratic. The numbers are minuscule, but they do not indicate a shift to Republicanism.[35] Indeed, they suggest that class, not party, is the crucial factor. Three middle class Irish residents indicated that they were no longer voting for the Democratic party but for the man, whereas a working class Protestant, traditionally Republican, chose the Democrats in Levittown because she felt closer to them. Insofar as the move itself was an expression of aspirations for social mobility, the change in voting is a byproduct rather than an effect of the move, the equivalent of an intended rather than an unintended change. If Levittown had an impact, it was to provide people from Philadelphia (then virtually a one-party city) with more choice among parties and the opportunity, as independents, to free themselves of party allegiance. Only time will tell, however, whether this is an effect of suburbia, or only of the newness of the community, that is, an expression of the desire to postpone a choice until party images have stabilized.

Despite their new status as tax-paying home owners and their better opportunity to get to know the candidates, the Philadelphians did not vote in larger numbers after moving to Levittown. Indeed, only 2 per cent reported not voting in Philadelphia elections, and 5 per cent in Levittown. The two Levittown elections about which respondents were reporting both drew a turnout of 90 per cent of registered voters, but in later elections, the percentages dropped to 71, 63, and 77 respectively. It seems doubtful, then, that the move to the suburbs increased voter interest, and a telephone survey I conducted the day after the 1960 election indicated that many had already forgotten the name of their candidate—even though (or, perhaps, because) it was Smith. Individual Levittowners did, however, develop an interest in politics for the first time in Levittown, and became active because the smallness of the community put them in direct contact with politicians.[36]

Spare-Time, Leisure, and Consumption Styles

Although the critics argue that suburban living deprives people of spare time, and 56 per cent of the random sample of Levittowners agreed, 35 per cent found they had more time now; only 9 per cent indicated that no change had taken place (less than for any other item in the interview schedule). Women had slightly less time now than men, childless couples reported no change, and those with one or two children also had less. Fully 83 per cent of families with four or more children reported an increase, however, so that becoming a parent and the children's ages are probably more important determinants of spare-time change than any other factor.[37] Indeed, the women give this as the principal reason. Those with children of school age now had more time; those whose babies had reached the "active" stage, less. Most who had previously been tenants also reported less spare time, but there was no difference between urban and suburban residents, indicating that home ownership, not the community, creates the impact. The new house was also the second major reason given for change; some women found it easier to take care of, but an equal number said it took more time. The journey to work did not cut into men's spare time, but among the women, the longer the husband's trip, the more who reported decreased spare time. The men said that job change was more significant; a new job might take longer or shorter hours.

Change in the kinds of leisure activities pursued is reported almost as often as time change (by 71 per cent of the respondents). Forty-two per cent of the women indulge in more social and game activities, mostly card playing, 21 per cent mention a shift to work around the house and yard, and 16 per cent to organizational participation. Among the men, 70 per cent have taken up house and yard work. All other changes are numerically insignificant. As might be expected, 83 per cent of people with more spare time mention activity changes, but so did 68 per cent with less time, demonstrating that activity change has little to do with available time. Some women organized their housework more efficiently now, partly because social opportunities and higher morale encouraged them to alter the daily routine to leave time for other activities. For most people, however, new pursuits are either required or facilitated by the move, and their effect on spare time is a matter of personal definition, those disliking the new activity finding that it cuts into their spare time.

Care of the yard is obligatory, and the work must be done during spare time. Whether gardening deprives people of leisure hours depends on how they feel about it. One man said sadly, "The house takes priority over fishing, boating, and hunting; I've sold my boat," but another said, "It's all lawn now. I don't do as much reading; I have no time. It doesn't bother me; my mind is more occupied here, I have more ambition and I am more active around the house." For the large majority, however, gardening takes away spare time, for 77 per cent of those who identify house and yard work as the principal activity change also say they have less spare time. Other activity changes, for example, more visiting, do not cut into it.[38] For example, 40 per cent of the residents—men (who do most of the yard work) as often as women—found time to add new magazines to their reading fare the first year. New magazines are taken most often by those who do less visiting, although not by those who are more bored in Levittown than they were before, but then they are usually poorly educated people who do not read much. Moreover, low-status respondents report both the least activity change and also the greatest loss in spare time, indicating that the yard may be more of a chore for them than for anyone else.

The move from city to suburb has had considerable impact on leisure time and activity, for 93 per cent of former city residents report changes in both.[39] Although former apartment dwellers and tenants indicate more change than former homeowners, the move from city to suburb is the crucial one, for regardless of house type, previous urbanites report change more often than suburbanites, at least in activities.[40] (If gardening were the only innovation, the change in house type would have been a more significant source, but former city dwellers also experienced increased social life and organizational activity, which are related to the change in settlement type.) In any case, their leisure pursuits have been transformed by the move, although some change may disappear as the novelty of house and community wears off. Since working in the yard and making new friends were included among aspirations before the move, the new activities were an intended change for many.

If the suburban critics are right, increased spare time and activity change should lead to more boredom, and bored Levittowners should have tried activity change to cut down ennui more than others. None of these predictions came to pass, however, for the proportion bored at least once a month is the same among people with more and with less spare time (20 per cent), and no Levittowner with added spare time is more bored than before.[41] Likewise, boredom is not associated with activity change; three fourths of the bored have taken on new leisure pursuits, but so have two thirds of those who are not bored. Neither leisure-time change nor activity change seems to have any effect on boredom.

Changes in leisure styles seemed minimal, for as I noted earlier, the Levittowners were not given to partying, and judging from my own visiting, the higher alcohol consumption and the accompanying shift from beer to cocktails attributed to suburbia did not take place.[42] Sunday afternoon trips to parks and beaches became rarer, for the greenery in the backyard and the neighborhood pools provided satisfactory substitutes within easy access and some people took to inspecting other new housing developments in the area. Except among the children, going to the movies became an unusual occurrence, even though Levittown eventually had two movie theaters, for television offered a more easily accessible and cheaper substitute. Going out for dinner, particularly on weekend nights, may have increased somewhat. Sometimes dining out was with other couples; more often it was a family affair to give the children a treat and relieve the housewife of the cooking chore. Like other suburbanites, however, Levittowners soon built backyard patios, and took to having outdoor barbecues, quite regularly for the family and occasionally for friends.

Thirty per cent of the random sample and 25 per cent of the city sample also responded positively to a question, asked of

women, whether "there had been any change in the style of furniture liked best after moving to Levittown." Fifty-four per cent
had shifted from modern to traditional, 15 per cent from traditional to modern, and the rest, from one type of traditional or
modern to another.[43] The principal impetus was the pseudo-
Colonial façade of the Levitt house, and 70 per cent of those
changing to traditional furniture chose "Early American." As
one woman said, "If the house had been Oriental, we would have
bought bamboo." Others cited personal esthetic preferences or
the greater comfort of traditional styles, and some ascribed the
shift to increasing maturity. "Being young, we liked modern
first," one explained. There was no relation between style change
and income, class, or even age. Former urbanites shifted more
often, but former renters, who would be most likely to buy new
furniture while moving, changed more often than former owners
only in the random sample group. The changers seemed to be
people dissatisfied with their life *before* Levittown, because those
bored in the previous residence and those wanting to make
changes in their way of living before arrival were more likely to
adopt new styles. Being bored *in* Levittown did not correlate
with change, however, and people with improved morale chose a
new furniture style more often than unhappy ones. Evidently,
the desire for change preceded Levittown, although the actual
change took place afterwards, the stimulus for the new style
preference often coming from neighbors, people liking the styles
they saw when they went visiting.[44]

Without a study of the distribution of furniture styles in the
community it is not possible to say whether the changes were impelled by Levitt's houses, by the neighbors, or by personal preference.[45] Undoubtedly, the Colonial style of the house made Early
American furniture seem most relevant to those already considering change, but then Levitt himself had adopted the Colonial
style while completing Levittown, Pennsylvania, and both he
and his customers were probably responding to a nationwide impulse that had nothing to do with the new Levittown. Since
modern style is associated with youth and traditional is associated
with maturity and residential stability, the preference for Colonial design may well be a function of the desire to settle down,
interpreted as a return to traditional values. Why some other
eighteenth or nineteenth century style was not chosen is probably explained by the high status associated with Colonial archi-

tecture and furniture and with its symbolism of rural and small-town America. These associations must not be exaggerated, however, for the majority of Levittowners seemed content to live with the furniture style they had brought with them from their previous residence.

Attitudes Toward Suburbs and Cities

Living in Levittown altered people's attitudes toward both the community and the city. The random sample was asked in two interviews how they liked living in Levittown; the majority liked it "very much" both times, none disliked it, and only a handful were ambivalent.[46] Even so, a third changed their opinions between interviews, 11 per cent being more pleased at the later interview than before, 23 per cent less. The major complaints, each voiced by a quarter of the complainants, were rising taxes, lack of public transportation within Levittown and to the city, and lot size or lack of fences. The last-named complaints expressed the wish of some to be separated from incompatible neighbors or desire for more acreage and the status that goes with it.[47]

Attitude changes over time are reflected in future moving plans. After two to three years in Levittown, most respondents still want to stay and only a fifth have changed their minds—not all of them to leave. In the random sample group, about three fourths planned to stay and the rest to leave; a total of 17 per cent had changed their original intent, 7 per cent to settle, 10 per cent to move.[48] When the Philadelphians first came to Levittown, half said they planned to settle, 20 per cent to move, and 30 per cent were undecided.[49] Three years later, 63 per cent planned to settle, 33 per cent to move, and 4 per cent were still undecided.[50] Most of the initially uncertain now want to leave, but of the rest, only 21 per cent had changed their minds, 14 per cent to move, 7 per cent to stay. Older, lower-status people were more likely to settle, younger, higher-status ones to leave. The latter want "a bigger and better house," or "a community that is not a development"—that is, a more settled suburban town of higher income and status. For most Mobiles, living in Levittown has not altered aspirations for a "better" suburb, but since these existed before arrival, neither has it created them.

Although no one planned to return to the city, 65 per cent of the women in the Philadelphia sample and half the men missed it. These people fall into three types.[51] Well-educated, city-bred women (many of them Jewish) miss its downtown cultural and shopping facilities. Low-status couples (particularly Italian women) miss people in the old neighborhood and downtown shops. Men, principally blue collar workers, miss trips that combined shopping and visiting.[52] Fifty-seven per cent of the women and 25 per cent of the men, usually the less educated, missed the old neighborhood.[53] No ethnic or religious group stood out, however. The neighborhood was missed for its people, 88 per cent pointing to relatives, neighbors, and friends in that order; and 6 per cent, for the neighborhood church. Thirteen per cent who came to Levittown from apartments missed them now, and 27 per cent missed their former row house. None of the men missed the apartment, but women recalled less housework there; a third of the men and 20 per cent of the women missed the row house, primarily because of lower heat bills.[54]

None of the Philadelphians who missed the city wished to move back, but 59 per cent of the women in the sample said they would like to live in the city "were it not for the children," almost three times as many as the 23 per cent who had answered the same question on the mail questionnaire before coming to Levittown. (Among men, the proportion increased only from 23 per cent to 29.) By and large, the women who would now choose the city if they were childless included, as before, the young, the well-educated, Jews, and Italians, but they have been joined by additional well-educated women, high school dropouts, partners in mixed marriages, and women who lived with parents or in-laws before Levittown.[55] Some were, once again, the socially isolated and extruded, but not all, for there was no association between boredom or loneliness in Levittown and wanting to live in the city.[56]

Of course, the interview question about a return to the city was hypothetical, and answers tapped the shortcomings of Levittown and an image of life without children rather than any great yearning for the city. As a result, reasons for the choice correspond closely to answers to a question on what urban facilities were wanted in Levittown—better transportation to the city, and more stores, entertainment, and cultural facilities.[57] The image of life without children came through in choosing where to live in the city. A few had dreams of urbane luxury, picking a Riverside Drive apartment in New York City or a town house in downtown San Francisco; others saw the move as an escape from housework and a chance to have more free time. Accordingly, 55 per cent of the respondents opted for an apartment, 14 per cent for a town house (all of them women), and the remaining 31 per cent for another single-family house. But the same impulse that brought Philadelphians out to the suburbs in the first place reasserted itself in their locating of these hypothetical residences; 58 per cent (63 per cent of the women) wanted to live in the outer parts of the city and only 42 per cent chose downtown. Perhaps the typical response was given by one woman: "a luxury apartment, but not in center city." The people who rejected the city even without children preferred the lack of congestion, outdoor living, fresh air, and the peace and quiet of the suburbs.

Even the teenagers, whom I had expected to be urbanites, do not want to live in the city. They miss downtown movie theaters, but previous city dwellers among them are only slightly more discontented with Levittown than the rest.[58] The adolescents' complaints about Levittown (other than "nothing to do") resembled those of the critics and reflected the adult suburbanity they hope to achieve. The few teenagers who commented on the community were unhappy about the look-alike quality of the houses and the rule against fences. Like their parents—but unlike the critics—some wanted lower densities and larger lots; one tenth-grade girl said, "I would like to have a big yard when I get married, because I don't wish the neighbors to hear my husband and me fighting."

To test attitudes about the house, suburbia, and the city further, the random sample was asked to choose between its Levitt house and a hypothetical ideal row house resembling the Levitt house in a Levittown-like community: if the community were only fifteen minutes from the husband's job; if it were a similar distance from downtown Philadelphia; and, if it were cheaper.[59] Although many planners argue that the row house is the answer to urban sprawl, and some predict it must become the major suburban building type during the next housing boom, most Levittowners were not interested. Altogether, 22 per cent chose the row house at least once, but no one for the house itself. Nine per cent picked it to reduce the man's journey to work—all of them women; 7 per cent, to be closer to downtown facilities, and 14 per cent, if it were at least $1000–2000 cheaper.[60] But most would not take the house at any price. "You'd have to give it to me," said one. "I figure I'm going to be ninety when I pay off this mortgage," said another, "and I might as well go first class." Even those who chose the row house said they did not want to live in one, and their choices really reflected dissatisfactions with Levittown.[61] The common and almost universal objection was lack of privacy. One Levittowner explained, "In a row house, you hear everybody's troubles. You are always hearing the other person's business and fighting about how much of the lawn and driveway is yours. You spend too much time with your ear against the wall." Freedom from the supervision and judgment of adjacent neighbors (and from the temptation to judge them) are more important than easier access to job or city. Unless future row houses are designed to maximize privacy, and can also overcome their present low-status image, they will not be very popular with the next generation of home buyers.[62]

Levittown has undoubtedly made an impact on people's attitudes, creating more favorable opinions toward the city than they held before. Even so, these reflect Levittown's drawbacks, particularly poor transportation to the city, rather than an endorsement of city living. Most Levittowners would probably move into a house in a low-density, suburban-like area in or near the center of the city, provided it cost no more than what they now pay. However, since this is out of the question, and the city does not lure them in the first place, they would gladly settle for more urban facilities and conveniences in suburbia. It may be premature to expect urban enthusiasm from a population just two years in its new suburban home, but judging by the pleasure which older Levittowners found in their houses, I doubt whether many young couples will consider a return to the city once their children have grown up, particularly as the house is then just paid for.

DOES SUBURBIA CHANGE PEOPLE?

The welter of statistics suggests that the move to the suburb and to a new community changes some people, but not in uniform ways. Church attendance may go up but it may also go down, and often it remains as it was before. The most frequently reported changes are not caused by the suburbs, but were reasons for going there in the first place. A smaller proportion are, however, unintended results of the move—some good, some bad.

Some people change more beyond the city limits than others. Women, particularly former urban ones, experience the most changes, as well as the most unintended changes and the most undesirable ones. So do people of least and most status and education, young people entering a new familial role, and of course the socially isolated. Urban men, former tenants, the people who share the dominant culture of the new community, and more generally, the majority of all who reported changes, experience desired and desirable changes.

Good or bad, many changes have nothing to do with the move but are related to factors of age, sex, class and ethnic culture, or occupation. Others are produced by the community's newness and will erode over time. The new house and home ownership create more change than the community; except for the physically isolated housewife, the woman who misses her parents, and the congenital urbanite, the important move is not from city to suburb but from one population mix to another. In fact, heterogeneity—even in the supposedly homogeneous suburb—is probably the major source of unintended change experienced by the Levittowners.

As I suggested before, Levittown's population mix is typical of new suburbs, but can also be found in other new settlements, and changes in population mix face many people who move. Usually, movers pick a new residence with some knowledge of the population mix, either "to be with the same kinds of people," or to have "better" neighbors. People in a new community, like those forced to relocate by urban renewal, lack this choice, but while the latter often suffer as a result, most Levittowners did not. Critics who think they *should* have suffered are only drawing conclusions about how they, as upper middle class cosmopolitans, would feel in a lower middle class, local, and home-centered environment. Undoubtedly they would have been depressed, bored, and lonely in Levittown—but then, Levittowners would have felt the same way if they had moved into the critics' midst.

Although I have emphasized the changes, the statistics also indicate that people's lives were not significantly altered by the move. As Table 7 shows, the "no change" percentage is usually the largest. Suburbia allowed people to live more comfortably and feel better, which is what they wanted. Some participated more (or less) in various aspects of community life, but the basic patterns of life in the family, in the home, and on the job remained much the same, and the routines and problems of daily existence were not affected. One Levittowner summarized it well: "I don't know how a new house changes your life. You have a pattern you go by, and that stays the same no matter where you live." The conclusion I reached in Part One of this book about the new community thus also applies to individuals: both carry on old ways in a new setting.

These findings corroborate other studies. For example, Berger discovered that a group of factory workers held to their working class ways of living when they bought homes in a new tract in suburban Milpitas, California, and remained steadfastly immune to both middle class and suburban styles which they should have adopted had they lived up to what he calls the "suburban myth." [63] He also found that the move had not engendered aspirations for occupational or social mobility, either for the adults or for their children, but had provided them—like the Levittowners—with a "new feeling of well-being." [64] Wilner and his associates, who studied a group of slum dwellers after their move into a new public housing project, discovered the same thing: people felt better, but had not developed new aspirations for work, children's education, or home ownership. [65]

Like my interviews, both these studies were conducted two to three years after the move, but Willmott reported that the people of Dagenham, a municipal housing project on the outskirts of London, maintained their working class ways during the twenty to forty years since they had left the slums of that city. Some critics have suggested that the real impact of the suburban move can only be seen in the next generation, and that the children will either want to escape, or will show the deleterious consequences of suburbia when they grow up. In Dagenham, only a few of the second generation wanted to leave; 28 per cent of the original settlers reported that married children had remained, and that many others would have if housing had been available. Willmott also found that at least a third of those who left would have preferred to stay in Dagenham. [66] Some did move out voluntarily, however, having adopted middle class life styles. An American study, by Zelan, found that graduate students raised in the suburbs did not differ in intellectual interests from those raised in the city, casting doubt on the charges that a suburban childhood leads to intellectual debility. [67]

THE SOURCES OF IMPACT

To understand Levittown's impact on its residents, the sources which do and do not bring about behavior and attitude change must be catalogued. Knowing these sources allows the planner or policy maker (I will use these terms interchangeably here) [68] to develop plans that will achieve the intended goal. The sources can be classified into pre-occupancy aspirations, post-occupancy conditions, and extra-community conditions. Among post-occupancy conditions, of most concern to the planner whose arena is the community, are: (1) the house (and the move from apartment to house); (2) the settlement type (and the move from city to suburb); [69] (3) the community layout; (4) community facilities, public and commercial; (5) and the low density. (These five sources encompass the physical characteristics of the community.) The social characteristics include: (6) the population mix and (7) the social structure or array of community institutions. An eighth source, not directly related to the community, is its newness. Among extra-community sources are the area housing market, the regional and national economy, and the national social structure and culture. A policy-oriented analysis must also identify spurious sources, which have nothing to do with change.

The House

The single most important source of impact is undoubtedly the house, even though most of the changes it encouraged in the lives of Levittowners were intended. The house is both a physical structure and an owned property. Among its physical characteristics, space was the most significant source of change, providing easier child-rearing, more room for family activities, and greater privacy to its members, thereby reducing family friction and increasing contentment. [70] Modernity encouraged improved housekeeping methods and allowed a bit more spare time for wives. Both house and yard offered opportunities for initial fixing and furnishing, and also for more lasting decorating, hobbies, and other kinds of cultural self-expression. They also had unintended effects: more family cohesion and change in spare time and spare-time activity.

Contentment results principally from home ownership, however, particularly among men. Aside from the acquisition of property and its monetary value, ownership brings the freedom to do as one pleases and to indulge in forms of self-expression inside and outside the house that are not available to a tenant; it permits or encourages familial "settling down" and provides a public symbol of achievement, "something to show for all your years of living," as one Levittowner pointed out.[71] Ownership also incorporates people into the block and gives some a feeling of community belongingness which may result in church, organizational, and political participation. These changes last only so long as people are satisfied with the house as a physical structure and with the community in which it sits, and, of course, they are most intense while the house and ownership are novel.

Settlement Type: Suburb and City

Generally speaking, the changes that could be assigned to the move from city to suburb alone were few; they came through most clearly in the poorer adaptation of the Philadelphians. Had similar changes been reported by urbanites in the random sample, they could be attributed to the change in settlement type, but for most Philadelphians it was not the move from city to suburb, but the loss of a specific set of social ties located in a specific city. They missed parents and old friends, but so did Transients who had grown up in small towns and suburbs from which their jobs had taken them. All in all, the city per se (and the leaving of it) had little impact on people's lives—and certainly not enough to encourage them to go back to it; the impact resulted, rather, from the people they left behind, Levittown's shortage of urban facilities, and lack of transportation to the city.

Conversely, the move to Levittown as a suburban settlement was a more important source of change. One consequence was the feeling of being stuck, which stems partly from the shortage of commercial "safety-valve" areas. Physical isolation is not limited to suburbia, however, for some women were stuck in the city. Sometimes, the lack of shopping and window-shopping opportunities impels neighboring, and lack of entertainment facilities encourages visiting with other couples. The discovery that visiting may be preferable to "being out on the town" qualifies as a significant unintended change of suburban living and of community newness.

Another consequence was the slowdown in the pace of living,

noted primarily by former city dwellers and men. It follows from the ability to spend more time in the house and yard, activities for which one can set one's own pace; the increase in outdoor living, which may reduce the energy and desire to do other things; and the availability of friendly people nearby, which eliminates visiting that requires travel. The men, who report increased relaxation more than women, could avoid participation in disliked parental and in-law activities and escape urban congestion. Both sexes also called attention to the satisfactions of clean air and greenery and the safety of the relatively traffic-free residential neighborhoods. But despite the feeling of greater relaxation, the suburbs actually reduced spare time and caused a major change in leisure activity; gardening (whether it was fun or drudgery) and social life replacing some mass-media and urban diversions.

Perhaps the most significant impact of the suburb was on family finances. Rising expenditures can be attributed to suburb-related transportation costs, higher taxes (which resulted primarily from community newness), to house-related expenses that come with a single-family house and home ownership, and to a higher standard of living that was partly intended, partly a result of norms set by the population mix of the community.

Finally, the suburban location meant longer commuting for some, and was a source (albeit a minor one) for a variety of consequences. Short work trips provided more time with the family and more joint activities, although increased ones did not reduce it, since men took time away from other activities instead. Even so, longer commuting did not affect their spare time or their social and organizational activities. Indeed, the main burden of commuting fell on the women; they reported less spare time and poorer dispositions when the man's trip is long. The men themselves were little affected by trip length, being content so long as they did not have to use public transportation. Since most were not faced with a significantly longer travel time to work after the move, its overall impact was negligible, and certainly not enough to make them unhappy about suburbia.

Levittown as a Community: The Physical Environment

Levittown is also a source of change as a physical and social community, but the various elements of the physical community have not produced a significant impact. Although they are laid out according to the precepts of the traditional neighborhood scheme, the individual neighborhoods do not affect people's lives. As I noted earlier, they are too large for social relations among their occupants, too similar to each other to encourage identification, and without distinctive social or political functions that might spawn neighborhood groups. The elementary school, located in the middle of each neighborhood, has not become a focal point. Although some students identify with their school, overcrowding has forced busing of students across neighborhood lines. School meeting rooms are used almost every night, but by community-wide groups, not neighborhood ones (except for the PTA).

The neighborhood pool *is* a center, but because admission cards are issued only to neighborhood residents. In theory, it provides an opportunity for members of the same neighborhood to meet, but most people come to the pool as a family or in cliques, and there is little incentive for strangers to become acquainted.[72] It has become a social center for teenagers, however, and has undoubtedly helped them find each other. Even so, I doubt whether the pool has created youthful friendships on the basis of neighborhood except, perhaps, among children of elementary school age, for older ones make community-wide contacts at school and at teenage social functions. The school playgrounds programs are restricted to neighborhood children, but afterhours informal use of the playground attracts only those who live close by; it is not interesting enough to draw neighborhood youngsters who live farther away. The small shopping centers, whether planned or unplanned, tend to be on the edges of two neighborhoods, and thus do not function as neighborhood centers, even for the teenagers who gather there. The road system, designed in conjunction with the neighborhoods to keep through traffic out of their streets, has made them safer for playing children, but it has also served to isolate people from other neighborhoods. The curvature of internal streets makes each neighborhood a maze, and it is easy for people to get lost outside their own. This has not prevented people from making friends in other neighborhoods, however, or restricted them to socializing in their own.[73]

The socially most significant unit is the sub-block, the sector of adjacent houses facing each other on the street, where most neighbor visiting and mutual help takes place. It exists because people need neighbors, but can develop only a limited number of social relationships, and because women and children are restricted in their mobility.[74] Of course, it is not a real physical unit, because its size and boundaries are unique for each individual, being determined by his gregariousness. Sometimes a social isolate becomes the boundary between sub-blocks, but sharp curves in the street that site houses away from each other create the only physical determinant of the sub-block (and then only rarely). When a set of neighbors is very friendly, the sub-block may become an in-group unit with which people identify, but this too is rare. More often, they see other blocks as out-groups, marked by quarreling or deviant behavior, perhaps to assure themselves that their own is friendlier than most.

Neither the sub-block, the block, nor any other element in the site plan is influential in determining friendships. Propinquity is a factor while people get to know each other, after which compatibility becomes the major criterion, but the spaces between houses and the gentle curvature of the streets put enough distance between people to allow them to ignore all but next-door neighbors. Even the mixture of house types on the street had little social impact. Although class differences existed between the buyers of different types, the variations in number of bedrooms encouraged people to make family-size rather than class distinctions.[75] Nor did people discriminate in their visiting on the basis of house type. As a result, the gap of $3000 between the cheapest and most expensive house on the block had no impact on social life or on neighbors' attitudes toward each other, suggesting that differently priced houses can be put next to each other without negative results. How wide the price gap can become before it has social consequences cannot be answered by my data. In a later development, Bel Air (near Washington), Levitt added a $25,-000 house to the street mix but was unable to sell it until he located it in a separate neighborhood. Presumably, people were unwilling to buy it amidst houses $5000 to $8000 cheaper, but no reliable data are yet available to determine how high a price difference will discourage mixing of housetypes, and whether it is an absolute figure or a proportion of house price. In any case, the Levittown experience suggests that mixing is feasible when the price gap between the most expensive and least expensive house on the street is 20 per cent.

Levitt's motive for mixing house types was esthetic; he wanted to avoid the criticism of architectural monotony aroused by earlier Levittowns. The critics never noticed his innovation, how ever, the Levittown stereotype having become firmly established by then, and the purchasers also paid little attention to it. People who had moved from the physically homogeneous blocks of Levittown, Pennsylvania, liked the mixture, but the rest were not concerned about architectural sameness. Actually, Levitt also used a highly variegated color scheme to increase diversity, so that only every 150th house was alike; besides, purchasers put their individual brand on the house and yard soon after they moved in. Their image of other houses was determined not by their façades, but by their occupants, so that (for neighbors at least) every house quickly became unique. None of the adults who thought Levittown dull ascribed the dullness to architectural homogeneity.

More important than site plan and street layout was the community's low density. Although it was not especially low as suburban areas go—most lots were only 6500 square feet—houses 10 feet apart gave people a sense of privacy. Even so, many Levittowners preferred a lower density, to put more space between them and incompatible neighbors and because lot size is an index of status in American society. The low density had some negative consequences for cultural minorities, separating them from compatible neighbors. For example, adolescent gathering places at the shopping centers were beyond walking distance, although many teenagers soon coped with it by acquiring bicycles.

Architects and planners insist that every community must have a single physical and symbolic center, but Levittown, like most suburban communities, lacked such a nucleus. The main shopping center was located at the edge of the community to attract outside purchasers, but since it was still under construction during the time of my study, its impact on people's lives was hard to define. It served not only as a shopping area but as a place where local businessmen (and mothers) could meet for lunch and as a location for occasional community ceremonies. City hall, closer to the geographical midpoint of the community, was its civic and political center, although the meetings of the Township Committee did not attract many residents; those meetings for which a large turnout could be expected were held in a school auditorium, as were school board meetings. Other centers were the high school athletic field, where varsity teams bearing the community's name performed, and the parking lot of the shopping center, where 15,000 people welcomed the late President Kennedy when he campaigned in Levittown.

It is doubtful whether Levittown needed a single nucleus, or whether its existence would have created a major impact on people's lives. Few events are of interest to a significant proportion of Levittowners, so that the community is not likely to come together as a group. In most cities, demand for and use of centers is generated by tourists, for the center is the area they want to visit. In a heterogeneous community, the center's historically and otherwise sacred landmarks may serve as a cohesive symbol for those few residents who need to identify with the community; more often, the center is most important to local interest groups who want to promote a cohesive feeling (civic pride) among citizens to obtain political support, hide community conflict, or reduce the dissension that comes with heterogeneity. Levittown has as much heterogeneity and conflict as any other community, but neither would have been reduced by a real or symbolic center. For most Levittowners, their own home was the center of the community, and that determined the town's social structure and politics.

The Social Environment

Most of the changes following upon the move to Levittown can be traced to the social community, to the impact of people on each other. The increased visiting, organizational activity, church attendance, altered leisure pursuits; the changes in health, morale, boredom, and loneliness; and even some of the new worries resulted neither from the move to the suburb nor from the suburbanness of Levittown or its physical environment, but from the contact or lack of contact with other people in Levittown, and this in turn can be traced ultimately to the population mix. The homogeneity of that mix was the major source of social life and the benefits to morale that followed; its heterogeneity was largely responsible for social isolation and the resulting emotional costs.

A second source of change was the social structure. The need for organizations to spring into existence brought about some of the increased organizational participation, and the desire of people to feel themselves a part of the community (by which they meant the social structure) encouraged it and religious activity as well. But the social structure was also a result of the population mix, for it determined what organizations and institutions were viable, and organizational participation in turn depended on whether members found each other compatible. The functioning of the social structure was enhanced by two other sources: the random settling of purchasers, that is, people's choosing their houses without knowing who would live next door; and the openness of the structure itself, which at first admitted everyone who wanted to participate. When people moved in, they were atomistic family units, placed together arbitrarily, who had to trust each other to be friendly and cooperative in order to set up the formal and informal groups that would eliminate the initial atomization. This could only be achieved by an open, universalistic, and achievement-oriented social structure, which judged people by what they did, not what they were. The random settling hastened the development of organizations for those who could not find compatible neighbors and was a direct cause of increased organizational activity. For those unable to join, random settling also produced physical and social isolation by scattering people with minority tastes, as well as those who had come out of cohesive ethnic and working class areas where settling had been anything but random. Even so, the openness of the social structure probably kept the number of social isolates to a minimum.[76]

The open social structure was, of course, a direct consequence of newness, as was some of the initial visiting, the unintended organizational participation, the reduced boredom and loneliness felt by Philadelphians, some of the joint family activity, and the change in spare-time activity. Newness alone was not enough to explain the increased social activity, however, for if the strangers who came together had been more heterogeneous in background and characteristics, the first meetings could well have resulted in conflict and a general retreat into the safety of home and family. Because people were sufficiently homogeneous to trust each other, they could share the common pains of newness and the needs of a new community and act together in the ways that produced the behavior changes here reported. *Ultimately, then, the primary source of change was the population mix of Levittown.*

THE AGENTS OF IMPACT

Behavior changes must be traced beyond sources, to agents and agencies that have some influence over them, particularly since

policies for change can be effective only if they can assign responsibility to agents within or without the community. Obviously,
Levitt was a major agent of change, for without him there would
have been no Levittown, but not all of the firm's decisions and
decision-makers were important. For example, those designing
the physical community were not, but those creating the Levitt
houses were crucial. Levitt's mass production techniques made
it possible to build an entire community, and at a price that provided the opportunity for home ownership to people who could
not have moved to the suburbs otherwise. Of course, the federal
government played a role as well, for without FHA insurance,
Levitt could not have kept either the price or the down payment
as low as he did. Mass production also made it possible to maximize the space of the house, which in turn enhanced family activities and individual privacy (for adults) and thus improved their
morale.

Since the behavior changes brought about by the house and by
home ownership were largely intended ones, Levitt did not really
change people's lives. He (and FHA) enabled people to achieve
their aspirations for home ownership, but he did not bring these
aspirations into being. The most important agents of change,
therefore, were the aspirations themselves and the processes of
purchaser recruitment that determined the population mix.
These processes cannot be ascribed either to Levitt or to any
other single agent. He designed houses that served the needs of
young families with children, but he made no effort to attract
young families and had in fact no policies of purchaser selection
other than race; until the community was integrated, he took all
whites who wished to buy and could pass the credit check. This
was standard suburban builder practice, as was the random
settling pattern. Both were, furthermore, responses to purchaser
preferences; houses were built for young families because they
have been the mainstay of the suburban housing market for over
a decade, and communities were settled randomly because people
came as individual family units. If they had come as a clan or as a
clique of friends, Levitt would have been glad to sell them an entire block or two. Even Levitt's decision to offer houses within a
narrow price range was a standard builder practice, which responded to property value and status concerns among the purchasers.

Thus, people's preferences as purchasers led to builder practices, which in turn produced the population mix. *Ultimately,*

*then, people were their own agents, and the changes that came
about as a result of the move were created by the pressures and
aspirations which led them to the suburban builders.* The principal pressures were the lack of space and modernity of today's
middle-income urban housing stock, the deterioration and congestion of the cities, and the normal and ceaseless processes of invasion and succession that bring about neighborhood population
change. Some Philadelphians were pushed by the expansion of
the Negro ghetto, others by the desire to escape from the parental
generation; the Transients were impelled by the needs of their
corporate employers. The principal aspirations were for a detached house, home ownership, and "outdoor" living. These aspirations and the conditions that made it possible to realize them
are the final source-and-agent of Levittown's impact, and they
can be traced back to more fundamental sources and agents outside the community, in the national culture and economy.

Many explanations have been offered for the intense desire for
home ownership and the single-family, low-density house. Some
have pointed to post-World War II government policies making
it cheaper to own than to rent. These policies encouraged people
to buy houses and discouraged apartment living, but they did not
create the desire. Others have argued that it results from mass
media depictions of an idealized suburbia. Admittedly, much of
the popular fiction, in print and on television, takes place in lo-
cales which cross the nineteenth century small town with the
modern suburb, but they do not therefore inspire their audiences
to move to the suburbs. For one thing, research shows that the
media are not very effective in changing important values. More
important, a historical analysis of the media would show that
they follow taste more often than they lead it. Women were
smoking in America before heroines of mass media fiction were
allowed to do so, and the dominant media audience had moved
to the suburbs before the popular dramas and situation comedies
followed them. Stories about upper class suburbanites have been
a staple of American popular culture for several generations now,
but media portrayal of lower middle class life has been located
in the suburbs for only a few years.

Another explanation proceeds from status: the popular desire
for suburban home ownership imitates the fashion-setting upper
and upper middle classes. This argument is historically more
viable than that of mass media imitation, because higher-income

groups have lived in the suburbs since before the turn of the century. The dream home of most Levittowners is not the Main Line or Westchester County suburban mansion, however, but "a bigger house with some acreage around it," a tiny farm (not to be farmed) with all the conveniences of urban and suburban living, including easy access to social life. This dream residence is not of recent origin, but is rooted in the cultures of most Americans, Protestant and Catholic, middle class and working class alike. Among middle class Protestants, the home-ownership aspiration can be traced back to the rural and small-town heritage of eighteenth and nineteenth century America and England; among working class Catholics, to the peasant settlements of continental Europe. Only the Jews did not share this rural heritage, and although acculturation has persuaded many to accept it, Jews are still more favorably inclined to city living than any other group.[77] The mass media have promulgated the Protestant and Catholic ideal, and in their own way, so have the upper classes —but they have not generated it, for it preceded them both. Even if the American upper classes had opted for an urbane existence in inner-city luxury apartment buildings, I doubt whether the desire for suburbia among the rest of the population would have been significantly reduced. Actually, even the ideal of the celebrities and performers who monopolize what little upper class fashion-setting exists is not apartment living, but a Manhattan townhouse and a weekend country mansion—also a single-family house aspiration.

The American economy of the nineteenth and early twentieth centuries made the traditional popular housing ideal unachievable, industrialization and urbanization forcing many rural Americans, like the European immigrants, into city tenements. They lived there out of necessity, and made the best of it, although some became confirmed urbanites and tenants. But the majority moved out at the earliest opportunity, first to row houses, then to single-family houses still within the city but farther removed from its center with every generation. After World War II, however, prosperity and government housing policy put suburbia within reach of the urban lower middle and working classes. Of course, if the government had decided to subsidize urban apartments instead, many would have moved into them. This would not have abrogated their aspirations, but only frustrated and postponed them. Government policy is not made *in vacuo,* however, and the elected officials who decided to sub-sidize suburbia were aware of their constituents' aspirations. Per-haps they could have ignored them, especially during the drastic housing shortage of the postwar era, but politicians are not given to crossing the voters unnecessarily, and there was no good reason for them to do so at the time.

The move to the suburbs was encouraged further by rapid so-cial change, which created large differences between generations, eroded the ties that held ethnic groups together, and encouraged young families to leave the parental environment. Young people have always been most mobile, but today they marry increasingly outside their own neighborhood and this too reduces loyalties to older areas. In addition, many want to give their children a "bet-ter start," so that they are almost inevitably led to a new environ-ment in the suburbs.

THEORETICAL AND POLICY IMPLICATIONS

The findings on changes and their sources suggest that the dis-tinction between urban and suburban ways of living postulated by the critics (and by some sociologists as well) is more imagi-nary than real. Few changes can be traced to the suburban qual-ities of Levittown, and the sources that did cause change, like the house, the population mix, and newness, are not distinctively suburban. Moreover, when one looks at similar populations in city and suburb, their ways of life are remarkably alike. For ex-ample, when suburbs are compared to the large urban residential areas beyond the downtown and inner districts, culture and so-cial structure are virtually the same among people of similar age and class. Young lower middle class families in these areas live much like their peers in the suburbs, but quite unlike older, upper middle class ones, in either urban or suburban neighbor-hoods.

The crucial difference between cities and suburbs, then, is that they are often home for different kinds of people. If one is to un-derstand their behavior, these differences are much more impor-tant than whether they reside inside or outside the city limits. Inner-city residential areas are home to the rich, the poor, and the nonwhite, as well as the unmarried and the childless middle class. Their ways of life differ from those of suburbanites and people in the outer city, but because they are *not* young working or lower or upper middle class families. If populations and residential areas were described by age and class characteristics, and by racial, ethnic, and religious ones, our understanding of human settlements would be much improved. Using such concepts as "urban" and "suburban" as causal variables adds little, on the other hand, except for ecological and demographic analyses of communities as a whole and for studies of political behavior.[78]

The findings also question a related theory, espoused by city planners, that the community, especially its physical component, is a significant determinant of behavior. The social community is important, of course, particularly in a politically autonomous settlement which can determine its own fate. Nevertheless the intended changes made by the members of that community came from their aspirations, which originated outside the community in national cultural patterns; even the unintended ones reflected social and organizational practices prevalent in national middle and working class cultures. For example, when low-status Levittowners became social isolates, they suffered from nationally determined status distinctions, and when Jews increased their synagogue attendance, they acted like all Jews who settle randomly amid a predominantly non-Jewish population.

Likewise, city planners overestimate the role of builders and designers as agents of change. Not only are builder policies a response to the demands of expected purchasers, but they are usually national practices, which in turn follow from national cultural patterns. Levitt's recruitment policies reflected national preferences for age and class homogeneity, and the breakup of extended families and ethnic enclaves. He could have developed an individual recruitment pattern, for example, to create a demographically "balanced" community, but only by luring presently recalcitrant urbanites out of the city and rejecting many willing young families. Even the subsidies and restraints with which he worked originated from federal and state more than local government. Moreover, the population mix he did recruit was only partially pulled by the house and community he offered, and often pushed by demographic changes in Philadelphia (again reflections of national trends), by the makeup of the regional housing market and its offerings, and by a regional and national economy that was shifting offices and factories to the suburbs generally and to South Jersey in particular.

Plans and policies aimed at changing people's behavior can

therefore not be implemented through prescribing alterations in the physical community or by directives aimed at builders; they must be directed at the national sources and agents which bring about the present behavior. The fact that policies for changing behavior must be based on other foundations does not mean, however, that policies with different aims, e.g. to minimize traffic congestion, and to regulate builder practices for other goals, e.g. to outlaw shoddy construction, should be abandoned.

Planning for Behavior Change

These conclusions may be truisms, but they have implications for the policy-maker who is seeking change in people's behavior or in the community. If he wants to change a social or physical component of the *community*, he must first determine whether it affects residents' crucial aspirations or values. If it does, he has three alternatives: to make no change, to alter the component so that it will achieve the aspirations in another way, or to alter aspirations so that people will accept the changed component he has in mind. If the component is not a source of valued behavior, the policy-maker has more freedom, for if his plan has no impact on people's lives, they will not care one way or the other. The city planner has often been able to make innovations in site plans and in the physical community for this reason.

If the policy-maker seeks to change a component of *behavior,* he must find out if it is valued or situational, i.e., a tolerated or un-wanted adaptation to necessity. If the behavior is valued, he must either satisfy or change the values; if it is situational, he is freer to plan. In either case he must, of course, orient his plan to the proper sources and agents of behavior. For example, a planner aiming for more community participation can try to change aspi-rations, which would be quite difficult, requiring a wholesale so-cial reorganization to transfer the emotional rewards of family and informal group life to the community. Or he can affect the sources of participation, by depriving a new community of insti-tutions so that people have to create them and by inducing com-munity crises, for these always stimulate participation.

The city planner has traditionally chosen the most difficult of his options: to change people's aspirations so that they will accept a community component he considers desirable. And he has chosen the most spurious of all solutions: to induce behavior change through a physical component. "Educating" people to accept the cultural, moral, or economic superiority of his ideal community has not been very effective, however, for preaching is rarely attended and few people are persuaded by an argument which attacks their behavior as inferior and their aspirations as unworthy. When the physical component and the behavioral-change goal turn out to be values of upper middle class professionals as well, other classes may reject the planner as well as his plan.

Aspirations are difficult to change deliberately; even advertisers have not yet come up with an effective method. This is just as well, for such power is awesome and likely to be misused more often than not. Most often, aspirations change as a result of necessary behavior change: if a transformation in the economy or the social structure requires people to act differently, their aspirations will eventually change accordingly. Necessity cannot often be manipulated by the policy-maker, however. Probably the best deliberate method of changing aspirations is to provide people with alternative opportunities that are by *their* lights clearly superior; this policy will result in behavior change and, eventually, in value change as well. New aspirations are formed out of new opportunities, provided these opportunities appeal to some present aspiration, for otherwise they will not be accepted. City planners are geared to providing new opportunities, but usually those *they* find desirable, and without concern about how other people feel. Often, they deny that people have aspirations, arguing that they do not know what they want, and will therefore be receptive to whatever the planner considers superior. Although people may not know what they want, they know what they do *not* want; more important, they are able to choose when choices are offered them. It is up to the planner to offer such choices, and if he proposes choices that reflect people's aspirations, they will be accepted; if not, they will be ignored.

Needless to say, the policy-maker must sometimes advocate policies that do not coincide with people's·aspirations, but are required by the public interest, for example, transportation facilities to prevent the future traffic congestion his studies predict. Preventive planning demands present sacrifices for future gain, a behavior change most people are unwilling to make, unless incentives, such as tax benefits for long-range planning, are provided. In appealing to the public interest, the planner must be careful, however, that he is not just imposing his own aspirations. If he considers traffic congestion or a long commuting trip un-

desirable, but the commuters do not, he must provide evidence
for his proposals. If he can prove that failure to plan will lead to
consequences which people consider harmful (for example, if a
long journey to work would eventually lead to chronic weariness
and family conflict), he is justified in trying to impose his plans,
although wise strategy would dictate combining them with other
plans that offer incentives. He can also insist on his ideas if he can
demonstrate that people will be pleased once they have made the
change. In both instances, however, he must be able to prove to
his clients that the outcome of his planning will accord with their
aspirations, not just his. But if there are no serious negative
consequences to a long journey to work, the planner cannot
expect people to make sacrifices just because he thinks a shorter
journey would be good for them.

The attempt to induce behavior change through physical components is of course likely to fail, because it deals with spurious
sources and agents. Indeed, the Levittown data make it clear that
the only physical planning which induces behavior change is
house-related. The policy-maker can increase contentment by
providing sufficient internal and yard space to afford family
members greater privacy and opportunities for more activity.
And if his house planning is superior, people may be willing to
accept innovations in the physical community, but if he suggests
innovations at the price of an inferior house, he is sure to fail. If
the policy-maker wants to increase neighborhood cohesion, however, physical solutions such as neighborhood schemes or the provision of plazas where neighbors can meet are irrelevant, for so
long as neighbors have no reason to meet, they will not do so.
Cohesion can only be increased by making the neighborhood a
political unit, or by so altering the family that people will derive
more satisfaction from being with neighbors than with spouse
and children. Such policies are not likely to be popular or feasible. If the policy-maker wanted to increase family cohesion or
contentment, however, his plans would probably be accepted.
But these would have to improve the house or deal with the social sources of family discontent described in the previous chapter: by finding ways of reducing physical and social isolation
among unhappy suburban housewives, eliminating husbands'
traveling on the job, and removing financial worries.

A good illustration of the various drawbacks in the city
planner's approach is his current advocacy of higher-density sub-

urban development. He and his colleagues argue for suburban row house and apartment construction because they believe that the single-family house wastes land, encourages urban sprawl, increases commuting, makes for a physically monotonous community, and discourages an urbane way of living. Few actual or potential suburbanites share these attitudes, because they do not accept the business efficiency concept and the upper middle class, antisuburban esthetic built into them. In this instance, the planner is asking people to change their aspirations to accept a physical community he considers desirable, demanding behavior change through a new physical form, and ignoring their own aspirations. Typically, he claims that if people would only try a modern row house, they would accept it, but he has not yet convinced them that it provides the privacy and status of the single-family house, and they are loath to give up private yards for more public open space, which would require them to sacrifice family privacy for involuntary interaction with neighbors.

Land shortages may well require the next generation of home buyers to live in row house suburbs, but if planning were sensitive to their aspirations, consumer research and design experimentation to develop plans that will please them would now be under way. If city planners were rational, they would also stop trying to impose their desire for urbanity, particularly through physical solutions. They could either retire this goal and design for improved "suburbanity," or they could begin to plan on the basis of the real sources of urbanity. Since it is to be found principally among upper middle class cosmopolitans, the solution is to develop ways of giving people upper middle class incomes and job opportunities and cosmopolitan schooling for their children.

So far, I have asked whether the planner *can* change behavior and aspirations, but have begged the question of whether or not he *should*. If Levittown were as harmful as the critics claim and as undesirable as the city planners believe, the answer would be obvious. Since this is not the case, however, the planner's decision about change should be governed by two assumptions: (1) in a pluralistic society, alternative ways of living—and community arrangements—are justified, provided they are not clearly antisocial or individually destructive; (2) the people for whom he is planning are on the whole the best judges of how they want to live. The planner may prefer urbanity, but unless he can prove other alternatives to be harmful, this preference only gives him the right to practice it himself. The key word is *prove,* for if people's wishes have harmful consequences, he ought to propose change and use all possible means to implement it. Even so, the consequences must be harmful for them and their aspirations and not just for his; or they must be demonstrably antisocial or self-destructive. Obviously, people's wishes to destroy themselves and harm their neighbors through drug addiction cannot be accepted, but their willingness to accept long work trips in exchange for lower residential density should be honored, unless superior ways of achieving the family goals that underlie the desire for low density can be found. Likewise, if the planner can prove that changes people consider undesirable may actually benefit them and the goals *they* value most, he ought to defend such changes. For example, if the planner can demonstrate that the introduction of apartments into a single-family house community—a change most suburbanites oppose—will reduce their taxes or permit improvements in municipal services of the kind they want, he is justified in proposing change. If people prefer, however, to pay higher taxes to maintain the status and other values they derive from limiting the community to single-family housing, they have the right to do so.

One problem remains: when people in a community do not all have the same aspirations and when the choice is not between the community and the planner, but between the community and a larger area. For example, some suburban residents may favor the introduction of high-rise housing, but when opinions vary, majority rule should prevail. A community may be united in its opposition to high-rise housing, but the region may need it and the best location for it may be in that community. There is no simple answer to this dilemma. The needs of the region ought to have priority over the community's, if only because of majority rule, but some minority rights must remain absolute. The desire to keep out apartments does not fall into this category, but the right of Negroes to enter a community when the majority of white residents opposes them is constitutionally inalienable. If behavior change must be imposed, however, it ought to include incentives. For example, when opposition to integration stems from fears of status deprivation the change ought to be planned so as to minimize it, by making sure the first Negroes are of high status, by helping newcomers with financial aid so that visible signs of low status can be removed, and by scheduling integration so that people of different status are not thrown together arbitrarily.

Planning values like neighborhood cohesion and urbanity are not absolute values, however, and cannot be used to justify rejection of people's aspirations. The city planner's professional status entitles him to apply his professional expertise and to propose his own values, but not to insist on them. These are rarely professional ones anyway, but those of the upper middle class culture from which he comes. More important, his approach often demands allegiance to such values from people who lack the economic and other opportunities that create them, so that he is demanding upper middle class standards—and using public power to back up his demands—without providing for upper middle class incomes. This is like insisting that poor people buy Cadillacs simply because they are demonstrably superior to Chevrolets. If the quality of life is to be altered, economic and other incentives ought to be made available. Voluntary and wanted behavior changes can be encouraged in other ways, but involuntary ones are difficult to implement, and their imposition should be limited to goals that reflect the public interest and minority rights.

NOTES

1. The principal studies are Mogey (1956), Young and Willmott, Hole, Ktsanes and Reissman, Mogey and Morris, Berger (1960), Willmott (1963), Dobriner (1963), and Clark.
2. In this analysis "community" is defined in the traditional sense to include all of the physical and social components of human settlements.
3. People were asked, "How has your life changed since you moved to Levittown?"
4. The major unintended changes at this point were increased joint family activity, organizational participation, and visiting.
5. Slum dwellers who moved to a new public housing project—but into apartments—showed an increase in a variety of measures of morale, but not much more than a control group moving into old private housing. See Wilner et al., Chap. 15.
6. Seventy-two per cent ascribed the increase in joint family activity to the house and yard.
7. Slum dwellers moving into new public housing apartments lacked

the stimulus of the house, for they reported almost no change in joint family activity and marital relations after the move. Wilner et al., Chap. 11.

8. In the first interview, 75 per cent of the random sample credited the house and 12 per cent the community; by the second interview, the percentages were 37 and 37. Among the Philadelphians, 54 per cent credited the house, 23 per cent credited the community.

9. Mogey (1955), p. 125; Mogey (1956), p. 72; Young and Willmott, p. 119.

10. Since husbands never missed relatives, this analysis was limited to women. Fifty-five per cent of those not missing relatives got along better with their husbands, as compared to none of those who did miss them.

11. Kiser's careful study of the number of third children born to a national sample discovered little difference in births between urban and suburban parents of the same religion, or between those moving within the city and from city to suburb.

12. Fifty-seven per cent of the Philadelphians with unplanned children were Catholics; 28 per cent were poorly educated non-Catholics. Even if one assumed that neither practiced birth control, this still leaves 15 per cent "accidents."

13. Seventy-three per cent of those wanting more neighboring reported an increase, and 75 per cent of those wanting less also got their wish. Altogether, 62 per cent of the respondents did the amount of neighboring they wanted. For couple visiting, the figures were slightly lower: only 53 per cent wanting more were able to achieve it; altogether, only 44 per cent got what they wanted.

14. Fifty-six per cent of changes in couple visiting were unintended. Thirty-one per cent of those who had wanted no change did more, and 10 per cent of those wanting more did less. Thirty-eight per cent of changes in neighboring were unintended, and 42 per cent of those wanting no change actually found themselves doing more.

15. In Levittown, Pennsylvania, 65 per cent of the women interviewed had wanted more evening visitors at home, but only 20 per cent reported more "than they were used to." Even so, 80 per cent reported having visitors and going to visit at least once a week. Jahoda et al., pp. 112–113.

16. In the random sample, 75 per cent of former city residents and 38 per cent of former suburbanites reported more neighboring, and 24 per cent of the latter, less, but two thirds of former suburban apartment dwellers and 84 per cent of urban ones did more neighboring in Levittown.

17. All in all, 41 per cent of the Philadelphians preferred old friends to Levittowners; 27 per cent preferred the opposite. (The rest were undecided or said both.) Among mixed-marriage partners, 67 per cent chose old friends and the rest could not decide. On the other

hand, among former Philadelphians who had become organization members, 31 per cent chose Levittowners, as compared to 9 per cent of nonmembers.

18. Similar friendliness is reported in a new high-rise apartment development in downtown Detroit by Wolf and Ravitz. Increase in visiting was also found among people moving into a new urban public housing project. Wilner et al., Chap. 12.

19. For an earlier finding on the role of predispositions in suburban sociability, see Fava.

20. A study of Dagenham, an English new town now forty years old, found that the longest residents reported their streets the friendliest. Willmott (1963), p. 69. In an American homogeneous community, long residence expanded the circle of acquaintances, rather than increasing the intensity of association. See Caplow and Foreman. Pierson's data from Levittown, Pennsylvania, indicated a decrease in neighboring over time, however, for 67 per cent of people living there two to three years were doing more neighboring than in the former residence, but only 15 per cent with six to seven years in Levittown were doing more; 62 per cent of the latter reported less neighboring than when they first moved in. The data cannot tell, however, whether the decrease resulted from the aging of the community or increasing incompatibility due to turnover of residents.

21. In the random sample, 78 per cent of the previously active and 77 per cent of the inactive were more involved in Levittown; in the city sample, the percentages were 41 per cent and 50 per cent, respectively.

22. People were asked whether they had "intended to join that organization or one like it before you moved out to Levittown."

23. Another 14 per cent were women who joined because their husbands were already active; a similar number joined because they were asked by the children.

24. In a working class suburb in California, 17 per cent reported joining more organizations than where they lived before, 20 per cent fewer. Seventy per cent belonged to none at all, however. Berger (1960), p. 59. Slum dwellers moving to a new public housing project reported a slight increase in organizational attendance, but hardly more than the control group moving to old housing. Wilner et al., p. 191.

25. Only 31 per cent were members at the first interview, but two thirds of the rest said they planned to join an organization in the future, and most later did so. In Levittown, Pennsylvania, Pierson found that membership increased with length of residence; 46 per cent of those living there three years or less were members, but 76 per cent of those living there six or seven years.

26. In a new working class suburb, 27 per cent reported more church attendance, 24 per cent less. Berger (1960), p. 45.

27. Thirty-three per cent of them now went to church less often, and

only 7 per cent more often. Among former tenants, on the other hand, 41 per cent attended more, and only 4 per cent less. One reason for reduced attendance is the loss of parental baby-sitters. The other group which reduced its attendance most were professionals, 29 per cent reporting a decrease as compared to 9 per cent of white collar workers and 14 per cent of blue collar ones.

28. Among Catholics in the Philadelphia sample, 14 per cent attended more often, 10 per cent less. Among the Protestants, 42 per cent attended more, 8 per cent less. Among the Jews, 67 per cent attended more, 17 per cent less. In the suburb studied by Berger, fundamentalist Baptists were the only group to go to church significantly more often after the move. Berger (1960), p. 48.

29. Even so, only 8 per cent of the Jewish synagogue members attended regularly.

30. The random sample intermarried group reported a 13 per cent increase; the Philadelphia sample, no increase but a 30 per cent decrease.

31. In the Philadelphia sample, two thirds of former apartment-dwelling Protestants went to church more, as compared to a third of those coming from row houses or detached ones. For the random sample, the percentages were 54 and 14.

32. Forty per cent of those increasing their church attendance also reported more couple visiting, but none of those who decreased it or did not change it altered their visiting. For neighboring, the percentages were 60 and 26 per cent respectively. Among random sample Protestants, differences were negligible. Unfortunately, the data cannot identify the causally prior factor.

33. Catholics did not make a single friend at church.

34. The random sample was asked about shifts in party allegiance between the first and second Levittown elections, when a likeable Republican amateur defeated a veteran Democratic professional politician. Sixteen per cent had shifted parties, 10 per cent of previous Republicans but fully 44 per cent of previous Democrats. There were no background differences between changers and stable voters, and many of the shifts were probably temporary, for the Republican lost decisively in the following election.

35. Similar party stability has been reported for Levittown, New York, by Wattel, p. 299; in other American suburbs, by Berger (1960), p. 3; Lazerwitz; Wallace; and in an English new town, by Willmott (1963), p. 105. See also Banfield and Wilson, pp. 16–17.

36. In a newly suburban working class population, 29 per cent said their interest in politics increased after they became home owners. Berger (1960), p. 36.

37. Fifty-nine per cent of the women and 50 per cent of the men reported less spare time; 4 per cent and 17 per cent reported no change. Respondents were also asked to answer the question for their spouses. Whereas the women judged changes in their husbands' spare time correctly, the men overestimated the decrease

and underestimated the increase in spare time reported by women. Evidently they thought Levittown had been harder on the women than was actually the case.

38. Of those reporting activity changes, 41 per cent also have more spare time, and 53 per cent less; among those reporting no activity change, only 23 per cent now have more time and 62 per cent have less.

39. For the random sample as a whole, Levittown's impact on spare-time change is less, 64 per cent of the reasons given being unrelated, 20 per cent related to the house, and 16 per cent related to the community. For activity change, only 7 per cent are unrelated, however; 50 per cent are house-related and 43 per cent are community-related.

40. As regards time change, the impact of moving to the suburbs and to a house is about the same for former urbanites, although former suburban single-family home occupants naturally report less time change than anyone else.

41. Among these with more spare time, 37 per cent are less bored now than they were in the former residence. Among those with fewer spare hours, 12 per cent are more bored, 56 per cent less.

42. In the California working class suburb, 29 per cent reported drinking less, and 4 per cent more, but otherwise there was little change in leisure styles. Berger (1960), p. 79.

43. Percentages are from both samples combined to obtain a sufficient number of respondents. The styles were named by the respondents, and "modern" refers to what professional designers call "Moderne" or "Hollywood Modern." The designers' conception of modern was described as "Danish Modern" by one respondent.

44. Some people derived their inspiration from Levitt's model houses, but since these were furnished in a wide array of styles, the builder gave them no single clue for furnishing his houses.

45. A study of Levittown, New York, suggests individual taste as the prime determinant. Wattel, p. 297.

46. The first time, 72 per cent liked it "very much," 23 per cent "quite a bit," and 5 per cent "don't care one way or the other." By the second interview, the percentages were 61, 32, and 7 respectively. The Philadelphians were less satisfied, 36 per cent liking it very much, 42 per cent quite a bit, and 22 per cent ambivalent. In both samples, low-status people tended to be most dissatisfied. The question was very general, came early in the interview, and required respondents to choose between fixed categories, so the figures themselves probably mean little. Despite the unwillingness to dislike Levittown, people did not hesitate to answer the next question: "Is there anything you don't like so well about Levittown?"

47. In the random sample, complaints about lot size came from former suburbanites, but the Philadelphians mentioned them too.

48. In the first interview, 73 per cent expected to stay, 19 per cent to

move, and 8 per cent were undecided. In the second, everyone had made up his mind, 74 per cent to stay and 26 per cent to leave. The initially uncertain were too few to be analyzed. Proportionately, more of the initially decided changed their mind in favor of staying, for of intended Settlers, only 13 per cent now want to move, and of Mobiles, half now expect to stay.

49. Since the Philadelphians were interviewed only once, these data come from respondents who had filled out mail questionnaires before arrival, and may be an unrepresentative fraction of the total sample.

50. Seventy-three per cent of the California working class suburbanites planned to settle, 21 per cent to move. Berger (1960), p. 109.

51. Altogether, young women, the college-educated, high school dropouts, blue collar workers, Italian and Jewish women, Irish men, first and second generation Americans, and partners in mixed marriages miss the city most often. Education was the determining factor; except among Italians and other Southern Europeans, the better educated missed the city more than the poorly educated; even among the Jews, who missed it more than other ethnic groups, the better-educated outnumbered the others. The longer people have lived in the city, the more they are likely to miss it, except again for the Italians. The latter also miss the city only for people they know there; all other groups did so even if they were not lonely for relatives and old friends.

52. Fifty-six per cent of all women mentioned missing downtown shopping, some adding cultural facilities as well. Sixteen per cent missed the old neighborhood or corner stores; another 16 per cent, their families. The men gave no dominant reasons, but shopping was mentioned alone or in conjunction with other things by 60 per cent, and 37 per cent mentioned relatives.

53. Seventy per cent who missed the neighborhood also missed the city, but 32 per cent who did not miss the city were lonely for the neighborhood. Some people missed the city but not the neighborhood; they were primarily short-term residents, well-educated people, Jews, mixed-marriage partners, and ethnic group members who lacked their own neighborhood (for example, Albanians).

54. Judging by their responses, they did not miss the row house as such, but were using the question to complain about high heating bills in Levittown.

55. Thus, 75 per cent of those not completing high school, 70 per cent of those who had attended college, but only 41 per cent of high school graduates chose the city. Women who had formerly lived with their parents and would have preferred the city if they had been childless seem to imply that conflicts about how to raise the children must have caused considerable trouble in the three-generation home.

56. Levittowners who missed the city wanted to move back without children, but those who missed people there did not.

57. Sixty-five per cent of the sample offered suggestions, and women did so more than men. It should be remembered that the interview took place before department stores and a movie theater were built in the Levittown shopping center. Another reason given by women for wanting to live in the city was job opportunities.

58. Thirty-seven per cent of the former urbanites dislike Levittown, and the same proportion of former suburbanites do. Among tenth- and twelfth-graders, 49 per cent of former urbanites and 39 per cent of non-urbanites complain about having nothing to do.

59. The description was as follows: "Now, I want you to imagine a row house, not the kind built in Philadelphia, but a modern one, with a 30-foot front, and with the same amount of space, the same layout, and same general design as your Levitt house. It would be just like your present house, except that it would be a row house. It would be built in rows of four on streets just like those in Levittown, and in a community just like Levittown in all other ways." The questions were: "A. Suppose you had a choice between your present house and this modern suburban row house, but the row house was only 15 minutes from the husband's work; which would you choose?" "B. . . .(If) the row house was only 15 minutes away from the stores and other facilities of downtown Philadelphia, which would you choose?" "C. Now supposing both were located in Levittown. If the row house cost $1000 less than your present house, which would you choose?" "Ca. . . . how about if the row house cost $2000 less than your present house?" "Cb. How much less would the row house have to cost before you would think seriously about it?"

60. Five per cent would take the row house for $1000 less, 9 per cent more for $2000 less. Another 4 per cent agreed for half the price of the Levitt house.

61. Despite my attempt to describe a superior row house model, the respondents were reacting to the row houses they had known. For this reason, the Philadelphians, many of whom had come from row houses, were not even asked this question.

62. For some hopeful trends in row house design, see Whyte (1964).

63. Berger (1960), Chap. 1.

64. Berger (1960), p. 93.

65. Wilner et al., Chap. 13.

66. Willmott (1963), computed from Table 8, and pp. 44–47.

67. Zelan's study also showed that students raised in the suburbs were more likely than urban ones to prefer suburban residence once they had married.

68. I do so for stylistic reasons, but also because I see no major difference between the two. A planner is a type of policy-maker, sometimes but not always concerned with long-range change, and a city planner is a policy-maker who works inside community boundaries. When I describe or criticize current city planning

practice, however, I shall refer explicitly to the city planner.

69. The mere act of moving may also be a source of change.

70. These effects of a new dwelling unit and its greater spaciousness were also the most significant changes reported by a sample of slum dwellers moving into a new public housing project. Wilner et al., Chap. 10.

71. Stability is not, however, intrinsic to home ownership; Transients may not feel it, and tenants may feel it as much as owners if they expect to live in the apartment and neighborhood for a long time —for example, the West Enders I studied and Manhattanites.

72. An exception is the wading pool, where mothers talk to others while watching their small children.

73. The minority churches tended to attract people from the neighborhood in which they were located, and insofar as they made friends at church, were thus limited to their own neighborhood.

74. The size of living rooms and the cost of entertaining also play a limiting role.

75. Even so, there were class differences. For example, only 21 per cent of the purchasers of the cheapest house had graduated from college, as compared to 30 per cent of those in the medium-priced one and 48 per cent in the most expensive.

76. It was infinitesimal, for example, when compared to what Young and Willmott (Chap. 10) found in a new English housing estate, where almost the entire population sat and suffered in individual loneliness for several years, unable to break the ice even with next-door neighbors.

77. In most American cities, the new downtown high-rise apartments attract a disproportionate number of Jews. Abu-Lughod, p. 406 and Fenmore. Fenmore reports on his unpublished study of a sample of suburban home owners near Philadelphia who, for various reasons, might be prospective residents of downtown apartment buildings. He writes: "The significant finding of the study is that almost all of the suburban non-Jews . . . wished to remain in their single-family homes, whereas the overwhelming majority of Jews either wished to or were actually planning to move into new urban high-rise apartments."

78. A more detailed treatment of these points can be found in Gans (1962b).

Part 3 ▪ THE DEMOCRACY
OF POLITICS

Chapter Twelve

POLITICAL COMMUNICATION

IN PART ONE OF THIS BOOK I CONCLUDED THAT THE ORIGIN OF THE community was determined more by the events which took place after its founding than by prior planning, and more by the people than by their leaders. In Part Two I suggested that people's lives were also shaped by what happened in Levittown, particularly by the other people they encountered. These conclusions lead logically to a related question: To what extent do government and politics reflect the goals and priorities of the people, and to what extent those of the decision-makers, the elected and appointed officials, party leaders, and influential interests who affect and make decisions in the name of the people? This then raises the question of whether or not government *should* be responsive to the people and, if so, how much.

THE STRUCTURE OF POLITICAL COMMUNICATION

At one level these questions are about political communication between decision-makers and citizens; the responsiveness of the former to the latter and the feedback from the latter to the former. In a democratic community the functioning of the decision-makers is affected by two obvious facts of life: that the voters have a life-and-death power over government through their periodic visits to the ballot box; and that between elections, they take only a minor role in government, so that their feelings about its decisions are unknown and unpredictable. Even so, government must be responsive to the citizenry; the people who run for office want to be elected, and the political party can flourish only if its candidates win. The candidates themselves want to be responsive too, at least in Levittown, where being an elected official is a part-time job. As a result they are and wish to remain amateur politicians, running for office not simply to further political careers but for personal goals (like bathing in the public spotlight) and for social ones (to do what they think is best for the community). Being amateurs, they believe that doing good is largely a matter of having the right intentions—which they usually feel they have. Indeed, much campaign disagreement is a result of differences among equally well-intentioned people over just what is best.

Once elected, however, the candidates' behavior changes considerably. Now they are part of a political system which can make decisions only by minimizing response to and feedback from citizens and by not raising (or taking stands on) issues. Only by keeping public disagreement to a minimum can it function as a broker and synthesizer between conflicting interest groups and voter blocs.[1] In other words, candidates become what Levittowners—like most Americans in other communities—deprecatingly call "politicians." The reasons for this change are quite simple. Between elections, the government gets little feedback, for the average citizen neither communicates with the government nor is interested in the government's communicating with him. All decision-makers in Levittown, whether elected or appointed, whether in municipal government, the school system, or any other public agency, invariably reported that only a handful of citizens ever approached them to discuss their decisions or to make requests. Meetings of elected bodies are poorly attended, and even public hearings usually draw badly, except when a fight is in the offing. As a result, the elected official gets feedback from only a few people: those personally and directly affected by government decisions, especially those deprived—and therefore angered—by current and proposed actions.

The lack of citizen communication and attendance is not a result of apathy but of two other factors. First, most governmental activities simply do not touch the everyday lives and concerns of the citizenry. Most Township Committee decisions dealt with internal matters, of interest only to it and its staff, with meeting the requirements of county and state governments, and with satisfying requests for approvals and licenses from the builder and businessmen. School board agenda were similarly removed from parental concerns with the school. In addition, many people were hesitant to communicate with elected officials. Whether they come from large cities or small towns, people know that politicians are not often receptive to criticism, that they will usually respond in vague generalities, and that only rarely can they be really helpful with individual requests.

The politicians' reluctance to pay attention to the citizenry is not caused by disdain or lack of interest, however, but by the very sparseness of citizen communication and participation. If most people do not participate most of the time, and if the community is at all heterogeneous (and most communities are), those citizens who *do* contact the decision-makers will have different and often conflicting interests, and will make contradictory demands, some for one decision, others for a diametrically opposed one.[2] This conflict places the decision-makers in a difficult and nearly impossible position, for they can make only one decision. Consequently, whatever they say and do will alienate someone, and their wisest course is to listen as little (or at least as impassively) as possible, and to say and do even less.[3] Since the angry citizen is more likely to remember his grudges at election time than the happy one his satisfaction, it is to the politicians' advantage to be noncommittal. But they are also faced with uncertainty; they cannot help displease some citizens, yet without adequate feedback they rarely know how many and who will remember till the next election. But their problem is much closer than even the next election. If they talk publicly and freely about the decisions they must make and what they are thinking, they open themselves to immediate attack from whichever side feels its case is being given short shrift and from the opposition party, which is always looking for disgruntled citizens and campaign issues. And if they exposed themselves to continual feedback, each side would bombard them with demands and arguments and no decision could ever be reached.

Communication is also inhibited by what might be called the norm of *altruistic democracy*. According to this norm, a keystone of popular democratic theory, citizens enter government to serve their fellows and the public interest. They are expected to be impartial, altruistic servants of the citizenry, sure of how the public interest is to be defined, who make morally proper decisions without concern for interest groups, for voter blocs, or for their own and their party's political future. Since actual decisions can rarely avoid such considerations, however, practicing altruistic democracy would not enable decision-makers to perform their duties. Yet if the actual decision-making process were made public, the decision-makers would immediately be attacked as immoral, self-seeking, and "political." With the opposition party always lying in wait for a campaign issue, the decision-makers' only solution is to hide the actual process from both their opponents and the public.

The deviation between the normative and actual decision-making process would not become a campaign issue, of course, if the citizens did not embrace altruism in government. Although they may sense that the theory does not work, many are nevertheless hopeful that when the incumbent rascals are turned out at the next election, things will be different. Indeed, voters are sensitive to personalities rather than issues because, in addition to lacking interest in most issues, they are looking for a candidate they can trust to act according to the normative model. Experienced politicians cater to this in their campaigning, trying to prove that the opposition candidate is self-seeking whereas their own is altruistic. The voters' ability to "believe" and to be suspicious at the same time is deeply imbedded in the country's cultural heritage. Americans are convinced that the normative conception of democracy is viable, and that it is not put into operation because of the corruptibility of the politician. At the same time, however, they also identify their own point of view—and their own interests—as altruistic, the opposition as selfish, and the politician as a hero or a villain depending on which side his decision falls.

Ultimately, this conception of the political process stems from people's lack of involvement in government. If they participated in its activities, they would soon realize how the decision-making process works and why so. They might not give up their faith in altruism, but they would somehow adjust their thinking to allow them to be able to function in government, just as they do in order to function in the midst of office and factory politics on the job. Moreover, in a community like Levittown most officials and party workers are not professional politicians, and so share the attitudes of the ordinary citizen.[4] They may understand the necessity of "politics" in their own agency or party, but they explain the actions of the opposition as a violation of altruistic democracy.[5]

The selective participation of citizens in government and their belief that it ought to be run by altruistic norms forces the government to protect itself from its constituents. The individual decision-maker restricts feedback and response, but this is not sufficient, for if a politician suddenly decided to seek greater political support by becoming more responsive to his constituents, his colleagues would have to follow suit, and as soon as conflicting demands were evoked, the decision-making process would be back in the same impasse.

Consequently, government must develop institutional means to shield itself from the citizens. In Levittown (and I suspect everywhere else) it does so by creating two governments, a *performing* and an *actual* one. The government with which the decision-makers confront the citizens is a performing government; its actions are *performances* that follow altruistic democratic theory.[6] The stage, designed according to this theory and legitimated by state and local statutes, is the public meeting of the governing body, where decision-makers listen to citizens' opinions and then appear to vote on a final decision on the basis of what they have heard. But this is only a performance, for the decision has already been made "backstage," in the secret deliberations of the actual government.[7] In Levittown, its major components are the caucus and the political party.

The caucus is a private arena where decision-makers can debate and agree on the decisions which they then announce at the public performance. The political party provides the individual decision-maker with the support he needs to function in both performing and actual governments. The elected government, open to public inspection and liable to turnover with every election, is socially and psychologically an extremely unstable base of operations. The individual decision-maker, like any other human being, needs an institution in which he plays a permanent role, can make a career, can be rewarded and promoted for successes (but be retained if he should fail temporarily), and—most important—where he can associate with people he can trust. Even in the government caucus, he can never be totally open with his colleagues, some of whom may represent present or future political opposition.

The party aids him in yet another crucial way. If he is to be re-elected, his decisions must reflect, at least to some extent, the wishes of his constituents. Since he is restricted in determining these wishes, the party provides a service to him by gathering feedback about citizens' ideas and feelings through its party workers. More important, it offers him another, simpler, criterion for decision-making—the welfare of the party. Since its welfare is, like his own, based on its ability to win elections, the party becomes a responsible partner in the decision-making process. Indeed, often the elected official is only a representative—sometimes even an errand boy—who carries the decision of the party leadership or caucus back to the government caucus.

The constituents who have definite opinions on the decisions government should make or who demand government action in their behalf are, of course, excluded from both caucuses. Even so, they must attempt to get around the performing government and reach the actual one, or rather, to communicate with the performing politician in such a way that their message will be considered by the actual government. Those who represent powerful interest groups and voter blocs have easy access to the actual government, but the powerless groups have considerable difficulty and must devise techniques that compel the actual government to pay attention. Such groups can put on their own performance, stating their viewpoint in public so that the decision-makers must acknowledge it, or they can bring a large number of citizens to the public meeting, putting on a show of strength to persuade the decision-makers to take them into account. If they know that they are not reaching the actual government, they can put on a *counterperformance*. They may get up at a public hearing and ask the decision-makers a series of questions to which they already know the answers, hoping that the counterperformance will gain them sympathy from other constituents and thus add to their strength. They may also try to make the decision-makers look foolish or contradict themselves, aiming to show that the whole operation is a performance and that the real decisions are made elsewhere. This too is intended to gain outside support, especially from among those who believe in altruistic democracy. Finally, they may try to force the decision-makers into a *performance break,* generating so much pressure that the latter lose their poise, depart from the previously agreed-on decision, and promise publicly to support the protesters. They are now not only

committed to a position they must take in the actual government, but they have also revealed the performance and thereby
ended it temporarily. Protesting citizens continually seek to create enough disagreement and conflict to end the performance
and force the actual government to reveal itself; the decision-
makers try to prevent conflict so that they can maintain the secrecy of the actual government and preserve their freedom from
pressure.

Most people, including even the decision-makers themselves,
are not entirely aware of the existence of performing and actual
governments.[8] Nevertheless they sense it, for they know that
politicians "talk out of both sides of their mouths," promise one
thing and do another, and cannot be trusted. Although their descriptions are couched in moral terms, they are referring to the
deviation between the politician's performing and actual roles.
Of course, performances are usually considered deceitful, and the
term itself is derogatory, but I do not use it in this sense. It
should be clear that I consider the performance a real and intrinsic
part of American politics, and although by no means desirable, it
is probably impossible to eliminate except through a radical
(and quite unlikely) change in the citizen-government relationship. In any case, I do not mean my observations to be read as an
exposé of the "immorality" of American governments, local,
state, or federal, for politics is too complex to be judged by norms
of personal or familial relationships.

The Functions of the Performing Government

A primary function of the performance is reducing uncertainty. When everything rides on the next election, every decision—indeed, every act of government—can result in unpredictable consequences. In a suburban community, where many
voters are independents, neither party can count on a sufficient
number of loyal adherents who will support it regardless of the
candidates or the issues, and there are too few patronage jobs to
provide workers and assured votes. In a new community, uncertainty is even greater, for no one knows the voters well enough to
predict how they will vote, and strangers may get up at public
meetings and throw them into an uproar. Also, when organizations are hurrying to establish themselves, normative democracy,
which posits open discussion, means inevitable delays. If just
enough democracy can be incorporated to mollify those who feel

it is as important as getting things done, then the actual practice of democracy can be avoided. Whether the group is new or established, the expression of democratic dissent is evidence of conflict, and this is often interpreted as a sign of organizational ineffectiveness. A proper performance, on the other hand, creates an image of efficiency and skill. Consequently, government tries to exclude uncertainty and open conflict from the political process wherever it can, and to plan and "stage" all its activities.

Particular care is taken in the staging of confrontations with citizens. Open meetings of public bodies are run with an agenda, which functions much like a script. In fact, when the school board was still composed of old residents, the superintendent prepared a virtual script, enabling the board members to read all their remarks off the agenda, except for their votes. The maintenance of the performance is enhanced by local and state ordinances, and by Robert's Rules of Order, which make it difficult for the audience to question the decision-makers. In New Jersey, the local governing body is not even legally obligated to hear citizens at its regular meetings, but Levittown's Township Committee allowed them to speak. Its counsel acted as a gatekeeper, however, using the laws governing public meetings to cut off comments that might erupt into argument and endanger the performance.

The main opportunity for people to offer feedback is the public hearing, but it too is set up as a performance. Citizens can make speeches and offer testimony, but questioning of the decision-makers is discouraged. The latter sit on the podium and listen (or appear to listen), absorbing testimony without any response, so as not to indicate how they are going to vote. During my study, the public bodies had decided how to vote before the public hearing, and simply sat through it as a legal requirement. Not that they rejected all comments, but usually they had heard them before, and the chance of learning anything new was small. Yet even if new facts or ideas were presented, and officials were influenced by what they heard, they tried to mask it.

The incentives for maintaining this performance become visible during the rare occurrences of performance breaks. When the ordinance to admit nonresident doctors was in public hearing, the opponents were putting intense pressure on the elected officials to table it. Stung by their angry remarks, one official suddenly announced that he was reversing his position and would go back on the caucus agreement to approve it, made before the public hearing. Having neither political ambition nor a firm base in his party, he was less insulated from pressure than his colleagues, who tried to restore the performance by keeping silent. His defection and continued audience pressure eventually also forced them to reverse themselves, however. Although the performance break achieved the opponents' demands, it only made them angrier, because they realized the public hearing had been "cut and dried." The supporters of the ordinance were angry too, demanding equal time at a later meeting. New political negotiations ensued to reduce the conflict and to construct a compromise, and later the performance breaker and his colleagues denied that they had given in to pressure, their denial illustrating once more how much trouble the break had caused them.[9] Another performance break took place at a school board meeting, when a large number of parents arrived unexpectedly to protest the actions of a teacher. The board members pointed out that they had not been briefed, meaning that without a caucus they were unable to prepare a performance demonstrating that the board had the situation under control and would take the appropriate actions. The parents insisted on an immediate answer, however, and the board members had to call on the superintendent to make a statement. This was a significant performance break because it violated the traditional performance in which the school board announced all policy decisions (implying thereby that it also made them) and the superintendent spoke only when asked for facts and technical detail.

Experienced politicians can perform without letting on, but nonprofessionals are less expert and less detached. They need the voters' approval more, and are more likely to give in to pressure. Seeing themselves as working hard for little financial or psychological reward (few voters ever praise them), they are especially sensitive to criticism, and the more strictly they adhere to the performance, the less their chance of being criticized. One elected official explained the necessity for the caucus as follows: "People on the board wouldn't speak freely at public meetings. They serve on a courtesy basis, and they wouldn't take that kind of punishment, the newspaper and other attacks that would follow if they spoke freely." Nonprofessionals fear unrehearsed confrontations of all kinds. They are apprehensive about making speeches, but these can be written out and rehearsed, and since people suspect overly glib speakers, a poor style is not a serious liability. Answering questions afterwards is another matter. Either uncertainty or evasion can make the politician look foolish, and if he tries to answer openly he may be trapped into a performance break. Professionals, on the other hand, are more adept at maintaining the performance, although they need it less psychologically, being less threatened by criticism and hostile questions.

A performance is most necessary if the actions to be taken publicly violate the democratic norm. When leaders of the two opposing Republican party factions met to make peace, new appointments to the party club and executive committee had to be arranged, and an hour of the meeting was spent in planning the "deal" so that it would not look like one to rank-and-file members. If important men suddenly resigned from party or government posts, performances had to explain their departure. The official reasons were usually "new business duties which prevent giving sufficient time to the community," to maintain the myth that politicians never squabbled or forced out dissidents. The individuals concerned could have told the real reasons, but only at the cost of losing their remaining party support and ending their political careers. So could the groups which had dismissed them, but only at great political risk; if the truth had come out, the opposing faction (or the other party) could have staged counter-performances to show that party bickering signified the leadership's incompetence. Although many Levittowners suspected the public explanations for dismissal, the safest course was to hold to them. Maintaining the performance might increase voter distrust, but this was less dangerous than giving opponents the opportunity to put on counterperformances. And once a false reason is given, it can be reiterated ad infinitum until even the most skeptical lose interest in questioning it.

Performances are not restricted to small-town local government; they are staged by state and national politicians, including Presidents of the United States, and by executives of large national corporations as well. A fascinating example took place during the 1964 Republican convention, when Governor Scranton was forced into a performance break that lost him what little support he had left for the nomination. After criticizing Senator Goldwater as impulsive, he sent him a letter attacking his stand on several issues, using stronger language than customary among party colleagues. When this departure from normal performance was criticized, Scranton explained that the letter had been written on the spur of the moment, allowing the Goldwater forces to describe *him* as impulsive. To make matters worse, he then indicated that an aide had drafted the letter, and that he had signed it without reading it, enabling his enemies to speculate whether he had ever written anything attributed to him, and more important, whether he ever read what he signed. Inevitably, a Goldwater supporter wondered publicly if Scranton would read the laws and policy documents he had to sign if he became President, putting an end to Scranton's performance portraying himself as an effective and unemotional decision-maker. Of course, the Goldwater group's reactions were performances too; every politician uses ghost-writers and signs his name to unread documents, but he maintains the public trust by not admitting that either happens.[10] Once there is a breach in performance, trust quickly evaporates, because people wonder whether the politician can take the proper actions in a crisis—including, among other things, maintenance of the necessary performances.

The performance is only one method of restricting feedback, and many others are used by decision-makers in confronting citizens. For example, if an angry citizen suggests that a decision was based on morally doubtful reasons, they will supply reasons quite in keeping with altruistic democracy. Unless the citizen has adequate information on their real reasons (and he rarely does), he cannot continue the discussion. If he appears frequently, and consistently questions actions and reasons, the decision-makers can charge him with being a crank or a "radical," and if he comes regularly to voice dissent, his fellow citizens may agree with them. If a large group of citizens appears in opposition, the decision-makers can restrict feedback by pointing out that they were elected to use their own best judgment to make decisions and that they will not be blackmailed into reaching a decision on the basis of "pressure," a performance statement that is made to reduce pressure, precisely because decisions *are* affected by it. To discourage petitioners, they suggest the threat to the social order that follows from "government by petition." Again, the response is a performance, for if the petitioning group is large and angry enough, its demands may be taken into consideration even while its right to petition is questioned.

Motivations also count; an individual who voices disagreement because of ideological concern and has no personal interest in the matter is likely to be ignored. This is ironic, because government is supposed to be run on an altruistic basis, but it is also pragmatic; the decision-makers know that people without personal stakes are not likely to be interested very long, and their comments can be rejected.[11] They will also ignore feedback if they believe it is "political," a performance staged by the opposition party to give it an issue for a future campaign. Finally, the most frequent device is to dismiss all public feedback unless the person can provide a legitimate reason for offering it. Because so few people volunteer feedback in public, decision-makers believe that those who do only get up "to hear themselves talk"—and the substance of their remarks can be set aside.

Of course, the decision-makers do not reject all feedback, for they must be able to judge the electorate's mood between elections. They prefer, however, to gather their own, and to do so privately, away from the public arena where it can upset the performance. This also enables them to structure the questions they ask their constituents, to get specific reactions to the alternatives open to them on crucial decisions. More general feedback from rank-and-file citizens is collected mainly by the parties' district representatives. The party leaders concentrate on the organizationally active, making sure that a high party member participates in every major civic and service club. Decision-makers often stay late in public meetings to listen to people who want to talk to them and invite calls at home or in the office, thus screening out all but those concerned enough to stay behind at the end of a meeting or to take the trouble of calling.

But the major means of discovering what the public is thinking is by a kind of clinical empathy which produces "anticipatory feedback." As part of his professional training, the politician learns how to understand his constituents—what they want, what angers them, and how intensely they feel about issues. Some politicians have "empathic personalities." By nature they are marginal people, detached from close ties (which makes them good observers) and able performers, who can draw people out and sense how their minds work. Nevertheless, most politicians have to learn such skills. They spend most of their waking hours meeting with people, and thus gather a great deal of information about them. They have also learned to be tough-minded, to see their constituents as defenders of their various self-interests, and to screen out the rhetoric with which voters confront them. Moreover, successful politicians usually—but not always— resemble their constituents and can sometimes use their own re- actions to an issue to judge how the voters feel.

The Functions of the Actual Government

The workings of the actual government are hard to fathom, for the caucus meets in total privacy, no minutes are kept, and no out- siders are permitted. The press cannot attend, and I was refused admission even though I promised not to publish anything on what took place. Its functions can, however, be described by its origin. When the township was rural, there was no need to divide government into performing and actual branches. Since everyone knew everyone else, feedback could be anticipated and did not have to be solicited or restricted. The only performance was to satisfy the statutory requirement of "the record," but in a one- party community the decision-makers did not require protection against the voters. No caucus was needed; when disagreements arose, township officials could talk them over informally and make the necessary compromises. After Levitt had purchased land for the new community, the volume of decisions increased. Differences of opinion developed, and decisions became raw ma- terial for pro- and anti-Levitt factions embroiled in primary elec- tion contests. Additional people had to be hired, and their quali- fications could not be discussed openly without hurting feelings or creating grudges that might become campaign issues. The new decisions also generated controversy, and as one old resident ex- plained, "People were in the audience who liked to hear them- selves think. They kept interrupting and this made for long meetings and nothing got done." As a result, the Township Com- mittee decided to hold what it called "conference meetings." "We work out our disagreements at the conference meetings," another Committee member pointed out. "We don't wash our dirty linen in public." The caucus was continued when the Levittowners took over the township government.

The importance of the caucus was illustrated in 1961, when the Township Committee consisted of two Republicans and a Democrat. The latter, realizing that he was a losing minority, decided to make political capital from it. One day he suddenly announced the existence of the caucus and his "resignation" from this secret and therefore undemocratic body. Although he

departed in well-publicized indignation, he returned quietly a
few weeks later. Given the widespread lack of interest in governmental activities at the time, no public outcry followed his exposé, and his absence only kept him out of the actual government.
The Board of Education delayed instituting the caucus until its
factions disagreed so much that it had no other choice. A year
later, when control of the board was taken over by two cosmopolitans from the Citizens Association for Public Schools, it was
dropped as undemocratic, but with many controversial matters
on the agenda so much time was spent on debate that few decisions were made. When community leaders began to say that the
board was unable to make up its mind and that its members were
acrimonious, the caucus was restored. Backstage, disagreement
was reduced, for without an audience, minority factions and politically ambitious board members could not put on a show of
intransigence to impress their supporters. Arguments did not
end, however, even at public meetings, for the board was too split
on some issues to maintain a harmonious performance.

The party plays many roles in the actual government. Party
caucuses precede governmental ones and constantly remind the
decision-makers that their individual decisions must be woven
into a pattern that can be used in election campaigns to remind
the forgetful voter and provide him with an image of the party.
The party workers act as brokers between the party and the
voters between elections, doing favors and providing an entree to
the actual government for individuals with personal requests. Although modern political science theory has it that the service-
giving functions of the political party are unnecessary in middle
class communities, this is not entirely true. The district leader
tells citizens which agencies of government can help him; he is
available in the evening when government offices are closed, and
can even offer to process a request when the citizen cannot take
time off from work to go to city hall. If a citizen is in trouble, a
kind word with the police or the judge cannot hurt, even if it
cannot help very much. And when unemployment strikes, the
politician may be able to come up with a temporary government
job or a business contact who is looking for workers. Since
elections are sometimes won by a small margin, the goodwill cul-
tivated by the district leader may be decisive.[12]

Party workers also function as a micro-electorate, as stand-ins
to test issues and candidates. If a candidate does not go over with

the party workers, he is unlikely to attract the voters, and if he wins the workers' favor, they will try harder to get him elected. Workers make good candidates, because of their party loyalty. Since a candidate, once elected, is formally free to arrive at his own decision, the party can advise and cajole, but it cannot dictate his actions. If the official is a loyal party man, however, the party can be sure of some influence in the workings of the actual government.

But the party's main function is campaigning. In a community of independents, every vote is unpredictable and campaigning never ceases. The formal election campaigns are of course crucial, for while they are performances, they decide the fate of the actual government. The party needs a good performer, a candidate who acts like a winner to enthuse the workers and who can attract loyal and independent voters. The voters, particularly the uncommitted, look for candidates whom they can trust as persons, and who would do the right thing for them in case they became interested in an issue or had to request a favor.

Voter demands result in a campaign which concentrates on personalities and party images. Personal qualities are hard to stage, so that a candidate must come across as stable, moral, honest, and trustworthy. For this reason, any hint of personal scandal is enough to exclude a potential nominee. Divorce, especially among women, is construed as a sign of instability and is a handicap even with non-Catholic voters. So is a sexually attractive woman candidate. Other women will oppose her for fear their husbands will vote for her sexual charm; men, for fear that she will use her attractiveness politically and throw government into an uproar. Dedication to altruistic democracy and the community's welfare is a must, and a previous history of service in community organizations and in church is required as evidence. The candidate who dwells on the community's troubles may be considered overly pessimistic; the voters seem to want an optimist who feels problems are solvable. In a community like Levittown, the candidate must be a family man, with somewhat more schooling than the voters but not too much more.[13] Candidates show off their families, and the campaign literature provides information about their education and occupation, allowing the voters to judge if they are in similar circumstances, and therefore likely to understand them and act on their behalf. For example, a housewife with a large brood of children and a blue collar worker husband needed few speeches to persuade the voters that she would vote to keep taxes low. Speeches are only words and promises, but personal characteristics are undeniable evidence.[14] The school board candidacy of a very popular but childless Levittowner was questioned, the feeling being that without children of his own, he might not represent parents properly. This set of criteria tends to select young, lower middle class people, and encourages salesmen—but not high-pressure ones—to run for office.[15]

Much of the campaigning is devoted to presenting the candidates as people, wherever possible through direct and informal confrontations with the voters. The rest consists of an endless stream of press releases proclaiming the moral virtues of one party and its opposition's corruption. Party public relations men, hired for the duration of the campaign, spend their time taking apart the opposition's every move and every statement to find charges. As a result, the campaign becomes a constantly escalating morality play, with each party attacking the other for acts which both would carry out without a second thought if they were politically desirable and if the party were protected by the privacy of the actual government. For example, in the fall of 1959, the Democrats attacked the Republican incumbent for "running a political employment agency" by appointing relatives and friends to township posts, then a standard procedure among the old resident elite. The Republican target described the charge as "tragically humorous" and "stupid," pointing out that the Township Committee, rather than he personally, appointed people, and that in any case, no new residents were available for appointments. The Democrats promptly called his statement "tragically unfunny," accused the Republicans of only appointing other Republicans, and charged that unqualified local people were being named to jobs for which experienced outsiders should be found.[16] At this point, the Republican declared that "he would engage in no more political infighting," and that "these assaults have been directed at me for purely political reasons." He described himself as being "township administrator" and said he had "neither the time nor the inclination to engage in political mudslinging." Then a Republican candidate for minor office took over the attack, accusing the Democrats of operating a political machine and waging a "smear campaign," and called on them to "stick to issues and cease resorting to personalities." "We," he continued, "are running on a sound platform of progress for the best interests of the community." The Democratic leader promptly responded by calling the smear "ridiculous." He added, "If that were the best that the Republican candidates could offer in the way of press releases, then their campaign must be pretty barren of intelligent thinking." He pointed out that lacking patronage jobs the Democrats could not possibly build a machine, and then repeated the political employment agency criticism, arguing that it was "a charge we supported with facts." He concluded by pointing out that the Democrats had offered constructive recommendations, whereas the Republicans said "that Levittown is a nice town, but not a word about what they propose to do to keep it that way." The Republicans then announced a ten-point program to "continue the best features of past and present programming." [17]

These exchanges are ritual performances, not expected to be read by the mass of voters and put on in the vain hope that they may persuade a few naive ones.[18] They serve no significant function except to offer constant evidence of the existence of the performing government (and to uphold the norms of altruistic democracy), but they are perpetuated because they take little effort and might just sway the small number that constitutes the margin of victory. The absence of evidence on the progress of the campaign forces both parties to use every possible technique and opportunity to change the voters' minds, and once one party sets off a volley of charges, the other must retaliate, for silence could be an admission of guilt and would be so interpreted in the opposition's next press release.

The entire process is less a conspiracy by the parties to put over their candidates than an attempt, however fumbling, to anticipate the demands of the electorate. The only point at which the parties refuse to respond to these demands is in taking stands on major issues. Taking stands is divisive and can lose as many votes as it gains, and the parties do not even force each other to do so, for that tactic would only boomerang; the challenging party would also have to take a stand. Instead, both limit themselves to generalities, noncontroversial issues like civil service, and those controversial ones which are already identified with the party position and image. On the rare occasions when many voters are, however, interested in an issue, they pressure the candidates and parties to take a stand. For example, at one candidates' night for the school board election, the hopefuls were asked whether or not they would vote for the school budget. Those without further interest in public office answered freely, but one politically ambitious man explained candidly that he had not yet decided, for either a yes or no would lose him votes. The audience rejected his answer and made him promise to announce a decision publicly, which he did after days of feverish conferences with his advisers.

The election is the point of maximum communication, feedback, and response, and once it is won or lost, these end abruptly. But even then, feedback is limited. People can only vote for a candidate, and unless he runs on one specific issue, the meaning of the vote remains unclear. If the party in power is turned out, people are obviously discontented, but no one knows—or can prove—the specific gripes, who shares them and how intensely. Unless there is a single overriding issue of deep and widespread concern, the electorate has not been able to tell the government what decisions it wants, if any; it has only chosen decision-makers who resemble it in a variety of personal characteristics and who have promised to do their best for it and the community. The diffuseness of the feedback is of course advantageous for the new officeholders; it frees them to function in the actual government and to adapt their decisions with an eye to the next election.

THE ROLE OF THE PRESS

Political communication is not restricted to government and citizens alone; the press also plays a role.[19] In theory, it is independent of government and politics, but in practice it is not, even contributing to feedback restriction somewhat by its tendency to report the activities of the performing government. Ironically, the reporters are interested in just the opposite; their professional norms, their prestige, and their feeling of accomplishment are nurtured by debunking performances and by describing what happened backstage, although they too believe in altruistic democracy, and their reportage of the actual government often emphasizes its deviation from democratic norms. This is the essence of the exposé. But the journalist and his newspaper are also part of the political institution. Publishers and editors are sometimes party or government decision-makers and often influential behind the scenes.[20] Even when this is not the case, the reporter becomes involved in a relationship with his news sources which ultimately forces him to cover the performing rather than the actual government.

The decision-makers want no news spread about the actual government, and if a reporter crosses them, he incurs their hostility (or at least loses their confidence) and may be punished by not being given good stories in the future. Yet if the reporter limits his coverage to the decisions and the performances that accompany them, his story will be dull and uninteresting. He is thus caught in the middle. If he alienates the decision-makers, he loses the only reliable source of news about the actual government; if he goes along with them, he will displease his editor and his readers. His only escape hatch is the decision-maker's need for him. If the decision-maker punishes a reporter by withholding information, the reporter can retaliate by not publishing something the decision-maker wants to get into the paper.

These conflicts of interest lead to the development of a *system of mutual obligation* between reporter and decision-maker, which incorporates the former into the political institution by inviting him backstage, but with the requirement that he limit his coverage of the actual government. The reporter learns all (or almost all), but cannot tell; the decision-maker tells all (or as much as he has to), but knows he will not learn about it in next morning's paper. The relationship is perhaps less a system than a tug of war, for the decision-maker is always trying to reveal as little as possible, and the reporter attempts to publish as much as he can without alienating his source.[21]

The tug of war begins as soon as the reporter is put on the city hall beat. At first, he gets only stereotyped interviews, but as he hangs around city hall he picks up bits of unauthorized information, gossip and rumors, and gradually begins to learn about the actual government. At this point, the decision-makers let him step behind the scenes to tell him what is happening in the actual government, usually warning that it is not to be published. If he does not reveal off-the-record information (which can be checked quickly if his paper comes out daily or weekly), he is likely to be taken further into their confidence, and for good reason. If the reporter were not told everything, he might find out anyway, and from hostile sources. The decision-maker who shares confidences can at least be sure that the reporter gets *his* version of the event.

The reporter benefits by understanding the political scene, which helps him make sense of it to his readers even if he cannot publish all he knows.

Sometimes he can report beyond the performance, by obtaining bits of information from friendly decision-makers he can use without attribution, or by finding one who has private reasons for letting himself be quoted. He can also speculate, incorporating material that may be far more than speculation among city hall insiders. His mere presence occasionally makes it impossible to keep backstage information secret; city hall insiders may talk so much about political dissension that rumors about it appear in the community, and then the reporter is not only free to cover it but is almost forced to, in order to show that the press is not holding back information. When a story is big, the reporter may risk angering his sources, particularly if he knows they will need him in the future. He can also plead the norms of his craft, for politicians know that professional reporters will reject any demand for overt censorship or self-censorship. Or he can argue that competing reporters may publish the story and he cannot let them scoop him.

Even if the reporter writes an article the decision-maker does not like, the latter cannot criticize too much, for if the reporter is angered he may dig deeper, get back at the decision-maker by revealing confidences, or obtain damaging material from his opponents. Since the decision-makers are the most avid readers of city hall news, a skillful newsman can include such material between the lines without actually reporting it, thus giving the decision-maker a signal to get back on good terms with the reporter before he resorts to more open coverage. Of course, decision-makers have ways of keeping the reporter in line, too.[22] They can criticize his articles and shame him into more friendly stories, they can forget to invite him to an important meeting or feed scoops to a competitor, and if necessary they can complain to the editor or publisher, although this will surely cause the reporter to retaliate. They can also wine and dine him or even try to establish a social relationship, but the experienced reporter knows how to avoid these traps.

The mutual obligation system was nicely illustrated during the 1960 election campaign when the Levittown Civic Association sought to hold a local version of the Great Debates. Local reporters were asked to question the Levittown candidates, but all refused. The dean of the local press corps explained: "The questions I really want to ask I can't ask in public, only in private, but if I ask innocuous questions, my reputation as a newspaperman is impugned." Eventually two Philadelphia reporters who covered Levittown as "stringers" and were not involved enough in local affairs to become part of the system of obligation agreed to serve.

Over time, the reporter becomes a part of the political institution, if only marginally, and his coverage begins to be selective, sometimes deliberately but more often unconsciously. Getting to know his major news sources well, he forms likes and dislikes which cannot help but influence his reporting. For example, one local reporter told me: "I would never publish anything nasty about C————. If he makes a mistake, either a political or a moral one, I tell him to watch out, but I don't put it in the paper." The reporter also begins to identify with the community, omitting uncomplimentary items, and helping people and causes he thinks deserve publicity.[23] For instance, one editor gave extra space to a Levittown organization and kept out stories of its internal conflicts, because it provided a worthy community service. He also proposed community programs he considered desirable or necessary, writing editorials about them and creating news stories by feeding his ideas to a community leader and then interviewing him. In addition to helping the community, such coverage aided the newspaper's reputation for community service, which in turn might attract more advertisers and readers. And when news was scarce—an almost constant problem in Levittown —planting ideas helped fill up the pages.

Of course, reporters also expressed personal prejudices. One, believing that elected officials deserved respect, described their critics as rabble-rousers, thus supporting the governmental performance and preventing the community from knowing the extent of dissatisfaction. He covered Levittown only a short time, and was also atypical, for most reporters enjoyed watching the decision-makers squirm under questioning and were especially pleased to report evasive answers to critics by those who had also evaded *their* questions. Another reporter, also temporarily in Levittown, remained outside the system of obligation altogether, leaving him free to slant the news in favor of the Democrats and his own point of view on the school budget.

It must be noted that most of the time the reporter's coverage is routine and does not involve the conflict with sources I have described. His everyday work is to cover the community and its myriad events, and he is not expected to delve deeply into government. In a small community, many decisions of the actual government have obvious or publishable explanations, and events that strain the system of mutual obligation are rare.

Yet even if that system did not exist, coverage of the actual government would still be difficult. For one thing, reporters are not admitted to caucuses and must get their information second and third hand. Accurate explanations for decisions are hard to come by, for even when a political event is not secret it is difficult and time-consuming to reconstruct what really happened and why, requiring interviews with many people to dig out reasons and motivations. Few newspapers have large enough staffs to do such legwork, and in a small community too many other events must be covered. The average reporter often looks in on several governmental and organizational meetings during the same night, even if they provide little news, in order to maintain his rapport with the people in charge. Since politicians and organizational leaders are quick to object to poor or insufficient coverage, the reporter spends much of his time on inconsequential stories which respond to a demand from his most loyal readers. Finally, few newspapermen have the training to analyze an event or to understand the social forces and processes that lead to a political decision.

Ideally, in order to give people the kind of information needed to participate effectively in government, it (but particularly the actual government) should be covered as a serial, in which the day-to-day reportage is part of an integrated analysis. Over the long run, the coverage should show—at least for major issues— what alternatives were open to decision-makers; why these; which ones they chose when they had a choice; and what social, economic, and political incentives and pressures brought about the choice. This kind of reportage would require a staff of skilled and dispassionate political scientists who would not make snap judgments about deviations from democratic norms. The available reporters are neither social scientists nor trained sufficiently in the social sciences, however. Experienced hands know the principles of political strategy, but even they rarely focus on the social system and on the processes which encourage or require these strategies. Reporters are, like their readers, believers in altruistic democracy, which is one reason why decision-makers try to keep them from reporting the activities of the actual government. Of course, they are more sophisticated and more skeptical than their readers and rarely cast politicians as heroes or villains as quickly or as permanently as citizens do. Moreover, they are trained to be objective, so that their evaluations are often implicit—and generally unconsciously so. Even so, reporters have political positions like anyone else, and a close reading of their articles (which is carried out only by the politicians they cover) would reveal these positions. However, the value judgments reporters make are more often based on their personal and professional relationship with the politicians they cover than on political ideology; they tend to favor the cooperative politician and to write negatively about the one who makes their work more difficult.

But more sophisticated coverage of the actual government is also held back by lack of incentives for doing so. Protests by politicians may contribute to the reporter's pride that he has done a good job, but they may also get him a warning from his editor. Professional rewards for scrupulous reporting and in-depth analysis are rare; the newspapermen who work for small-town dailies and weeklies are not read widely enough by their professional peers or in the executive suites of top papers and magazines to bring the better job offers that follow superior performance in other occupations.

Still, the main obstacle to better reporting—and the main withholder of incentives—is probably the audience. Many readers want to know what is happening in the actual government, but their interest, like their political participation, is intense only when a topic concerns them personally—which is why local papers devote much space to social columns. The rest of the time they are curious rather than concerned, reading the news only "to keep up with events." As a result, Levittown's reporters and editors received no more feedback than the decision-makers. Readers wrote in occasionally, but as is so often the case, many letters came from a few regular correspondents, some cranks, others defined as cranks simply because they wrote in so persistently. For these reasons, letters were considered a poor source of feedback. So were circulation figures, because many papers are distributed without charge. Consequently, newspapers know little about their audience and rely on professional intuition and what they can pick up at random about its interest in the news. Even so, editors took audience interest into account, and a matter thought to be of minor interest would generally get little space unless news was in such short supply that everything had to be printed.

Generally speaking, an event was thought to be interesting to the readership only if excitement or conflict developed around it. For example, when the builder persuaded both political parties to support a referendum to change the township's name to Levittown, the absence of visible resident opposition led one editor to conclude that his readers did not care. Personally, he was against the name change and tried hard to find politicians who would take a stand against it or give him a quote around which he could build a critical article. Unable to get either, he gave the matter only routine coverage. When the name change was approved by just a hundred votes, he was sorry he had not written about it in more detail, feeling—perhaps justifiably so—that additional coverage would have produced the votes needed to reject the change.

In this instance, the editor misjudged potential (although not actual) reader interest, but normally, his paper covered political news in more detail than Levittowners seemed to want. And even when they were interested, they used the press for other functions than information; they also wanted a performance that would give the outside world an idealized picture of Levittown. If an event reflected negatively on the community, many readers preferred to have it hushed up. For example, when a teenage fight broke out, many people wanted to read about it, but were also sorry it had to appear in print. Likewise, a neighbor was unhappy about a survey of Levittown's racial attitudes which appeared in the Philadelphia papers because she did not want the world to know that many Levittowners had doubts about integration. Organizational leaders are even more insistent than ordinary residents that the press cover the performance. Voluntary associations flooded the papers with publicity releases written to attract new members and were angered by articles about internal strife, arguing that the papers should be supporting their organizations instead of tarnishing their reputations by playing up discord. The demand for performance reporting even extended to' noncontroversial matters. When a photographer came to do a picture story on everyday activities in the local pools, a school official posed the children in a well-organized swimming and diving exhibition, belying the near-anarchic playing and splashing that normally occurred in a crowded pool too small for much real swimming. Organizational leaders and amateur politicians felt more compelled to ask for friendly coverage and were more upset by critical reporting than the professionals, who knew that pressuring newsmen for printed praise would be likely to boomerang.

The net outcome of the reporting process is that the public does not get the kind of news it would need if it decided to participate in government and politics. Only when an issue of widespread concern develops and people begin to participate can the reporter spend the time and energy to improve his coverage in both quantity and quality. Even though he responds to, rather than initiates, reader interest, such coverage can have significant impact, providing the already interested with information to participate effectively and perhaps motivating others to join them. When citizen protest becomes sizeable, he can go beyond the governmental performance, reporting counterperformances and other signs of the public's concern. He can critically analyze official reports and public statements for errors or contradictions, thus exposing the performance if only by implication. He can also do surveys within the community to reveal the extent of citizen dissatisfaction. But even when the reporter's sympathies are with the citizens, he can help them only up to a point, for his permanent ties are with his city hall sources. When the issue has been resolved or public interest has waned, he must face the decision-makers again, and alone. If the public were interested more often, he would have more power within the system of mutual obligation, and the decision-makers would treat him more respectfully even if he publicized the actual government. This happens to few reporters in few communities.[24]

When reportage diverges regularly from actual events, people in the know become skeptical of press competence and honesty, and when the divergences become sizeable, an information vacuum develops which not only increases skepticism but generates rumors to fill the vacuum. It also encourages informal communication systems, like the community grapevine that serves the residents, and private ones developed by decision-makers to keep in touch with events outside their own circles. For instance, a young lawyer-politician developed an extensive personal information network by exchanging free legal advice to public officials and organizations for information he needed to function politically.

The reporter's skepticism about the divergence between events and his coverage is even greater. The conflict between his desire to write about the actual government and the need to stress the performance leads to a low opinion of his sources, whom he sees as vain and dishonest, and of his readers, whom he sees as headline-scanners and cranks. Popular fiction often describes the reporter as a cynic, and the stereotype has some validity, although more often he just becomes discouraged and angry. The hostility and frustration he feels every day is expressed openly once a year at press banquets, where reporters perform skits which tell with only thinly veiled animosity what they think of the politicians and the politics they cover. The mutual system of obligation requires the politicians to attend the banquets and to suffer the attacks in good humor. Once a year, then, the newspaperman gets even with his sources.

NOTES

1. This view of the political system draws on the concepts and findings of Meyerson and Banfield, particularly Chap. 9; Banfield (1955); Banfield (1961); and Dahl.
2. Community heterogeneity has many political ramifications. For example, a study of librarians showed those in heterogeneous communities were less likely to buy controversial new books than those in homogeneous communities. Fiske, p. 67.
3. Banfield (1961), pp. 252–253.
4. See the discussion by Dahl on the professional's monopoly of political skills, particularly pp. 279–280 and Chap. 27.
5. This has some positive functions. For one thing, it spurs the party workers on to greater effort to defeat the opposition. For another, it allows the professional politicians to test issues to be used in the campaign on the workers before taking them into the general community.
6. The concept of performance, and of other dramatic terms used in this analysis, are taken from Goffman, especially Chap. 1. I use the term "performance" somewhat more narrowly, for he defines it as "all the activity of a given participant on a given occasion which serves to influence in any way any of the other participants" (p. 15), whereas I am thinking primarily of the attempt to impress an audience that decisions are made in ways other than they really are made.

My first perception of the performance took place at a township meeting in which I watched two lawyers debating angrily with each other over a decision, only to greet each other in the most friendly fashion after the meeting was over. I am not sure whether they "really meant" the anger, but the point is that they impressed the audience with the intense defense of their views. Of course, the change in behavior can also be described as a shift in role from political antagonists to professional colleagues, just as the difference in performing and actual behavior among government officials can be described as the difference between the roles of elected official and decision-maker. Both concepts are valid, but performance is more useful for understanding the relationship between government and citizen.

7. Dahl distinguishes between the ritual and the reality of power, p. 159.
8. The awareness of performances in everyday life is discussed by Goffman, p. 17.
9. The performance was restored in the minutes, which did not mention the incident. The secretary explained she omitted it so that "when people fifty years later read this, they won't laugh at us."
10. Top leaders admit that they use ghost-writers to write their speeches, but always qualify the admission by indicating that they go over the final drafts themselves. They may not actually do so, but this maintains the performance that the speech is their personal product.
11. Meyerson and Banfield, pp. 70–71.
12. The leader who wants to rise in the party must carry his own district, and there, with the margin of victory being even smaller, every favor counts.
13. One aspiring candidate was rejected because he had gone to Harvard Law School, and in one school board election I analyzed, candidates with high school diplomas fared better than those who had gone to college.
14. When the Good Government slate offered to serve without pay, the voters concluded that it was made up of high-income people who did not need the small salaries attached to public office, and so were unlikely to share their financial worries.
15. As a result, upper middle class Levittowners were continually upset about the lack of "qualifications" among the candidates. Looking for officeholders of their own socioeconomic level, they complained about the candidates' low level of education, absence of professional skills, poor speaking style, vagueness on issues, and of course their lack of interest in nonpartisan good government, long-range planning, and quality schools.
16. A year later, the Democrats were charging that Republicans preferred outsiders to local people.
17. The quotations are from the *Levittown Herald*, September 24, 1959 to October 15, 1959.

18. On "election rituals," see Dahl, pp. 112–114.
19. At the time of my study, Levittown news was published by a county daily, the Levittown (now Burlington County) Times; a weekly, the Levittown Herald; and by occasional reportage in the Philadelphia, Camden, and Trenton papers. In 1961, a weekly called Levittown Life was founded by a resident and his friends. It supported C.A.P.S. and generally spoke for the upper middle class point of view until it went bankrupt in 1963. It was then purchased by a local Democratic leader and became a Democratic party organ to counteract the Times and the Herald, both of which were usually Republican. The original founders of Levittown Life bought a weekly in a neighboring town of Beverly from which they commented on events in Levittown. By 1964, it too went under. So did Levittown Life, which was merged with the Burlington County Times. Later that year, a suburban chain began to publish the Willingboro Weekly, retitled the Willingboro Suburban in 1966.
20. This aspect of the relationship between politics and the press is discussed in Banfield and Wilson, pp. 28–29 and Chap. 21.
21. Gieber and Johnson.
22. The restraints placed on journalists to maintain good relations with their sources are described in more detail by Rosten, pp. 107ff.
23. Normal self-censorship also takes place. Coverage of municipal court proceedings in Levittown papers excluded domestic conflicts, because they were considered private affairs, and sordid events were toned down for "family newspapers." Nervous breakdowns which took place in public were reported as arguments, and the case of a man who took his underage cousin to a motel was described only as a disorderly charge. The story of a teacher's breakdown in class was quashed by all reporters at the suggestion of the town's senior reporter because he felt that both the school system and the individual teacher would be hurt badly, while the newspapers would not gain sufficiently by having published it.
24. If it did happen, their reportorial performance would probably be affected. Indeed, the only journalists with such political power are columnists and commentators who do not have to gather the news themselves.

Chapter Thirteen

THE DECISION-MAKING
PROCESS

JUST AS DECISION-MAKERS CONSTANTLY SEEK CERTAINTY IN A PO-litical system marked by uncertainty, so they attempt to avoid decisions in a governmental system which requires decisions. Government is organized toward bureaucratic routine; it aims to carry out municipal services entrusted to it in such a way that appointed officials will hold their posts and elected ones will be re-elected, and that criticism and conflict are minimized between elections. The ideal is a situation in which precedent can rule and no new decisions are needed.

But new problems arise and decisions must be made. Broadly speaking, the decision-making process is ruled by four criteria. *First,* government is normally passive; it waits for issues to come to its attention. In Levittown, the decision-makers initiated action only on internal governmental expansion necessary for the smooth functioning of the bureaucratic apparatus; on state or federal statutory requirements; on issues which required little effort, cost, or structural change and resulted in favorable public-ity; on matters which benefitted Levittown as a whole in the con-tinuing competition with other communities; and when they had no choice but to act. For example, the Township Committee initiated a polio vaccination program without citizens' asking for it, because it was easy to do and earned political goodwill, and the school board raised school budgets because the increasing number of students left it no other alternative.

Second, government avoids or postpones decisions that cannot be resolved without conflict or that expose the gap between the actual and the performing government. The Township Committee tried to bring ordinances out of the caucus to the public meeting only when unanimity had been achieved. *Third,* government gravitates toward decisions with immediate payoffs, avoiding those which produce mainly long-run effects. Government is reluctant to establish new precedents or set into motion irreversible policies that may restrict its flexibility in the future. For this reason, if no other, long-range planning and the formulation of permanent "policy statements" are discouraged. Of course government does plan, but principally for goals of its own choosing—for example, the staging of performances and the adaptation of decisions to future election campaigns. It also sets policy (albeit unwritten) when government agencies develop working routines. But long-range plans that require higher current expenditures to produce a result 5 or 10 years later (for example, to forestall future school overcrowding) are only implemented if outside funds are available or if community pressures give the decision-makers no other choice. By and large, however, planning and explicit policies are advocated by voters whose demands are being ignored in current decisions and unwritten policy, their hope being that these demands can be included in long-range plans.

Fourth, the decision-making process is structured so that, whenever possible, every elected official is free—or feels he is free—to reach the decision dictated by his conscience and by his desire to benefit the community. Whether or not he is ever really free is debatable, but the feeling of being so allows him to claim that he is not required to pay attention to citizen pressure, to include his own values in his decision, and to identify these as the public interest. Feeling free to vote "according to his conscience" allows him to make decisions that will please his reference groups and the constituents from whom he gets the most votes.

The application of these criteria resulted in decisions which: (1) maintained Levittown's governmental bureaucracy and municipal services up to voter expectation; (2) aided the party in power; (3) benefitted large or otherwise influential voter blocs and satisfied interest groups that were either in constant contact with the government, could apply pressure on it, or had campaign funds to contribute (or withhold); (4) represented pet projects or vested interests of individual decision-makers.

Obviously, the decision-makers used their decisions to improve their own and their parties' election chances. Although citizens' requests were few, they carried out those easily satisfied and those from large or visible voter blocs. Demands from the Catholic leadership group always received attention because the Catholic population was large, and the Democrats tried to satisfy requests from the Jewish community because it was well organized and therefore assumed to be a cohesive voter bloc.[1] Unorganized residents were similarly favored if their demands were modest, considered desirable by the decision-makers, and not likely to arouse opposition from more powerful voters or interest groups.

But most decisions, other than housekeeping ones, were made for the interest groups closest to government. At the time of my study, the most demanding one was the Levitt organization, which needed frequent approval of its building program and made demands and suggestions on a wide variety of issues. In fact, the builder was consulted so often that for all practical purposes he was a member of the actual government. In addition, most decision-makers accepted the builder's claim that what was good for him was also good for the township. For example, Levitt was able to persuade the Utilities Authority not to link competing small shopping centers to the water and sewer lines he had built until he turned the lines over to the township. In the early years, the decision-makers even checked with the builder on decisions in which he had no interest. Lacking staff aid of their own, respecting the know-how of Levitt executives, wanting to make sure the firm would not oppose their final decision, and believing that Levitt had the right to be consulted on everything, they sought his advice on a wide variety of topics.

Paying close attention to the builder was also dictated by political considerations. Not only could he exert power at all levels of government, but many Levittowners were favorably inclined toward him, so that political incentives for opposing him were few. Working class residents were grateful for the opportunity to buy a suburban house they could not have afforded otherwise, and middle class residents, though less grateful, went along with his demands as long as they meant lower taxes or affected yet unbuilt neighborhoods. Only the cosmopolitans opposed him, for, being able and willing to look further into the future, they could see that Levittown could not solve its tax problems so long as he continued building, thus minimizing their chance to obtain schools and other municipal services that met their upper middle class standards.

The other major interest group was made up of businessmen who had bought land in Levittown and wanted to build stores and shopping centers. Here, too, the municipal government was generally eager to please. Wanting more taxables in the township, it welcomed the arrival of new businesses—so much so that Planning Board meetings were sometimes set to accommodate the schedules of applicants for licenses and zoning changes.

Finally, the decision-makers supported each others' pet projects; protected the vested interests, political domains, and private businesses each had staked out; and went along with colleagues' personal grudges.[2] Even when beset by internal strife, the decision-making bodies always united to defend members against attack from citizens. For example, school board members allowed a colleague to continue his advocacy of municipal recreation although the school system wanted to retain control of recreation facilities; and the Township Committee did not interfere with one committeeman's personal vendetta against another leading politician, even though it was politically ruinous.

Nevertheless, the model that best describes decision-making in Levittown is "political benefit–cost accounting," for, generally speaking, the decision-makers tried to evaluate the costs and benefits of any decision for their own and their party's political future.[3] Of course, they did not apply such a model systematically, but acted intuitively. Sometimes they had too little information about even the obvious costs and benefits of their decisions, and rarely were they aware of the subtler and long-range ones. Lacking sufficiently detailed feedback, they did not know which voters might be affected by a specific issue and how they would react. Moreover, the personal values of the decision-makers and their conceptions of the public interest were added to the mix, so that often decisions only approximated those suggested by the model.

The Responsiveness of the Decision-making Process

Although Levittown's public decisions were made by a handful of elected officials, responding principally to demands and pressures from a small number of citizens and interest groups, many decisions were remarkably responsive to the rest of the citizenry, particularly the lower middle class majority.[4] While I could not compare residents' attitudes with decision-maker actions on every decision, the data I have support the hypothesis of responsiveness. The random sample was asked for its views on seven major issues, and in all but two the majority of respondents supported the governmental decision. For example, 89 per cent favored (or had no opinion on) the desirability of a city manager, 56 per cent were concerned about rising taxes, and 73 per cent went along with changing the name of the township from Willingboro to Levittown.[5] On the question of doctors purchasing homes for office use, 36 per cent were in favor, 15 per cent had no opinion, and 49 per cent were opposed—suggesting why the final decision of government was a compromise that restricted two nonresident doctors to a house. Likewise, an almost even split between those for, against, and undecided about racial integration suggests why the township government and both political parties refused to get involved in the issue.[6]

Decisions and citizens' attitudes diverged on liquor, and Levittowners' opposition to the Township Committee's approval of a wet community contributed to the incumbent committeeman's defeat at the next election.[7] The reduction of the kindergarten entry age, which the school board rejected, was favored by a slight majority, but most had no opinion, and the divergence can be attributed to the school board's minimal contact with its constituents at the time of decision.[8] A 1964 survey of attitudes on school policy among a much larger sample showed that the residents usually favored the status quo or had no opinion, thus producing convergence with school board decisions.[9] For example, 29 per cent wanted smaller elementary school classes, 18 per cent wanted larger ones, but 53 per cent preferred no change or had no opinion. Likewise, 30 per cent favored higher expenditures for education; 16 per cent, lower ones; but 54 per cent wanted no change or expressed no opinion. No wonder the school board felt it had a mandate for a policy of minimal change. These data cannot *prove* decision-makers' responsiveness, for the surveys were conducted after the decisions were made, did not limit themselves to voters actually concerned about the issue, and did not measure the intensity of their concern. Perhaps the best illustration of the overall responsiveness to the majority is that whenever the decision-makers went against majority opinion, they promptly lost the next election. Only Levitt usually received what he wanted, but when his demands were opposed by the residents, they voted out the decision-makers who went along with him.

The pattern of responsiveness can be traced back to the election system.[10] The selection of candidates assured officeholders who were representative of the large mass of voters, and their handling of issues reflected the vagueness and confusion which the voters themselves felt. Moreover, both parties agreed substantially on basic assumptions. Both came out for low taxes, a minimal role for government, and decisions that would favor the majority whenever possible; both opposed the demands and political styles of working class people and upper middle class cosmopolitans. Of course, the fit between candidates and community was hardly perfect, and most of the time Levittowners felt they were choosing the lesser of two evil ones. They grumbled about politics, but they were not dissatisfied enough to act and did not support minority factions or independent slates. After all, decision-makers rarely had significant impact on the really important aspects of their lives; they could not solve the community's central problem, taxes, and they were not expected to solve the financial, job, family, and child-rearing problems of individual Levittowners.

But if the decision-makers were responsive when the majority demanded it, they were anything but responsive to other than the powerful minorities. The election's diffuse and general feedback apprised the politicians of the majority opinions, but it did not inform them of minority demands. Nor were the performing and actual governments attuned to these demands, for the performance was structured to assure the majority that all was well, and the caucus and parties sought decisions that would attract the majority at the next election. Moreover, the decision-makers could not represent minorities either. A Township Committee of three men (and later of five) and even a school board of nine made it impossible to elect minority representatives to the actual government, and since decision-makers sought unanimity before passing ordinances, there was little room for the consideration of powerless minority opinion. Even when decisions were reached by majority vote, the decision-making body and the issue itself had to be structured so as to create a dichotomous (or at best

entrance age because the advocates were consistently able to bring 20–30 people with them. The decision-makers will, of course, try to find out whether those who attend are serious or whether they have come only as a favor to a friend or neighbor.

Petitions also involve large numbers of people in the intervention process, but the decision-makers know that many people sign them only to please the circulators or to get them out of the house. Unless the signers come to a public meeting, it is assumed that the signatures themselves do not indicate serious interest. For example, when the opponents of nonresident physicians presented a petition with over 400 names, the nonresident physicians brought in 1200. Their use of a commercial signature-collecting agency neutralized their numerical superiority and in the end the Township Committee ignored the petitions altogether and effected a compromise between the two points of view.

For interveners who are small in number, low in power, and unable to generate widespread public support, the most effective method is probably to insert new "facts" or "ideas" into the decision-making process. By facts and ideas, decision-makers mean three things primarily: political or other consequences of a decision, viewpoints of groups not previously considered, and suggestions for compromise. Of course, intervention appeals are always filled with facts and ideas, and most of the time, the decision-makers have heard them all or are not interested. They are not impressed by unprovable consequences or long-range ones; even when they ask for new facts, they may reject those not to their liking, as they did when the kindergarten interveners supplied scientific findings which disproved their beliefs. Of course, asking for new information is also one way of postponing a decision; often decision-makers (and interveners) call for a study to obtain time for enrolling further support for their own position. If the decision has not yet been made, the decision-makers may be receptive to new data, but their receptivity varies with the situation. If a compromise is called for, they may be eager for solutions; otherwise, they usually pay attention only to new information about important political or community implications of alternative decisions.

In the last analysis, the most effective method of intervention is the demonstration of visible political support. In Levittown, what impressed decision-makers most was a sizeable and repeated turnout of personally concerned citizens. For example, if the issue dealt with education, they had to be parents whose children would be affected; if it concerned a zoning change, they had to live in the area under discussion. The larger the turnout the better, of course, but no absolute number can be predicated, for the figure varies with the amount of change being demanded.[15] For example, a half-dozen complaints about the bus service from Levittown to Philadelphia were sufficient to persuade the Township Committee to ask the bus company for additional buses. A group of four residents was enough to have six small neighborhood shopping areas which had been proposed in the master plan eliminated through a zoning ordinance revision. They called and wrote to the builder, the Township Committee, the township building inspector, and the Governor, and they submitted a petition signed by all residents adjacent to the proposed sites. Although they exaggerated their actual support, Levitt's reluctance to displease people who had already purchased homes and his lack of enthusiasm about the proliferation of neighborhood shopping areas suggested by the township's planning consultant resulted in successful intervention. In this instance, then, determined activity by a concerned handful which accorded with the preferences of the agencies making the change was sufficient.

Conversely, almost 400 petition signatures and 20 to 30 interveners who attended school board meetings regularly were not enough to alter the kindergarten entry age, because it required a change in attitude on the part of school board members and, more important, a change in established school board policy which contradicted the policies of other boards in Burlington County and the recommendations of the State Department of Education. On the other hand, 150 angry Levittowners at a public hearing effected a compromise on the nonresident doctor issue, but a slightly smaller number could not convince the Township Committee to keep Levittown dry. In the doctor issue, a compromise did not require thwarting the builder; in the liquor issue, no compromise was possible, and evidently the interveners were not numerous enough to convince the Township Committee to cross the builder. Six hundred even angrier citizens who attended the 1961 school-budget public hearing were unable to force a further reduction in the budget because this would have required the school board to increase class size, thus alienating teachers and the State Department of Education.

Only an intensive study of many issues would make it possible to determine accurately the numbers needed for successful intervention. Levittown experience shows that a small number can sometimes achieve its aim, but that in order to reverse a major government decision, concerted intervention from at least 5 to 15 per cent of the community, (above and beyond constant interveners, clearly identifiable minority voters, and opposition party members) is necessary, and probably a larger proportion for more permanent policy change. These figures suggest that intervention can be effective and can even overcome the wishes of the majority on some issues. If interveners demand significant structural change in government, however, they must have support from at least a majority of the population or more, because such change has repercussions on outside governments and political systems, which will exert pressure on local politicians to prevent alterations in the status quo.

What Levittown experience cannot show is the effectiveness of intervention methods such as demonstrations, protest marches, sit-ins, and riots. Middle class suburbanites are unlikely to use such methods, but if these became necessary, they would perhaps be met first with frenzied performances to maintain equilibrium, and then with repression, after which the decision-makers would slowly begin to make concessions in the most face-saving manner possible, provided, of course that such concessions did not generate a yet larger group of people opposed to them. If they do, the decision-makers are caught in the middle and may resort to performance solutions which try to persuade the interveners that government is on their side, and convince the opposition that it will not make basic changes. Local government's power to change society is limited, and intervention for this purpose ought to be directed against the federal government and the corporate economy. The former will only be impressed by an intervening group of massive proportions, however, and the latter does not need to be responsive to interveners at all unless they can mount a sizeable work stoppage or consumer boycott. Local intervention can only hope to affect the national bodies if it takes place in several communities at once, and cannot be explained away as an effect of distinctively local political or economic conditions.

TYPES OF INTERVENERS

Most of the groups who sought to intervene in Levittown were ad hoc. Indeed, permanent ones tended to become interest groups which were consulted before a decision relevant to their concerns was reached. One permanent though unorganized group was not consulted regularly, however, and became a consistent and active intervener—the cosmopolitans.

The Cosmopolitans

The cosmopolitans are college-educated and are usually professionals with upper middle class life styles. Although they are quite active locally, their approach to the community is extra-local; they seek to realize an ideal community which stems from a nationwide and even worldwide culture.[16] The ideal places a high value on education. Cosmopolitans want a high-quality school system to prepare youngsters for the best universities and professional careers, as well as facilities for adult education, educational kinds of recreation, and high culture. Government and politics, they feel, should be liberal and reform, with emphasis on progressive public welfare, medical and mental health services, decision-making by experts and technicians rather than by politicians, a nonpartisan political structure that follows the norms of democratic theory, long-range and master planning, and a maximum of intense and selfless citizen participation. Their community should be governed by liberal-professional upper middle class values.

Cosmopolitans can be found in every community, but they are particularly visible in new communities and in those where the majority is of lower income and status.[17] There, the cosmopolitan "set" is small and scattered and the mutual antagonism that develops in relationships with lower-status neighbors soon forces them to find friends outside the block and to set up community-wide organizations that express their values. Since they enjoy civic participation and are often highly skilled in fact-gathering and political advocacy, they frequently become active in the community and in its government long before other groups do. For example, in Park Forest, Illinois, they pressed for the incorporation of the new community as a village, organized its first government, and stayed in power for several years, even though the community had meanwhile become predominantly lower middle class.[18]

In Levittown, the prior existence of governing bodies forced the cosmopolitans to become interveners from the start. Although their main concern has been with education, they have also been active in recreation, planning, racial integration, mental health, "the juvenile problem," and social welfare.[19] They established or helped to establish the League of Women Voters, the Citizens Association for Public Schools, the Burlington County Human Relations Council, and a Good Government slate that ran unsuccessfully in the 1961 election. They ran individual candidates for Township Committee and the Board of Education and tried to influence the activities of many other groups.

Considering their numerical strength, their ability to intervene was surprising. There were probably not more than a hundred cosmopolitans in Levittown during the time of my study, and less than a third of these were active interveners.[20] Although their demands were usually rejected, they were able to negotiate some successful compromises. For example, a handful of cosmopolitans eventually obtained a settlement from the school board by which children who passed entrance tests could be admitted to the kindergarten before the age of five. They persuaded the school system to raise its academic standards somewhat and to develop formal policies for its operations. In 1961, two cosmopolitans ran for the school board and temporarily dominated the majority faction, but they never persuaded either the board or the staff to endorse their ideas for upper middle class education. In township affairs the cosmopolitans were less successful; although they frequently appeared as critics of the Township Committee and the Planning Board, they lacked the party ties and political strength needed to force the decision-makers into compromises.

The cosmopolitans were most successful when they were in accord with the rest of the community and functioned as technicans and experts in behalf of majority demands or as initiators of actions that the majority would eventually support. For example, an active cosmopolitan sat on the Government Study group that recommended the city manager form of government, and its final report was based largely on his recommendations. Another lobbied almost singlehandedly in Trenton to reduce residence requirements for school board members from three years to two. The same two people initiated the campaign that changed the township's name back to Willingboro and spearheaded the successful attack on the Township Committee to revoke an ordinance permitting garden apartments in Levittown. They also tried to fight Levitt's plan for the routing of a new state highway through the community, and even sought to call a halt to his building program until tax receipts could catch up with the expanded municipal services they deemed desirable, but on these issues they could not generate community support.

The cosmopolitans were skilled interveners because they had a strong and continuing interest in a number of important issues, were well equipped to argue their case, could propose new facts and ideas to the decision-makers, and were able to enroll support from like-minded Levittowners. But their persistence, their ability to debate, and their reluctance to give in also created antagonism that sometimes reduced their effectiveness. For one thing, the cosmopolitans seemed to be involved in everything. Their constant and dedicated activism confounded the decision-makers, who expected citizens to participate only sporadically. And since most of the cosmopolitan activity was generated by a few people, they were highly visible. When conflict arose and tempers grew heated, it was easy to think of them as malcontents and agitators.

Their style of intervention added to the antagonism. They considered themselves idealists, defending the public interest of the community against selfish forces. Like everyone else, they assumed that their values were the only desirable ones; they could not see that what they considered the public interest was often only an impersonal, but nevertheless upper middle class (and therefore self-) interest. But as idealists, they felt themselves also to be morally and otherwise superior, and as well-educated people they believed the opposition (and the decision-makers) were acting out of ignorance—and this attitude upset everyone with whom they disagreed. Yet for all their education, the cosmopolitans were as ethnocentric as other Levittowners; the repugnance they felt toward their neighbors' way of life was at least as strong as the neighbors' for cosmopolitan culture.

Their consistent appeal to idealism, principle, and morality typed their opponents as expedient, unprincipled, and immoral, and naturally produced considerable hostility from them. And since they argued from principle they confused the decision-makers, who were looking for more personal forms of self-interest. For example, they argued for long-range planning even when they expected to leave Levittown in a few years. Nor could the decision-makers bargain with them; the cosmopolitans saw their priorities as absolute values, rejecting all others and precluding compromise. While this was good strategy for a counterperformance, it was hardly an effective method of intervention for a politically weak minority. As idealists, the cosmopolitans did not think in strategic terms, however; they stuck by their principles and almost welcomed the resulting antagonism as a validation of their own goals.[21]

Part of the conflict must be ascribed to cultural differences. The cosmopolitans were of higher socioeconomic level than the decision-makers, and they communicated this without ever saying so. They did not defer to them as people or as officeholders, but confronted them as equals or betters. They could not be intimidated by power and were sometimes accused of lacking respect for authority. Their inability or unwillingness to realize that they had no power made their demands seem even more impertinent, and their tone grated on the decision-makers, who retaliated by flexing their political muscles in public confrontations. The decision-makers argued that Levittown was not Brookline, and privately they muttered that these people should not have bought homes in Levittown in the first place. Their hostility built up over the years, and eventually resulted in a smear campaign against one of the leading cosmopolitans which almost forced her out of public office and led to her defeat at the next election.

Even so, the cosmopolitans could not be dismissed altogether, even by the decision-makers. If they insisted on trying to have their own goals adopted for public policy much of the time, they were also calling attention to crucial community problems which the elected officials, responding to the voters' demands for optimism, did not want to discuss. For example, when the cosmopolitans advocated higher school budgets and long-range planning, they were not only proposing an upper middle class set of municipal services, but were also pointing to the need to do something about the inadequate tax base; and when they criticized Levitt's power, they were raising questions that also bothered the decision-makers. As a result, they were sometimes consulted privately by the same officials who rejected their intervention in public.[22]

The cosmopolitans' overall effectiveness as interveners is not easy to evaluate. On the one hand, the hostility they created testifies to their ability to raise issues and plant seeds of doubt in the decision-makers' minds. On the other hand, they might have been more successful had some of the cultural differences that aroused hostility, but were tangential to the issues, been mini-

mized. If the cosmopolitans had been more relativistic, distinguishing between demands which reflected only their upper middle class values and those which were shared by lower middle
class Levittowners, they might have been able to establish coalitions with the latter. Had they been more sensitive to the way
they threatened the decision-makers, they might have let others
do the public intervening on issues not limited to upper middle
class demands. And if they had been less certain of the universality of their principles, they might have implemented more of
their ideas through compromise, although they might also have
been coopted or dismissed entirely because of the smallness of
their numbers.

Yet the very "idealism" and intractability which brought forth
so much hostility also generated the motive power, the dedication, and the persistence with which they intervened. If they had
been less convinced of the myth that they alone were fighting for
Levittown's salvation, they might not have been able to continue
the battle. Asking them to be relativistic and realistic might have
dampened their spirits and caused them to give up when the odds
were against them. Moreover, in order to generate public support, some people have to take purely moral stands, although if
they are to be effective interveners, others on their side have to
act strategically, to incorporate the moral stand into the intervention process. "Radicals" who put moral pressure on the Establishment are consequently as necessary as "coalitionists" who
work for change within "the system." The cosmopolitans were too
few in number to take both moral and strategic roles, and besides, if they had taken the latter, they might have been punished
for selling out by moral advocates in their group. Principled in-
tegrity was one of the cosmopolitans' strongest weapons, and if
they failed, the fault lay also with other political minorities in
Levittown who did not know how to use their help in battles of
community-wide significance. But the class differences were just
too great to be hurdled even for political advantage.

The Individual as Intervener: The Role of the Expert

American democratic theory is staunchly individualistic; it
asserts that the lone political leader, aided only by the *deus ex
machina* called "leadership," can divert government from its accustomed path, and that the individual citizen can intervene successfully in the affairs of government provided he is determined

enough and has right on his side. Levittowners, sharing this faith wholeheartedly, were disappointed when leaders did not lead, and disturbed when decision-makers did not do their bidding. They could not see that a governmental change affecting many thousands of people will not be undertaken just because an individual desires it, and they failed to realize that politics is a group game which pays little attention to an individual intervener. When the community is new, however, and political organizations and communication systems are still fledglings, the individual may have a chance. For example, Levittown's Superintendent of Schools could institute a comprehensive reading program virtually by fiat, and William Levitt was similarly able to decide that house types should be mixed on the streets of his new community. Even so, both men had to check out their decision with others. Levitt's executives argued strenuously that mixing house types would hurt sales, and if they could have proved their case, Levitt might have had to agree. Although he owned the firm, he could not insist on change that might alienate his staff. Once the community is established, few individuals can "buck the system." Even a politician who campaigns on a single issue and wins office in a landslide can only implement his mandate if he has the authority and the power to force change on the bureaucracy—and with the electorate behind him, he is hardly acting as an individual.[23] The lone intervener is only deceiving himself if he expects to change his community all by himself.

Perhaps the most effective individual intervener is the expert. If he comes from outside the community, he is thought to be free of political entanglements and can use his technical skills and professional reputation to urge change. Experts are normally hired for purposes other than intervention, but in a middle class community, they are brought in as interveners as well, because middle class citizens believe that facts and expertise can overcome politics.[24] Working class people are more skeptical, and also distrust the expert, sensing rightly that his expertise usually results in recommendations that favor the middle class.[25] Yet even middle class people will reject the expert when his solutions do not agree with their goals. When he is called in to solve a so-called technical problem—for example, to advise on the number of Sunday school classrooms needed by a church—his intervention is accepted, not only because he has the technical answers, but because of consensus on the desirability of maximum religious education. When the Library Association called on the county librarian's expertise to help plan a local library, however, her advice was ignored when it became evident that the library she had in mind was much bigger and more costly than that her sponsors envisaged.

Most experts are professionally committed to the activities and institutions about which they possess expertise; they recommend the best and most expensive programs, defending these with technical data and "standards" (for example, those requiring one acre of playground for every 800 residents) which are made up by associations composed of fellow professionals. If an expert upholds these standards as inviolable and proposes decisions which the community is unwilling to adopt, opposition is sure to develop. At first, the attacks are likely to be apolitical; in Levittown, they questioned the expert's mystique, arguing that "he cannot be controlled" or "he is too egocentric." If the expert admits that the standards are too high and bargains for the best compromise, he begins to play a political role, leaving himself open to charges of political interest. He often avoids this position by defending the standards but suggesting that their full achievement take place gradually. Even so, he may not be able to escape political entanglement. If there is opposition to his sponsors or his ideas, the other side will find experts with different recommendations. When the kindergarten issue was being debated, the interveners collected expert advice favoring early entry, but the school board came back with other experts who proved it was harmful. Later, when C.A.P.S. proposed a consultant who had served the Brookline schools, the board argued that Levittown needed experts accustomed to advising less affluent communities. Experts of unquestioned national repute can sometimes make recommendations stick merely on the basis of their reputations, but such men are not likely to be consulted by small communities. If their fame is limited to cosmopolitan circles, lower middle class people may not be impressed at all. When Levittown's Human Relations Council brought in a group of nationally known race relations experts to speak to a workshop on integration, some attending Levittowners dismissed their remarks as those of unknown outsiders brought in to convert them to tolerance.

Expertise alone is thus rarely sufficient for successful intervention, because even its detached and scientific aura is not strong enough to overcome political considerations. The expert has more power than the resident intervener, but his "intervention potential" is translated into effective intervention only when political support is generated behind his advice. Without it, the expert can do little to change the decisions of the actual government.

DECISION-MAKING, INTERVENTION, AND THE POWER STRUCTURE

The ongoing decision-making process in a local community is best described as a dialectic, in which the decision-makers seek to maintain the actual government in equilibrium, and the interveners, to upset it.[26] The aims of equilibrium are the preservation of order and the retention of power; those of intervention, to disturb the actual government (and its associated performances) sufficiently to force the decision-makers to restore order by acceding to intervener demands. In this process, interveners are aided by the opposition party, which shares their strategic aims but not their substantive demands. It tries to upset the equilibrium by finding weak spots in the performance that will enable it to demonstrate the incumbents' ineffectiveness or dishonesty, and by giving political aid to interest groups whose demands or power are threatened by the decision-makers. The opposition constantly challenges the incumbents in symbolic ways, accusing them of partisanship or neglect of the public interest in the hope that it will evoke political support. Interest groups and voter blocs may play the same game, testing the decision-makers to determine whether their power is still being recognized. For example, when community ceremonies were scheduled in Levittown, civic groups and service clubs scrambled for prominent places in the program to demonstrate their power in much the same way as Soviet officials do when they line up to greet visiting heads of state at a Kremlin reception.

The outcome of the never-ending dialectic is a constant struggle for position which involves not only decision-makers, interveners, and political parties, but also other organized elements in the community. Every action, be it a government decision or a voluntary association officer's resignation, is interpreted as a political move, even when it is not. The participants in the dialectic always seek total victory, for compromise is viewed as a defeat by the holders of power, as "selling out" by the interveners, and as a "deal" by the uninvolved citizenry. Consequently, all relationships take place in an atmosphere of suspicion and tension. Experienced politicians, whether in city hall or in a voluntary association, are accustomed to this state of affairs, and the amateurs eventually become resigned to it, but the citizens see it as shot through with dishonesty and hypocrisy. Since it does not concern them vitally, however, they play the bemused bystanders, and chalk it up to "politics." [27]

This view of the decision-making process departs somewhat from the contemporary political science conception which emphasizes the role of power structures, informal bodies that monopolize or dominate community decision-making. One theory isolates permanent power elites, composed of a small set of individual leaders and interest groups (mainly from the business community) which has sufficient power to make decisions without paying attention to the citizenry.[28] Another—more reasonable—theory identifies a number of individual (and often temporary) power structures, each generated by a specific issue, with some overlap in membership depending on the total array of issues and the distribution of power in the particular community.[29] This model leaves more room for citizens, since the politicians representing them can incorporate their demands in the decision-making process.

My analysis tends to follow the second theory, but being concerned not only with how decisions are made but also with the responsiveness of the process to the community, I have placed more stress on the role of citizens. Their activities do not, however, preclude the existence of a power structure in Levittown, for the incumbent party leaders, elected officials, and the Levitt organization constituted such a structure. Indeed, as I noted in Chapter Seven, the builder's imposing influence, the power of the Democratic party leader and the Catholic bloc, as well as some distinctive features of the community, have made the power structure somewhat more monolithic than those found by political scientists in established communities, although its members tend to be leading citizens, politicians, and municipal officials rather than business leaders. As a purely residential community, Levittown lacked the array of commercial and industrial interests that are usually found at the top of the political pyramid, and gave a larger role to organizational officers and vote-bloc leaders.

Since the community was still under construction, the builder played an unsually prominent role; and since the community was still new, political issues had not yet become sufficiently diversified to generate a wide variety of power structures. Also, as a suburban middle class community, Levittown was without the low-income, nonwhite population which makes up a sizeable proportion of the urban constituency, but is nevertheless largely excluded from the decision-making process by poverty, segregation, low political skill, and its habitual support of Democratic machine candidates. Even the most excluded interveners in Levittown were therefore more adequately represented in the decision-making process than are the Negro lower class citizens of Chicago or New Haven.

IMPROVING THE DECISION-MAKING PROCESS

The picture I have drawn of Levittown's politics and decision-making is not a pretty one, and it would be easy to charge the community's political institutions with being undemocratic and ineffective. To do so would be to assume that they could function according to formal democratic theory, but the self-righteousness of such an assumption will not eliminate the conflicting realities of American political behavior. If a community is heterogeneous, and if the citizens restrict their participation to periodic balloting except when their personal interests are at stake, yet expect the decision-makers to observe altruistic democracy, the resulting political system will produce decision-makers and decisions that cater to majority wishes at election and powerful minority demands between times, hiding the process behind the performing façade. However flawed this system may be, people will be willing to maintain it—even while grumbling about its faults—so long as they need or want to maintain heterogeneity, nonparticipation, and the electoral system of majority rule.

Politics could only be different if people's political behavior and values or government's functions would change. If citizens were so homogeneous that differences about issues were minimal, feedback restriction, the performance, and other means of coping with heterogeneity would be unnecessary; the voters could simply hire the best trained or most highly motivated among them to carry out the popular consensus. If everyone participated in government as intensely as in the family, all decisions would receive considerable discussion, decision-makers would be more responsive to the constituency, and performances to hide disagreement would no longer be needed, although some form of caucus might be required to hammer out agreement among heterogeneous citizens. Conversely, if government were radically different, if it were like the family and provided emotional support, and if the political leader were really a father figure, people would presumably participate more, more informally, and without such diverse interests. And if it were like the church, they would participate with less insistence on having their own personal interests satisfied.

Such medieval alternatives are abhorrent. More constructively, Paul Goodman has long argued for small communities and governmental decentralization so that people can participate more directly; he advocates, among other things, a school of one hundred students, to be run by their parents.[30] If people were required to participate, they undoubtedly would, but if a heterogeneous group of parents set up a school, they might argue indefinitely about what it should teach and how, and the school would never be built. Goodman would argue, and justifiably so, that the process of setting up the school will be more educational than its actual operation—but then he is not particularly interested in children learning the technical skills for functioning in the larger society. Even so, his idea deserves to be tried, although it may happen that parents and children with less intense interest in education than Goodman himself would eventually delegate the task to their more highly motivated neighbors, who would then function much like a school board and staff.[31]

That a small community and a decentralized government alone would increase participation is also doubtful. The Israeli *kibbutzim* achieved almost total member participation in government during the early years, but as soon as the recurring crises which threatened their existence had passed, many settlers handed the decision-making responsibility to people who were interested in being leaders, and spent their free time in the same individual and family pursuits found in an American suburb.[32] What the well-educated, culturally and ideologically homogeneous, and politically sophisticated *kibbutz* members were unwilling to do cannot be expected from American suburbanites.

Yet even if people like the Levittowners were dissatisfied enough with the status quo to demand or accept decentralization, the decision-making process would not change significantly so long as they believe that altruistic democracy ought to determine governmental operations. This belief stems from three sources: the schools, the citizens' detachment from the political process, and their application of primary-group morality to it.

The modern public school was founded as part of an intensely antipolitical nineteenth century social movement; it has therefore taught altruistic democracy for over a hundred years, keeping the realities of politics out of its courses. Many teachers assume naively that if students learn only an ideal concept of politics, they will put it into practice when they become adults, and thereby reform society. Educators are also often conservative; they see government itself as nonpolitical, and think only those who question its decisions are acting politically. Politics being evil, the efforts of the interveners are left out of the curriculum.[33] More sophisticated teachers can be found here and there, but schools are not supposed to generate controversy, so that social studies courses favor history and antiseptic descriptions of current events.[34] In many communities, teachers who bring political controversies into the classroom have found that disagreeing parents communicate their opposition to the school board, forcing them to go back to teaching noncontroversial ideals.

What students fail to learn in school they pick up later when they need it, and if the civics curriculum has any influence on adult beliefs it is largely because most citizens are so untouched by governmental activities that they have no need for more realistic beliefs. Faith in altruistic democracy is a direct consequence of the irrelevance of government to their everyday lives and aspirations. As a result, they apply primary-group morality to politics, believing that politics should be guided by the same norms that rule family relationships and friendship, and that deviations can be explained by the personal dishonesty of individual politicians. In the process, their lack of consciousness about self-interest in primary-group relations is transferred to their political role as well.

The alternative to this state of affairs is not relinquishing of faith in democracy or morality, but for the citizenry to be "politicized"—to learn that politics is a universal phenomenon; that all matters about which disagreement exists are by nature political; that the resolution of disagreement is the role of the politi-

cian, and that this role is guided by nonfamilial norms. Politicization requires a relativistic outlook, the pluralistic assumption
that other people's interests may be as moral as one's own, and
the ability to accept compromise. In addition, people have to
realize that everyone's demands are a mixture of self-interest and
community concern, and to restrain the temptation of condemn-
ing nonaltruistic demands. For example, Levittowners should
have been pleased rather than disturbed that self-interest by voluntary associations motivated them to provide community services that would not have existed otherwise. Unfortunately, altruistic democracy encourages people to judge political events by
the motives of the participants, instead of by their actions. The
goodness of a decision cannot, however, be determined from the
decision-makers' motives—even if these could be identified—but
only from the consequences of that decision for the individual
and the community.

Politicization, pluralism, a broader view of self-interest, and
the substitution of action for motive in judging decisions would
make for *effective democracy*. Politics would become more open
and above board, and disagreement and conflict would be accepted without the undesirable side effects that develop when
these are repressed through performances. Distrust of politicians
would also be reduced, and once people realize that politicians
usually act as they do because of the pressures on them, they
would learn in yet another way that they have to intervene in the
decision-making process themselves if they want change.

Beliefs cannot be altered by demonstrating their inapplicabil-
ity or irrationality, however, and new ones cannot be created by
appealing to people to be sensible. They usually change when
the situations and institutions in which people participate undergo change, for people generally adopt the beliefs that support
actions needed to achieve goals. Consequently, politicization
would best be achieved if people were required to participate
more directly and actively in politics—but this process requires a
drastic reorganization of government, and of the government–
citizen relationship, which is not likely to happen.

More feasible changes can perhaps be implemented. People
might begin to see politics differently if reporters would cover
the actual rather than the performing government, and if they
described it in terms of the resolution of conflicting interests, relating decisions to the interplay of interests and to the perspec-

tives, political positions, and background characteristics of inter-est groups. Some reporters and columnists already cover federal politics this way, although primarily for well-educated readers. A drastic revision of social studies and civics courses, particularly at the high school level, would also help, but students would learn most effectively by doing—by participating in municipal govern-ment as interns or administrative aides or undertaking studies of local politics and decision-making. This approach might also be politically less risky than classroom discussion of controversial topics, but ultimately, the schools must be pressed (and enabled) to give up the idea that education is above politics. Pluralism is already being taught, at least with regard to racial and religious differences, but the more crucial pluralism of class (and all its cultural and political implications) is now discussed only in some college sociology courses, and then only in the more cosmopol-itan universities. Moreover, pluralism is not produced just by teaching it, and unfortunately, it seems to be more acceptable with regard to matters in which people are less intensively in-volved, such as religious doctrine.[35]

None of these proposals will have much impact, for the politi-cal belief system I am advocating is presently held only by profes-sional politicians, whose activities require that they think this way. Ultimately, all suggestions for improvement require greater political participation, and this solution is illusory. In an affluent society, people like the Levittowners get what they want from the corporate economy, from a federal government which subsidizes that economy for their benefit, and from local governments which they elect to protect their residential status. Unlike poor people, who are increasingly dependent on government for jobs and incomes, middle class people have no need to participate or intervene, except on the rare occasions when government de-prives them of goods, status, or privileges they have come to take for granted.

Some Modest Proposals for Change

If "radical" solutions are often mere dreams that only uphold the radical requirement for total change of "the system," more modest proposals for improvement may, however, have a chance. Political communication can be increased in several ways, not to eliminate feedback restriction or even to increase voluntary citi-zen feedback (both of which seem utopian), but to generate involuntary feedback and to upgrade its diversity so that decision-makers are forced to notice all possible viewpoints in the population. One solution would be the establishment of a civic association which, like traditional ones, allows people to air their opinions on important issues, but which also solicits them through a community public opinion poll that regularly reports the views of a random sample of residents on current issues and new policy proposals. The poll could be financed by selling its reports to the local press and by also doing special studies for local organizations and businesses. Its operating costs could be reduced by having high school students do the research as part of their social studies courses (which would also give them a useful and educational community function), and whatever deficits remained could be met from municipal subsidies. The association could also publish its own newspaper, giving a few pages in each issue to the political parties to add diversity (albeit partisan) to the exchange of ideas, and allowing more citizen feedback by publishing letters of ideas and grievances.[36] The information vacuum created by the actual government and the resulting rumors could be alleviated by a regular column which publishes the current rumors, together with whatever facts are available to support, reject, or correct them.

The proposed civic association can only succeed if it decides from the start to be political, rather than "above" politics. It need not take sides, but it must draw members and officers from all political groups, including party factions; otherwise, it will become the satellite of a single political group which will then do its utmost to exclude opposition groups. The association must also obtain authority, either by force of law or by attracting widespread citizen support, so that decision-makers will be required to pay attention to its activities and findings.

Communication from government to citizens can be improved by increased press coverage, particularly of the actual government, although outside funds from foundations or the federal government would be needed to hire more and better-trained reporters. The system of mutual obligation between reporters and their sources could be made less pervasive if local reporters were organized into a guild, so that politicians who threaten to withhold news from particularly inquisitive newsmen could not favor more cooperative ones from competing papers. A more effective solution would be to bring in outside reporters periodically to cover the local community for a short time. They would function like the expert or the stranger who can offer a fresh view, and being outsiders, they would be free of the system of mutual obligation and could not be punished for their reportage. To prevent local reporters from sabotaging outsiders for making them look incompetent, the system would have to be reciprocal, with two communities exchanging reporters. If the local press is unwilling to print the outsiders' stories—as it well might be—they could appear in the civic association paper or in the press of a nearby city which is not obligated to local political institutions.

But perhaps the best way of improving both communication and decision-makers' responsiveness would be to enlarge the elected bodies. Three or five or even nine men cannot adequately represent the diversity of a typical community, particularly its minority elements, and yet less so when they stand for re-election only every second or third year. If the municipal government, the school board, and other public bodies were manned by 15 to 20 officials, the voters could express their views of government operations more regularly and more quickly, and minority positions would receive more adequate representation. Responsiveness would increase further if the heads of all municipal agencies were also elected, offering their policies for citizen review and enabling candidates with alternative policies to compete for the office. Even the city manager and planner might stand for election, provided candidates who ran against them were equally qualified professionals and if their departments included appointed technical directors to provide some continuity. Making more offices elective could result in more partisan decisions, and would eliminate appointed officials who are now politically free to pursue the public interest and attend to minority demands, but these costs are balanced by the benefit of a more explicitly political and representative government. Safeguards to protect the public interest and minority needs would be necessary (see Chapter Fourteen), as would new incentives to recruit candidates. Being an elected official in a small community is a thankless task, for the financial rewards are minimal and emotional ones are almost nonexistent. Like actors, politicians are bathed by the public spotlight, but unlike actors, their audiences neither pay nor sit politely to watch them perform; they come, instead, to demand and complain. As long as the politician must reconcile conflicting interests, there is no way of making his role more respected or satisfying, although a higher salary might compensate for its emotional burdens and raise the status of the office.[37]

Citizen participation could be increased somewhat by electing citizen advisory committees to every municipal agency, although it might be difficult to recruit enough ordinary citizens and prevent domination by political party members. A more feasible solution, based on the assumption that people participate only when personal interests are at stake, would be to adapt the concept of "maximum feasible participation" of the antipoverty effort or the concept of the civilian review board that oversees the police to the entire community, providing for the participation or representation of affected citizens in welfare, public health, recreation, education, planning, and other public agencies. If students, as well as more parents, participated in school board decisions, public education might not be better by academic standards, but it would be more responsive to their needs. Of course, it might also deteriorate, for parents and students would rarely opt for the public interest or long-range school needs, and the majority might vote against satisfying the educational needs of a minority—but these are the costs of local democracy.

The decision-making process and the qualities of the decision-makers are not easily changed, and criticizing their shortcomings is unproductive because it does not get at the real problems. They act as they do because they must resolve conflicting demands, and if they are poorly trained, shortsighted, uninterested in long-range planning, and overly concerned with their political party and the next election, they only reflect the values of the voters they represent and the political system in which they must function. Radical solutions could of course be proposed, either an elitist one in which trained experts replace the elected officials or a pure democracy in which people are somehow encouraged to make their own decisions, but the first is undesirable and the second is not feasible.

A more practicable solution is to recruit professional politicians for the decision-making roles. Much of what is wrong with government in Levittown is that the present incumbents are amateurs who share the voters' naiveté about the political process and cannot cope with the realities of decision-making when they are elected. Believing in the theory of altruistic democracy even while defending their own and their constituents' interests, they identify these with the public interest. As a result, the decision-making process becomes a debate among unself-conscious, well-intentioned, but unsophisticated amateurs who behave in ways that they consider undesirable and undemocratic because they have little choice to do otherwise, and then take out their frustrations on the interveners. Unable to deal with the emotional conflict between what they have to do and what they think they ought to do, they seal themselves off from feedback more than is necessary, try to stifle disagreement, and cut down on the effective democracy that is possible.

The professional politician, whether a full-time or part-time practitioner, sees decision-making as a vocation, rather than as a duty and a cause. He is politicized and pluralistic, and can function as a broker between groups. But the qualities of the professional have some disadvantages too. The detachment that breeds a political other-directedness which sensitizes the professional to the conflicting demands of a pluralistic constituency also makes him less responsive to the problems of the community as a whole and to long-range needs, to demands of powerless minorities, and indeed, to all issues in which conflicting pressures are absent or irrelevant. In situations where the decision-maker is free to act as he sees fit, the morally committed amateur may come up with a more desirable decision than the professional.

Moreover, the professional politician will probably be no better than the amateur in decision-making skill. Neither his role nor his personality motivates him to undertake systematic analyses of community problems or to develop policies that deal with causes of problems. His approach to policy is likely to be even more intuitive and unsystematic than the amateur's and most sensitive to the political currents that flow around him twenty-four hours a day. The professional may also be cynical and personally unreliable, making different promises to different people, and telling voters only what they want to hear—all without excessive personal guilt. Perhaps this is the price of reaching decisions in a heterogenous community.

The alternative, then, is between the committed amateur who can respond best to the wishes of his own group and the detached professional who can shape conflicting interests into a workable compromise. The former is most effective under conditions of consensus; the latter, under conditions of conflict. Since issues on which there is consensus are rare, the drawbacks of the professional politician are less serious than the amateur's. This choice may well violate the faith of democratic theory in the ability of the disinterested citizen to produce democratic government, but then this theory was itself formulated in reaction against the professional politicians who ran the governments, parties, and political machines (rural as well as urban) of eighteenth and nineteenth century Europe and America.

Nevertheless, whether the decision-maker is an amateur or even an expert, his decisions will not differ significantly from the professional's, for these are largely determined by his political role rather than by his personality or training. Significant change can take place only if new and different pressures impinge on the decision-makers. Improved political communication will help, and so would more electoral offices and elected citizen advisors, but the burden must fall largely on intervention. *Interveners must realize that change is likely to come about only as a result of their efforts to upset the political equilibrium.*

Intervention can be improved in a variety of ways. Formal devices include more opportunities to hold referenda, giving citizens the right to introduce legislation, and (in communities larger than Levittown) decentralizing municipal functions and powers so that government becomes more accessible to the average citizen. Educating people about the importance of intervention and about its most effective methods would help, for example, by teaching leaders the significance of organizing and bringing significant numbers of citizens to governmental meetings instead of relying on moral appeals and angry attacks. And if residents could be encouraged to direct the complaints they now make largely to friends and neighbors to the decision-makers themselves, everyday gripes would become instruments of intervention. Complaint bureaus serve this function, but nothing is more successful than direct confrontations with the governing body. Interveners must also be trained to concentrate on introducing new facts and ideas into the decision-making process. A community opinion poll would isolate the distribution and diversity of views, enabling interveners to show the decision-makers when they are not sufficiently informed about citizens' feelings.

But the most badly needed facts are on the consequences of alternative decisions. Here decision-making is presently most deficient, for neither decision-makers nor interveners make any real effort to catalog the consequences, political and nonpolitical, long-range and short-range, of alternative decisions. Such a task is probably too complex for either decision-makers or interveners. They and their community would be helped by an agency which systematically developed cost-benefit analyses for major alternative decisions, even on a rough and imprecise basis. This function might be taken on by the civic association (aided by high school students to carry on the needed research), but a professional agency could do it better, and a regional one which serviced local communities with such analyses would do it most effectively. In theory, this task is the proper function of a planning agency, for benefit-cost analysis is a major component of the modern planning method.

More effective intervention is no cure-all, and the interveners may not succeed very often, but sometimes the Davids *do* defeat the Goliaths. No one, not even the decision-makers themselves, knows in advance how much pressure or what new facts and ideas may cause them to change their minds. They may be impressed by an argument or a show of strength; they could get an idea for a better compromise, and they might help the interveners to gain support from a new constituency. Even if the odds seem doubtful, there is no other choice but intervention. Most of the time, interveners will lose, but sometimes they can win, and no one can predict when.

NOTES

1. Most Jews were Democrats, but there was no evidence of the existence of a "Jewish vote," particularly since no issues arose to generate such a vote.
2. Several elected officials and party leaders earned their livings as real estate or insurance brokers and, of course, sought (and obtained) municipal contracts whenever possible.
3. The idea of applying this economic analogy to the political process stems from Banfield (1955), pp. 304–312. See also Downs, and Banfield (1961), Chap. 11.
4. Other studies reporting responsiveness or convergence of opinion between community leaders and residents are by Dye (1963b) and by Levine and Modell. Divergence was reported by Sigel and Friesema.
5. Forty-two per cent were in favor, 9 per cent were undecided, and 22 per cent had no opinion. Republicans in the sample were opposed to the name change, but the party was too disorganized to

realize how its members felt or to resist the builder's pressure for the change. In the 1963 referendum to change the name back to Willingboro, the party went along with its adherents.

6. The percentages were 30, 37, and 26; only 7 per cent had no opinion.

7. Fifty-three per cent opposed the sale of liquor, 33 per cent favored it, and 14 per cent had no opinion.

8. Thirty-four per cent were for lowering it, 20 per cent were against, and 46 per cent had no opinion.

9. Dux. The tabulation combined those favoring no change and voicing no opinion.

10. See also Dahl, p. 101.

11. Crozier, pp. 235–236.

12. The term is taken from Banfield (1961), p. 241.

13. Exaggeration can—and often does—develop unintentionally in the heat of political battle.

14. After C.A.P.S. met with the school board, its members were invited to help the school staff by doing research—the former hoping that the proper facts would result in a change of school policy, the latter intending to keep them busy so that they would stop questioning the school board policy. In the end, neither group achieved its aim.

15. It is also affected by the other sources of available feedback, for the kindergarten entry age issue showed that the less the decision-makers know about how the community feels, the smaller the number of interveners needed.

16. The nature of cosmopolitan participation in local communities is described in detail by Merton (1957). See also Dobriner (1958) and Dye (1963a).

17. In older suburbs they are frequently newcomers. Merton (1957), p. 400, Dobriner (1958), pp. 138–139.

18. See Gans (1953).

19. See also Merton (1957), pp. 399, 402–406.

20. In the analysis that follows, I treat the cosmopolitan group as more cohesive than it actually is, and neglect some of the differences of opinion among individuals.

21. These principles were also a source of cultural differentiation which allowed them to maintain their status position. For example, their belief that they were more civic-minded than other Levittowners enabled them to retain their sense of personal worth, and the hostility they generated as a result allowed them to feel that they were of higher status, regardless of how much they were scorned for advocating "Brookline values."

22. Of course, in some cases, the decision-makers were just checking to find out where the cosmopolitans stood on an issue so that the latter could be more easily neutralized when they began to intervene publicly.

23. Even the President of the United States has limited ability to persuade the government to bend to his wishes. See, e.g., Sorenson.

24. An expert may also be hired by decision-makers to legitimate a decision they have already reached and by interveners to support their demands with facts and expertise. Under these conditions, he functions as a resource person; he is an intervener only if he comes with an opportunity to make or change a decision that diverts the actual government from its routine path, regardless of who sponsors him.

25. When he is willing to conform to working class values, however, his advice may be accepted. For example, a Levittown working class politician who opposed the city manager, because he expected him to eliminate patronage jobs usually taken by working class constituents, was quick to call in an expert to set up the fire company he had organized.

26. See also Dahl's distinction between "legitimists" and "dissenters," pp. 323–324.

27. For a comparison of decision-maker and citizen views of the suburban political process, see Dye (1962).

28. This theory is argued by Hunter, and by Mills.

29. Among its many advocates are Dahl, and Banfield (1961).

30. See, e.g., Goodman (1965). His school proposals are described in Goodman (1964).

31. A more detailed discussion, set off by a debate about the schools of Levittown, is to be found in Goodman (1961), and in my response in the "Letters" section of *Commentary*, Vol. 32 (November 1961), pp. 436–437.

32. See, e.g., Vallier.

33. Friedenberg, pp. 138–140.

34. Levittown's social studies courses emphasized the Indians who once lived in the area more than current problems in the community. They also dealt as much with the history and geography of foreign countries as with American society.

35. For example, working class people, who are usually little interested in civic affairs, view society more relativistically as composed of people "all trying to get their own," as one Levittowner put it, and deceive themselves less than middle class people about the possibilities of altruistic democracy. A number of studies have shown that cynicism is lower among the affluent and well educated. Milbrath, p. 80.

36. Such a newspaper could also be subsidized by the community. A community radio program in which listeners could call up to voice their ideas and complaints would also be useful. Such a program has been on the air in Levittown, Pennsylvania, for years.

37. Higher salaries might also increase citizens' resentment, for, lacking understanding of the politicians' functions, people do not see how they "earn" the low salaries they now get.

Chapter Fourteen

POLITICS AND PLANNING

THE PROPOSALS MADE IN THE PRECEDING CHAPTER FOR IMPROVING the decision-making process would not change it significantly; it would still be *political* and would most often result in "popular" decisions. Since such decisions may lead to tyranny of the majority and neglect of the public interest, one must ask whether *nonpolitical* decision-making processes and "unpopular" decisions are possible in a political system like Levittown's, and under what conditions they are desirable. In order to answer these questions, it is useful to begin with a brief evaluation of decisions reached by political means.

POLITICAL AND NONPOLITICAL DECISION-MAKING

Among the politically reached decisions during the time of my study were: the sale of liquor, the admission of nonresident doctors, the kindergarten entry age, the tax rate, and "the juvenile problem." The liquor decision was, in my opinion, handled poorly, for the decision-makers arbitrarily rejected majority opinion, although the citizens were able to overturn them because New Jersey law permits referenda on this issue. The "wets" were not really inconvenienced, however; they only had to go to the next township to find package stores and taverns. The nonresident doctor issue was resolved more adequately, for the citizenry seemed to be ambivalent, and the decision-makers reached a compromise, permitting some nonresident doctors (including the specialists who would otherwise not have come), yet without creating commercial enclaves in residential areas and thus threatening those fearing a reduction in property values and status. The kindergarten controversy was also resolved adequately, for people who wanted to keep their children home as long as possible were satisfied, but so was the minority, which was eventually able to enroll children earlier through a voluntary testing program.

The several tax rate decisions were handled poorly, but I doubt whether the decision-makers had any other choice. They raised taxes because they had to, but as little as possible to satisfy the antitax majority. Their decision-making process was erratic, but then the intensity of majority feelings varied from year to year, and so did the intervention of the minority favoring higher municipal budgets. Although the initial popular opposition to taxes stemmed primarily from the precipitous increase in the tax rate brought about by the builder's withdrawal of subsidies to the school budget, the fact remains that he provided considerable sums to keep taxes low in the first two years. After the tax rate stabilized at the higher level, popular opposition decreased somewhat, but principally because the decision-makers knew that the voters would not tolerate further tax hikes. The community's tax base was simply insufficient to raise the level of municipal services (particularly of schools) to minority demands and still keep the majority of voters happy.

As a byproduct of the tax debate, the majority got the lower middle class schooling it wanted for its children, but the cosmopolitans were deprived. Since the ideal solution, satisfying both majority and minority, was impossible, one cannot quarrel with the final solution. It seems wrong to argue, as did the cosmopolitans, that all children should be exposed to an upper middle class education. Parents have the right to socialize their children in their own class, provided some alternatives are available for the mobile (both upward and downward). Without an intensive study of the Levittown schools, it is impossible to say whether they provided enough educational diversity (for both upper middle and working class aspirations). However desirable, such diversity is difficult to establish in a small community and hard to finance when the majority of voters want lower taxes.

Possibly, the lower middle class school system which the majority wanted for its children was not good enough by its standards either, particularly for career preparation. It seemed good enough for now, for its graduates entered lower middle class colleges, and would eventually qualify for the technical and other white collar jobs they wanted in order to finance the lower middle class life styles for which they had been raised. Whether or not their education was good enough to train them sufficiently for an automating economy with radically altered job opportunities is hard to say. No one knows today what jobs will be available in the future or whether the youngsters now sitting in Levittown's classrooms are learning enough to qualify for those jobs. Since no one could prove that the school system was clearly inadequate by this criterion, one need not be surprised that neither decision-makers nor parents were willing to change the system—even if they had known how to do it.

The "juvenile problem" was handled most poorly of all. The final decision—to do nothing—was popular, of course; not enough voters wanted adolescent facilities, citizen intervention was minimal, no expert interveners were brought in to testify to adolescent needs, and the decision-makers acted accordingly. Even so, the means proposed to achieve the popular goal of reducing delinquency were irrational. No one distinguished between serious delinquency and vandalism, and no one sought to find out how the latter could be eliminated. Neither the Juvenile Discussion Group, which asked voluntary associations to sponsor adolescent recreation activities, nor the Youth Commission, which set up a Teenage Panel to punish the vandals who were caught, ever considered the needs of the teenagers or looked into ways of giving them a social function in the community. The final solution, a patchwork of voluntary but adult-run activities and more police supervision, did not attack the basic causes of the problem and was inadequate, because something could have been done to satisfy both adults and adolescents. Teenage gathering places could have been provided away from residential and shopping areas, and the teenagers could have established their own center, much as working class adults built themselves a firehouse with private fund-raising and their own labor. The primary obstacle was not cost, but adult fears, which might well have been reduced if adults and adolescents had sat down together. The decision-making process was inadequate and undemocratic, however, for the adolescents were not represented and could not even intervene to state their demands or apprise adults of their feelings.

A comparison of the five issues shows that political decisions can be both good and bad, and my cursory evaluation suggests some criteria for judging them. They must respond first to majority demands, but the more they can also satisfy minority demands, the better. Often, they can also be rational without political ill effects; they ought to address themselves to the causes of problems, and unless popular demand for irrational solutions is politically overpowering, experts can be used to bring solutions as close to rationality as possible.[1] Minorities have to rely on intervention, but it must be effective, so that the minority's power is expressed to the fullest. It can also be rational, using experts to expose majority irrationality and to propose compromises that would optimize benefits on both sides. Above all, the decision-making process must be representative; the people affected by an issue must have the opportunity to state their demands and exert political pressure. They may not be successful, but if they are excluded from the start, as the adolescents were, the decision-making process is not even properly political.

Nonpolitical decision-making processes rely principally on expertise and systematic planning to come up with decisions that may not please or interest the majority. In order to consider how they can be effective in a political system that caters to the majority, I want to resort again to case studies, analyzing two such processes in some detail.

THE RACIAL DESEGREGATION OF LEVITTOWN [2]

Levittown's desegregation was accomplished through nonpolitical means, enforcing a decision made outside the community, and, like most nonpolitical decisions, it was not favored by the community's majority. Even so, effective expertise and rational planning produced an outcome that guaranteed minority rights without harming the majority, and indeed, even pleased the people who had been opposed to integration.

The question of desegregating Levittown came up before any purchasers had arrived, and was raised by the builder himself. In spring 1958, at a press conference to publicize the imminent beginning of the new community, William Levitt permitted himself to be questioned by reporters. They knew that the firm had not previously sold to Negroes; that Levittown, Pennsylvania, had experienced a racial disturbance when a Negro family bought a house from a white Levittowner; and that New Jersey law made it illegal to practice discrimination in housing supported by federal subsidies. Nevertheless, Levitt declared publicly that he would not sell to Negroes in Levittown, New Jersey. Reactions were not long in coming. Senator Case requested the Federal Housing Administration (FHA) to refuse mortgage insurance to Levittown; Governor Meyner was asked to enforce the state law, and set the State Division Against Discrimination (SDAD) to work; and a Burlington County Quaker group picketed the model homes on opening day and for the next few weeks. Soon afterwards, two Negroes who had not been allowed to buy brought suit against Levitt in the state courts, arguing that the availability of FHA mortgage insurance for Levitt houses constituted government support.

The Levitt decision had not been easy. The firm was under pressure from the national Jewish community to integrate, and Levitt had even made vague promises to pro-integration groups to admit Negroes after the first neighborhoods had been settled. Skeptics thought these promises were intended to reduce pressure on Levittown, Pennsylvania, where the firm was then having trouble selling the last of its houses. In any case, the firm decided that the first priority was economic, and that immediate integration of the new Levittown would hurt sales to whites. Bressler writes: "In defending his policy of racial exclusion, Levitt had often had occasion to assert that both as a Jew and a humane man he sympathized with the plight of struggling minorities, but that economic realities reluctantly compelled him to recognize that 'most whites prefer not to live in mixed communities . . . the responsibility for this is society's . . . it is not reasonable to expect that any one builder could or should undertake to absorb the entire risk and burden of conducting such a vast social experiment.' " [3] One of the Levitt executives put the firm's position to me this way: "Our firm is liberal and progressive, but we don't want to be singled out or used as the firm which should start the other builders off. If there is no other builder who can keep Negroes out, we will not do so either; we will go with the group if the state makes us, but we don't want to lose millions by being the first . . . we could not afford to take such losses."

Although the Levitt family had not been very active in behalf of minorities—many years earlier the firm discouraged Jews from an expensive housing development on Long Island—there was some justification for the charge that they were being singled out. SDAD and pro-integration groups were concentrating on Levittown because it was by far the largest new suburb in the state and because they felt that if Levitt would integrate, other builders would follow suit.[4] Presumably, being the biggest builder in the East, he could pay the costs of integration—if indeed there were any—more easily than smaller ones. Moreover, Levittown had become a national symbol of suburbia and a brand name in housing generally, so that the publicity value of its integration would be considerable. One could even argue that the firm had attracted more purchasers and profit because its communities had become national symbols, and that it therefore deserved being singled out. Even so, the builder felt he had been picked on unjustly.

As a result, Levitt decided to fight the suit brought by the two Negro applicants, arguing that FHA mortgage insurance did not constitute government support of housing, but represented a contract between the FHA and the individual buyer. Meanwhile, Levitt salesmen assured prospective white buyers that, "It's all politics; the other Levittowns are all white and this one will be too." In some instances the "politics" was attributed to Communists, in others, to politicians campaigning for votes in the Negro slums of Newark and Jersey City.

The suit against Levitt dragged on inconclusively for most of 1959, without causing much overt concern among potential buyers or residents. Participant-observation data and my attempts to start conversations on the topic suggest that the majority of Levittowners were uncomfortably ambivalent about the issue. Some were hostile and threatened to move or to protest violently. These were primarily working class people who had left the city because their neighborhood was becoming predominantly Negro.[5] Unable to afford another move, they were fearful that the same mass invasion of lower class Negroes would occur in Levittown, confronting them with a sudden and visible decline in property values and status. Having just achieved suburban home ownership, and being at the top of the working class socially and occupationally, they sensed that such an invasion could only pull down their prestige. A smaller group (mainly the cosmopolitans) was very much in favor of desegregation and many of them became active in the Burlington County Human Relations Council. Principally Jews, Quakers, and Unitarians, some had been active in integration efforts in former residences.[6] The majority of Levittowners stood between these poles. An attitude survey would probably have shown that they did not favor desegregation, but also believed Negroes had a right to live in Levittown.[7] They too feared a lower class invasion, but were able to distinguish between middle class Negroes, "those who are more like us," and slum dwellers, common sense telling them that the latter could not afford to buy in Levittown. Some feared intermarriage. Seeming to believe that once Negroes moved in, they would be integrated socially, white parents were afraid their daughters would date Negro boys.[8]

Despite the fears, integration received little attention throughout 1959. Minority factions in two organizations unsuccessfully proposed by-laws to exclude Negroes, dissatisfied buyers joked about revenging themselves on Levitt (or their neighbors) by selling to Negroes, and there was a brief panic one Sunday when a group of Negroes came to look at an empty house, until it was learned that they were there to clean it for a new white buyer. Meanwhile, some Negro maids had been living "in" without adverse comment, and others came into town daily as part-time domestics. But then, they were clearly servants and threatened no one's status.

When the Appellate Court ruled late in 1959 that the State Division Against Discrimination could hold public hearings on the case, Levitt went to the state Supreme Court. Knowing that once public hearings were held he would probably be judged in violation of the state antidiscrimination law and forced to desegregate, he promised that if the Supreme Court upheld the lower court, he would desegregate without further delay, even before public hearings. The firm's decision was based on its longstanding belief that all but the most favorable publicity about Levittown should be discouraged, and that, in this instance, the publicity from the public hearings could only scare away more white buyers. Meanwhile, Levitt had attempted to obtain postponements from the lower courts, hoping to sell an all-white community to as many people as possible before a higher court finally ruled for integration.[9]

In March 1960, the state Supreme Court issued a stay on the case until April, but toward the end of March ministers and township officials were summoned to a number of conferences at the Levitt office building. On Sunday, March 29, all the ministers announced during church services that the Court stay would end April 15, and that even if it were prolonged while the builder took the case to the U.S. Supreme Court, desegregation was inevitable.[10] Consequently, the builder had decided to desegregate voluntarily and asked the community to prepare itself to welcome Negro residents. The decision was accepted quietly, partly because it came from the ministers, partly because the community had accepted the inevitability of integration. Moreover, people knew that it would not take place in their own neighborhoods, but in the new one under construction. Also, the announcement stressed the desirability of peaceful integration—and as it turned out, Levittowners favored peace and order even more than segregation.

The desire for order was a direct outcome of the racial disturbance in the Pennsylvania Levittown. On its arrival there, the Negro family was met by a milling crowd of about five hundred angry people, and when the local police was unable or unwilling to restore order, the state police had to be summoned. Although there was no violence and only two stones were thrown, the disturbance was thereafter described as a stone-throwing riot, giving the older Levittown a worldwide reputation as a riot-torn community and placing a blot on its escutcheon which the residents of the newest one wanted desperately to avoid.[11] In fact, in later years, people distinguished the older Levittown from their own as "the one that had the riot." The Levitt organization also wanted to avoid another disturbance, fearful that a riot would hurt sales more than desegregation itself. Believing that the Pennsylvania disturbance had been caused by the surreptitiousness of Negro purchase, it sought to make sure that the New Jersey community would be desegregated publicly, and therefore set in motion a planning program to achieve this aim.

Planning for Desegregation

The builder's first step in planning the desegregation process was to hire an expert consultant, a recently retired director of SDAD. Given a free hand by the firm, he developed a five-point program: the announcement of the Levitt decision by community leaders; a thorough briefing program for the Levitt sales force, government officials, the police, and the press; an attempt to discourage anti-integration activities, informally called "Operation Hothead"; the formation of a community Human Relations Council; and careful screening of the first Negro applicants to make sure that they would be middle class people.[12]

The township governing body was initially asked to announce the Levitt decision, but its members were not especially eager to do so. Some were personally opposed to integration, but all feared association with the decision would hurt them politically, particularly since neither party would take a stand.[13] The ministers then volunteered to make the announcement. Most favored integration, and several knew that like-minded colleagues in Levittown, Pennsylvania, had been forced out of their pulpits over this issue. If they made the announcement in unison, no congregation could condemn its own minister, and no individual minister could invite anti-integrationists to his church to exploit the then lively competition for congregants.[14] The more fervent pro-integration ministers took leadership positions on the Human Relations Council, organized at the same time, and also placed some of their lay supporters on it.[15]

The police briefing stressed methods to ensure the peaceful settling of the first Negro purchasers, to head off anti-integration demonstrations, and to prevent the police laxity that had existed in the older Levittown. Although the force was not especially enthusiastic about desegregation, the police chief was vitally interested in making his department the best in Burlington County. Since a riot would have left a permanent mark on his record, he cooperated completely. The press briefing was also influenced by events in the older Levittown. Several papers in the Levittown, Pennsylvania, area had played up the integration issue and had reported the address and arrival time of the first Negro buyer, thus facilitating crowd formation for the disturbance. In Levittown, New Jersey, the newspapers agreed to limit their coverage, and eventually reported only the signing of the deed by the first Negro family. Press cooperation was easy to obtain; the publisher of the local daily also owned the erring Pennsylvania one and was eager to make amends. The Levittown editor of the Burlington County weekly, having seen the disturbance in the older Levittown at first hand, helped brief his colleagues and advised the consultant in other ways.

"Operation Hothead" was organized by the consultant; aided by ministers, reporters, and others who knew the community well, he made up a list of known militant segregationists. These were then lectured sternly by their respective ministers and firmly discouraged from organizing anti-integration protest. The screening of Negro applicants sought middle class people able to withstand the hostility and isolation that might come their way. Although this process reassured the builder and local leaders that Levittown would not be invaded by poor Negroes, the community was never told about it. Screening was abolished after the first Negroes had moved in, and the unscreened purchasers who came later were quite like the screened ones.

The integration process was also aided by the plan by which Negroes chose their homes. The builder and his consultant agreed that Negroes should be scattered around the community (if possible, only one per block), and that under no circumstances should two Negroes be permitted to buy adjoining houses. This prevented anyone from imagining that groups of Negroes were invading the community or that a Negro subsection might develop, and made it impossible for white buyers to ask to be located in an all-white section, thus facilitating the task of the sales force in implementing integration.

Needless to say, the sales force was briefed intensively. Every salesman was instructed that, "At no time would he, directly, or indirectly, raise the issue of race; that when questioned by a prospect he would react without evasion, defense, or apology but with a manner that suggested to the questioner that the matter was not of specific concern to him or the firm." [16] A deliberate decision not to attempt to convert the salesmen to a personal belief in integration and a two-week research program, which showed that few prospective white purchasers brought up the race issue, seems to have altered the behavior of the sales force quickly and quietly.[17]

Although many whites were willing to live in an integrated Levittown, some were hesitant about buying next to a Negro family. To overcome this problem, the Levitt organization developed an ingenious system for choosing lots, giving first choice in each neighborhood and its subsections to Negroes. Like other purchasers, they naturally preferred a private lot, one backing up on woods, creeks, or open space rather than on other houses. Consequently, Negroes automatically located themselves at the edge of neighborhoods, where they would be adjacent to fewer white purchasers than they would have been in the middle, and where they might be less visible to hostile whites. It also forced whites who chose lots after them to decide whether they wanted a private lot next to a Negro family, or a less desirable one in all-white company.[18] If a white purchaser chose a lot adjacent to one selected by a Negro family, he was told so and given the option of changing to another lot. Most white buyers preferred privacy with Negro neighbors to interior lots, and even when the few "private" lots were gone, only about 20 per cent who had chosen next to a Negro picked another lot.[19] As a result, few houses adjacent to Negro-owned ones remained unsold.[20]

The large majority of Levittowners were not affected by these aspects of the desegregation process; they were to be involved through the Human Relations Council, which made plans to publish pamphlets, visit concerned white and Negro residents, and hold school programs and community workshops on integration. Of these, only the workshop materialized, for by the time the Council began to meet regularly, the first four Negro families had moved in without incident, and Levitt felt that further Council activities would only draw undue publicity toward the presence of Negroes in Levittown. The workshop was to be attended by representatives from every voluntary association in town, but drew more from those favoring integration. The workshop program consisted of lectures by outside name experts, which were unsuccessful because they assumed the Levittowners were prejudiced and demanded a change in attitude; and of post-lecture "buzz groups," which were quite successful, because people saw their neighbors had similar doubts about integration and were thus able to talk freely about the problems that really concerned them—property values and intermarriage. The discussions did not convert anyone to integration, but the provision of new facts in the right setting stilled some fears.[21]

The arrival of the first Negro purchaser in June, just after the final session of the Workshop, proceeded quietly, uneventfully, and almost unnoticed. The family was personally welcomed by a Levitt vice-president and even by the Mayor (but without publicity). A brief flurry of concern arose when a milk salesman tried to organize a boycott against the company serving the Negro family, but a call from the Human Relations Council to his employer put an end to the matter. A week later, some pro-integration residents, believing that in the other Levittowns no Negro had ever dared enter the pool, made elaborate plans to take the family swimming, but this turned out to be unnecessary, for the day before, the children next door had casually taken their new neighbors with them to the pool. Other families moved in equally quietly, and by the time the fifth one had arrived, even those who followed integration closely no longer kept track of the newcomers. As of 1964, the number of Negro families was estimated at around 50, more than in the two other Levittowns combined, but no one knew—or seemed to care—about the exact number.

The integration of Negro residents into community life also proceeded without incident, although slowly. They were welcomed as church members in their own denominations; individual Negroes became active in a number of organizations, such as the Chamber of Commerce and the Democratic party, but membership in more explicitly social organizations was rarer. Neighbor relationships between whites and Negroes were cordial, but there was little sociability across racial lines. Only Negro cosmopolitans found the relaxed and intensive sociability that spells real integration, for the white cosmopolitans, themselves an isolated minority in the community, incorporated them into their organizational and social activities.

Shortly after my fieldwork was concluded in 1961, two Negro families purchased houses in one of the all-white neighborhoods settled before integration. The resales were made privately, without any involvement by either human relations agencies or real estate brokers, and they too took place without incident, although not without some tension. The real estate agencies were in fact the only group to discriminate openly, refusing to show houses for resale to Negro buyers. Competition between brokers was intense, and they figured that whites might not give their house for sale to brokers who had previously sold to Negroes. And they knew that white customers would outnumber Negroes for a long time to come. Most whites who got along well with their neighbors were reluctant to sell to Negroes if the neighbors opposed it, and giving the house to a real estate agency which did not discriminate might anger the neighbors.[22] Some Levittowners were not yet ready to live next door to a Negro, and others were afraid that they would have difficulty selling a house in the extremely soft resale market if the adjacent house was Negro-occupied. The real estate salesmen therefore considered it good business to deal only with whites.[23]

All things considered, the desegregation of Levittown turned out to be successful. True, only a relative handful of Negroes did buy. The vast majority could not afford even the inexpensive Levitt house, and some of those who could were not yet emotionally ready to move into what was still a 99 per cent white community. The county Human Relations Council always had more difficulty in finding Negro buyers than white sellers. The only one for whom integration was not a clear success was the builder. Even before integration, sales had begun to slow down, and the drop-off continued afterwards. What portion of the reduction resulted from integration is difficult to establish. If one compares the number of move-ins just before and after integration, there is no indication of any direct and immediate relationship.[24] Sales did drop sharply in the years that followed, but the drop occurred during a period when the area housing market had become saturated and county employment had been reduced.[25]

Although Levitt officials felt that integration had made it difficult to attract Philadelphians who were themselves escaping racial change in the city, and attributed 20 per cent of the sales decline to integration, I suspect that this estimate is too high.[26] Levitt's publicity policy did not help either, for the Philadelphia area was never told that integration had been peaceful and had attracted only a handful of middle class Negroes. If would-be buyers thought Levittown was overrun with lower class Negroes or beset by racial strife, and therefore refrained from even considering moving there, no one ever set them straight.

In any case, Levitt's experience with New Jersey's Fair Housing Law did not discourage him from building two other subdivisions in the state, both integrated. Conversely, in his Bel Air, Maryland, subdivision near Washington, D.C., Levitt announced from the start that he would go along with local "customs" and would not sell to Negroes, thus once again inviting court action and demonstrations by local pro-integration organizations.[27]

Reasons for the Success of Desegregation

Had it not been for the state law banning discrimination in government-supported housing developments and the court's interpretation of FHA mortgage insurance as a form of government support, Levittown might still be an all-white community today. When the builder decided to anticipate the court's decision, however, an effective decision-making apparatus for implementing integration was quickly established. Moreover, Levitt used two methods for which he had previously shown little enthusiasm: the employment of outside experts and deliberate planning, primarily to avoid a repetition of the events in Levittown, Pennsylvania. In many ways, then, the successful integration of Levittown, New Jersey, was a direct consequence of the racial conflict and ensuing publicity in the older Levittown.

Major credit must be given to the consultant, however, and particularly to his approach. He did not attempt to change community attitudes, but systematically confronted the major participants in the process (as well as possible sources of conflict), and persuaded them to adopt behavior patterns that would assure the success of the venture, yet without requiring them to surrender their own major goals. Writing about an orientation session with the Levitt sales staff, he described his approach as follows:

> [It was] designed to accomplish two principal missions: (1) to obtain through discussion some measure of the responsiveness of this highly influential group of opinion-makers to the new policy, and (2) to enable the consultants to present the inevitable situation which conditions and the law imposed. There was no hope of converting those holding negative views. The session was geared to reinforce the official position of the employing firm with fact and research findings, and information as to the legal aspects of their own acts as agents of a building firm.[28]

Aware that order was the goal of highest priority, he developed a consensus among the relevant community officials and leaders, and communicated it to the residents. The mechanism was a new, short-term institution devoted solely to the implementation of integration, made up of existing community institutions which were in turn in contact with many residents. This new institution had both an actual component—sets of instructions and pressures placed on participants to conform to the integration plan— and a performing component, the Human Relations Council, which sought to demonstrate that most Levittowners were not opposed to integration. In peopling this institution, the consultant provided positive roles for those willing to participate and gave the unwilling an opportunity to stay on the sidelines. The ministers were able to develop a united front for their churches, the police chief got a chance to demonstrate his department's professionalism, and the politicians were allowed to stay out to prevent the issue from hurting them politically. Finally, the consultant was able to persuade a community most of whose residents were opposed to integration to accept it without visible reaction. The ministers added a moral imperative to the legal imperative supplied by the law, making it difficult for anyone to come out publicly against integration. Opposition was thus restricted to private grumbling, and it was dissipated between the time integration was announced and the first Negro family arrived.

Even so, desegregation might not have proceeded so smoothly had it not been for the willingness of Levittowners to cooperate. Five factors were responsible: the legal imperative, the absence of status threat, the class level of both white and Negro purchasers, the physical layout of the community, and its newness. Undoubtedly, the court decision set the stage for a positive climate, and so did Levitt's decision to integrate "voluntarily" after previous vigorous opposition. Levittowners realized, I think, that Levitt stood to lose many white sales, and felt that if he nevertheless went along voluntarily they had no good reason to do otherwise.

Still, they might have objected to the possible loss of community status. Of course, only the new neighborhoods were involved, but even so, everyone knew that from now on, the outside world would consider the entire community integrated. But the arrival of Negroes was not interpreted as a major status threat, principally because Levittown was—and would remain—a predominantly middle class town. Higher-status people had not yet begun to leave, and the fears of property value and status decline that threatened working class people in Levittown, Pennsylvania, and contributed to its racial disturbance were not present.[29] Even though residential turnover and tax problems were serious enough to frighten both working class and lower middle class residents, they did not panic. Many knew that racial conflict might well begin to reduce Levittown's prestige, and even those who opposed integration often said that it was preferable to a riot. If they had felt really threatened, however, these considerations would have been ignored in the heat of panic.

One reason people did not panic can be found in their own socioeconomic position and in their expectation that the Negro newcomers would share it. Research on prejudice and racial conflict has demonstrated that these are less intense at higher socioeconomic levels, and the white New Jersey Levittowners were more affluent than the Pennsylvanians. The Negroes who came were clearly and visibly middle class people, with more education, better jobs, and higher family incomes than most whites, but the white Levittowners did not know this in advance. Even so, most were convinced that poor Negroes could not buy in their community and that the builder would not admit slum dwellers. Although the belief that only a few atypical Negroes could afford Levittown was a way of reassuring oneself of the community's high status, the fact that people were convinced of this without data to back up their feelings suggests again the lack of intense status fears.

The physical layout of Levittown into separate neighborhoods made it possible for segregationists in the existing ones to feel secure in the knowledge that their own areas were still white, and that the Negroes were geographically and socially far away.[30] The mixture of house types on the block scattered low-income residents throughout the community, and segregationists among them, living amid people who favored integration or order above all, probably never knew how many others shared their feelings and were willing to act on them. In the older Levittown, one-price neighborhoods concentrated such people and made it easy for them to get together with like-minded neighbors. One Levittowner who had lived in the Pennsylvania community during the disturbance described her block there as "very negative; nice neighbors became ugly, took their kids evenings and went over to the [Negro] house to throw stones."

Finally, the success of integration must be traced also to the community's newness. Levittown, Pennsylvania had been in existence for six years when the first Negro arrived, but the New Jersey community had only been established for two, another reason why status decline had not yet begun. The desire to be law-abiding, orderly, and idealistic was typical of a new community, and so was the police department's desire to be the best in the county. The politicians' reluctance to participate in the integration process can be attributed to newness as well, for they did not yet know their constituents well enough to take a stand. Had they been aware of a significant bloc of anti-integration opinion, one of them might have been tempted to exploit it for political benefit. And the newness of the neighborhood into which the first Negroes moved made it impossible for segregationists to recruit their neighbors for opposition. In an already settled neighborhood, they would have known similarly inclined residents.

In fact, the positive role of the community's newness raises the question whether integration should not have been instituted at the very start. Pro-integration groups in the Philadelphia area had urged this step on the builder, and if it had been taken, there would have been no need for advance planning to prevent a disturbance. Moreover, the housing market was healthier then, and the Levitt house a better bargain in 1958 than in 1960. Although the builder would have lost some sales among militant segregationists, most of them would really not have had an alternative source of new, low-priced homes. Moreover, voluntary integration would have avoided a court case, saved legal costs for the builder, and brought a number of symbolic rewards—and favorable national publicity—for a progressive and courageous act.

There are, however, some good arguments against initial integration. When Levittown was first occupied, the state law had not yet been tested in the courts, and the legal imperative was still lacking. Consequently, antagonistic Levittowners who later wished to be law-abiding might have been less reluctant about acting out their prejudices. Organizations badly in need of members might have turned away Negroes for fear of scaring off potential white members, and the politicians, then terribly short of issues, might have made one out of integration. Since neither Levitt nor community leaders would have known the community, it would probably have been impossible to plan against such occurrences, and without the positive community climate, interested Negro buyers, not knowing what they would face in Levittown, might have been discouraged from coming.[31]

Comparing the benefits and costs of initial and later integration is difficult, but I suspect that in the absence of legal inevitability in 1958, opening the community to Negroes from the start would have been more problematic. This conclusion applies only to Levittown; other communities might well benefit from initial integration. Even so, the choice between the two alternatives is less important than the fact that even after Levittown was opened to Negroes, only a handful came. Results of successful integration experiences ought to be better publicized so that other communities can use them to plan, and so that Negroes who are justifiably concerned about the hardships of moving into an overwhelmingly white community can learn that they have less to fear than they think. But the main problem is to do away with the economic inequities that now prevent so many Negroes from affording suburban homes or decent shelter of any kind.

THE QUALITY OF COMMUNITY PLANNING

The activities of the community's Planning Board and its professional consultant provide a less happy illustration of nonpolitical decision-making. As I noted in Chapter One, the Planning Board had been set up before Levitt purchased land, and it, together with its consultant, cooperated fully with Levitt's efforts and plans. Once the community was occupied, the old residents who served as board members were replaced by newcomers—party workers who were being rewarded for their campaign contributions and engineers and real estate salesmen who had (or were thought to have) some expertise on planning matters. Like most other municipal agencies, the Planning Board initiated little activity of its own, but responded to requests that came before it, most of which were for approval of small shopping centers on land not owned by Levitt. For example, from January 1960 to May 1961, 46 per cent of the items on the board's calendar fell into this category, and another 15 per cent dealt with the proper size of signs for stores and gas stations. Only 11 per cent of the agenda dealt with more general planning topics, the major one concerning the number of gas stations to be permitted in Levittown.

Since the board members knew little about planning, they usually gave the consultant free rein to propose what he thought best, adopting his recommendations as their own except when they became controversial. The consultant's main function was to check shopping center plans to make sure that they were in accord with municipal ordinances, had enough parking space, and were designed for efficient traffic circulation. He also advocated changes in the community's planning ordinances, among them that stores and gas stations should be built in Colonial style so as to coincide with the design of the houses and that signs by which stores advertised their presence should be limited in size.[32] Both proposals were bitterly fought by the applicants for sites, especially by chains which wanted the same elevations and signs they built elsewhere in the nation, but eventually they went along with the board because they had no other choice.

The builder and the Planning Board supported the consultant because they agreed that the community should be esthetically pleasing and that this could be achieved by architectural harmony of the kind he proposed. The residents were primarily concerned with status protection and wanted to make sure that commercial establishments did not infiltrate residential areas. Indeed, their concern for protection—also shared by most of the board members—was strong enough that sometimes the Planning Board went beyond what the planner had proposed. When some residents objected to the number of gas stations being built in the community, the planner was asked to write an ordinance limiting them, and the Planning Board was able to persuade Levitt to put just one gas station on any intersection he owned. The consultant was overruled only when his proposals generated political opposition, for example, his recommendation to let all nonresident doctors purchase homes for offices and his rejection of a variance request by the powerful VFW to build a clubhouse near a residential area.

One of the planner's most important duties was to prepare a community master plan to regulate future growth. Since there was little community interest in a master plan, and not many people knew what ought to go into it, he had considerable leeway to make—or at least propose—decisions about the community's future. Of course, he was limited by the small budget allocated for township planning, by the builder's role in the community's future, and by his own decision to coordinate his master planning with the builder's. As I indicated in Chapter One, the planner's sympathies were more with Levitt than with the residents. He believed fervently in what he defined to be good planning, saw his role as "trying to teach good planning to the Planning Board and the Levitt Company," and felt that "the best kind of planning was that which also made good business sense." His planning philosophy and his judgment of where the power lay dictated that he work closely with the builder in planning for the township, and that he adapt his recommendations to the builder's proposals. As a result, the preliminary plan, completed in 1959, coincided closely with Levitt's own scheme. Both it and the final plan, published in 1964, proposed and located future community facilities ranging from schools to shopping areas and utility systems, suggested some revisions in the design of residential areas, and advocated improvements in some municipal services.

The final plan deserves detailed examination as a case of poor nonpolitical decision-making. It ran to two volumes, but one was taken up with "basic studies" of the community which told

Levittowners little they did not know already.[33] The second volume was devoted to a "Suggested Development Plan," and in accordance with contemporary planning thought, proposed a number of "community objectives" and policy proposals to achieve them. Community objectives are of great significance, and one would need to know how they were determined. If they were really community objectives, the planner should have interviewed a sample of citizens, or if lack of funds made this impossible, at least the political leaders. The report does not indicate how the planner determined them, and states only, "the development plan has formulated objectives which all citizens and officials should strive to achieve." [34] Since the planner gathered most of his information about Levittown from the U.S. Census, he could not have learned the objectives from the community. Judging by their content, some came from the decision-makers, some from the builder, but the majority were his own.[35] Actually, most were such general and vague statements that one suspects no analysis of any kind went into their formulation. As a result, the objectives were not ranked in any order of priority to indicate which were of most urgency, and, of course, they paid no attention to the community's diversity, thus giving residents no opportunity to debate alternatives. Since their generality made them virtually useless for planning purposes, the main weight of the plan fell on the policy proposals, but these also seemed bereft of analysis and bore no logical or empirical relationship to the objectives they were supposed to achieve. If they were intended as means to community goals, the plan provided no evidence that they could or would realize these goals.

These deficiencies can be illustrated by an analysis of some of the plan's ten objectives and the relevant policy recommendations: [36]

> Objective 1: Achieve an environment for the people of Willingboro by providing for the human activities of work, leisure, play, rest, education, religion and esthetic fulfillment.

This statement, although typically found in planning reports, is so general as to be meaningless. It fails to define an "environment," or to indicate what kinds of work, leisure, play, etc., are wanted by various sectors of the population and which are desirable by other criteria.

The plan's policies for achievement of this objective deal with only a few "human activities." Leisure needs are to be met by township parks, playgrounds, playfields, tot-lots, walking areas, a marina, and a golf course. However desirable, these offer only athletic outdoor recreation, principally for children (especially boys), for men, and for families affluent enough to own a boat. No provision is made for nonathletic forms of leisure, such as commercial entertainment, and nothing is said about facilitating sociability and reducing the social isolation which I reported on in earlier chapters. Also, there is no plan for the needs of teenagers, other than to suggest a "Teenage Center" as part of the public library, to be located near the senior high school. A moment's observation is enough to show that adolescents would look skeptically on a center located in the library—an institution that demands quiet from its users, or one sited next to the high school—an institution that discourages precisely the kind of recreation teenagers want. Moreover, the plan is silent about the activities of the center, whether it would be run by teenage or adult rules or what it would do to give teenagers a function in the community.

Esthetic fulfillment is to be provided through the establishment of parks and the preservation of "natural features" of the original rural landscape. The plan offers no evidence for (or against) the assumption that a significant number of people derive esthetic pleasure from looking at or being in parks, and no provision is made for other forms of esthetic pleasure-seeking, be they museums or movies. The plan argues that "the park should be designed to give the residents an opportunity to get away from the noise and rush of traffic and enjoy contact with nature once again." [37] It offers no data, however, that Levittowners want to escape from local noise and traffic (which were, of course, minimal), that they want to enjoy contact with nature, or that they prefer to do this in a park rather than in their own gardens or at a beach.

Planning for education is limited to listing the number of needed schools, suggesting their acreage, and locating them on specific sites on the "Development Plan Map." There is no discussion of what kinds of education are wanted by the residents (or even by the planner), or why the elementary school needs to be 15 to 20 acres, and the senior high school 40 to 50. Such acreages may be desirable and necessary, but the community might also want to spend scarce funds on other educational objectives.

Planning for work is touched on only in a brief statement about industrial facilities that reads: "The present nature of the township would seem to dictate that any industry in Willingboro should be of the quiet type, . . . research and development laboratories and administrative offices, light manufacturing processes and warehousing and storage." [38] The plan says nothing about whether Levittowners want to work in their own community or not, and if so, what kinds of work they would like to have or are qualified for, and whether it could be provided in Levittown.

> Objective 2: Establish local commercial shopping center sites in the Township and at the same time set a policy which discourages strip commercial development off Route U.S. 130.

This objective is a policy statement which does not refer to any broader goal, but reflects the planning consultant's intense dislike of strip shopping. It is clearly his own goal, and although a shopping center may well be preferable to stores strung along the highway, there is no evidence either in his report or in my observations that Levittowners were very much concerned about what kinds of stores they shopped in.[39] If they had shopping goals of their own, these probably had to do with low prices, and the availability, accessibility, and variety of stores.

> Objective 4: Provide the foundation for a sound and functional municipal service program.

This objective is meaningless unless the terms "sound" and "functional" are defined. Policies related to the statement are limited to a suggestion that water and sewer facilities are in good order, that more policemen and a second fire station are needed, that the public works department requires more storage space, and that a township medical building (the functions of which are not specified) ought to be attached to the existing hospital. Nothing is said about what kinds of new services the community wants or should have, or how existing services might be improved. For example, the expansion of the police force is proposed without questioning whether the town's crime rate or traffic problems justify it. Similarly, nothing is said about the

kinds of medical services residents want and need, about counseling and mental health facilities, or about how to pay for them.

> Objective 8: Develop a program to help balance existing
> and future residential development with ap-
> propriate ratables that will: provide lands
> for future industrial and commercial expan-
> sion, offer recommendations for future con-
> trol of highway development off U.S. Route
> 130, provide sites for local planned shopping
> centers, establish certain remaining tracts for
> a lower density pattern of residential develop-
> ment.

This objective is deficient on several grounds. It is unclear, making it impossible to tell whether the primary aim is to "balance"
existing and future residential development or to solve the tax
problems of the community. Moreover, no evidence is given that
providing land for commerce and industry and doing away with
strip shopping will create either "balance" or "appropriate"
ratables. Nothing is said about the community's unwillingness to
pay higher property taxes or about feasible alternative sources of
public funds, given the likelihood that sufficient industry cannot
be attracted to Levittown. In fact, the plan does not concern itself with the tax problem at all, except to provide a detailed analysis of current sources of municipal income and expenditure patterns and to point out repeatedly that "the only recourse available
to lessen the burden of the individual taxpayer is the addition of
profitable ratables to the Township's tax base." [40] The Suggested Development Plan does not even raise the tax base issue,
and does not suggest how Levittown can solve its financial dilemma.

Admittedly, one should not expect the planner to solve the insoluble, but then he should have indicated that no solution
existed and that Levittown could choose to increase the tax rate
further, keep it at its present level and restrict future expenditures accordingly, or lobby for state and federal subsidies. The
planner should also have estimated the costs of his various proposals and, since Levittowners object to higher taxes, indicated
which were of greater urgency than others in case not all could
be financed. Instead, the report concludes hopefully: "In short,
the Planning Board realizes that it cannot wave a magic wand
and make new industry flock to Willingboro, but that honest and

steady work by the Planning Board, the Industrial Development Committee, Town Council, and the public will result in substantial gains for the Township." [41]

Despite the community's great concern over taxes, the actual plan is most detailed about policies for future residential development. In describing these policies, the planner adds a new objective, for he suggests: "A prime objective of the Township's development plan is not only the recognition of continued development of single-family houses but to recommend a wider diversification of future residential lots and dwelling types that will accommodate a possible 50,000 people." [42] No reason is given why such diversification is desirable, or why the town should eventually have a population of 50,000.[43] The policies themselves call for the construction of houses on larger lots, which presumably means more expensive houses as well, although this is not stated. There is no discussion of whether Levittown could attract high-income residents, a particularly important omission since Levitt has so far been unable to do so. Nor is there any indication of the virtue of such an approach or of whether it would help provide significant additional tax revenues.

Instead of dealing with such questions, the plan proposes that many of the future houses be sited in "cluster subdivisions," a series of cul-de-sacs surrounded by public open space, instead of in "conventional" subdivisions of houses placed side by side on curving streets. The planner's argument for this innovation, a current fad in site planning, sometimes borders on the ludicrous. It indicates that conventional subdivisions create urban sprawl, "provide row upon row of stereotyped houses, many with unsightly and unkept yards . . . and utility poles weave a tangled web of wires." [44] The cluster, on the other hand, "helps reduce the dangerous intersections and streets found in conventional subdivisions, [is] uncluttered with overhead utility wires, [provides] greater variety of house styles, nearby open space, and prevents children from playing in the streets." [45]

The plan offers no evidence for these statements. In actual fact, urban sprawl is caused by speculative land acquisition which often leaves vacant and unbuildable spaces between subdivisions, but has nothing to do with the site planning of specific subdivisions. Moreover, there is no reason why houses need be stereotypes in the conventional subdivision or more varied in the cluster style; this is a function of builders' practices and house price decisions. Unsightly yards can exist in any site plan, and whether utility poles are located above or below ground is a function of cost (and house price) and not of the site plan. Also, no evidence is offered that either plan will prevent children from playing on the streets (they actually play mainly on the sidewalk and very little on the grass) or that the conventional subdivision has created traffic accidents and danger to children, at least in Levittown. Finally, there is no evidence that buyers want more public open space or are willing to pay the taxes to have it maintained.

Whether or not the cluster plan is superior to the conventional one is not at issue here; what matters is that the planner is proposing a scheme requiring more expensive houses without commenting on either their feasibility or desirability. Moreover, if industry is to be attracted, it might be argued that Levittown should provide less expensive houses so that workers in these industries can live there, especially since a firm's location decision today often hinges on the provision of housing and other facilities for its workers.

> Objective 10: Develop a plan for the health, safety and general welfare of all the people of Willingboro that promotes good civic design, stresses the efficient expenditure of public funds and recommends provision of necessary public services and facilities for the future.

This final objective illustrates the deficiencies of the plan as a whole. Despite its claims, the plan has not concerned itself with the health and safety of all the people, nor has it sought to determine their welfare, i.e., their goals and problems. Instead, it has accepted some of the builders' and the municipal agencies' demands, and combined them with standard planning proposals (such as large acreages for schools) and with current site-planning fashions, which are equated with "good civic design." The plan does recommend public services and facilities, but its definition of "necessary services" is based on the growth demands of various municipal agencies, and not on what Levittowners need, want, or are willing to pay for. Also, no evidence is given for the claim that the plan achieves the aim of efficient expenditure of public funds. It fails to define efficiency or to identify the goals in relation to which efficiency is to be determined and neglects to offer alternative schemes which might be more efficient in achieving even the goals that the planner has set for the community. For example, if the plan wants to maximize the welfare and safety of the community, it would be more efficient and more welfare-oriented to provide for the needs of the teenagers beyond an obviously inadequate Teenage Center than to increase the size of the police force.

The plan's lack of interest in the citizens' objectives was compounded by the planner's failure to pay attention to citizens' opinions. He spent little time in the community, and judging by his occasional appearances at public hearings, made no effort to understand them. He first made people unhappy when he failed to question the location of a gas station immediately adjacent to a church. At a hearing on the preliminary plan, he antagonized his audience by his unwillingness to discuss the bases for his recommendations, justifying a particularly controversial one by asking people to accept "thirteen years of experience and long discussions with the Planning Board" instead. Following a public meeting on the final plan, a local columnist took him to task for blithely jumping to conclusions about controversial community issues, such as the then bitterly fought garden apartment ordinance. In a caustic column which also questioned his presentation of obvious facts in the guise of technical jargon and his reliance on outdated census statistics, she reported him as saying:

> A community of young children requires "increased schools, police, fire protection, recreation and garbage disposal" [in THAT order?]. He then added that a higher tax levy would be required. [There were only seven in the audience and nobody stood up and cheered.] Just after that I caught a phrase pregnant with meaning . . . "more intensive residential use." Is this a sophisticated way of saying apartments? [46]

The planner often appealed for popular support of planning through "citizen participation," but he gave people no opportunity to participate, and his actions indicated that he only wanted their assent to his proposals. In fact, Levittowners who wanted to talk with him found it difficult to see him, and when they succeeded, he was insensitive to their concerns. He failed to explain his close working relationship with the builder and took little interest in zoning issues. He never quite understood people's status fears, and could not fathom why some objected to nonresident doctors, clubhouses, or gas stations, and why they did not embrace his vendetta against strip shopping and hot dog stands. And he was totally unaware of the living patterns, the problems of social and physical isolation, and the community-related worries which I described in earlier chapters. His inability to comprehend even the Levittowners' occupational and class level is underscored by a sentence in the planning report which suggests that, "Results [in attracting new industry] are also obtained when the residents of the community . . . in their daily contacts with businessmen, industrialists, and investors make their community interests known." [47] I doubt whether even William Levitt himself had such daily contacts, but then the planner was interested in land use, not people; in efficiency and "balance," not in people's demands and needs; in site plans and community facilities, not in how people live.

As a result, the community gave him little support. Of course, uninformed about planning, people could perhaps not have distinguished between good and bad master plans. But the planning they received all dealt either with future community facilities, of interest only to later arrivals, or with vague generalizations about the community's problems, which they could not get the planner to discuss openly. Admittedly, long-range planning rarely interests many people, but when the planner ignores their present problems, it is not surprising that they care little about long-range ones. And when the planner is not trusted by the community, he loses the support of even the cosmopolitans, who are usually the most enthusiastic advocates of planning.

The planner's approach and his master plan are not unique; the Suggested Development Plan is quite typical of those prepared for small (and even large) communities all over the country, and the lack of contact with the citizens and the concentration on future physical development are common as well. So are the undue reliance on census data, the concern with professional objectives, the proposal of policies which are professionally fashionable but bear no logical or empirical relation to the objectives they are supposed to achieve, the failure to provide evidence for crucial points in the argument, and the sloppy methods of analysis and synthesis which go into the policy proposals.[48] It is no wonder, then, that planning remains a poorly budgeted municipal activity, thought to be of little relevance to the real problems of the community.

LOCAL DEMOCRACY AND CENTRAL PLANNING

The success of desegregation and even the failure of master planning demonstrate that nonpolitical decision-making—or, to call it by its rightful name, planning—can be implemented in a local community when properly handled. Of course, it is not entirely fair to compare the two processes, for the planner had a much more complex assignment. The integration consultant had to deal with a single issue; the decision that generated the plan had already been made, and the power of the state and the builder stood behind it. The planner, on the other hand, had to determine community objectives on a variety of issues, make decisions about them, and use what little power the Planning Board had or could give to demand their implementation—and all this with probably less money than was spent for integration.

Even so, the fact remains that the integration consultant planned well and the master planner did not. The former evoked the latent community consensus for order, used it by organizing optimum communication between community leaders and residents, kept the issue out of the political arena, developed rational policies which were logically related to the goals he sought, and implemented them by demanding behavior rather than attitude change and by maximizing benefits and minimizing costs for all participants wherever possible. The master planner did just the opposite. He made no attempt to look for consensus and kept communication with residents to a minimum. Although he saw his role as nonpolitical, he could neither keep major issues out of the political arena nor restrain himself from judgments about controversial ones. His policies were irrational, and they asked attitude as well as behavior changes from people, requiring their conversion to his vision of the community without taking their demands or needs into account. If benefits and costs had been computed, the former would clearly accrue to the planner (insofar as the plan realized the kind of community he wanted) and the latter would be borne by the residents who would be both paying for the changes he proposed and altering their life styles to fit the plan.

Successful planning requires at least six ingredients: (1) sufficient local consensus or outside power to initiate the process; (2) an expert who has the resources, skills, and information to determine community goals and find the proper policies to achieve them; (3) a set of policies which maximize benefits and minimize costs for those sectors of the local community whose cooperation is needed; (4) an overall organizational approach which isolates the process from day-to-day politics; (5) a communication system which provides for maximum feedback and response among the participants in the process; and (6) enough local consensus to implement the final product, or power from outside the community to do so when consensus is lacking. The most necessary—and perhaps even the sufficient—ingredient is outside power, for it can insist on many kinds of local action, short of major behavior and attitude change on the part of the population.

When such power ought to be used and when nonpolitical decision-making has priority over the local political process is another matter. An age-old question with far-reaching implications, it involves a choice between politics and planning, democratic and elite decisions, majority rule and the public interest, politicians and statesmen—and also between home rule and regional or national policy. It is even at the heart of the suburban critique, in the choice between the suburbanites' satisfaction with their community and the critics' evaluation which considers such satisfaction irrelevant. Proper treatment of this question and its various dichotomies requires a thorough philosophical discussion which is out of place in the framework of a community study. Yet since my research in Levittown raised the question in my mind, I feel compelled to conclude with at least a cursory attempt at an answer.

Obviously, dichotomizing the question is dangerous; the choice is not between politics or planning, etc., but between their relative priorities in different situations. The real issue is: When should outside or central planning replace local democracy. By "local democracy," I mean a government with equal representation for all, maximal decision-maker responsiveness, optimal feedback and intervention opportunities, and an electoral system that prevents well-organized minorities from voting in their candidates and policies. Levittown fell short of this ideal, what with Levitt's power and the government's pervasive feedback restriction. But if the community is genuinely democratic, I would begin with the value judgment that local democracy is of high priority, and that its costs must be accepted along with its benefits. If people are entitled to determine their own destiny and to do so by majority rule, the right of lower middle class citizens to run their community by lower middle class priorities must also be granted, even when this results in decisions that are undesirable from another perspective. If democracy is important, one cannot set up another, nonpolitical criterion for decision-making every time the decision goes the wrong way. The suburban critic, the city planner, and anyone else whose conception of the good and well-planned community deviates from that, say, of lower middle class Levittowners, must therefore consider whether his vision is so perfect and therefore so universal as to justify the downgrading of local democracy.

My feeling is that no such conceptions have yet been put forth; upon analysis, all the utopias and even the more modest community plans turn out to reflect the philosophies and styles of life of one or another sector of the cosmopolitan upper middle class. Whatever their virtues—and these are many—they assume either a cosmopolitan population or a wholesale and magical conversion of noncosmopolitan people to cosmopolitan culture. Since more than 95 per cent of Levittowners (and the rest of the world) are now not cosmopolitan, the assumption does not speak to present policy alternatives.

Consequently, the guidelines I suggested in Chapter Eleven apply here as well; people of every culture have the right to choose what they want, and unless it can be proven that their choices are harmful to other important values they hold or are clearly self-destructive and antisocial, they also have the right to use local democratic government to achieve their public wants. The key word is *antisocial,* for it holds the clue to possible limitations of majority rule. Antisocial choices, I would argue summarily, are those which ignore the public interest, violate minority rights, and prevent the achievement of minority demands.

The nature and boundaries of the public interest have been debated as long as mankind has lived in communities, but I would take it to be either an interest that is *consensual,* shared by all or almost all people in their role as community members, or *holistic,* so important to the community as a whole that it must override the conflicting personal or communal interests of individual members.[49] Moreover, each must be divided into two levels, the *absolute,* which outweighs all other interests, and the *relative,* which requires a determination whether the public interest is actually more important than the diverging personal or community interests of its members. A matter of absolute public interest would override the individual interests of members; a relative one might not.

The consensual public interest of either level can be determined through the political process, for in casting their vote, people can presumably decide whether the issue is important enough to override their individual interests. Instances of the consensual public interest are few and far between, for rarely do people have enough in common to unite for one goal. Perhaps Levittowners came close to consensus in wanting to avoid racial conflict, and there being few personal interests in the way, they could consider it a matter of absolute public interest. They probably also agreed that the community should obtain industry to reduce taxes, but here the issue is one of relative public interest, for once the means of obtaining industry are considered, other concerns may get in the way. For example, it is questionable whether Levittowners would willingly pay such costs as a beneficial tax rate to industry, the publicly financed construction of industrial buildings, and the provision of low-priced housing for workers. These costs would reduce not only the ultimate tax benefits, but also the community's status, and only a detailed benefit-cost analysis could tell voters whether obtaining industry fits the consensual public interest more closely than a reduced program of municipal services.

Issues in the holistic public interest are also rare. Although interveners often claimed their own demands were so important that they justified the rejection of individual interests, I cannot think of a single issue in this category in Levittown's short history. A clear case of the absolute holistic public interest is the survival of the community and all its residents, and martial law is readily invoked in dealing with a natural disaster. But other instances are hard to find. If the community as municipality went bankrupt, and if state or federal funds were not available to rescue it, one could argue for a drastic tax increase, although even then one might want to give residents the alternative of disbanding the community altogether. Conversely, the holistic interest does not justify repression of riots. It (and the consensual interest) allows actions to prevent bloodshed, but rioting itself is clearly a desperate method of minority intervention when the government has been insufficiently responsive, and must be treated as a political issue, to be resolved by eliminating community-based grievances.[50] The relative holistic public interest is hardest to determine, for it requires the comparison of benefits and costs to the community as a whole with those of people as community members and individuals. But the most important benefits and costs are almost impossible to measure.

The public interest is so easy to claim and so difficult to determine that once one proceeds beyond consensus and community survival, the pluralism of American society soon interferes with the assumptions of value agreement and value priority inherent in the two kinds of public interest. Communities could, of course, go through the complicated process of determining what values its members share and what community values are so important that they outweigh all others, but populations and values are not always stable. Perhaps the only solution is to put one's faith in the local political process (assuming it is genuinely democratic), letting decision-makers and interveners use their conception of the public interest as a campaign or intervention strategy, and hoping that the voters will opt for the public interest as they see it.

A special case of the public interest is the community's long-range development, which requires a determination of whether future consensual or holistic public interest is important enough to justify short-range sacrifices. I would argue that long-range *needs* deserve implementation if there is substantial proof that they accord with present public interest or majority values, but that it is unwise to give up important current priorities for goals in the uncertain future. Some needs can be proven; present population data provide unmistakable evidence of the need for future classrooms, but a long-range land acquisition program for local suburban parks would require some evidence that such parks will be used adequately; otherwise, the money might better be spent for other needs. Of course, land can always be purchased by the government and later turned to other uses or even sold to private developers, but given low suburban densities, I would doubt whether the demand for future park use is high enough to divert money now, say, from building more classrooms and establishing smaller classes. Long-range *planning* (which demands no significant current sacrifices) is always desirable, provided it addresses itself to issues of the kind I have described, rather than to the realization of minority demands in the guise of long-range thinking.

Minority interests must be divided into demands and rights. In a genuinely democratic community, minority demands have lower priority than those of the majority, although the ideal is a compromise that optimizes the achievement of both. When it comes to minority rights, however, the line must be drawn firmly and their priority over majority values must be asserted. Such rights are guaranteed by the Constitution, and whether they are those of nonwhite people to live where they choose or of individuals with deviant opinions to utter them freely, they cannot be abrogated by the community.

Up to this point, the argument has assumed local autonomy: that the public interest and the definition of majority and minority are determined by the boundaries of the local community. That assumption is justified on issues affecting only the people living within these boundaries, but these are increasingly rare. When so much of community life is shaped by forces and agents impinging from the outside, no community can be an island. This is particularly true of suburbs, whose political boundaries were drawn in rural times and are constantly crossed by the social and economic forces that make them interdependent with cities. The principle of majority rule alone would justify that the majority demands or the public interest of the larger area take precedence over the community; but what might be true in theory breaks down in practice, for there are few political units or governmental bodies with enough authority or power to act in behalf of metropolitan areas or the social and economic regions to which cities and suburbs belong. The limitations of the local community and the artificiality of its boundaries are obvious enough, but this does not thereby generate the political power needed to establish new governmental bodies. So long as local government's prime function is to protect property and status values, voters will not support metropolitan or regional governments. Consequently, state and federal governments are presently the major resource for outside intervention.

The Case for Outside Intervention

I pointed out earlier that the most important ingredient for nonpolitical decisions was outside power, and when this was exerted, Levittown's decision-makers acted accordingly despite strong local political pressures to act otherwise. State and federal action are therefore most effective for realizing what are by local standards nonpolitical decisions. Admittedly, such action is political as well and depends ultimately on voter approval, but it is easier to obtain at the state and federal levels than at the local level. The final question then is: How much and what kind of outside intervention is desirable in the local community?

Generally speaking, outside agencies ought to be empowered to carry out the local (and the extra-local) public interest when the local community is unwilling to do so. Similarly, they must enforce the minority rights guaranteed by the Constitution and by federal and state laws. Yet another function is to help local minorities attain their demands. If a minority of Levittowners wanted a more cosmopolitan school, outside aid would be desirable to enable the local school board to provide it as part of its system or as a separate school. Such a solution is possible only if the minority demand does not conflict with the majority one; it would not work for a minority wanting to drive on the left side of the street. More important, since not all minority demands can be satisfied from the outside, criteria are needed for choosing those deserving of outside financial aid or political support. Three such criteria can be advanced, two related to the community, and one external to it.

The first is the correction of the imbalances and inequities that result from local autonomy and majority rule. Outside power and aid should be used to satisfy those demands which can be met through governmental action, provided they cannot be satisfied privately by these minorities, and provided, also, the minorities represent a significant enough proportion of the community. For example, a minority which cannot afford to pay for its needs in the private economy deserves governmental aid before a more affluent one, for government ought wherever possible to correct the inequities of the private economy. But since it cannot satisfy all demands, it ought also to give priority to those of a larger minority than before those of a smaller one. A second criterion is the outside correction of local irrationality. Short-range political considerations encourage local governments to find stop-gap solutions, but an outside agency can demand rational ones in exchange for financial aid. For example, if it proposes to help eliminate juvenile delinquency, it can more easily set standards to assure programs that aid adolescents and to discourage irrational adult repression.

But given the shortcomings of local democracy and the limited role of local communities in the lives of their residents, the most important criterion must be external: the goals of the outside agency itself. A state agency ought to use its funds and authority to achieve state aims; a federal one, federal aims. The federal government usually has a broader perspective than the local community, as well as more power to correct its shortcomings, and most state governments should be in a similar position after reapportionment. They are able to see that regional needs may require apartments in single-family home suburbs, or that the automating economy demands changes in local schools. Of course, outside agencies pursue their own political and bureaucratic priorities before attending to more general state or national goals, and the ideal is a state (and national) plan that sets priorities for what local facilities and services are to be affected and subsidized by the state or federal government. Such a plan would enable the federal government to decide, for example, that given the prospective changes in the economy and its job structure, educational subsidies to a suburban school system are more important than recreational subsidies, but that if work time is reduced a generation hence, recreational ones may become more urgent than others; or that subsidies to suburbs are less important than to the cities and their low-income populations.

Like all arguments for planning, mine ultimately requires a central national plan which determines what goals and policies are of highest priority. But central planning requires a consensus on national goals and needs, and agreement about the shape of the future, and these are hard to achieve. The increasing role of the federal government in the affairs of local communities suggests that such a plan will be developed eventually, if only to guide the federal Bureau of the Budget in its allocation decisions. Nor is such a plan as impossible as it seems, for on those issues on which consensus is lacking, the goals of a pluralistic society suggest that the demands of different groups ought to be satisfied as much as possible. If they know what they want, these wants are at least given. When unanimity is not possible, the best solution is to encourage diversity.

I have tried to argue that as long as local governments make predominantly political decisions, outside agencies must require or encourage the local community to make nonpolitical ones. Even then, opportunities for local planning will be limited, but national planning for local communities may be feasible. Given the increasing interdependence of the local community and the national society, and the relative insignificance of local communities in the lives of their residents, outside agencies are justified in protecting the public interest and minority rights, in looking after minority demands, and in implementing regional, state, and federal priorities.

In coming to this conclusion, I have proposed a number of absolute values which take precedence over the workings of the political process and limit majority rule. The fundamental philosophical problem remains: once politics, democracy, and majority rule are accepted, it is difficult to insist on exceptions, for who is to say—and by what external criterion—which absolutes take precedence. In a democratic society which is also pluralistic, every act and every value must become political, and seemingly nonpolitical absolutes may only reflect the interests of one or another sector of the population. If one's choice of absolutes is itself political, depending on the values of whatever economic, cultural, or philosophical interest group one belongs to, then social scientists or cosmopolitans are likely to insist on absolutes different from those of low-income Negroes, for example. The search for truly nonpolitical absolutes must go on, but it may well be that none exist beyond the survival of the individual, the community, or the nation. Then, one can only insist on a single absolute; a genuinely democratic society. The virtue of such a society is that it gives one the right to fight politically for the other absolutes of one's choice; the drawback, that if one knows oneself to be in a minority, these absolutes are not likely to be accepted by the majority.

NOTES

1. I define rationality here as the determination of the most effective means of achieving a stated goal; it refers to the methods for bringing about a goal rather than to the choice of goals or the process of determining this choice.
2. Although I use the terms "desegregation" and "integration" interchangeably for stylistic reasons, I am describing how Negroes ob-

tained the right to purchase houses in the community, rather than their social integration into it.

3. Bressler, p. 127.

4. This assumption turned out to be inaccurate, for when Levittown was integrated, the salesmen of smaller subdivisions told potential customers hair-raising and totally inaccurate stories about the amount of integration, conflict, violence, and blight that had taken place, promising them that the small subdivisions would remain totally white. Eventually, SDAD acted to halt this practice, and the Burlington County Human Relations Council made special efforts to find Negro buyers for every small subdivision in the area.

5. As I pointed out in Chapter Two, 1 per cent of the buyers (3 per cent from the cities) volunteered racial change as their main reason for leaving their former residence, and 9 per cent (about a fifth of city dwellers) checked it as an important reason on a fifteen-item list.

6. Not all Jews supported desegregation. I was personally quite shaken by a bitter attack on it by a Jewish leader who had survived the German concentration camps. The majority Jewish view was probably like that of one Levittowner, who told me, "I don't want Negroes in Levittown, and I don't want Jews associated with interracial attempts, but I won't picket. We are a minority too."

7. A door-to-door survey made by a local paper with a more randomly chosen sample than is usually the case showed that in 1959, sixteen Levittowners interviewed were opposed to integration, while only two favored it.

8. Fears of intermarriage undoubtedly also fed on the powerful white fantasy about Negro sexual potency.

9. Also, some lawyers felt that he had a good case for his interpretation of FHA insurance and that it might be upheld by the U.S. Supreme Court.

10. Later, a company official explained to me that if the state Supreme Court should unexpectedly find for Levitt, the company could always reverse itself and not sell to Negroes. In July 1960, the court ruled 8 to 0 against Levitt, however, and since Levittown had by then been desegregated peacefully, the firm did not take the case to the U.S. Supreme Court.

11. Despite the lack of violence, the disturbance and integration split the community politically for several years. The effects of the disturbance are described by Bressler.

12. For another report on Levittown's integration, prepared by the consultant, see U.S. House and Home Finance Agency.

13. The politicians had been burned the previous year by cooperating with Levitt on the liquor issue and the name change, and were loath to help out again, especially on this seemingly more explosive issue.

14. Reluctance about integration came from ministers whose congre-

gants were of lower socioeconomic status, especially the fundamentalist ones. Interestingly enough, the decision to announce
integration on a Sunday left out the two rabbis, for they would
not meet their congregations again until the following Friday.
Evidently no one was much concerned about opposition from the
Jewish community.

15. On the other hand, township officials made sure that people opposed to or ambivalent about integration were also seated on the
Council, for they feared that they and the Council would otherwise be described as tools of the integrationists. Anti-integrationists were, however, outnumbered in the Council.

16. U.S. Housing and Home Finance Agency, p. 23.

17. The survey showed that only 11 per cent of all prospects indicated
any interest in the question of racial occupancy. Furthermore, 4
per cent registered mild disapproval, 2.4 per cent were unwilling
to buy a house next to a Negro family, and only 1.7 per cent "gave
evidence of holding uncompromising views in opposition to racial
inclusion and therefore might be considered to be 'lost' prospects."
U.S. Housing and Home Finance Agency, p. 23.

18. Since the private lots were more desirable and slightly more expensive, they also had a higher resale value. This not only made
them easier to resell, but also prevented generalizations that
Negroes reduced property values and resale prices.

19. This figure was reported to me by a sales manager and includes
some who changed their mind for reasons other than the color of
their neighbors.

20. A May 1963 survey showed that only three houses were vacant
adjacent to the 32 Negro families. U.S. Housing and Home Finance Agency, p. 19.

21. The experts were ineffectual also because it was thought they
were hired by the builder to "brainwash" opposition to his decision, because they were outsiders and ignorant of local conditions—many describing Levittown as culturally and socially homogeneous—and because they talked down to the audience. The
only lecturer to make a favorable impression was a Negro social
worker who, according to one participant, "gave us the facts and
no propaganda." He was dark-skinned (thus providing many
Levittowners their first opportunity to meet "a really black Negro"), talked in a mild tone, and was not insistent on attitude
change.

22. Neighbor social pressure not to sell to Negroes was quite intense.
When I prepared to sell my own house, I was made aware that
most of my neighbors were opposed to integration. Since I was
friendly with many pro-integration leaders, a rumor swept my
block that I had sold my house to a Negro family. Although I
thought about doing so, I decided not to, mainly because I
planned to continue the fieldwork for another year and felt it
would be endangered.

23. One of the two resales to a Negro family had earlier been listed with a local realtor who had forgotten to take down his sign. When he heard that the house had been sold to a Negro, he hurriedly removed his sign, but for a while his competitors gleefully spread the false rumor that he had been responsible for the sale.

24. A comparison of the number of move-ins during the same months of 1959 and 1960 shows that from January to March 1960, arrivals were 50 per cent of those in the same months in 1959. Between April and June, when integration had been announced, they rose to 106 per cent of 1959 arrivals; but between July and September, they dropped to 40 per cent and from October to January to 45 per cent of the preceding year's arrivals. This was only 5 per cent less than in the three months preceding the integration announcement, however.

25. In the last half of 1958 Levitt had sold 487 homes, and in 1959, 2174, but in 1960 sales dropped to 848; in 1961, to 729; in 1962, to 575; in 1963, to 416; and in 1964, to a low of 336. In 1965 and 1966 sales began to rise again, to about 800 per year.

26. The federal study of Levittown's integration came to no definite conclusion about the impact of integration on sales. U.S. Housing and Home Finance Agency, pp. 17–19.

27. In 1966, William Levitt testified personally and enthusiastically before the Congress in favor of an open-occupancy clause in the 1966 Civil Rights Act, arguing as he had in the past that no builder will desegregate his community unless all builders are required to do so.

28. U.S. Housing and Home Finance Agency, pp. 21–22.

29. Bressler, p. 33.

30. Indeed, I doubt whether more than 1 or 2 per cent of the white adult population has ever met any of the Negro Levittowners.

31. Of course, it could be argued that initial integration would have discouraged militantly segregationist purchasers, which in turn might have attracted more Negroes. But the latter could not have known this; besides, hostility toward them would have come not from the militants, but from a community climate which permitted the militants to express their opposition. The community climate might have been poorer if more Negroes had purchased, although their number would have had to increase tenfold before it would have deteriorated significantly. Actually, so few Negroes can afford to buy in Levittown that I doubt whether initial integration would have increased their numbers materially.

32. The main, Levitt-owned, center was built in contemporary style, however, since the idea for Colonial elevations was not proposed until after it had been started.

33. See Township of Willingboro. For unfathomable reasons, most master plans begin with a community description which is written, not for the residents who must pass on the plan, but for someone who has never been in the community.

34. Willingboro Township Planning Board, p. 1.
35. For example, two of the ten objectives deal with shopping centers, a subject on which the planning consultant had strong beliefs.
36. The objectives are quoted, in order of their presentation from Willingboro Township Planning Board, pp. 12–13. Those omitted here are either obvious or deal with minor and local technical matters.
37. Willingboro Township Planning Board, p. 25.
38. Willingboro Township Planning Board, p. 21.
39. Actually, by the time the plan came out, almost all the Route 130 frontage was developed with strip shopping, and the consultant's proposal could only have been implemented by tearing it all down and starting over. He did not suggest this, however.
40. Township of Willingboro, p. 74.
41. Willingboro Township Planning Board, p. 21.
42. Willingboro Township Planning Board, p. 14.
43. Levitt's original plan was to build at least 12,000 houses for about 50,000 people, and another 4000 houses if the market held up. Evidently the planner has accepted Levitt's minimum projection.
44. Willingboro Township Planning Board, p. 16.
45. Willingboro Township Planning Board, p. 17.
46. Rondum. Emphases and parenthenthetical phrases hers.
47. Willingboro Township Planning Board, p. 21.
48. For a more detailed case study of such deficiencies, see Piven, and Altshuler, Part I.
49. For a more detailed discussion of types of public interest conceptions, to which my own analysis is heavily indebted, see Banfield (1955), pp. 322–330. Banfield distinguishes between the communalist public interest, involving ends which community members share as community members, and the individualistic public interest, involving ends which community members share as individuals (pp. 323–324). Since both conceptions require consensus, I have lumped them here, although people's interests as community members may conflict with those they hold as individuals.
50. Even looting can be interpreted justifiably as a method of economic intervention, to make up for the lack of equitable income distribution and responsiveness in the economic system.

Chapter Fifteen

LEVITTOWN AND AMERICA

I BEGAN THIS STUDY WITH FOUR QUESTIONS, THE ANSWERS TO WHICH can be generalized to new towns and suburbs all over America. *First,* a new community is shaped neither by the builder, the planner, and the organizational founder, nor by the aspirations with which residents come. A builder creates the physical shell of the community; a founder, the social one; but even when organizations and institutions are initiated by national bodies outside the community, they can only survive by attracting people and responding to their demands. If residents lack choice among churches or clubs, individual founders can impose their will or their vision of the community on the residents, but such lack of choice is rare. Aspirations of residents are usually limited to the house, family life, neighboring, and friendship; people have few that concern the larger community and the demands they make on it emerge after they have settled down. Only when they have lived on their blocks for a while can they decide what functions must be filled by the rest of the community, and only when they have met their fellow residents can they determine where compatible people are to be found and how they want to sort themselves. In short, their choices of (and within) community institutions are basically a function of the population mix they encounter.

These choices are not made in a vacuum, but involve values and preferences which people bring with them. Perhaps the most significant fact about the origin of a new community is that it is not new at all, but only a new physical site on which people develop conventional institutions with traditional programs. New towns are ultimately old communities on new land, culturally not significantly different from suburban subdivisions and urban neighborhoods inhabited by the same kinds of people, and politically much like other small American towns.

Second, most new suburbanites are pleased with the community that develops; they enjoy the house and outdoor living and take pleasure from the large supply of compatible people, without experiencing the boredom or malaise ascribed to suburban homogeneity. Some people encounter unexpected social isolation, particularly those who differ from the majority of their neighbors. Who will be socially isolated depends on the community; in Levittown, they were older couples, the well educated and the poorly educated, and women who had come from a cohesive working class or ethnic enclave or were used to living with an extended family. Such people probably suffer in every suburb; even though they want to escape from the close life of the "urban village," they miss their old haunts, cannot find compatible people, or do not know how to make new friends. But the least happy people are always those of lowest income and least education; they not only have the most difficulty in making social contacts and joining groups, but are also beset by financial problems which strain family tempers as well as family budgets. And if the suburb is designed for young adults and children, the adolescents will suffer from "nothing to do" and from adult hostility toward their youth culture and peer groups.

People's lives are changed somewhat by the move to suburbia, but their basic ways remain the same; they do not develop new life styles or ambitions for themselves and their children. Moreover, many of the changes that do take place were desired before the move. Because the suburb makes them possible, morale goes up, boredom and loneliness are reduced, family life becomes temporarily more cohesive, social and organizational activities multiply, and spare-time pursuits now concentrate on the house and yard. Some changes result from the move: community organizational needs encourage some people to become joiners for the first time, ethnic and religious difference demands more synagogue attendance, and social isolation breeds depression, boredom, and loneliness for the few who are left out. But change is not unidirectional; different people respond differently to the new environment, and the most undesirable changes usually stem from familial and occupational circumstances.

Third, the sources or causes of change are not to be found in suburbia per se, but in the new house, the opportunity for home ownership, and above all, the population mix—the people with whom one now lives. They bring about the intended increase in social life, the unintended increase in organizational activity, and, of course, the equally unintended social isolation. Some changes can be traced to the openness of the social structure in a new community and people's willingness to accept and trust each other, as well as to the random settling pattern which requires them to make friends with strangers next door or to leave the block for the larger community to find compatible people. But most result from the homogeneity of age and class of the population that buys into a new suburb. Indeed, the basic sources of change come from goals for home ownership, a free-standing house, outdoor living, and being with people of similar age and class, which have long been basic aspirations of American working and middle class cultures.[1] Even unintended changes could be traced finally to national economic trends and cultural patterns that push people out of the city and provide incentives for builders to construct communities like Levittown. Ultimately, then, the changes people undergo in the move to the suburbs are only expressions of more widespread societal changes and national cultural goals.

Fourth, the politics of a new suburb is no more distinctive than the rest of its life. In any heterogeneous community, conflicting demands from the voters force the decision-makers to set up a performing government which observes democratic norms, freeing them to reconcile these conflicts in a backstage actual government. Their decisions are, more often than not, responsive to the majority of voters when that majority makes demands, but are unresponsive to powerless minorities, which therefore have to intervene—to upset the normal decision-making process in order to get satisfaction. Since they fail more often than they succeed, local government generally neglects minority demands and rights, and the public interest as well. Experts with sufficient consensus, skill, and power can implement decisions unpopular with the majority, but on the whole, such decisions have to be enforced by nonlocal agencies. Of course, suburbs like Levittown have few of the problems that face American cities, dying small towns, or stagnant rural areas, so that local governments can meet the limited needs of at least their dominant constituents. Supra-local governments must be developed, however, to deal with the problems generated by the myriad of suburban sovereignties and the artificiality of suburban boundaries.

THE POTENTIAL FOR INNOVATION AND CHANGE

My four initial questions were joined by a common theme: To what extent is a community made by its residents and to what extent by leaders, planners, and other experts who want to stimulate innovation and change? The findings, I would suggest, demonstrate again an important sociological truth and truism, that what happens in a community is almost always a reflection of the people who live in it, especially the numerical and cultural majority. That majority supports the organizations and institutions that define the community; it determines who will be enjoying life and who will be socially isolated; and it forms the constituencies to which decision-makers are responsive. In the last analysis, then, the community (and it origin, impact, and politics) are an outcome of the population mix, particularly of its dominant elements and their social structure and culture.

The processes by which this community outcome is achieved are conflict-ridden. A modern community is not like a folk culture, in which congruence between the community and its population is achieved by a widespread consensus about behavior and values. In Levittown, the congruence is much less perfect, and is produced by power struggles, which are constantly resolved by compromises so that institutions and organizations can function in an orderly manner. These struggles are unending, for every compromise solves only the immediate conflict, and new issues arise all the time. Whether the compromisers are parents, organizational leaders, or elected officials, they spend a great deal of time and energy in averting what they define as crises, and preserving the fragile equilibrium by which congruence between community and society is engineered. As a result, all other issues are pushed into the background, including innovation and change. And when decision-makers cannot satisfy everybody, there is rarely time or energy for any but the most numerous, powerful, or vocal constituents.

Under these conditions, founders, innovators, and individual "change agents," expert or otherwise, can do little. They may suggest new ideas, but before these are implemented, they have been altered to make them responsive to important constituencies. Without initiators, nothing can begin, but once the initiative has been taken, the social process transforms it. People who can initiate successfully and anticipate the required transformations are made leaders and often get credit for the workings of the social process—and those who want to be leaders learn quickly what will be successful. Only rarely is such a role awarded to innovators.

These findings could easily be used to justify the status quo, but that is not my conclusion or my purpose. The study suggests that change and innovation are always possible, but not easily achieved. No group or community is impervious to change, but neither is it an aggregate of open-minded people who do not know what they want and can be persuaded to shed their past. Consequently, advocates of innovation and change cannot be satisfied (as they so often are) with appealing for something new or by demanding conformity to their ideas (as they so often do) because they are convinced of the superiority of what they propose. Groups and communities are fluid systems, with leaders who have some—but precious little—leeway in their decisions. If that leeway is to be used for innovation, change agents who lack the power to insist on change or the resources with which to reward people for undertaking it must offer distinctly superior alternatives to present arrangements. No community and no social arrangement satisfies everyone, and as the data on Levittown make persuasively evident, even when most people are happy with their new community, some are not. The best approach to change, therefore, is to give up the single solution that compromises between the wants of different groups, and to experiment with new solutions for dissatisfied groups and cultures in the total population. This means a diversity of housing, living arrangements, and institutions, either within the same community or in separate ones, keyed to the diversity of background, culture, and aspirations relevant to community life.

Conflict, Pluralism, and Community

Although a part of my study was concerned with the possibilities of change and innovation, I do not mean to suggest that Levittown is badly in need of either. The community may displease the professional city planner and the intellectual defender of cosmopolitan culture, but perhaps more than any other type of community, Levittown permits most of its residents to be what they want to be—to center their lives around the home and the family, to be among neighbors whom they can trust, to find friends to share leisure hours, and to participate in organizations that provide sociability and the opportunity to be of service to others.

That Levittown has its faults and problems is undeniable, and I have described them in previous chapters: physical and social isolation, familial and governmental financial problems, insufficient public transportation, less than perfect provision of public services, inadequate decision-making and feedback processes, lack of representation for minorities and overrepresentation for the builder, and the entire array of familial and individual problems common to any population. Many of them can be traced back to three basic shortcomings, none distinctive to Levittown or the Levittowners.

One is the difficulty of coping with conflict. Like the rest of the country, Levittown is beset with conflict: class conflict between the lower middle class group and the smaller working and upper middle class groups; generational conflict between adults, children, adolescents, and the elderly. The existence of conflict is no drawback, but the way conflict is handled leaves much to be desired. Levittowners, like other Americans, do not really accept the inevitability of conflict. Insisting that a consensus is possible, they only exacerbate the conflict, for each group demands that the other conform to its values and accept its priorities. When power is a valuable prize and resources are scarce, such a perspective is understandable, but in Levittown the exercise of power is not an end in itself for most people; they want it mainly to control the allocation of resources. Since resources are not so scarce, however, the classes and age groups could resolve their conflicts more constructively than they do, giving each group at least some of what it wants. If the inevitability of conflicting interests were accepted, differences might be less threatening, and this would make it easier to reach the needed compromises. I am not sanguine that this will happen, for if people think resources are scarce, they act as if they are scarce, and will not pay an extra $20 a year in taxes to implement minority demands. Even so, conditions to make viable compromises happen are more favorable in Levittown than in larger or poorer communities.

The second shortcoming, closely related to the first, is the inability to deal with pluralism. People have not recognized the diversity of American society, and they are not able to accept other life styles. Indeed, they cannot handle conflict because they cannot accept pluralism. Adults are unwilling to tolerate adolescent culture, and vice versa. Lower middle class people oppose the ways of the working class and upper middle class, and each of these groups is hostile to the other two. Perhaps the inability to cope with pluralism is greater in Levittown than elsewhere because it is a community of young families who are raising children. Children are essentially asocial and unacculturated beings, easily influenced by new ideas. As a result, their parents feel an intense need to defend familial values; to make sure that their children grow up according to parental norms and not by those of their playmates from another class. The need to shield the children from what are considered harmful influences begins on the block, but it is translated into the conflict over the school, the definitional struggles within the voluntary associations whose programs affect the socialization of children, and, ultimately, into political conflicts. Each group wants to put its cultural stamp on the organizations and institutions that are the community, for otherwise the family and its culture are not safe. In a society in which extended families are unimportant and the nuclear family cannot provide the full panoply of personnel and activities to hold children in the family culture, parents must use community institutions for this purpose, and every portion of the community therefore becomes a battleground for the defense of familial values.

This thesis must not be exaggerated, for much of the conflict is, as it has always been, between the haves and the have-nots. Even if Levittown's median income is considerably above the national average even for white families, no one feels affluent enough to let other people determine how their own income should be spent. Most of the political conflict in the community rages over how much of the family income should be given over to the community, and then, how it should be used. In fact, consensus about municipal policies and expenditures exists only about the house. Because many Levittowners are first-time homeowners, they are especially eager to protect that home against loss of value, both as property and as status image. But every class has its own status image and its own status fears. Working class people do not want to be joined by lower class neighbors or to be forced to adopt middle class styles. Lower middle class people do not want more working class neighbors or to be forced to adopt cosmopolitan styles, and upper middle class people want neither group to dominate them. These fears are not, as commonly thought, attributes of status-seeking, for few Levittowners are seeking higher status; they are fears about self-image. When people reject pluralism, they do so because accepting the viability of other ways of living suggests that their own is not as absolute as they need to believe. The outcome is the constant search for compatible people and the rejection of those who are different.

When the three class groups—not to mention their subgroupings and yet other groups with different values—must live together and share a common government, every group tries to make sure that the institutions and facilities which serve the entire community maintain its own status and culture, and no one is happy when another group wins. If working class groups can persuade the Township Committee to allocate funds for a firehouse, middle class groups unite in a temporary coalition to guarantee that a library is also established. When the upper middle class group attempts to influence school policy to shape education to its standard, lower middle class residents raise the specter of Levittown aping Brookline and Scarsdale, while working class people become fearful that the schools will neglect discipline or that taxes will rise further. Consequently, each group seeks power to prevent others from shaping the institutions that must be shared. They do not seek power as an end in itself, but only to guarantee that their priorities will be met by the community. Similarly, they do not demand lower taxes simply for economic reasons (except for those few really hard pressed) but in order to be sure that community institutions are responsive to their familial values and status needs. Obviously, power sought for these ends is hard to share, and decisions for levying and allocating public funds are difficult to compromise.

The third shortcoming of the community, then, is the failure to establish a meaningful relationship between home and community and to reconcile class-cultural diversity with government and the provision of public services. Levittowners, like other Americans, not only see government as a parasite and public services as a useless expenditure of funds better spent privately, but they do not allow government to adapt these services to the diversity among the residents. Government is committed to the establishment of a single (and limited) set of public services, and its freedom to do otherwise is restricted by legislation and, of course, by American tradition. Government has always been a minor supplier of services basic to everyday life, and an enemy whose encroachment on private life must be resisted. The primary source of this conception is the historic American prejudice against public services, which stems in part from the rural tradition of the individual and his family as a self-sufficient unit, but which is perpetuated by contemporary cultural values, and made possible by the affluence which enables at least middle class families to live with only minimal dependence on local government. The bias against public services does not interfere with their use, however, but only with their financing, and their extension and proliferation. Nor does it lead Levittowners to reject government outright, but only to channel it into a few limited functions. Among these, the primary one is the protection of the home against diversity.

Government thus becomes a defense agency, to be taken over by one group to defend itself against others in and out of the community. The idea that it could have positive functions, such as the provision of facilities to make life richer and more comfortable, is resisted, for every new governmental function is seen first as an attempt by one community group to increase its dominance over others. Of course, these attempts are rarely manifest, for the political dialogue deals mainly with substantive matters, but when Levittowners spoke against a proposal, they were reacting principally against those who proposed it rather than against its substance.

Until government can tailor its actions to the community's diversity, and until people can accept the inevitability of conflict and pluralism in order to give government that responsibility, they will prefer to spend their money for privately and commercially supplied services. Unlike city hall, the marketplace is sensitive to diversities among the customers and does not require them to engage in political conflict to get what they want. Of course, not all people can choose the marketplace over city hall, but Levittowners are affluent enough to do so. Moreover, until parents have steered their children safely into their own class and culture—or have given up trying—they are likely to seek out relatively homogeneous communities and small ones, so that they have some control over government's inroads against personal and familial autonomy. This not only maintains the sovereignty of hundreds of small local governments but also contributes to the desire to own a house and a free-standing one.

LEVITTOWN AS AMERICA

The strengths and weaknesses of Levittown are those of many American communities, and the Levittowners closely resemble other young middle class Americans. They are not America, for they are not a numerical majority in the population, but they represent the major constituency of the largest and most powerful economic and political institutions in American society—the favored customers and voters whom these seek to attract and satisfy. Upper middle class Americans may spend more per capita and join more groups, but they are fewer in number than the lower middle classes. Working and lower class people are more numerous but they have less money and power; and people over forty, who still outnumber young adults, are already committed to most of the goods, affiliations, and ideas they will need in their lifetime.

Even so, Levittowners are not really members of the national society, or for that matter, of a mass society. They are not apathetic conformists ripe for takeover by a totalitarian elite or corporate merchandiser; they are not conspicuous consumers and slaves to sudden whims of cultural and political fashion; they are not even organization men or particularly other-directed personalities. Clearly inner-directed strivers are a minority in Levittown, and tradition-directed people would not think of moving to a new community of strangers, but most people maintain a balance between inner personal goals and the social adjustment necessary to live with neighbors and friends that, I suspect, is prevalent all over lower middle class America. Indeed, the inability to empathize with diversity would suggest that inner-direction may still be a much stronger pattern among the Levittowners than it was among the upper middle class people studied by Riesman and his associates.[2] Although ethnic, religious, and regional differences are eroding, the never ending conflicts over other differences are good evidence that Levittowners are far from becoming mass men.

Although they are citizens of a national polity and their lives are shaped by national economic, social, and political forces,

Levittowners deceive themselves into thinking that the community, or rather the home, is the single most influential unit in their lives. Of course, in one way they are right; it is the place where they can be most influential, for if they cannot persuade the decision-makers, they *can* influence family members. Home is also the site of maximal freedom, for within its walls people can do what they want more easily than anywhere else. But because they are free and influential *only* at home, their dependence on the national society ought to be obvious to them. This not being the case, the real problem is that Levittowners have not yet become aware of how much they are a part of the national society and economy.

In viewing their homes as the center of life, Levittowners are still using a societal model that fit the rural America of self-sufficient farmers and the feudal Europe of self-isolating extended families. Yet the critics who argue about the individual versus mass society are also anachronistic; they are still thinking of the individual artist or intellectual who must shield himself from a society which either rejects him or coopts him to produce popular culture. Both Levittowners and critics have to learn that they live in a national society characterized by pluralism and bureaucracy, and that the basic conflict is not between individual (or family) and society, but between the classes (and other interest groups) who live together in a bureaucratized political and cultural democracy. The prime challenge is how to live with bureaucracy; how to use it rather than be used by it; how to obtain individual freedom and social resources from it through political action.

Yet even though Levittowners and other lower middle class Americans continue to be home-centered, they are much more "in the world" than their parents and grandparents were. Those coming out of ethnic working class backgrounds have rejected the "amoral familism" [3] which pits every family against every other in the struggle to survive and the ethnocentrism which made other cultures and even other neighborhoods bitter enemies. This generation trusts its neighbors, participates with them in social and civic activities, and no longer sees government as inevitably corrupt. Even working class Levittowners have begun to give up the suspicion that isolated their ancestors from all but family and childhood friends. Similarly, the descendants of rural

Protestant America have given up the xenophobia that turned previous generations against the Catholic and Jewish immigrants, they have almost forgotten the intolerant Puritanism which triggered attacks against pleasure and enjoyment, and they no longer fully accept the doctrine of laissez faire that justifies the defense of all individual rights and privileges against others' needs.

These and other changes have come about not because people are now better or more tolerant human beings, but because they are affluent. For the Levittowners, life is not a fight for survival any more; they have been able to move into a community in which income and status are equitably enough distributed so that neighbors are no longer treated as enemies, even if they are still criticized for social and cultural deviance. By any yardstick one chooses, Levittowners treat their fellow residents more ethically and more democratically than did their parents and grandparents.[4] They also live a "fuller" and "richer" life. Their culture may be less subtle and sophisticated than that of the intellectual, their family life less healthy than that advocated by psychiatrists, and their politics less thoughtful and democratic than the political philosophers'—yet all of these are superior to what prevailed among the working and lower middle classes of past generations.

But beyond these changes, it is striking how little American culture among the Levittowners differs from what De Toqueville reported in his travels through small-town middle class America a century ago. Of course, he was here before the economy needed an industrial proletariat, but the equality of men and women, the power of the child over his parents, the importance of the voluntary association, the social functions of the church, and the rejection of high culture seem to be holdovers from his time, and so is the adherence to the traditional virtues: individual honesty, thrift, religiously inspired morality, Franklinesque individualism, and Victorian prudery. Some Levittowners have retained the values of rural ancestors; some have only begun to practice them as affluence enabled them to give up the values of a survival-centered culture. Still other eternal verities remain; class conflict is as alive as ever, even if the struggle is milder and the have-nots in Levittown have much more than the truly poor. Working class culture continues to flourish, even though its rough edges are wearing smooth and its extended family and public institutions are not brought to the suburbs. Affluence and better education have made a difference, but they have not made the factory worker middle class, any more than college attendance has made lower middle class people cosmopolitan.

What seems to have happened is that improvements and innovations are added to old culture patterns, giving affluent Americans a foot in several worlds. They have more knowledge and a broader outlook than their ancestors, and they enjoy the advantages of technology, but these are superimposed on old ways. While conservative critics rail about technology's dehumanization of modern man, the Levittowners who spend their days programming computers come home at night to practice the very homely and old-fashioned virtues these critics defend.[5] For example, they have television sets, but they watch much the same popular comedies and melodramas their ancestors saw on the nineteenth century stage. The melodramas are less crude and vaudeville is more respectable; the girls dance with covered bosoms, but Ed Sullivan's program is pure vaudeville and "the Jackie Gleason Show" even retains traces of the working class music hall. The overlay of old and new is not all good, of course; the new technology has created methods of war and destruction which the old insularity allows Americans to unleash without much shame or guilt, and some Levittowners may find work less satisfying than their ancestors. But only some, for the majority's parents slaved in exhausting jobs which made them too tired to enjoy the advantages of suburbia even if they could have afforded them. On the whole, however, the Levittowners have only benefitted from the changes in society and economy that have occurred in this century, and if they were not given to outdated models of social reality, they might feel freer about extending these benefits to less fortunate sectors of American society. But whether people's models are anachronistic or avant-garde, they are rarely willing to surrender their own powers and privileges to others.

LEVITTOWN AND THE FUTURE OF SUBURBIA

Presently available data make it certain that another suburban housing boom will take place during the next ten years. As the children born during the period of high family formation and fertility after World War II become parents, they will need housing to raise their own children, and will almost surely want to find it in the suburbs.[6] Unless a sharp economic downturn reduces middle class employment opportunities and either slows down the rate of family formation or forces young families to double up with their parents, yet another ring of suburban communities will spring up around most American cities.

The form the newest suburbia will take is as yet unknown. In most metropolitan areas, the current building of subdivisions, one by one, will probably continue. Where land for suburban development is running short, the single-family house may give way to the row house; where land is plentiful (as in the West) more comprehensively planned new towns with their own sources of employment are possible.[7] In big cities like New York and Chicago, where the remaining vacant land is more than forty miles from downtown, future suburban growth may be reduced by the unwillingness of commuters to travel over an hour each way, although this may in turn generate more support for high-speed mass transit. But the present trend of industrial decentralization is likely to increase as well, so that more job opportunities will be available in the suburbs themselves, bringing yet more vacant land into the range of an acceptable journey to work. And if the decentralization of industry is accompanied by the decentralization of offices, nothing should impede further suburbanization in all American cities.

This likelihood is already being viewed with alarm in some quarters. Advocates of the city are fearful that further suburban development can only result in added physical, financial, cultural, and political deterioration of the cities. They are joined by opponents of urban sprawl and by conservationists who are afraid that new suburbanization will further reduce rural acreages and may even cut into the forests and wildernesses that now provide recreational opportunities and land reserves at the edges of many metropolitan areas. In this coalition can also be found the critics of suburbia, concerned that an undesirable way of life will proliferate even further in the next generation.

Some of these fears may be reasonable, but none justify halting suburbanization. The inaccuracy of the suburban critique indicates that if the suburbs have positive consequences for the present generation of young parents, they will have similar ones for the next generation. Although suburbanization may further increase residential segregation by class and race, class segregation may be reduced as class lines within the middle class and between the lower middle and working class are blurred. And if future suburbanization takes the form of new towns and large subdivisions, these will be (like Levittown) more heterogeneous than small subdivisions and urban neighborhoods—which have often been one-class and one-race areas.

The fear of more urban sprawl also seems exaggerated. Urban sprawl is an inefficient use of land rather than the absolute evil it has been labeled, but it also promotes flexibility of growth.[8] If employment opportunities continue to decentralize, the wasteful features of urban sprawl may be reduced, partly because vacant areas will be filled in, but mostly because new suburban centers with industry and offices as well as shopping centers will develop all over the metropolitan area.[9] Indeed, in the future, the present mononuclear metropolis, with a downtown center surrounded by a disordered mass of urban and suburban areas of low density, is likely to become a multinuclear one with many centers, of which downtown is only the oldest and most important.

Probably the major disadvantage of urban sprawl is the proliferation of small local government.[10] Although it provides people with considerable control over their own destinies, it discourages public action on the many metropolitan-wide problems. A logical case can be made for some form of metropolitan government, and the case has been made logically since the beginning of the twentieth century. Unfortunately, its advocates often see only the advantages for the larger area, but ignore the very real disadvantages for local communities. These have opposed metropolitan government in the past as a trespass on local autonomy, and for fear of domination by predominantly white Catholic or non-white working class urban voters. (On the other hand, as suburbanization continues, city residents may begin to oppose it for fear of domination by white middle class suburbanites.) If the elements of metropolitan government can be separated into those badly needed and universally wanted, those which only increase governmental efficiency and economy at the cost of local autonomy, and those which are made unworkable by intense class and race conflicts, it may be possible to promote the first. Federal subsidies, now already beginning to flow, may make it worthwhile for suburbs to band together with other suburbs and with the city on selected problems and public services. But further suburbanization would not affect the chances of metropolitan government. The suburbs of the next decade and generation may strengthen existing small communities, but they will not add many new ones to the welter of local government. They will not cut down governmental sprawl, but neither will they increase it.

The reduction in open space is even less serious. Despite the uproar over "megalopolis," there is an immense amount of vacant land even within that alleged belt of city running from Boston to Norfolk. Most of America is less densely settled than the Eastern seaboard, and as Hans Blumenfeld once pointed out, the country is so rich in land that all Americans could be housed at suburban densities in the buildable parts of California. The disappearance of farmland near the big cities is irrelevant now that food is produced on huge industrialized farms, and the destruction of raw land and private upper class golf courses seems a small price to pay for extending the benefits of suburban life to more people.

More recreational acreage will be needed with increasing leisure time, but principally as small parks in the dense portions of the city and as larger ones for weekend and vacation trips. The latter can be located at the edge of the metropolitan area, where they can be made accessible by expressways and mass transit. Moreover, parks are much less important than beaches, lakes, amusement areas, camping sites, and motels with adjacent recreation facilities. Wildernesses provide a desirable recreation resource, but they are used by relatively few people per acre. Making inexpensive and efficient transportation available to distant wildernesses would be more sensible than preventing many people from living in the suburbs in order to retain a wilderness nearby in which a handful can seek solitude a few times a year.

Actually, the conservationist opposition to further suburbanization rests less on the need for recreational land than on a desire to reserve vacant land for future generations, and this in turn is based less on accurate predictions of actual land needs than on a value judgment that the preservation of open land is more important than the current needs of people. Although land should be saved for requirements of ecological balance and for the use of future generations if current needs are not urgent, I believe that restricting current development for an unpredictable future is undesirable. We do not know today how Americans will want to live fifty years from now, or where. By then work and play patterns may have changed so much that many people will want to live a hundred miles or more beyond the city limits. Transportation methods may be available to bring a wilderness five hundred miles away within easy and cheap reach of every metropolitan area resident, and economic and technological devices for rapid land-use changes may have been created. Consequently, ignoring the present demand for land in order to save it for an unknown future demand by our grandchildren cannot easily be justified.

For this reason, I suspect that conservationist opponents of suburbanization are less concerned with future land needs than with a desire to preserve land from people. Many—although not all—of the advocates of wilderness preservation are ideological descendants of the nineteenth century conservatives who opposed European immigration because they did not want America to become a country of non-Puritan city dwellers. In preserving open land, they also wanted to preserve America as a predominantly rural, predominantly Protestant society in which they held political and cultural power. The idea that America ought to be a country of open spaces rather than one of people deriving maximum utility and pleasure from the land still exists today and is manifested by opposition to proposals that virgin lands (note the phrase) be opened up for intensive recreational use. Opponents fear that the land will be "spoiled" by unappreciative (read urban middle and working class) populations. They choose to bar people instead of demanding sufficient funds to remove the garbage left behind by people who have engaged in the very "constructive and wholesome" recreational pursuits that wilderness advocates also favor.

The final source of opposition to further suburbanization comes from the defenders of the city. As the white middle class continues to leave the cities, these become more and more the residence of a small number of rich people—at least in the biggest metropoli—and of a large number of poor people, many of them nonwhite. This trend is alleged to destroy cities as centers of civilization, on the assumption that culture can be created only in the city. Cities were centers of culture in the past, not because they were cities, but because they housed the upper-income populations who supported the creators of culture. The current flourishing of culture in many American cities denies the traditional assumption, for while its supporters have been living in the suburbs for more than two generations, they have not only returned to the city to use its cultural facilities, but have also generated suburban facilities, a trend that will increase more rapidly in the next decades. Whether or not the dominance of poor people in the cities will affect the creators of culture is harder to judge, but many who supply the middle class with culture are already living in suburbs and exurbs without loss of creativity, while new urban (but not middle class) culture is coming into being for the ever larger pool of poor people.

As more middle class taxpayers move beyond the city limits, they will reduce the tax income of the city even as a further influx of poor people increases the need for costly municipal services. The next round of suburbanization should not worsen the situation, however, for many of the young people who will want suburban houses in the coming years are already in the suburbs. Even so, it is obvious that urban governments are in poor economic health and that something has to be done. The solution is not, however, to attempt to reverse a residential process that is not really reversible, but to find new sources of income for the cities. Recent federal legislation has established the principle that cities must be subsidized by federal funds, and some cities are already levying payroll taxes that require suburban commuters to pay for their use of city services and income taxes that counteract the decline of receipts from the property tax. The best solution, however, is probably a single federal income tax, a portion of which would be distributed to the taxpayer's community. This would not only eliminate the need to raise property tax rates as property values decline, but would also result in higher tax levies, for there is less public opposition to federal income taxes, and tax receipts go up with increasing incomes.

The political feasibility of this solution is not enhanced by further suburbanization, however, for as more and more white middle class people move to the suburbs they will be extremely reluctant to support legislation to subsidize the urban nonwhite poor. This possibility is frightening, but it cannot be dealt with by attempting to prevent further suburbanization. If the next generation of young families wants to live in the suburbs and can afford to do so, it will vote down any programs that restrict its freedom of residential movement. Some young people may be persuaded to remain in or return to the city by urban renewal programs, but their numbers are not likely to be large, for even with increasing college attendance, the proportion of city-loving cosmopolitans remains minute. The only solution I can see is to permit further suburbanization, but in ways which prevent further economic deterioration of the city. Payroll and income taxes are one answer, but federal subsidies to the city, sweetened by grants for services wanted by suburbs and commuters, may be able to obtain the "suburban vote."

All of these problems are immensely complicated by the racial difference between city and suburban residents, by the persistent increase in the proportion of nonwhite residents in the city and the equally persistent ability of the suburbs to maintain racial exclusion practices. If suburbanization continues on the present basis, an increasingly nonwhite city surrounded by rings of white suburbs may make efforts to solve the problems of the city even more difficult than they are today. Even so, one little-recognized obstacle to the solution of these problems is the very image of the predominantly nonwhite city—as a bankrupt, disintegrating, violent and corrupt municipality. This image is a fantasy, a reflection of white middle class fears, felt most strongly by white suburbanites who will have to commute to the stores, offices, and cultural facilities of the city. In reality, such a city will not be chaotic, and for nonwhite residents, it may well be more desirable than today's nominally integrated city.

Although there are many Negroes, middle class or with middle class aspirations, who want to live in an integrated suburb, there are many more, not yet middle class, who would favor further white suburbanization because they would be able to leave the slums for better urban neighborhoods deserted by the whites. Moreover, if they became a political majority in the city, they might be able to elect officials more sensitive to *their* needs for public services and *their* priorities for the allocation of public funds than the present white incumbents are. A predominantly nonwhite city would be even poorer than today's city, but Negroes are voters, and if they can only give up their habitual allegiance to the urban Democratic machines and threaten to bolt the national Democratic party, whichever party is in power in Washington will be motivated to increase federal subsidies to the city. If they can also persuade Washington to develop effective antipoverty programs that will create better jobs and higher incomes, they will be able to achieve a higher standard of living and will be less angry and hostile toward middle class whites than they are today. Since white anxieties about the predominantly nonwhite city are ultimately based on class rather than race, these anxieties would be reduced considerably. Indeed, those suburbanites who prefer the city but shun it now because they do not want poor neighbors may return to take advantage of its urbanity.

Opponents of further white exodus also argue—as they have for generations—that it means a loss of "civic leaders" to the city and less concern for the city on the part of upper income people with downtown property holdings. From the point of view of the remaining white middle class residents, this loss is real, since the civic leaders represent some of their interests in the city power structure. The low-income population may see it otherwise, however, for control of public welfare and private charity by these civic leaders has only helped to keep it a proletarian underclass. And whether the owners and managers of downtown real estate would act differently if they lived in the city has yet to be shown. Most likely, their behavior is determined by profit potential and property tax rates.

The possibility that a city governed by the leaders of the non-white poor population may have advantages for that population does not, however, reduce the urgency of the need to integrate the suburbs. Not only will the number of nonwhites who want to live in the suburbs and in integrated communities on either side of the city limits increase in the years to come, but the continuing exodus of job opportunities into the suburbs makes it essential for nonwhite workers to be able to live near these sources of work. Consequently, present and future suburbs *have to be* opened to nonwhite residents. Indeed, the goal is not to hold back further suburban development, but to make sure that its benefits are extended to all parts of the population, regardless of color and class.

The implementation of racial integration in the suburbs is almost as difficult as the restriction of future suburban growth. Although Levittown accepted the peaceful integration of a handful of Negro middle class families once state law had made it mandatory, I doubt whether it or any other suburb would voluntarily open its doors to larger numbers of nonwhite people, especially those of lower income and status. The only solution is federal action. When it becomes politically feasible for the federal government to require "open housing," either through legislation or executive order, not only will the legal imperative persuade many suburbanites to accept the inevitable, but if all communities must integrate, no one can expect to live in all-white communities.

But legal integration is not sufficient, for only a small proportion of the total nonwhite urban population can afford to live in the suburbs. Consequently, the federal government must also mount a massive housing program, combining rent subsidies, builder subsidies, and perhaps even direct federal construction to enable nonwhite city dwellers to move to the suburbs.[11] A similar program should enable others to move to better urban neighborhoods and yet others to new and rehabilitated housing in the ghetto. Many liberals have debated long and earnestly whether new, or rebuilt, housing should be provided in the ghetto as long as white opposition makes integrated housing impossible, *or* whether new housing should be built only outside the ghetto and even outside the city to prevent the perpetuation of segregation, even if this means less new housing for Negroes in the short run. But this dichotomy is false and dangerous. Residential integration is a highly worthwhile goal, but it is not the only goal, particularly since so far it has helped mainly middle class Negroes and has often decreased available inexpensive housing for poorer Negroes, for example, when urban renewal displaces them to make room for integrated middle and high income projects. Moreover, not all Negroes want to move to the suburbs today; some want to stay in the city, and some even in the ghetto, although unfortunately no one knows what proportion of the ghetto population wants (or can afford) each of the three alternatives. There is no reason why better housing cannot be built in the ghetto and the suburbs integrated concurrently.

The process of integration (suburban and urban) would have to be planned and paced to avert white panic over racial invasion and status decline. Levittown's successful integration is evidence that such planning is possible. Since the first nonwhite suburbanites will undoubtedly be middle class or aspiring middle class people, and since the kind of lower class Negro whom suburbanites fear would probably be neither willing nor able to move to the suburbs for another generation, the real difficulties of integration are much smaller than the imagined ones. It seems hard to believe that the lower class Negro family without job security or the unmarried mother would have much incentive to move to the suburbs even with federal housing subsidies; both want to leave the slums, but for better housing in the city.[12]

The costs of federal programs to improve living conditions and public services in cities (and suburbs) will be high, and they have to be paid with public funds. Some of these funds ought to come from suburbanization itself, and specifically from the huge increases in land values that accompany residential development. In the past, the federal government has supported suburban growth through FHA and VA mortgage insurance, tax writedowns to builders, and the construction of expressways, but neither it nor local and state governments have obtained their share of the increase in land values or of the speculative profits created as rural land became suburban. High speculative profits are often justified by the amount of risk in residential development, but these risks have been reduced to near-nothing in the past two decades. Since the new suburban boom is virtually a certainty, and since it can only take place in a relatively small number of locations in most metropolitan areas, risks will be even smaller in the future, especially if rent subsidy programs are added to the present array of mortgage insurance and other forms of risk reduction for developers and builders. Consequently, governments should be participating in the "profits" that come from land turnover and suburban building. Indeed, it would be desirable to work out a formula by which taxes on land use change increase as risk is decreased; and these taxes ought to help pay for governmental subsidies.

The Suburban Community of the Future

Although a number of changes should be made in the next round of suburbanization, I can see no reason to oppose its occurrence or to discourage the building of more Levittowns. Whether or not the Levitt organization will or should build more Levittowns is not the issue; I would argue, rather, that more communities like Levittown are desirable if people want them. Not only are they more efficient than a myriad of smaller subdivisions, but they permit the builder to install community facilities because of the economics resulting from the scale of his operation.

Of course, future new communities should learn from and improve upon Levittown. For instance, prior planning should occur, particularly to anticipate tax problems, and more physical facilities should be installed before the community is occupied. Not only should builders be expected to include some of the capital and operating costs of these facilities in the house price, but federal, state, and local housing agencies should subsidize those facilities which cannot be provided by the builder without a drastic increase in the house price. Federal or state planning powers and subsidies should also encourage the coordination of residential construction with industrial location, to encourage factories and offices that can share the tax burden. Even so, most new suburbs will be without industry, and federal aid to schools and other municipal services will probably be needed to provide those rejected by local voters. Here too, financing local services from a diverted federal income tax would be helpful.

The suburban facilities which ought to be subsidized first are those needed or demanded by minorities but not likely to be provided either by the builder or by voters once the community is occupied. Among these are higher-quality schools, meaningful activities for teenagers, and more comprehensive programs of public health. Community medical health insurance programs in lieu of or in addition to federal Medicare schemes would be desirable to reduce the high cost of medical care for families with young children.[13] Community mental health clinics and agencies that will provide personal and family counseling are needed, as are community credit unions which can provide low-interest loans to people under financial pressure, and local newspapers and other media to increase both social and political communication within the community. Needless to say, better transportation (both within the community and to the outside) than was available in Levittown during the time of my study is a necessity. As the boundaries of the metropolitan area expand, all suburban communities and urban neighborhoods ought to be accessible to each other and to the downtown and suburban centers of employment, entertainment, and shopping. Finally, local and regional planning agencies which can provide benefit-cost analyses for the solution of intracommunity and intercommunity problems ought to be established.

If government took a major role in the preplanning of community facilities, the power of a single builder over the community would be reduced. The problem is to maximize his freedom to build a large-scale venture and to innovate, while supervising him sufficiently so that he will provide for community needs that purchasers cannot voice until they have moved in. For example,

Levittowners had no chance to determine the size of the schools, and while most were satisfied with what Levitt provided, they should have had some choice in the matter. Ideally, Levitt should have been required to build larger schools at the start or to include a higher portion of municipal services in the house price, with any needed increases in house price made up by federal subsidies for facilities. Or Levittowners could have decided among themselves after they moved in whether they wanted smaller classrooms, and then resorted to public controls on the builder and federal subsidies to provide them.

But perhaps the best form of control over the builder is choice. If people are told what community plans and what level of services they are buying when they purchase a house, and if they have alternative choices in different communities, then their decision to buy assumes agreement with the proposed level of services. Planning for the next round of suburban communities should reflect the increasing diversity of life styles and should ensure that many different kinds of communities are built. Some might be like today's Levittown, others might be equipped with more social and recreational facilities (like Reston, Virginia, and Columbia, Maryland), and some might have only the barest minimum of facilities for buyers who want to use the superior facilities of the city. Similarly, there ought to be new towns which provide jobs for people who want to keep their commuting to a minimum. Variations in density and house style should also be encouraged. Row house and garden apartment communities ought to be built for people who prefer to do less gardening and home maintenance, and quasi-rural communities might be constructed to allow people to do some farming in a basically suburban environment. Small communities like those suggested by Paul Goodman might be founded for people who want to participate directly in government and want to run their own school systems and municipal services. Many of these alternatives will not be politically or economically feasible, but they ought to be tried out on a small scale, perhaps in a section of an otherwise typical suburb. Government funds ought to be made available for such experiments, so that it is possible to determine which can be built on a larger scale.

But the most important priority for future suburban planning is the population mix, for ultimately it determines the quality of suburban living. In suburbia *sui generis*, the population mix must be broadened to make the opportunity for suburban living available to everyone who can and wants to come. Individual suburbs need not be balanced to parallel the metropolitan area population, but as long as local taxes pay for most municipal services, communities must be economically diverse enough to prevent the creation of low-income communities which cannot provide the array of public services their residents need more urgently than affluent people. Communities must also be planned to provide the block homogeneity and community heterogeneity I described in Chapter Eight, which allows for compatible neighbors, yet makes room for all kinds of people in the community as a whole—allowing diverse groups to live together peacefully and still have the social contacts and institutions each needs for a full life. How such communities can be achieved is the prime future challenge for professional planners. They must de-emphasize sterile physical planning questions and deal with social questions: how to program diversity so as to optimize both social compatibility and individual freedom; with economic ones; how residents and government can pay for the private and public requirements of suburban living; and with political ones: how to find ways of opening the suburbs to all comers.

It is easy to propose community improvements and even utopian communities that will make Levittown seem obsolete. Yet I should like to emphasize once more that whatever its imperfections, Levittown is a good place to live. Consequently, it is much less important to plan for new or improved suburban communities than to make sure that more people are able to live in suburbs like those now being built. Specifically, the most urgent priority is to make the benefits of suburban living available to the poor and nonwhite families, now condemned to slum ghettoes, who want to give their children and themselves a better life beyond the city limits. Building more Levittowns which are open to these families would be preferable to schemes for building more diverse suburbs, for these may require higher house prices, which would restrict suburban living to the white middle class for yet another generation. The ideal solution is more, better, and more variegated new towns and suburbs, but the first priority in the years to come is more such communities for the less affluent.

NOTES

1. There is some evidence that the desire for the single-family house is international, and even exists in countries which cannot afford to satisfy it. I found it among Swedes who must live in apartment complexes (albeit well-planned ones); it is reported in England by Orlans, pp. 106–107 and in Ghana by Tetteh, p. 25.
2. Riesman (1950).
3. The term is borrowed from Banfield (1958), p. 10.
4. Compare, for example, the picture of late nineteenth century class relationships in a small New England town. Thernstrom, Chaps. 1 and 2.
5. See, for example, Ellul.
6. If one assumes that parents become first-home buyers at about age twenty-five, the new suburban building boom can be expected to begin in earnest about 1972, twenty-five years after the start of the postwar increase in family formation and fertility.
7. For example, two sizeable new towns, Columbia, Maryland, and Reston, Virginia, are now being built near Washington, D.C. For a study of these and of the many proposed California new towns, see Eichler.
8. Lessinger, Greer (1962), Chap. 7.
9. See, e.g., Gutkind.
10. See, e.g., Banfield and Grodzins, Wood (1961), and Greer (1963).
11. For a more detailed analysis, see Gans (1965).
12. Many suburbs have their own Negro slum ghettoes, and suburban slum dwellers obviously need the same kinds of assistance as urban ones. Some can be helped to move to the better side of the suburban tracks, especially if local employers will integrate their labor force, and some may prefer to live in the cities.
13. James Rouse, the developer of Columbia, Maryland, has proposed the establishment of community health insurance that would automatically cover every purchaser and his family.

Appendix

THE METHODS OF
THE STUDY

SINCE SOCIOLOGICAL FINDINGS ARE THE RESULT OF THE RESEARCH-
er's methods, I must describe my specific methods and their shortcomings in more detail than was possible in the Introduction, in
order to give a fair picture of the reliability, validity, and limitations of the data.

THE MAIL QUESTIONNAIRE SURVEY

As I noted in the Introduction, I had to resort to a mail questionnaire in order to obtain data from the Levittowners before
they moved to their new community. The mail questionnaire ran
to four pages, and included a covering letter explaining why it
was being sent out by the builder and why it was to be returned
to the University of Pennsylvania. The letter said: "We want to
emphasize this is a University research project. The Levitt firm
sends out our questionnaire in order to protect your anonymity,
but the filled-out questionnaire comes back to us here." It was
signed by the Director of the University's Institute for Urban
Studies, since I did not want to be identified in Levittown as
being connected with the survey. Although some people thought
it was a Levitt promotion or inquiry, most accepted it at face
value.

The questionnaire bore a code number based on the lot number of the house, so that reminders could be sent to people who

had not returned theirs.[1] Although this created some suspicion that I knew people's names, I actually did not, and as it turned out, the reminders were quite effective. The original questionnaire was returned by 45 per cent of the buyers, and two reminders brought questionnaires from another 14 per cent and 7 per cent respectively, thus giving a total return rate of 66 per cent.[2] The first reminder was sent by the Levitt firm to the previous residence; the second one was sent by the Institute for Urban Studies to the occupant at his Levittown address, usually about a month after people had moved in.

Originally, I had decided to ask women to fill out the questionnaires because I felt they had more time to do so than their husbands, although they were asked to check with their husbands on questions pertaining to them. Later, the choice of who would answer was left up to the respondent, but even then, women filled it out more often than men. In the final sample of analyzed questionnaires, 60 per cent had been filled out by women, 32 per cent by men, and 8 per cent by a joint effort. If women had a different point of view about the move to Levittown, the questionnaire data undoubtedly reflect a female bias, but on important questions, I asked for both the wife's and the husband's point of view. I did not do any comparative analysis to check for female bias on other questions, but most questions asked for information rather than attitudes, and thus are not especially affected by sex differences. Moreover, because of the inherent limitations of asking people questions by mail, personal questions were reduced to the absolute minimum. Even so, only 11 per cent of the respondents refused to give their income, always the most difficult question for which to get answers.

Since I could not afford to analyze all of the 2100 returned questionnaires, I decided to draw a sample. From a comparison of some demographic data collected by the builder on all purchasers, it was apparent that, despite the high return rate, older people, blue collar workers, and the poorly educated were not adequately represented among the respondents.[3] Consequently, I decided to draw a sample based on the characteristics of the entire population rather than one based on the characteristics of only the questionnaire respondents.

Because women had answered the questionnaire more often than men, and because I felt education was a significant determinant of whether the questionnaire would be answered, I stratified the sample by women's education and by a variable that had some relation to age and income, the type of house bought in Levittown. Interviewers were sent to a 15 per cent random sample of houses in the first three neighborhoods, and data were obtained on women's years of schooling. This provided a frequency distribution of years of schooling by house type in each neighborhood. On the basis of this distribution, I then selected a sample of questionnaires to represent 30 per cent of all households in the first three neighborhoods, and obtained a set of 952 questionnaires which reflected the distribution of house types and of women's years of schooling in each of the neighborhoods. The final sample still did not represent the population exactly. It could not correct directly for age, sex, income, and men's education—or for those unknown factors that make one Levittowner with ten years of schooling return his questionnaire and another not. As a result, the findings probably still underrepresent the older and lower-income purchasers to some extent.

THE INTERVIEW STUDY

As I indicated in the Introduction, I thought that as a participant-observer I could not conduct formal interviews with people, because personal questions are answered more easily if they come from a stranger than from a resident of the community. I had enough funds to interview a 10 per cent sample of the first neighborhood (of 670 houses) and selected a random one stratified only to include the proper proportion of the three house types. Half the respondents were to be men. Of the 65 households in the sample, seven could not be found at home after five callbacks, a couple refused, and in some instances, wives had to be interviewed because the men could not be reached. Of the remaining 58 people, another 13 were lost over the two years before the reinterview. (Eight had moved, one was never home, three refused, and one had become senile.) The final sample thus consisted of 27 women and 18 men, each interviewed twice. The Philadelphia sample of 65 was also selected from the first neighborhood, to make sure that it would include only people who had lived in Levittown at least two years. It was originally random, but a high refusal rate eventually resulted in a final sample of 55, 37 of them women, 18 men.

In both samples, the refusals came primarily from men and

from older, poorer, and poorly educated purchasers. Wherever possible, the data were analyzed by sex, age, occupation, and education to determine how these affected the answers, but when I report figures for the entire sample, women, and younger, more affluent, and better-educated people are somewhat overrepresented.[4] Although this understates the extent of dissatisfaction and worries somewhat, the undersampling of men (who generally reported less dissatisfaction) overstates it, so that the two may cancel each other out. Moreover, since all respondents came from Levittown's first neighborhood, and later purchasers were of higher socioeconomic level, the class bias in the samples may thus make them more representative of Levittown as a whole.[5] Of course, the data are limited in that they apply only to the first buyers in Levittown. Although later buyers might react differently on some questions, I doubt whether time of arrival affected the amount and direction of behavior change. I analyzed some of the data to check for differences between those who had lived in Levittown two years and those who had been there for three, and found none. Moreover, an initial draft of the mail questionnaire, sent to the first 300 purchasers in the first neighborhood, had asked whether they felt themselves to be pioneers, but so few answered this question positively that it was dropped from the final version.

I did not attempt a systematic study of why so many former Philadelphians refused to be interviewed, but many of the men (who did most of the refusing) indicated they could not spare the time for the interview. The poor transportation between Levittown and Philadelphia made it difficult to find interviewers who could work evenings and weekends to contact the men, and some had trouble in obtaining interviews.

The more important questions used in the interview schedule have been included with the findings in the text. Most dealt with behavior and attitude change and typically asked people whether an activity had increased or decreased since they had come to Levittown. Since the easiest response would have been to say "no change," I left it out of the question, requiring people to volunteer it. Consequently, I believe I got a fair estimate of the change which took place, or rather, of the change people thought had taken place. The questions were carefully worded to make sure that no answer was morally or psychologically more desirable than any other, and questions about negative feelings, such as boredom, were always introduced with a sentence telling people that boredom existed and they were not alone in feeling it. Even so, some respondents undoubtedly emphasized favorable and underemphasized unfavorable change, although they were not at all reluctant to criticize Levittown or to talk about what worried them. The reinterview schedule repeated the questions asked initially, and the schedule for the ex-Philadelphians used the same questions wherever relevant. In some instances, respondents were asked to report on behavior and attitude change for their spouse as well, in the hope that this would enlarge the sample. When I analyzed these questions, however, I found that answers about husbands given by wives differed considerably from those of the men in the sample, and evidently people misperceived their spouses' feelings.

The interview findings could not be tested for statistical significance because of the size and imperfect randomness of the samples, but the consistent patterns in many answers suggest that the findings are not a result of chance and that it is possible to carry out useful quantitative analyses with small samples. Even so, the results should be considered as illustrative evidence rather than scientific proof.

THE PARTICIPANT-OBSERVATION STUDIES

My major research activities as a participant-observer included the following:

1. As a home owner and a resident, I lived in the community and used its social and physical facilities like everyone else. I could study my own residence in the community and observe that of other Levittowners.

2. As a resident of a specific block, I could both act as a neighbor and observe my own actions, and also study my neighbors in their relationship to me and to other neighbors.

3. I attended meetings of all organizations about which I knew and at which I could be present without being overly visible. I also attended almost all meetings of public agencies and many of the meetings of social, civic, political, and cultural groups. I could not attend meetings of women's clubs, and I did not attend many religious functions (except in the Jewish community), partly because of lack of time, partly because people knew I was Jewish and I felt I would be intruding in a Christian religious

service to no useful purpose. I did, however, attend at least one service in almost every church. I also attended other public gatherings, such as community ceremonies, social functions put on by organizations, high school football games, and local art shows, and even dropped in on a couple of teenage dances.

4. I conducted two types of informal interviews. I talked with people about specific events, for example, to find out the reasons for things that had happened at meetings I had observed. I also interviewed regularly a large number of informants in all major institutions and groups in the community. Like a newspaperman, I "made the rounds," checking regularly with one or more informants in the governmental agencies, the voluntary associations, churches, and political parties. I also maintained continuing contact with ministers, doctors, lawyers, and realtors, the local newspapermen, Levitt executives, store managers, residents in different parts of the community, and some of the pre-Levittown residents as well. Keeping in contact with informants and keeping abreast of events took most of my research time.

5. I visited with people socially as a resident, and since Levittown was always an important topic of conversation, I was able to collect data on these occasions.

These activities cast me in three types of research roles: *total researcher, researcher-participant,* and *total participant.*[6] As a total researcher I observed events in which I participated minimally or not at all, for example, as a silent audience member at public meetings. As a researcher-participant, I participated in an event but as a researcher rather than as a resident, for example, at most social gatherings. As a total participant, I acted spontaneously as a friend or neighbor and subsequently analyzed the activities in which I had so participated. The total participant role is the most honest one, and insofar as I was myself affected by the events in which I was participating, the most productive one for understanding a social situation. It is difficult to carry out, however, because it is almost impossible to lose consciousness of one's research role, and if one does lose it, one also becomes less observant of what is happening. Most of my data I gathered as a total researcher or researcher-participant, and only when I was involved in activities which I did not expect to produce relevant data would I relax into the total participant role.

Roles develop not only out of the participant-observer's activities, but also out of how people view him. When the researcher is very different from the people he studies, he is permanently an outsider, as I was in the Italian working class neighborhood I had studied in Boston.[7] In Levittown, however, I had bought a house like everyone else, was about the same age as most of my neighbors, and was not different ethnically or in terms of income. Like them, I was a resident, home owner, neighbor, citizen, and friend—as well as a researcher, which resulted in some role conflicts, partly for myself, but also for the people I was studying.

One of these was on my own block, and as I noted in the Introduction, I decided from the start not to act like a researcher there. I kept my formal research activities on the block to a minimum and tried to be a total participant as often as I could. Even so, occasionally my neighbors were ambivalent about my role. Once, a neighbor invited my wife and me to a meeting of her church fellowship to show us what the church was like, but asked me to take no notes. Away from my own block, I always announced myself as a researcher as soon as I could, so as to prevent uncertainty about my role. As I indicated earlier, people were as interested in my topic of study as I was, and revealing myself as a researcher did not affect their willingness to be studied. Indeed, if I had asked questions without explaining why I was so curious, people might have been more suspicious, especially if the questions would have been impertinent when asked by a nonresearcher. Also, they might have found out later that I was a researcher and thus been angry with me the next time. Unless there are pressing reasons to the contrary, complete openness and honesty is always the best policy.

If I aroused suspicion, it was about getting to know too much of the less ethical or respectable aspects of community life. I reported before that some politicians wondered if my book would be like *Peyton Place*, and another resident asked me if I had found any of Whyte's "organization men" in the community. People also became upset at my presence if they were not on their best behavior. When I attended private political meetings, I would always explain why I was there and that I would not be taking notes or mentioning names in the book. And I recall attending a picnic once, in which a community leader showed up in a rather outlandish pair of walking shorts. One of the picnickers suggested to a newspaper columnist that she put this in her column. She indicated that she would not, since she was not working on Sundays, but pointed to me and said, "You have to be careful of him, he writes everything in the annals of history." I could only sputter that I was not working on Sundays either.

Because I knew all the community's leaders, I aroused some status anxiety among my neighbors. I was occasionally kidded about having a front seat at important community events and was once asked jokingly whether I could do someone a favor at city hall. (I made it clear that I had absolutely no influence in the community—as, indeed, I did not.) To reduce their anxiety, I refrained from establishing social relations with community leaders. I did not invite them to my house, but then I was not much of a party-giver anyway, and the few parties which I held were limited to people on the block. Although my neighbors thought I had higher status in the community than they, I always felt that I had less than the leaders whom I interviewed, because even if I had a more prestigious job, I was not a real member of the community.

Actually, much of the role conflict developed because people wanted me to take nonresearch roles. I mentioned earlier that because of my planning background, I was asked to become active in the community, and was once offered a position on the Planning Board. I considered taking it, but felt it would conflict with my research role and would be unfair to the community, since I was not a "total" resident. Community leaders sometimes asked me to listen to their troubles, making me take a quasi-therapeutic role, and one thanked me once for being a "wailing wall." More often, they used the interview to think through their own problems and to test out ideas. Aware that this might affect their subsequent activities, I made as few comments as possible, and when asked for advice, I gave it only when it involved a technical point or a matter of no great importance. I usually explained that as a researcher I could not participate in the community in any way, and that if I gave advice to one person or group, I would have to do so for all others. Most people understood my neutral stance and did not insist.

Political leaders sometimes tried to get me to reveal findings. They knew I was talking to their opponents and sought to find out what I had learned. I was also asked and sometimes even pressured to take sides on community issues, and again I refused. People knew that I was often well informed and that my opinion might thus be based on information they did not have. Some were annoyed by my constant neutrality (and evasiveness) and tried to tease or shame me into taking a stand. At election time, members of both parties were curious about how I would vote. Although I did have preferences, I revealed them only once, shortly after my fieldwork began. As a political independent who generally voted Democratic, I found myself uncomfortable in the all-Republican and often quite conservative circles of the pre-Levittown residents. When I learned that a Democratic party had been organized and ran into a couple of the organizers, I was so pleased that I said I welcomed the event and would like to help out. Afterwards, I realized that I had revealed my political sympathies, and if these became known, I would no longer get data from the Republicans. I went back to the two organizers, withdrew the offer, and asked them to keep the entire conversation secret. They understood my dilemma, honored my request, and as far as I can tell, no one knew where I stood politically as long as I lived in Levittown.

This event was, of course, a performance break in which I dropped my role as researcher and acted as a person. Although the strains of being a performer often tempted me to other breaches, I was able to resist. The temptation was strongest with people whose values I shared, particularly the cosmopolitans. Consequently, I had to repress the urge to share my findings or to talk about how they could be more effective politically, but to have given in to the urge would have been unfair to other Levittowners. Instead, I relied on my wife and academic colleagues outside Levittown for the pressing need to talk freely about my study and to act as a person rather than a participant-observer.

The various roles I took and the various roles in which I was seen undoubtedly affected the kinds of data I was given, but it is difficult for me to judge how. Since the participant-observer must "sell" himself to get his data, how he comes across as a person and a role player may influence what people tell him. I pointed out in the Introduction that I became a bland and neutral person so as not to alienate people with different opinions, but this *persona* also reduced my own activity in a relationship and gave the informant more opportunity to talk. Indeed, quite often I purposely "played dumb" in interviews, giving the impression I knew less than I actually did, so that people would give me a fuller description of their activities and of their attitudes. Once I had obtained such a description, I could ask more specific questions, even about contradictions in the informant's description.

This posture was not entirely artificial; I often did feel dumb, and was always surprised how little I knew about the community and how poor I was at predicting future events. As a result, I had good reason for being humble (and neutral) with informants.

This is only one way of relating to informants, and I sometimes thought that if I took a more active role in the relationship and voiced my own opinions, particularly deviant ones, I would learn something I would not find out in polite conversation. In the end, I decided that getting into an argument might alienate me from people I wanted to talk with in the future. Moreover, as a person, I was more comfortable in an unassertive role, and acting otherwise would only have increased the strain of being a participant-observer. Yet perhaps the most important factor in the researcher-informant relationship is status, and a researcher of higher or lower status than his informant obtains different data than a researcher who is felt to be of equal status. As I indicated, I always sought to reduce status discrepancies and to treat my data sources as equal—or as superior, because they had information I did not have.

The extent to which my own values affected my findings is also difficult to judge. Coming to Levittown with the hypothesis that the suburban critics were wrong may have blinded me to some contradictory data, but it also made me feel more sympathetic to the Levittowners and more receptive to how they thought and felt. So did my belief in pluralism and relativism. Yet none of these values caused me to overidentify with my sources of data. Overidentification is a major problem for the participant-observer, which may create such strong attachments to the population he studies that he fails to see undesirable elements in their behavior.[8] The West Enders I lived with in my previous study were poorer than I and were facing destruction of their neighborhood by an urban renewal project which would eventually replace them with high-income tenants. They were underdogs, and I identified with them as such.[9] The Levittowners were neither poor nor threatened, and I had no reason to feel sorry for them.

I probably identified most with some of the working class residents who had financial and other problems or were struggling against the lower middle class climate of the community, partly because they resembled West Enders I had liked, partly because they were underdogs, and partly because I was not always happy with the political conservatism and moral restrictiveness of some lower middle class Levittowners. I did not like all the working class people I met, however, for some were openly anti-intellectual, opposed to racial integration, narrowly patriotic and hawkish about the "H" bomb, and politically no more liberal than the lower middle class. And I was also uncomfortable with some of the more mobile working class people who were trying hard to shed the informality and skepticism that prevails in working class culture. But I was more uncomfortable with lower middle class people who had graduated from college yet had retained the social and political conservatism of less educated people. Occasionally, I had to remind myself that I was judging them from my own class position as a university professor and from my own preference for cosmopolitanism and was lapsing into the rejection of middle class culture that is endemic to intellectuals. As I got to know people better, to understand their ways, and to see how these related to their own background, much of my discomfort and disapproval disappeared. Since most Levittowners were not status-seekers or anxious conformists, it was easy to like them even when I disagreed with their ideas. Indeed, I was perhaps most critical of the cosmopolitans, because they felt themselves to be liberals and intellectuals, but were not quite ready to practice what they preached and were particularly intolerant of their lower-status neighbors. Agreeing with them about some issues, I was ready to be more critical of them when I disagreed. I assumed (perhaps wrongly) that well-educated people should and could be more pluralistic and less intent on defending their own class interests than others.

The values (and feelings) which most affected my fieldwork concerned the deceptions required to be a participant-observer. They generated the guilt and anxiety I described in the Introduction, and sometimes made me feel I was using people for my own purposes. Although I told people I was a researcher at the start, I realized that they soon forgot this, so that they did not really know how much they were being observed; and among my immediate neighbors, I was collecting data when I appeared to act as a resident. This problem is endemic to participant-observation, and I cannot find a way of eliminating it. If the researcher is completely honest with people about his activities, they will try to hide actions and attitudes they consider undesirable, and so will be dishonest. Consequently, the researcher must be dishonest to get honest data.[10] If this leads to guilt feelings, it can affect findings, for it may discourage him from being critical of the people he has deceived and used. Fortunately, these feelings decrease once fieldwork is over, and their potential effect on the findings can be dealt with during the analysis and writing period. They never disappear entirely, however, and one must either live with them or stop doing research.

The researcher can protect his informants by making sure that the data he gathers will not be used against them. He need not mention names, and in any case, his publication usually appears years after the research, making it unlikely that the data can be used against anyone. Even if a researcher decided that the behavior of those he studied was so unjust that he felt impelled to reveal it, he would still withhold names. Such problems aside, the researcher acts on the faith that the advantages of his research to the people studied will outweigh the possible disadvantages of their being described in a published report, or the more subtle disadvantages of having been deceived by the researcher.

Still, the main shortcomings (and biases) of participant-observation result less from the researcher's roles and values than from the structure of the community he is studying. If the community is suspicious of outsiders, he will have difficulty in gaining entry and in observing a representative sample of the population. In a new town, conflict between the builder and his purchasers may force him to become identified with one, thus losing rapport with the other.[11] Neither problem existed in Levittown. Because the community was new, its social structure open, and its residents interested in a history of the community building process, I had no trouble in gaining cooperation or access (except at caucuses and some private political meetings). Community boosters are, of course, the most helpful (if not always the most accurate) informants,[12] but once I got to know them and had other sources of information about their groups, they were usually willing to talk about organizational conflict as well. But even the less enthusiastic Levittowners were willing to help me, partly because they could use me to get their gripes off their chest. My contacts with the Levitt organization were too infrequent and the purchasers' dissatisfaction with the firm too rare to cause any problems, although in this instance as in many others, being a homeowner with the same house-and-lawn problems as other residents made it much easier for me to obtain rapport with the Levittowners than for an outside observer.

Consequently, I did not have to worry about talking with a representative sample. I kept no record of how many people I interviewed informally during the three years of fieldwork, but I maintained frequent contact with at least fifty to seventy-five, and probably talked altogether with four or five hundred—at least one member from about 15 percent of the families in the first three neighborhoods. Moreover, since I was not doing a general community study, but was usually researching specific topics, the people to whom I talked were defined by the topic rather than by my ability to obtain access and rapport. Thus, there was less opportunity for the bias that develops unintentionally when a researcher talks to more people of his own class and educational level. Even so, in my general participant-observation activities, I probably talked with proportionately more middle class people than working class ones, and with more upper middle class ones than lower middle class ones. Fortunately, however, I had considerable contact with working class Levittowners who lived on my own block.

Actually, the most difficult research problem was untangling political events. I could not always get honest responses from some politicians; even when I did, they saw things so much from their own perspective that I was always faced with the problem of reconciling conflicting accounts. The difficulty was not so much in finding out *what* happened as *why*. Political strategies are very complex even in a small community, the motivations that create these strategies are often unfathomable, and politicians are not always willing (or able) to reveal their motives and goals. One solution is to talk to their opponents, ask them to explain an action, and then confront the original actor with this explanation. Usually this produces denials, but sometimes it results in more detailed explanations than would otherwise be given, and these can then be checked out with others. Another solution is to find a trustworthy person who is marginal to the group being studied and depend on him for final verification. Such people are rare, however, for if one is involved in politics it is difficult to remain marginal. I was fortunate in being able to find a couple of marginal people, as well as a local newspaperman who was "in the know" but sufficiently detached from the political process to serve as an informant. When these sources were not available, I had to rely on the information given me by people whom I trusted, and while this may have introduced some bias into the data, because I was more likely to trust people I liked and those of my own educational background, I had no other alternative. Sometimes, what really happens in politics is virtually unknowable to an outsider, and the only solution is for the researcher to become a participant and keep notes in the process.

In one sense, the mystery of politics is deceptive, however, for the unknowable is restricted to motives and to illegal or disapproved activities, neither of which is as important as one thinks they are while one is doing fieldwork. Illegal and disapproved activities usually play only a minor role in the politics of a middle class community. The need to know about them stems from the uncertainty of the political process, which breeds the desire (and the curiosity) to remain up to date and well informed, and from the rumors about corruption, graft, and deals that come up all the time and have to be checked out. Curiosity about motivations comes from the same uncertainty, but if the researcher is patient, he will usually find that later actions by politicians indicate which motives were at play in earlier ones.

ANALYZING THE DATA

Although I had hoped to analyze the mail questionnaire data and the first interview with the random sample before getting deeply involved in the participant-observation and before drafting the second interview schedule, the rapid pace at which the community developed and the slow pace at which data must be analyzed when funds for research assistance are lacking made this impossible. I was able to do some preliminary analysis of early questionnaire data with the help of students, and I knew how the first interview was answered before I made up the second schedule, but most of the data were analyzed after the conclusion of the fieldwork.

The mail questionnaire data were tabulated by IBM machines, but the interview data I coded, tabulated and analyzed myself. Although this took considerable time, it also made me quite familiar with the contents of each interview, and with the interviewees as people—at least, to the extent that they described themselves by their answers—making it methodologically and psychologically safer to attempt a quantitative analysis of a small sample.

The participant-observation data were originally recorded in a diary, but as soon as I had translated my initial study questions into a set of topics, I gave up the diary, and put my field notes on 5 × 8 sheets, one per topic. A single meeting or interview often produced data on half a dozen topics, and recording them by topic was a real time-saver in the analysis, for I did not have to take apart or index the diary to synthesize data on each topic. Eventually, I had many thousands of sheets, all filed by topic, and I drew my findings from an intensive and oft repeated reading of them. I made no real attempt to integrate the findings reached by the three different methods, except when I had developed interview questions to test an idea learned in participant-observation. More such integration would have been desirable, but I had such vast amounts of data that it took me a long time even to organize them into a single narrative.

The findings presented here have all the faults of the methods by which they were reached. Often, the resulting generalizations are examples of what Merton calls "post factum sociological interpretation"; they have been developed after the observations were made and are not tests of prior hypotheses.[13] I therefore conclude with the same remarks with which I ended my earlier book:

> This, then, is not a scientific study, for it does not provide what Merton has called compelling evidence for a series of hypotheses. It is, rather, an attempt by a trained social scientist to describe and explain the behavior of a large number of people, using his methodological and theoretical training to sift the observations, and to report only those generalizations which are justified by the data. The validity of my findings thus rests ultimately on my judgments about the data, and of course on my theoretical and personal biases in deciding what to study, what to see, what to ignore and how to analyze the products. Properly speaking, the study is a *reconnaissance,* an exploration of a community to provide an overview, guided by the canons of sociological theory and method, but not attempting to offer documentation for all the findings. I do not mean to cast doubt on the conclusions I reached (I stand behind them all) or on the methods I used. Participant-observation is the only method I know that enables the researcher to get close to the real-

ities of social life. Its deficiencies in producing quantitative data are more than made up by its ability to minimize the distance between the researcher and his subject of study.[14]

The mail questionnaires and interviews provided more systematically collected data, and are thus more scientific in one sense, although less so in another, for they can report only what people say they do and feel, and not what a researcher has seen them say, do, and feel.

NOTES

1. The numbers were masked slightly, but not enough to prevent their identification by some people, who either tore off the number or returned blank questionnaires. I received about a hundred of these, 3 per cent of the total. If the code number had been masked even more, fewer people might have been suspicious, but the Levitt clerks' task of sending out questionnaires and reminders would have been more difficult. I was not happy about having to number the questionnaires, but there was no alternative if reminders were to be sent out.

2. In the first neighborhood, the return rate was 57 per cent; in the second, 66 per cent; in the third, 70 per cent. In a seventy-house section of the first neighborhood built after the completion of the third one, it rose to 79 per cent. One of the reasons for the low return rate in the first neighborhood was some initial difficulty in routinizing the process of sending out the questionnaires.

3. In a specially selected random sample of Levittowners, 27 per cent of those answering the questionnaire, but 51 per cent of those not doing so were women over thirty-five. Similarly, 16 per cent of the returnees, but 36 per cent of nonreturnees, were blue collar workers; and 13 per cent of returnees, but 32 per cent of nonreturnees, were women with less than a high school diploma.

4. The only data comparing residents of the first neighborhood and my interview respondents in the random sample are by education, and show that 26 per cent of the women in the neighborhood had less than twelve years of schooling, 52 per cent were high school graduates, and 21 per cent attended or graduated from college. In the interview sample, the proportions were 18 per cent, 67 per cent, and 15 per cent, respectively.

5. For example, 18 per cent of the men in the first neighborhood had less than twelve years of education, as compared to 13 per cent in the second, and 10 per cent in the third.

6. These categories are adapted from Junker, pp. 35–40. See also Schwartz and Schwartz, pp. 348–350, and Gold.

7. Gans (1962a), pp. 338–340.
8. See Schwartz and Schwartz, pp. 350–352.
9. Gans (1962a), pp. 342–344.
10. This deception is not limited to participant-observation, for interview questions often hide the intent of the research. The interviewee can refuse to answer, however, whereas the person studied by the participant-observer cannot step out of the event in which he is acting. The ethical problems are discussed by Erikson.
11. On this problem, see Merton (1947b), p. 306.
12. Merton (1947b), pp. 308–311.
13. Merton (1957), pp. 93–94.
14. Gans (1962a), pp. 349–350.

References

Abu-Lughod, Janet. "A Survey of Center-City Residents," in N. Foote, J. Abu-Lughod, M. Foley, and L. Winnick, *Housing Choices and Constraints*. New York: McGraw-Hill, 1960, pp. 387–447.

Allen, Frederick L. "The Big Change in Suburbia," *Harper's Magazine*, Vol. 208, June 1954, pp. 21–28, and Vol. 209, July 1954, pp. 47–53.

Altshuler, Alan. *The City Planning Process*. Ithaca: Cornell University Press, 1965.

Anderson, Judith, and Settani, Nicholas. "Resales in Levittown, Pennsylvania, 1952–1960." Unpublished paper, Department of City Planning, University of Pennsylvania, 1961.

Banfield, Edward C. "Note on Conceptual Scheme," in Martin Meyerson and Edward C. Banfield, *Politics, Planning and the Public Interest*. New York: Free Press of Glencoe, 1955, pp. 303–330.

Banfield, Edward C. *The Moral Basis of a Backward Society*. New York: Free Press of Glencoe, 1958.

Banfield, Edward C. *Political Influence*. New York: Free Press of Glencoe, 1961.

Banfield, Edward C., and Grodzins, Morton. *Government and Housing in Metropolitan Areas*. New York: McGraw-Hill, 1958.

Banfield, Edward C., and Wilson, James Q. *City Politics*. Cambridge: Harvard University Press and M.I.T. Press, 1963.

Berger, Bennett M. *Working Class Suburb*. Berkeley and Los Angeles: University of California Press, 1960.

Berger, Bennett M. "Suburbia and the American Dream," *The Public Interest*, No. 2, Winter 1966, pp. 80–92.

Blake, Peter. *God's Own Junkyard*. New York: Holt, Rinehart and Winston, 1963.

Blake, R., Read, C., Wedge, B., and Mouton, J. "Housing Architecture and Social Interaction," *Sociometry*, Vol. 19, June 1956, pp. 133–139.

Blood, Robert O., Jr., and Wolfe, Donald M. *Husbands and Wives*. New York: Free Press of Glencoe, 1960.

Bressler, Marvin. "The Myers Case: An Instance of Successful Racial Invasion," *Social Problems*, Vol. 8, Fall 1960, pp. 126–142.

Burton, Hal. "Trouble in the Suburbs," *Saturday Evening Post*, Vol. 228, September 17, 1955, pp. 19–21, 113–118.

Caplow, T., and Foreman, R. "Neighborhood Interaction in a Homogeneous Community," *American Sociological Review*, Vol. 15, June 1950, pp. 357–366.

Citizens Committee for a Better Levittown. *A Preliminary Report of Your Self Survey*. Levittown, N.Y.: The Committee, February 1956, mimeographed.

Clark, S. D. *The Suburban Society*. Toronto: University of Toronto Press, 1966.

Crozier, Michael. *The Bureaucratic Phenomenon*. Chicago: University of Chicago Press, 1964.

Dahl, Robert A. *Who Governs?* New Haven: Yale University Press, 1961.

Danhof, R. H. "The Accommodation and Integration of Conflicting Cultures in a Newly Established Community," *American Journal of Sociology*, Vol. 9, July 1943, pp. 14–23.

Dean, John P. "Housing Design and Family Values," *Land Economics*, Vol. 29, May 1953, pp. 128–141.

Dean, John P. "The Neighborhood and Social Relations," *Forum on Neighborhoods, Today and Tomorrow*. (Philadelphia Housing Association) No. 3, April 1958.

Dobriner, William M. "Local and Cosmopolitan as Contemporary Suburban Character Types," in William M. Dobriner, ed., *The Suburban Community*. New York: Putnam, 1958, pp. 132–143.

Dobriner, William M. *Class in Suburbia*. Englewood Cliffs: Prentice-Hall, 1963.

Downs, Anthony. *An Economic Theory of Democracy*. New York: Harper, 1957.

Duhl, Leonard J. "Mental Health and Community Planning," in *Planning 1955*. Chicago: American Society of Planning Officials, 1956, p. 31–39.

Duncan, Otis D., and Schnore, Leo F. "Cultural Behavioral and Ecological Perspectives in the Study of Social Organization," *American Journal of Sociology*, Vol. 65, September 1959, pp. 132–155.

Dux, Henry E. "Levittown New Jersey: A Statistical Report." November 1964, mimeographed.

Dye, Thomas R. "Popular Images of Decision-Making in Suburban Communities," *Sociology and Social Research*, Vol. 47, October 1962, pp. 75–83.

Dye, Thomas R. "The Local-Cosmopolitan Dimension and the Study of Urban Politics," *Social Forces*, Vol. 41, March 1963(a), pp. 240–246.

Dye, Thomas R. "Leadership and Constituency in Fifteen Suburban Communities." Paper presented at the 1963 meeting of the American Political Science Association. 1963(b).

Eichler, Edward P. (with Marshall Kaplan). *The Community Builders*. Berkeley and Los Angeles: University of California Press, 1967.

Ellul, Jacques. *The Technological Society*. New York: Knopf, 1964.

Erikson, Kai T. "A Comment on Disguised Observation in Sociology," Paper presented at the 1965 meeting of the Society for the Study of Social Problems, 1965, mimeographed.

Fava, Sylvia F. "Suburbanism as a Way of Life," *American Sociological Review*, Vol. 21, February 1956, pp. 34–38.

Fenmore, Donald M. "Comments on Hoffman's 'Outlook for Downtown Housing'," *Journal of the American Institute of Planners*, Vol. 27, November 1961, p. 334.

Festinger, Leon. "Architecture and Group Membership," *Journal of Social Issues*, Vol. 7 (Nos. 1 and 2), 1951, pp. 152–163.

Festinger, L., Schachter, S., and Back, K. *Social Pressures in Informal Groups*. New York: Harper, 1950.

Field, Dorita E., and Neill, Desmond G. *A Survey of New Housing Estates in Belfast*. Belfast (Northern Ireland): University of Belfast, 1957.

Fiske, Marjorie. *Book Selection and Censorship*. Berkeley and Los Angeles: University of California Press, 1959.

Form, William H. *Sociology of a White Collar Suburb*. Unpublished Ph.D. dissertation, Department of Sociology, University of Maryland, 1944.

Form, William H. "Status Stratification in a Planned Community," *American Sociological Review*, Vol. 10, October 1945, pp. 605–613. Reprinted in William M. Dobriner, ed., *The Suburban Community*. New York: Putnam, 1958, pp. 209–224.

Form, William H. "Stratification in Low and Middle Income Housing Areas," *Journal of Social Issues*, Vol. 7 (Nos. 1 and 2), 1951, pp. 109–131.

Fried, Marc. "Grieving for a Lost Home," in Leonard J. Duhl, ed., *The Urban Condition*. New York: Basic Books, 1963, pp. 151–171.

Friedenberg, Edgar. *Coming of Age in America*. New York: Random House, 1965.

Fromm, Erich. *The Sane Society.* New York: Holt, Rinehart and Winston, 1955.

Gabower, Genevieve. *Behavior Problems of Children in Navy Officers' Families as Related to Social Conditions of Navy Life.* Washington: Catholic University of America Press, 1959.

Gans, Herbert J. "Park Forest: Birth of a Jewish Community," *Commentary,* Vol. 11, April 1951, pp. 330–339.

Gans, Herbert J. "Planning and Political Participation: A Study of Political Participation in a Planned New Town," *Journal of the American Institute of Planners,* Vol. 19, Winter 1953, pp. 3–9.

Gans, Herbert J. "Progress of a Suburban Jewish Community," *Commentary,* Vol. 22, February 1957, pp. 113–122.

Gans, Herbert J. "The Origin and Growth of a Jewish Community in the Suburbs," in Marshall Sklare, ed., *The Jews: Social Patterns of an American Group.* New York: Free Press of Glencoe, 1958, pp. 205–248.

Gans, Herbert J. "Planning and Social Life: Friendship and Neighbor Relations in Suburban Communities," *Journal of the American Institute of Planners,* Vol. 27, May 1961 (a), pp. 134–140.

Gans, Herbert J. "The Balanced Community: Homogeneity or Heterogeneity in Residential Areas?" *Journal of the American Institute of Planners,* Vol. 27, August 1961 (b), pp. 176–184.

Gans, Herbert J. *The Urban Villagers: Group and Class in the Life of Italian-Americans.* New York: Free Press of Glencoe, 1962(a).

Gans, Herbert J. "Urbanism and Suburbanism as Ways of Life: A Re-Evaluation of Some Definitions," in Arnold M. Rose, ed., *Human Behavior and Social Processes.* Boston: Houghton Mifflin, 1962(b), pp. 625–648.

Gans, Herbert J. "The Split-Level Trap" (Review), *Journal of the American Institute of Planners,* Vol. 28, February 1962(c), pp. 47–49.

Gans, Herbert J. "The Failure of Urban Renewal," *Commentary,* Vol. 39, April 1965, pp. 29–37, and "Controversy: Urban Renewal," *Commentary,* Vol. 39, July 1965, pp. 77–80.

Gieber, Walter, and Johnson, Walter. "The City Hall 'Beat': A Study of Reporter and Source Roles," *Journalism Quarterly,* Vol. 38, Summer 1961, pp. 289–297.

Goffman, Erving, *The Presentation of Self in Everyday Life.* Garden City, N.Y.: Doubleday Anchor, 1959.

Gold, Raymond L. "Roles in Sociological Field Observations," *Social Forces,* Vol. 36, March 1958, pp. 217–223.

Goodman, Paul. "Utopian Thinking," *Commentary,* Vol. 32, July 1961, pp. 19–26.

Goodman, Paul. *Compulsory Miseducation.* New York: Horizon Press, 1964.

Goodman, Paul. *People or Personnel.* New York: Random House, 1965.

Gordon, Richard E., and Gordon, Katherine N. "Psychiatric Problems of a Rapidly Growing Suburb," *A.M.A. Archives of Neurology and Psychiatry,* Vol. 79, May 1958, pp. 543–548.

Gordon, R., Gordon, K., and Gunther, M. *The Split Level Trap.* New York: Geis, 1961.

Gouldner, Alvin W. *Enter Plato.* New York: Basic Books, 1966.

Greer, Scott. "Socio-Political Structure of Suburbia," *American Sociological Review,* Vol. 25, August 1960, pp. 514–526.

Greer, Scott. *Governing the Metropolis.* New York: Wiley, 1962.

Greer, Scott (with Norton Long). *Metropolitics.* New York: Wiley, 1963.

Gruen, Victor. *The Heart of our Cities.* New York: Simon and Schuster, 1964.

Gruenberg, Sidonie M. "Challenge of the New Suburbs," *Marriage and Family Living,* Vol. 17, May 1955, pp. 133–137.

Gutkind, Erwin A. *The Twilight of Cities.* New York: Free Press of Glencoe, 1962.

Gutman, Robert. "Population Mobility in the American Middle Class," in Leonard J. Duhl, ed., *The Urban Condition.* New York: Basic Books, 1963, pp. 172–183.

Haeberle, Ann. *Friendship as an Aspect of Interpersonal Relations: A Study of Friendship among Women Residents of a Small Community.* Unpublished Ph.D. dissertation, New York University, April 1956.

Henderson, Harry. "The Mass Produced Suburbs," *Harper's Magazine,* Vol. 207, November 1953, pp. 25–32, and December 1953, pp. 80–86.

Hole, Vere. "Social Effects of Planned Rehousing," *Town Planning Review* (London), Vol. 30, July 1959, pp. 161–173.

Honigmann, John J. "Patterns of Eskimo Deviance in a New Eastern Arctic Town," *Research Previews* (Institute for Research in Social Science, University of North Carolina), Vol. 12, January 1965, pp. 5–15.

Hoshino, Ikumi. "Apartment Life in Japan," *Journal of Marriage and the Family* (Tokyo), Vol. 26, August 1964, pp. 312–317.

Hunter, Floyd A. *Community Power Structure.* Chapel Hill: University of North Carolina Press, 1953.

Infield, Henrik F. "A Veterans' Cooperative Land Settlement and Its Sociometric Structure," *Sociometry,* Vol. 10, February 1947, pp. 50–70.

Institute of Urban Studies. *Accelerated Urban Growth in a Metropolitan Fringe Area.* Philadelphia: The Institute, 1954, mimeographed.

Jahoda, M., Walkley, A., Walkley, R., Hopson, A., and Haeberle, A. *Community Influences on Psychological Health*. New York: New York University Research Center for Human Relations, 1954, mimeographed.

James, T. F. "Crackups in the Suburbs," *Cosmopolitan*, Vol. 149, October 1960, pp. 60–65.

Junker, Buford H. *Field Work*. Chicago: University of Chicago Press, 1960.

Keats, John. *The Crack in the Picture Window*. Boston: Houghton Mifflin, 1956 (Ballantine Books paperback 1957).

Kiser, Clyde V. "Residence and Migration," in C. Westoff, R. Potter, and P. Sagi, *The Third Child: A Study in the Prediction of Fertility*. Princeton: Princeton University Press, 1963, Chap. 10.

Kornhauser, William. *Politics of Mass Society*. New York: Free Press of Glencoe, 1959.

Ktsanes, Thomas, and Reissman, Leonard. "Suburbia: New Homes for Old Values," *Social Problems*, Vol. 7, Winter 1959, pp. 187–194.

Kuper, Leo. "Blueprint for Living Together," in Leo Kuper, ed., *Living in Towns*. London: Cresset Press, 1953, pp. 1–202.

Larrabee, Eric. "The Six Thousand Houses that Levitt Built," *Harper's Magazine*, Vol. 197, September 1948, pp. 79–88.

Lazerwitz, Bernard. "Suburban Voting Trends, 1948–1956," *Social Forces*, Vol. 39, October 1960, pp. 29–36.

League of Women Voters, Willingboro, New Jersey. *Know Your Town*. Willingboro: The League, second edition, 1965.

Lessinger, Jack. "The Case for Scatteration," *Journal of the American Institute of Planners*, Vol. 28, August 1962, pp. 159–169.

Levine, Gene N., and Modell, John. *Community Leaders' Reactions to the Fallout Shelter Issue*. New York: Bureau of Applied Social Research, Columbia University, September 1964, mimeographed.

Levitt, Alfred S. "A Community Builder Looks at Community Planning," *Journal of the American Institute of Planners*, Vol. 17, Spring 1951, pp. 80–88.

Levitt, William J. "What! *Live* in a Levittown?" *Good Housekeeping*, Vol. 147, July 1958, pp. 47, 175–176.

Levitt and Sons. "Levitt's Progress" and "Most House for the Money," *Fortune*, Vol. 46, October 1952, pp. 151–169.

Liell, John T. *Levittown: A Study in Community Development and Planning*. Unpublished Ph.D. dissertation, Department of Sociology, Yale University, 1952.

Liell, John T. "Social Relationships in a Changing Suburb: A Restudy of Levittown." Paper presented at the 1963 meeting of the American Sociological Association.

Lipset, S. M. *Political Man*. Garden City: Doubleday, 1960.

Martin, F., Brotherston, J., and Chave, S. "Incidence of Neurosis in a New Housing Estate," *British Journal of Preventive and Social Medicine*, Vol. 11, October 1957, pp. 196–202.

Merton, Robert K. "The Social Psychology of Housing," in Wayne Dennis, ed., *Current Trends in Social Psychology*. Pittsburgh: University of Pittsburgh Press, 1947(a), pp. 163–217.

Merton, Robert K. "Selected Problems of Field Work in the Planned Community," *American. Sociological Review*, Vol. 12, June 1947(b), pp. 304–312.

Merton, Robert K. "Patterns of Influence: Local and Cosmopolitan Influentials," *Social Theory and Social Structure*. New York: Free Press of Glencoe, 1957, pp. 387–420.

Meyersohn, Rolf, and Jackson, Robin. "Gardening in Suburbia," in William M. Dobriner, ed., *The Suburban Community*. New York: Putnam, 1958, pp. 271–286.

Meyerson, Martin, and Banfield, Edward C. *Politics, Planning and the Public Interest*. New York: Free Press of Glencoe, 1955.

Michelson, William M. *Adult Voluntary Associations in Levittown*. Unpublished senior thesis, Department of Sociology, Princeton University, April 1961.

Milbrath, Lester W. *Political Participation*. Chicago: Rand McNally, 1965.

Mills, C. Wright. *The Power Elite*. New York: Oxford University Press, 1957.

Mogey, John M. "Changes in Family Life Experienced by English Workers Moving from Slums to Housing Estates," *Marriage and Family Living*, Vol. 17, May 1955, pp. 123–128.

Mogey, John M. *Family and Neighborhood*. London: Oxford University Press, 1956.

Mogey, J., and Morris, R. "Causes of Change in Family Role Patterns," *Bulletin of the Research Center on Family Development*, Vol. 1, Winter 1960, pp. 1–9.

Mumford, Lewis. *The City in History*. New York: Harcourt, Brace and World, 1961.

Olsen, William. "The Location of Children's Birthday Party Attenders in Levittown, New Jersey." Unpublished paper, Department of City Planning, University of Pennsylvania, 1960.

Orlans, Harold. *Utopia Limited: The Story of the English Town of Stevenage*. New Haven: Yale University Press, 1953.

Orzack, Louis H., and Sanders, Irwin T. *A Social Profile of Levittown, New York*. Ann Arbor: University Microfilms, O.P. 13438, 1961.

Pearl, Arthur, and Riessman, Frank. *New Careers for the Poor*. New York: Free Press of Glencoe, 1965.

Pederson, Frank A., and Sullivan, Eugene. "Effects of Geographical Mobility and Parent Personality Factors on Emotional Disorders in Children." Washington: Walter Reed General Hospital, 1963, mimeographed.

Pierson, Alice D. *Survey of Levittown, Pennsylvania, 1960.* Unpublished bachelor's thesis, Department of Sociology, University of Pennsylvania, May 1960.

Piven, Frances F. *The Function of Research in the Formation of City Planning Policy.* Unpublished Ph.D. dissertation, Department of City Planning, University of Chicago, 1962.

Practical Builder. "P.B. Reveals Levitt's Building Methods," Vol. 23, August 1959, pp. 80–91.

Rainwater, Lee. "Fear and the House-as-Haven in the Lower Class," *Journal of the American Institute of Planners,* Vol. 32, January 1966, pp. 23–31.

Rainwater, L., Coleman, R., and Handel, G. *Workingman's Wife.* New York: Oceana Publications, 1959.

Recreation. "Competitive Athletics for Boys Under Twelve," Vol. 45, February 1951, pp. 489–491.

Recreation. "Are Highly Competitive Sports Desirable for Juniors?" Vol. 46, December 1952, pp. 422–425.

Reiff, Robert, and Riessman, Frank. *The Indigenous Non-Professional: A Strategy of Change in Community Action and Community Mental Health Programs.* New York: National Institute of Labor Education, November 1964, mimeographed.

Riesman, David (with N. Glazer and R. Denney). *The Lonely Crowd.* New Haven: Yale University Press, 1950.

Riesman, David. "The Suburban Dislocation," *The Annals,* Vol. 314, Fall 1957, pp. 123–146. Reprinted in David Riesman, *Abundance for What?* Garden City: Doubleday, 1964, pp. 226–257.

Riesman, David. "Flight and Search in the New Suburbs," in David Riesman, *Abundance for What?* Garden City: Doubleday, 1964, pp. 258–269.

Rondum, Rita. "Rondum at Random," *Levittown Life,* June 27, 1963.

Rosenfeld, Eva. "Social Stratification in a Classless Society," *American Sociological Review,* Vol. 16, December 1951, pp. 766–774.

Rosow, Irving. "The Social Effects of the Physical Environment," *Journal of the American Institute of Planners,* Vol. 27, May 1961, pp. 127–133.

Rossi, Peter H. *Why Families Move.* New York: Free Press of Glencoe, 1955.

Rosten, Leo. *The Washington Correspondents.* New York: Harcourt Brace, 1937.

Schorr, Alvin L. *Slums and Social Insecurity.* Washington: Social Security Administration, 1963.

Schwartz, Morris S., and Schwartz, Charlotte G. "Problems in Participant-Observation," *American Journal of Sociology,* Vol. 60, January 1955, pp. 343–353.

Seeley, J., Sim, R., and Loosley, E. *Crestwood Heights.* New York: Basic Books, 1956.

Sewell, William H., and Armer, J. Michael. "Neighborhood Context and College Plans," *American Sociological Review,* Vol. 31, April 1966, pp. 159–168.

Sigel, Roberta S., and Friesema, H. Paul. "Urban Community Leaders' Knowledge of Public Opinion," *Western Political Science Quarterly,* Vol. 18, December 1965, pp. 881–895.

Sills, David. *The Volunteers.* New York: Free Press of Glencoe, 1957.

Sklare, Marshall. *Conservative Judaism.* New York: Free Press of Glencoe, 1955.

Sorenson, Theodore C. *Decision-Making in the White House.* New York: Columbia University Press, 1963.

Southworth, Robert E. "Adult Social Activities in Levittown, New Jersey." Unpublished paper, Department of City Planning, University of Pennsylvania, 1961.

Spectorsky, A. C. *The Exurbanites,* Philadelphia: Lippincott, 1955.

Srole, L., Langner, T., Michael, S., Opler, M., and Rennie, T. *Mental Health in the Metropolis.* New York: McGraw-Hill, 1960.

Stein, Maurice. *The Eclipse of Community.* Princeton: Princeton University Press, 1960.

Strauss, Anselm L. *Images of the American City.* New York: Free Press of Glencoe, 1961.

Taylor, Lord, and Chave, Sidney. *Mental Health and Environment.* Boston: Little, Brown, 1964.

Tetteh, Austin. "Social Background of the Kumasi Plan," *Ekistics,* Vol. 14, July 1962, pp. 22–25.

Thernstrom, Stephan. *Poverty and Progress.* Cambridge: Harvard University Press, 1964.

Thoma, Lucy, and Lindemann, Erich. "Newcomers' Problems in a Suburban Community," *Journal of the American Institute of Planners,* Vol. 27, August 1961, pp. 185–193.

Thomas, Wyndham. "New Town Blues," in *Planning 1964.* Chicago: America Society of Planning Officials, 1964, pp. 184–189.

Township of Willingboro. *Willingboro Development Plan: Phase One, Basic Studies.* Willingboro, New Jersey, no date.

Ubell, Earl. "Marriage in the Suburbs," *New York Herald-Tribune,* January 4–8, 1959.

U.S. Housing and Home Finance Agency. "Changing a Racial Policy,

Levittown, N.J.," in *Equal Opportunity in Housing*. Washington: H.H.F.A., June 1964, pp. 17–27.

Urban Studies Center. *Problems of Migration Among the American Middle Class*. New Brunswick: The Center, January 1962, mimeographed.

Vallier, Ivan. "Structural Differentiation, Production Imperatives and Communal Norms: The Kibbutz in Crisis." *Social Forces*, Vol. 40, March 1962, pp. 233–242.

Vidich, Arthur J., and Bensman, Joseph. *Small Town in Mass Society*. Princeton: Princeton University Press, 1958.

Wallace, David. *The Second Tuesday*. Garden City: Doubleday, 1964.

Wattel, Harold. "Levittown: A Suburban Community," in William M. Dobriner, ed., *The Suburban Community*. New York: Putnam, 1958, pp. 287–313.

Webber, Melvin M. "Order in Diversity: Community Without Propinquity," in Lowdon Wingo, Jr., ed., *Cities and Space: The Future Use of Urban Land*. Baltimore: John Hopkins University Press, 1963, pp. 23–54.

Wechsler, Henry. "Community Growth, Depressive Disorders and Suicide," *American Journal of Sociology*, Vol. 67, July 1961, pp. 9–16.

Whyte, William H., Jr. *The Organization Man*. New York: Simon and Schuster, 1956.

Whyte, William H., Jr. *Cluster Development*. New York: American Conservation Association, 1964.

Wilensky, Harold L. "Life Cycle, Work Situation and Participation in Formal Associations," in Robert W. Kleemeier, ed., *Aging and Leisure*. New York: Oxford University Press, 1961, pp. 213–242.

Williams, Robin M., Jr. "Racial and Cultural Relations," in Joseph P. Gittler, ed., *Review of Sociology: Analysis of a Decade*. New York: Wiley, 1957, pp. 423–464.

Willingboro Township Planning Board. *Suggested Development Plan: Willingboro Township, New Jersey*. Willingboro, New Jersey, May 1964.

Willmott, Peter. "Housing Density and Town Design in a New Town," *Town Planning Review* (London), Vol. 34, July 1962, pp. 115–127.

Willmott, Peter. *The Evolution of a Community*. London: Routledge and Kegan Paul, 1963.

Wilner, D., Walkley, R., Pinkerton, T., and Tayback, M. *Housing Environment and Family Life*. Baltimore: Johns Hopkins University Press, 1962.

Wilson, Alan B. "Class Segregation and Aspirations of Youth," *American Sociological Review*, Vol. 24, December 1959, pp. 836–845.

Wolf, Eleanor, and Ravitz, Mel. "Lafayette Park: New Residents in the Core City," *Journal of the American Institute of Planners,* Vol. 30, August 1964, pp. 234–239.

Wood, Robert C. *Suburbia.* Boston: Houghton Mifflin, 1959.

Wood, Robert C. *1400 Governments.* Cambridge: Harvard University Press, 1961.

Wyden, Peter. *Suburbia's Coddled Kids.* Garden City: Doubleday, 1960.

Young, Michael, and Willmott, Peter. *Family and Kinship in East London.* London: Routledge and Kegan Paul, 1957.

Zelan, Joseph. "Intellectual Attitudes and Suburban Residence." Paper read at the 1963 meeting of the American Sociological Association, Chicago: National Opinion Research Center, August 1963, mimeographed.

INDEX

Actual government, 308, 317, 339; reporters and, 323, 324, 326; *see also* Performing government

Adolescents, 206–12; boredom of, 206; attitudes toward Levittown, 206; sex and, 207, 209, 210, 211; adults and, 207; site planning and, 207; schools and, 208; adults' attitudes toward, 208–9; attitudes toward city living, 273; master plan and, 388; *see also* Juvenile delinquency

Agents of change, 284–5; Levitt & Sons as, 285; population mix as, 285–6; aspirations as, 286

Altruistic democracy, 307; sources of, 357

American culture: and Levittown, 186–7, 196, 417; as source and agent of change, 289; and suburban move, 410; changes in, 418–20; *see also* National society

Architectural homogeneity, attitudes toward, 282

Architectural styles, attitude toward, 270–1

Architecture, sense of community and, 146

Art, attitudes toward, 203

Aspirations, 37–41; family life and, 38; social life and, 38–40; community participation, 40; house-related, 40–1; community-related, 41; community origin and, 138, 141; as agents of change, 286;

planning for change in, 291; planner's values and, 291–2, 295

Autonomy: conformity and, 180; national planning and, 400

Bedroom community: class structure, 133; power structure, 135; sense of community in, 145

Behavior change, 275, 409; intended, xx, 252–3; unintended, xx, 253, 254; planning and, 252, 290; sources of, 252, 277; agents of, 252; newness as source of, 254; house as source of, 254; population-mix impact on, 275

Bias: in mail questionnaire study, 436; in interview study, 438; in participant-observation, 444, 446; of findings, 449

Block: homogeneity and, 172; social control and, 177; *see also* Propinquity, Sub-block

Block culture, 144, 150, 161, 173; origin of, 47–8; lawn care and, 48, 177; social life and, 48–9; evolution of, 51; conformity and, 176

Boredom, 228–9; of adolescents, 206; amount of, 228; reasons for, 228–9; changes in, 229; loneliness and, 230; class and, 248; impact of houses on, 255; sources of change in, 255; community impact on, 255, 258; leisure and, 269

Bureaucracy, 418